Free to Hate

Free to Hate

THE RISE OF THE RIGHT IN POST-COMMUNIST EASTERN EUROPE

PAUL HOCKENOS

ROUTLEDGE   NEW YORK   LONDON

Published in 1993 by

Routledge
29 West 35th Street
New York, NY 10001

Published in Great Britain by

Routledge
11 New Fetter Lane
London EC4P 4EE

Library of Congress Cataloging-in-Publication Data

Hockenos, Paul, 1963–
Free to hate : the rise of the right in post-communist Eastern
Europe / by Paul Hockenos.
p. cm.
Includes bibliographical references and index.
ISBN 0-415-90824-8 (cl.)
1. Fascism—Europe, Eastern. 2. Nationalism—Europe, Eastern.
3. Post-communism—Europe, Eastern. 4. Europe, Eastern—Politics
and government—1989– I. Title.
JC481.H56 1993
320.5′3′0947—dc20 93-1847
CIP

British Library cataloging information also available.

To the others, who are many

CONTENTS

CONTENTS

ACKNOWLEDGMENTS

Unfortunately, it is impossible for me to thank all of the people who in some way contributed to the writing of this book, from the support of my friends to complete strangers who provided me with a bed for the night. The kindness and sincerity of a great many of the people whom I met during my travels in Eastern Europe contradict the impressions and simplistic conclusions that could easily be drawn from this book.

Nevertheless, I do here thank the people who contributed most directly to the final product. Among them I am grateful to Bob Cohen, Lázár Ildikó, Marc Woodworth, Carol Fiedler, Bánszegi Láci, Mary Ellen Fischer, Helga Doblin, Stephanie Baker, Daniel Balmuth, Bernd Siegler, Erich Rathfelder, and Max Zutty. I would also like to thank all of the superb journalists at *Die Tageszeitung*, and in particular Randy Kaufman for his generosity in opening its archives to me, as well as Sheryl Larson, James Weinstein and Beth Schulman at *In These Times*. I mention also Wade Green for arranging some financial support for the project.

Special thanks goes to William Totok for his invaluable assistance on the Romania chapter. Also, I am deeply indebted to Jasper Tilbury for his insightful comments on the text and collaboration on the Poland chapter; that chapter is as much his as it is mine.

If I had to single out only one person to thank, it would have to be Adam Blauhut, whose open criticisms, comments, and encouragement find their echo throughout the book.

Last but definitely not least, I thank my parents, without whom this book would never have happened.

That things continue on this way *is* the catastrophe.

Walter Benjamin

INTRODUCTION

If I had to trace the germ of this book to a specific time or event, it would be a visit to the Malibu *Jugendklub* in East Berlin on Christmas Eve 1989, a month and a half after the opening of the Berlin Wall. I had spent the day in West Berlin between my laptop and the kitchen radio, listening to the latest broadcasts from Romania about the revolution there. Despite the initial, exaggerated reports of "tens of thousands" of massacred protestors, I was thrilled to hear that the Dictator, as Romanians referred to President Nicolae Ceauşescu, had been overthrown. There would be plenty of rejoicing this Christmas in Romania, and the euphoria was palpable everywhere that the walls and their architects had fallen.

The excitement over the changes in the German Democratic Republic (GDR) had naturally infected West Berlin, where the cafés and bars were crowded, the mood inside light and cheerful. But I had begun researching a story on Skinheads in East Germany, and that Friday evening I had plans to visit a certain disco in the outlying East Berlin district of Hellersdorf. The "youth club" was a well-known hang-out for young neo-Nazis and fascist Skinheads. It was rumored that a Mozambican guest worker had been murdered there two years ago, al-

1

though neither the East nor West German press had made mention of the killing.

Nearly an hour's trip away on the *S-Bahn*, the commuter railroad, the Malibu lay at the base of a labyrinth of tall, cement-gray high rises, the kind of Stalinist housing projects that dominate East Berlin beyond its refurbished tourist center. Inside the disco, a sparse, box-like room that served as a cafeteria by day, a strobe light flashed wearily to some 1970s pop hits. A rotund man in his mid-thirties, perhaps a communist youth functionary a month ago, presided over the turntables as a handful of teenage girls danced with one another. There were no Skinheads to be seen, but outside on the terrace, a group of young guys in collarless "baseball jackets," with short haircuts and thin moustaches, stood about smoking cigarettes. Some sat on the dirty steps, while others paced anxiously back and forth, disappearing inside for a few minutes and then reappearing. The boys shared a similar nervousness in their movements and blank, cruel gazes. They had about them an aura of adolescent meanness, anger, and restlessness.

The boys recognized me at once as a stranger. Though wary, they seemed curious enough about my presence in Hellersdorf on Christmas Eve to agree to chat. No, they said, they hadn't been following the events in Romania. Yes, they agreed, the opening of the Berlin Wall was a fine thing, even if it was only the first step to ousting the communists once and for all. As for politics, they didn't have much use for them, and none of them identified with any of the political parties, East or West. At the same time, they all considered themselves "right wing," which translated first into being anti-communist and second into wanting the reunification of Germany. Finally, they said, they could be "proud to be Germans again."

They knew the Skinheads who frequented the Malibu, who would usually show up later in the evening and start fights or shout "Sieg Heil!", "Foreigners Out!", and other such slogans. The adolescents in the baseball jackets weren't fascists, but they didn't have anything against the Skinheads either. "On some things, like the niggers and the *Fidschis* (Asians), the Skins say it like it is," said one of the guys, a pimple-faced teenager a bit more talkative than the others. "They come here from the third world and get everything that they want, just because they're communists. But now that's come to an end." When I asked, they said that they knew about the murdered Mozambican. The worker, one said, had been "harassing all of the local girls."

I naturally had no idea at the time that in a few years the aggression against foreigners in eastern Germany, as well as in the western states, would climax in a string of vicious pogroms, arson attacks, and dozens of deaths, events that would shake the very foundations of the newly united Germany. There had been a small underground neo-fascist movement in the GDR since the early 1980s, and racism against people of color was nothing new in any of the communist countries. These guys from the Hellersdorf projects weren't committed Nazis, however, but more or less average teenagers, born and raised in the GDR. They clearly had little in common with the dissidents and intellectuals who were basking in the world spotlight at the moment, touting ideas of civic democracy and human dignity. They were frustrated and bored, looking at a future that had even less to offer than they imagined at the time. Like their peers throughout Eastern Europe, they had pinned their hopes for a new future on a swift transition to capitalism, which, they were convinced, would put their living standards on a par with that of the West Germans in just a few years' time. But how would they react if these expectations failed to materialize? If they found themselves unemployed upon finishing vocational school instead of pulling in comfortable West German salaries?

Communism's capitulation freed the East Germans and their Soviet bloc partners from the constraints of the police states, but it also handed them responsibility for filling its void. Although most of the people who lived under communism never identified with its rule, two generations had been socialized under its supervision. What would these people choose to replace the imposed ethic of the "real, existing socialism"? How had their experiences prepared them for the dramatic changes that would affect their lives? Also, the intensity of the Hellersdorf youths' racism was frightening in light of the paltry number of foreign nationals in the GDR. Where did this racism come from, and how far into mainstream society did it reach? On the way back to West Berlin I thought about these questions. I looked into the faces of the people coming and going from the S-Bahn and asked myself what forty years of dictatorship had made of the citizens of Eastern Europe.[1]

These thoughts and others crossed my mind as I traversed the region as a journalist, and it didn't take long before ethnic violence in western Romania's Transylvania region, and in Kosovo, Serbia's Albanian-populated southern province, confirmed some of my initial doubts. But as early as 1989, excessive pessimism was out of place. The "democratic revolutions" had swept communism from history's stage in Eastern Europe, and their symbols—toppled Lenin statues, dissidents-turned-politicians, free elections and national flags—expressed the hope of the moment. The people had thrown off single-party rule for a Europe of constitutional democracies based upon multi-party elections and accountable parliaments. Eastern Europeans seemed to speak in a common language about "a return to Europe," "a united Europe" no longer partitioned along the fronts of the Cold War. At the Conference on Security and Cooperation in Europe (CSCE) summit in Paris in 1990, West and East European leaders toasted a European House united by the common values of democracy, pluralism, human rights, and the rule of law.

The air was electric with potential and promise. Czechoslovak President Václav Havel spoke of Central Europe's unique opportunity to "approach a rich Western Europe not as a poor dissident or a helpless amnestied prisoner, but as someone who brings something with him: namely spiritual and moral incentives, bold peace initiatives, untapped creative potential, the ethos of freshly gained freedom, and the inspiration for brave and swift decisions." In their own countries, Havel saw the new elites' task to instill "spirituality, moral responsibility, humaneness, and humility" into politics. An era of dictatorship had ended, and a new one of democracy had begun.

The burst of creativity and democratic inspiration that Havel envisioned never materialized. If 1990 was a year of hope, 1991 was one of uncertainty, and in 1992 the idea of a united, democratic Europe perished for good in the mountains of Bosnia-Herzegovina. The Soviet empire's collapse and the dissolution of the police states reopened a Pandora's Box of age-old antagonisms, ethnic racisms, and historic rivalries. The consequences of nationalism reverberated across Eastern

Europe, the Balkans, and the Soviet Union. It's centrifugal forces fractured populations along ethnic fault lines, where those lines existed. Few of the nationalities in Eastern Europe, however, are so fortunate as to have homogeneous ethnic populations within undisputed borders. In ethnically mixed nation-states, nationalism distinguishes minorities and majorities, setting the stage for conflicts immeasurably easier to ignite than extinguish. By 1993, half-a-dozen wars alternately flickered and blazed on the territory of the former Soviet Union, with as many more waiting to flare. In former Yugoslavia, the world watched on as Serb—as well as Croat—forces systematically expelled and slaughtered the Bosnian Muslims in Bosnia-Herzegovina, reviving memories that we had prematurely consigned to history books.

With communism barely behind them, Eastern Europe's democrats confronted an adversary more unpredictable and incalculably more menacing than the unpopular dictatorships that had collapsed like houses of cards. Across the region, deeply conservative, radical nationalist, and even neo-fascist movements arose from communism's ruins. A diverse spectrum of right-wing forces surfaced in every country, each brandishing nationalist ideologies with authoritarian and racial underpinnings. A new, charged discourse of ancestry and tradition, of suffering and fate, of lost territories and thwarted ambitions replaced the stale rhetoric of Marxism-Leninism. Along with the national pageantry, some of the now-free press flaunted anti-Semitism and ethnic chauvinism that rivaled the tone of the interwar years. The darkest names of that period also reemerged after their decades-long banishment— Tiso in Slovakia, Antonescu in Romania, Pavelić in Croatia, and even Hitler in Germany. On the streets, racist violence erupted against foreigners, native Roma (Gypsies) and third world students. With their arms outstretched in the Nazi salute, young neo-fascists in the newly united Germany fire bombed the hostels of political asylum seekers. Most chilling, the wars in former Yugoslavia illustrated the consequences of national extremism when turned into a political program. Half a decade after Auschwitz and Treblinka, a fascist politics was possible again on European soil.

The Eastern Europeans filled communism's vacuum with the most convenient ideology at their disposal—nationalism; and in almost every country, the first free elections since the 1940s brought conservative nationalist leaderships to power. In and of itself, nationalism does not preclude the creation of democratic institutions or the guarantee of basic rights. While all of the far right movements in Eastern Europe are nationalist, not all nationalism is right wing. The free expression of national identity and culture also has a place—and arguably a constructive one—in modern societies. But, with the exception of the Czech lands, the historic nationalisms of Eastern Europe have never yielded healthy democracies.

The former communist countries now all boast constitutional democracies, regular elections, and varying measures of press freedom. In one sense, most of Eastern Europe has never been so democratic. The kind of democracy that has emerged, however, is a far cry from that in postwar Western Europe. For democrats, the break with communism implied the nurturing of western-style democracies and market economies in countries that, most of them admitted, lacked such traditions. For nationalists, the termination of Soviet occupation opened the way for a return to the national traditions and myths that communism had either swept aside or incorporated into its own ideological framework. The ghosts of the past reappeared in the garb of modern democracy, with thinly cloaked philosophies of organic society, ethnic superiority, and national destiny. Like those of the past, the nationalisms of postcommunist Eastern Europe inherently contradict the assumptions of liberal democracy and a united Europe.

Nationalism and extremist right wings also exist in Western Europe and the U.S. In 1991, former Ku Klux Klan chief David Duke garnered thirty-nine percent of the Louisiana vote in his run for governor. The past five years have seen the National Front in France, the Republican Party in Germany, the Northern League in Italy and other like-minded "New Right" movements in Sweden, Austria, and Belgium score unprecedented victories. With a potent mixture of racism and economic populism, these parties have effectively exploited the anxieties of the lower and middle classes, making their way into parliaments at the expense of the traditional conservative and center parties. In some cities and towns, they take over a quarter of the vote. In 1993, the Northern League emerged from the Italian corruption scandals as the most popular party in northern Italy. Yet, however ugly their message and worrying their electoral gains, their political relevance, for the moment at least, is on a wholly different scale than that of the undemocratic right-wing forces in Eastern Europe. Ideologically, the Western European New Right has much in common with the rights in Eastern Europe. The New Right parties, though, dwell on the periphery of the political process. They have their seats in the legislature and agitate in their publications. And although their demagoguery inevitably taints political discourse, they are in no way positioned to come to power in the foreseeable future. So far, all of the traditional parties, including conservatives, have strictly ruled out cooperation with the ultra-right.

In Eastern Europe, parties with similarly racist and even shriller nationalist rhetoric find themselves squarely within the political mainstream, if not in power. They are talked about as "normal" and "natural" phenomena (like nationalism itself), as part and parcel of democracy, and not as threats to it. The strength of nationalism and the shape of the far right varies from country to country. Where nationalist parties dominate discourse, such as most of the former Soviet Union or the Balkans, they define the nascent political culture, undermining all but the formal motions of the democratic processes. In Poland, Slovakia, Hungary, and Slovenia, national populist forces compete with viable democratic movements and reform communist parties. In Romania, Bulgaria, and Serbia, the former communist parties are the ultra-nationalists. An ultra-right populism of a different stripe has made advances in the independent Czech Republic. In former East Germany, a militant neo-fascist movement, supported by organized Western radicals, uses the streets as its political stage. The right incorporates all of these diverse actors, from Polish President Lech Wałęsa to neo-Nazi Skinheads. That in no way makes them the same, or their implications for democracy comparable. At the same time, there are assumptions that link the array of right-wing forces, and indeed, that penetrate to the very center of society.

Since this book is about the right in Eastern Europe, it requires an explanation of exactly who and what falls under the heading of "right." The task is all the more complex in light of the tangled notions of right and left that have emerged from the Cold War. In the West, the right has become identified with the ideals of the free market, restricted government, and an emphasis on the individual in society. Two prominent figures of the Western right, for example, are Ronald Reagan and Margaret Thatcher, both outspoken advocates of free market competition and opponents of welfare systems, social spending, and so forth. They are both "conservatives" although they presided over periods of radical change.

The right in Eastern Europe looks very different. The movements examined in this book are undemocratic movements, ones that fall outside the established parameters of Western democracy. In this sense, neither Reagan nor Thatcher would qualify as "right." In fact, I refer to those political ideologies that embrace free-market versions of capitalism as "liberal," in the sense of classic nineteenth-century English liberalism. On the other hand, Western Europe's "ultra-right," such as the National Front or the Republicans, would come under this definition of "right."

This more traditional definition of "right," which I use, is limited by not taking into account the authoritarian and racist aspects of Western conservatives. It tends to hold up liberal Western democracy as the reference point from which all other ideologies are evaluated. Although I concede this shortcoming, I also feel that the democratic ideals of the CSCE Paris Charter are positive, and that Western democracy should be looked at as a minimal standard rather than as an ideal in itself. Also, my omission of the likes of Reagan or Thatcher is offset by the fact that they have few equivalents in Eastern Europe. There are exceptions, such as Czech Prime Minister Václav Klaus, a radical free marketeer in the Thatcherist mold with authoritarian leanings and a questionable commitment to human rights and democratic procedure. Nevertheless, I decline to put Klaus in the league of Eastern Europe's old school nationalists and extreme rightists. This is not to say that someone like Klaus or Reagan (or better yet Patrick Buchanan) couldn't overstep the line that I have drawn. A slick, modern ultra-rightism with a liberal economic program could potentially be even more dangerous than the brittle nationalism that prevails now. Just such a party, the Freedom Party in Austria, was the most successful ultra-right party in Western

Europe in the 1980s. And, surely, it is only a question of time before the Eastern Europeans spawn similar offspring.

The term "fascism" too requires a brief explanation. All of the ultra-right and extreme nationalist movements in Eastern Europe have "fascistic" elements to them, and perhaps "fascistic" is more appropriate in most cases than "fascist" or "neo-fascist." I employ those labels however for the most extreme of the far right movements, to those who not only endorse genetic hierarchies, greater national states, authoritarian regimes, and so forth, but also demand that those theories be put into practice, either through legislation or extra-parliamentary force. Political parties that advocate laws which would empower local authorities to expel Roma from their communities or to ban the parties of national minorities would fall under this heading. In Bosnia-Herzegovina, the "ethnic cleansing" of Bosnian Muslims from areas controlled by Serbs and Croats is clearly fascist. I also put the racist violence of Skinhead gangs in this category. Contemporary neo-fascism can take the diverse forms of neo-Nazi youth gangs, national populist parties, fundamentalist religious movements, intellectual circles, fascist exile groups, armed militias, or even reorganized communist parties and cliques. Often, but not always, the most reactionary of these movements fall back on explicitly fascist traditions, which serves as a useful indicator of their intentions.

The conservatism that has taken shape in transitional Eastern Europe is of a different ilk from that which has matured in postwar Western Europe. Although not free of the past, conservative parties in the West, even those in present-day Germany, Spain, or Italy, have come around to the basic tenets of European democracy. In Germany, forty years of supervised democracy has transformed most of mainstream conservatism into modern, more or less self-conscious political ideologies. The single-party states in Eastern Europe, on the other hand, blocked a parallel development, suppressing independent expressions of nationalism and political conservatism as best they could, or appropriating those traditions for their own use when it proved expedient. When the dictatorships fell, nationalists had recourse to two intertwined sources of conservatism. One was that of the communist parties, which nationalists quickly stripped of its Marxist-Leninist trappings. The second was to the nationalist ideologies of the interwar period that the communists had vilified as "fascist" and "bourgeois-nationalist."

Neither of these traditions has much in common with modern, Western conservatism. In fact, Eastern Europe's nationalists harbor profound suspicions of three of the Western right's most sacred principles: the market, freedom of the individual, and limited government. Rather, it is some of today's most prominent democrats—"the liberals"—who most enthusiastically embrace laissez-faire economic policies and libertarian notions of freedom. The right in Eastern Europe calls upon a conservatism with its roots in rural, peasant cultures, traditions that emphasize prewar notions of nation, family, religion, and strong national states. It is a conservatism distrustful of modernity and the secular values of postwar Western Europe. The East European nationalists reject the Enlightenment values of progress, technological advance, human equality, urban-based culture, the individual, and self-expression. Theirs are the pre-modern values of a romantic national Golden Age, when their proud nation flourished as never before, and never again.

The ideological cornerstone of this conservatism is the Nation, and whether the issue is press freedom or the family, minority rights or parliamentary procedure, the logic of the right emanates from its understanding of the Nation. This does not mean that its spokesmen are true believers in their own creed. For the most part, they are the same apparatchiks who for years invoked the name of the working class to maintain their privileges under communism. But now the Nation serves as their all-purpose recourse to legitimize their autocratic grip on power, to attack political pluralism, to muzzle the press, and to justify strong military and police apparatuses.

In the lively academic discourse that has grown around nationalism, scholars distinguish two general concepts of the nation: the civic or democratic, and the ethnic.[2] The civic definition, with its roots in the French Revolution, uses "nation" to refer to a body of citizens whose collective sovereignty constitutes a state. In other words, it is "nation" as the term is commonly applied in the West, referring to all of the people who live within a state, regardless of their ethnicity, language, or other characteristics. The underlying principle of the civic nation is citizenship, and all citizens are afforded equality under the law. The civic nation-state is thus synonymous with constitutional democracy, the rule of law, and human rights. In German, the term is *Rechtsstaat,* and *Rechtsstaaten* were expressly what the East Europeans called for in 1989, when "class justice," privileged cadre, and secret-police terror were still fresh in their minds.

The ethnic nation, on the other hand, is a folkish community, bound not by a common legal code or state borders, but by descent, language, customs, and history. What defines membership in this kind of nation is ethnicity. This nation is a community of "pure-blooded" Germans or French or Romanians, for example, from which all other peoples of different lineage are excluded. The primacy of blood establishes a racial hierarchy of peoples, particularly when more than one people live in a given state. Rights and privileges are acquired by birth into the ethnic nation, and not upon citizenship. For ethnic nationalists, the nation is a natural unit, which evolves according to its own biological laws and inner rhythms. Each nation has its own unique, mystical destiny toward which it aspires, and which other nations impede at the cost of war. One critical aspect of that destiny, common to all ethnic nations, is that all of the members of their national community must live within the borders of one state.

The ethnic nation is at odds with the premises of a democratic, integrated Europe, and presents a certain recipe for conflict in the combustible multinational potpourri of Eastern Europe. Its ideology, as we shall see, sanctions autocracy, racism, ethnic hatred, expansionism, and revanchism. All modern states today contain elements of both civic and ethnic nationalism. Modern nationalism—both ethnic and civic, however, arrived late to Eastern Europe, and when it did it tended to take particularly unsavory ethnic forms. The dismantlement of the four empires, the German, the Habsburg, the Russian, and the Ottoman, in the aftermath of World War I brought national states to life that were burdened with weak and nonexistent democratic traditions, large national minorities, competing territorial claims, and socioeconomic poverty. The attempt to carve ethnically based territorial states from the "beltway of nations" in Eastern Europe was flawed from the beginning, and reached its tragic conclusion in World War II. The fragile interwar democracies buckled under the internal pressures of nationalism, finally succumbing in one form or another to the will of Nazi Germany.

Although, fortunately, there exists no equivalent to Third Reich Germany on the horizon, the scenario today for Eastern Europe is no less perilous. The same dynamic is at work that led the post-WWI successor states down the road of extreme nationalism and war. The dissolution of the Soviet empire has cast the small, poor, ethnically mixed states out on their own once again. And, again, in brazen defiance of history, their first impulses have been toward national identities and national states. Where extreme nationalists take the logic of the ethnic nation to its radical conclusion, as in former Yugoslavia, the result is the forging of an all-inclusive, homogeneous ethnic nation-state. The price, again, is war, complete with forcible mass expulsions, concentration camps, and genocide. In other cases, such as the Baltics, Slovakia, Romania, or Bulgaria, where significant national minorities live, the majorities have tightened the screws on their cohabitants through cultural repression and restrictive citizenship laws. Under fire, the minorities react with nationalisms of their own, which often take the form of separatist ambitions. In response, the dominant nationalities crack down all the harder on the "disloyal" minorities. The heightened tension can bring in the minorities' "mother states," usually all too willing to come to the rescue of their national kin, in regions they often consider their own anyway. The action-reaction spiral of nationalism plays itself out whereever ethnic nationalism is the order of the day.

For Westerners, one of the most confusing aspects of the postcommunist right is its antipathy to free-market economics. Whatever they may say, nationalists tend to think of capitalism as a Western (ultimately Jewish) ideology designed to strip the nation of its wealth and culture. Historically, the nationalist right saw industrial capitalism and its culture of technology and profit clashing with its folkish ethics. Also, a certain populist egalitarianism infuses the concept of the ethnic nation, which capitalism of course undermines. In classic populist terms, traditional nationalists believe that wealth should benefit the whole nation, and not just a certain strata, much less foreigners or other "aliens." Nationalists and populists today argue either to slow the pace of privatization or, in some cases, to halt it altogether. The "slow approach" is entirely in their interests. A centralized, managed economy implies a strong state that keeps economic power firmly in their hands. It means the maintenance of economic privileges, which denationalization, the process of selling off state property to private investors, would naturally jeopardize.

When the revolutions of 1989 brought down the East bloc regimes, they swept away the facade of historical half-truths, distortions, and lies upon which the ruling elites justified their power. Understandably, the East Europeans' "longing for the truth," as Havel phrased it, has led them to reexamine their histories, to recover what was valuable but had been lost. In their quest to recapture that "truth," however, the Eastern Europeans have accepted new historical fictions, no less ominous in their implications for democracy.

The national myths that every country has resurrected play important functions in postcommunist society. For one, the nation offers a redemptive panacea for peoples burdened with legacies of opportunism and collaboration. Nationalists cast their embrace of the past as a return to an era of national glory that Soviet-imposed communism had artificially stifled. As in all national communities, the easily sold fairy tales of a great national history give people a common sense of historical purpose, pride, and continuity. In Eastern Europe today, the embellished histories of the "good" and "long-suffering" nation also serve to relieve individuals of responsibility for their actions (or inactions) during communism. Admittedly, if the average person wished to live a normal life, he or she was forced to collaborate in some way with the system—as fellow-traveller, obedient onlooker, bureaucrat, or informant. Popular uprisings against the regimes were unsparingly crushed. Grudgingly or not, the overwhelming majority of people struck their compromise with power. The dissidents were the precious few.

The nationalist right portrays the history of postwar communism as a forty year struggle of their democratic nation against the Soviet-occupation regime. In 1989, so the story goes, the people finally triumphed, breaking free from the fetters of foreign rule. Under the mantle of the nation, which has supposedly fought courageously against all forms of foreign rule since time immemorial, the individual's legacy of collaboration is transformed into his victory, as a participant in the nation. If the Hungarian nation was always "good" and we're Hungarians, runs the logic, then "we" couldn't possibly share responsibility for communism, any more than for WWI or the Hungarian Holocaust. The rationale is popular throughout Eastern Europe, not least among careerist politicians. The logic raises grave questions for democracy however since it absolves the individual-as-citizen from responsibility and obligation, both in the past and in the future too. The individual acts not as a citizen with a duty to participate in (or protest against) the actions of the state, but as a subject of the nation, to be ruled from above by a nationalist leader. As part of the nation's collective past and future destiny, the individual's interests become synonymous with the will of the nation.

The nationalists also herald themselves and their historical forefathers as the purest champions of anti-communism, which, amidst the resentment flush in postcommunist Eastern Europe, has an attractive ring. The right itself poses as the antithesis of communism, the highest form of opposition to the "internationalist," ideals of the disposed regimes. I argue, however, that while the swing to the right is a reaction to four decades of communism, it fails to break with either the totalitarian ethic of Stalinism or the ideologies that preceded it. Rather, there exists a clear continuity in the values and political cultures of the right and the communist systems. On the one hand, this is hardly surprising since so many of today's most outspoken nationalists had been loyal communists until only a few years ago. Those that came to power tried their best to revamp but keep the institutions of the Leninist states—government-controlled presses, strong security services, and state-run economies—under new names, with a new operative logic. Although they broke with communist ideology, they could not, and indeed had no interest in, divorcing themselves from its essential structures.

In part, even nationalism is something that today's right inherited from the deceased systems. Although communism boasted of its final victory over national ideology, it routinely resorted to nationalism to bolster its legitimacy. In the aftermath of the Stalinist 1950s, every East bloc country turned to nationalism in one form or another. Nationalism, as Misha Glenny says, was "refracted through the prism of Stalinism," and the product was a grotesque hybrid of both ideologies. When necessary, populist wings within the communist parties resorted to the most plebeian of their countries' traditions—although always under the banner of communism. Polish and Czechoslovak communists ruthlessly instrumentalized anti-Semitism to discredit their enemies inside and outside of the party. In Romania, Ceaușescu exploited the most extreme brand of "national communism," which was similar in content to Romania's virulent interwar nationalism. The communist governments fanned nationalist emotions from above, while simultaneously suppressing their expression from below. When nationalism raised its head as anti-communist opposition, as happened time and again, the police states brutally quashed it, condemning the movements as "fascist" and "counter-revolutionary." In East Germany, Poland, Czechoslovakia, and Hungary, neo-fascist currents surfaced in underground youth subcultures that survived throughout the 1980s despite the state's repression. For most people, however, pent-up national feelings and resentments festered beneath the surface, captive until the regimes crumbled.

The communist regimes preserved and perpetuated the undemocratic, authoritarian features of national traditions. In the postwar haste to consolidate power, they refused to confront the historical and social-psychological roots of fascism's fruition in their countries during the 1930s and 1940s. Communism had defeated fascism once and for all, they claimed. Trials were held and the ringleaders executed. The communist leaderships went leniently on their peoples' often ignominious wartime legacies, attributing the atrocities to the Germans or isolated native "fascist cliques." One only had to declare oneself a communist to be relieved of responsibility for previous actions. The regimes papered over the truth of collaboration and the resentment that lingered between neighboring peoples.

The appeal of nationalist and far right ideologies in Eastern Europe is rife with contradictions. Although nationalism is a critical component of identity and deeply imbedded in culture throughout Eastern Europe, opinion polls consistently show that only small minorities of the populations agree with the ideas of the most radical nationalist and extreme right movements. The wars in Croatia or Bosnia never had the support of the majority of Serbs, much less the Croats or the Bosnian Muslims. A year before the division of Czechoslovakia, over seventy percent of Czechs and Slovaks supported the continuation of the federation. All of the mixed and neighboring nationalities have both histories of animosity and long traditions of peaceful cohabitation. In the cellars of Sarajevo, Serbs, Croats, and Muslims linked arms in solidarity, sharing their last scraps of food with one another. What is it then that compels a Croat farmer to take up a gun against the man he has shared a tractor with for twenty years? Or a Serb doctor to rape his Muslim neighbor's wife? Why would a Slovak, content with the Czechoslovak federation, vote for a nationalist party plotting its dissolution?

The freedoms of new liberty and self-expression, and the turbulence of change and uncertainty, came abruptly to Eastern Europe. Overnight, worlds were turned upside down, and for the first time in many peoples' lives they had to choose the course of the future for themselves. Communist rule, however, had left most people woefully unprepared for building democracy from scratch. The first years of democracy have shown the peoples of Eastern Europe easy prey for demagoguery that addresses their fears and anxieties. Although the different nationalities and ethnic groups may have lived together harmoniously under communism, latent suspicions continued to exist. The same Serbs who said that they opposed war openly degrade the Muslim or Croat cultures and insist that the safety of the Serb minorities cannot be insured in independent Bosnian or Croatian states. The average Slovak may have lived peacefully with the Czechs, but was always resentful of their greater wealth and elitist airs. The prejudices and hatreds of the past were *available* to manipulation, and manipulate them nationalist politicians have, with consummate skill. The most radical extremists are a tiny minority with an influence far disproportionate to their numbers. What they have successfully done is to stir up latent fears, shift debate, and win themselves a place at the center of the political stage.

The mounting economic misery in every former communist country has provided the right with plentiful ammunition to assault their market-oriented democratic opponents. While economic deprivation is not the source of right-wing extremism, it acts as a catalyst that radicalizes hopelessness and prejudice. Right-wing populists with pseudo-leftist economic demands and national jingoism have found an ear not only with the dispossessed but also with the lower and middle classes.

The Eastern Europeans departed from communism with naive hopes for a speedy transition to prosperous market-based economies. Since the late seventies and early eighties, growth in the East bloc economies had slumped badly, and living standards had dropped everywhere. In 1989, many people perceived capitalism as an instant remedy which would produce results in a year or two's time. But even four years after the changes, all but a few of the numbers are grim. The eastern economies have been unable to compensate for the loss of the rouble-based Comecon market with equivalent exports to the highly competitive and restrictive Western markets. Since 1989, overall production, industrial output, and real wages have fallen dramatically in all of the former Comecon countries. The sale and closure of many "inefficient" state-managed enterprises has produced previously unfamiliar phenomena—unemployment, homelessness, high criminality, and new levels of poverty. From next to nothing, the jobless figures have crept steadily into the double digits in most countries. In former East Germany, where unification dealt a swift blow to the GDR economy, unemployment soared to forty or fifty percent in some badly hit cities. The capital necessary to fund the drastic structural overhaul has failed to materialize from the West. Western investment and aid has been only a fraction (about a tenth) of what the new democracies had anticipated.

Instead, the West has lent Eastern Europe its advice. The International Monetary Fund (IMF) and the World Bank accepted most of the Eastern Europeans into their ranks at the price of compliance with their standard guidelines, the same applied in Latin America and Africa with such disastrous results. The IMF shock therapy programs cut the quickest road from the centralized, state-run economies to market economies, sacrificing the short-term casualties of "belt-tightening" for a promised future of prosperity. All of the postcommunist governments in Eastern Europe, whether IMF members or not, have dutifully implemented the general conditions of the IMF's program: monetary restriction, price liberalization, deregulation, and privatization. The austerity packages include massive cuts in domestic expenditures—from investment to food subsidies—in order to insure that the countries meet their balance-of-payment targets. Should they fail to meet those preset targets, as they often do, the IMF freezes access to its reserves. Many elements of the IMF packages had been on the East Europeans' agendas anyhow, and in some cases had even been gradually introduced during the final years of communist rule. Every government in the former East bloc ultimately aspires to the goal of some kind of market economy. The question is how radically to proceed with the transitions, or—as it is put behind closed doors—how hard to push the people without sparking revolt. Although politicians often contest the IMF austerity deals when in opposition, they find their hands bound once they reach office. No government feels that it can afford to lose the IMF's blessing, which is the seal of approval for private bank loans and foreign investment.

The economic transitions have made winners of some and losers of others. Glitzy shopping streets in central Warsaw or Budapest sparkle with Western consumer goods and new wealth, testimony that some have benefitted from the economic restructuring. Not so far from the main thoroughfares, however, the run-down neighborhoods and high-rise projects like Hellersdorf tell a different story. There futures look bleaker than ever before. The disappointments of the economic transition have provoked anger, resentment, envy, and anxiety. Disillusionment has replaced the brief euphoria following communism's postmortem. The market and democracy were synonymous in the minds of many people, and for them the failure of one spells the failure of the other.

Under communism, the East Europeans grew used to the security of the state, and today a strong egalitarian streak surfaces again and again in their protests. The situation is ripe for right-wing populists with easy answers, who promise everything and blame peoples' misfortunes on other people—on foreigners, Jews, Roma, the West, or neighboring countries. They appeal to those hit hardest by the economic reforms, to a large extent the workers, the traditional territory of left. The reform communist parties, sometimes armed with nationalisms as vicious as those of the right, have targeted the same people, and with surprising success so soon after their unceremonious departures. Still weak and undefined, diminutive progressive left or social democratic parties have been unable to compete against the roar of nationalism, their intentions suspect as a "better Bolshevism."

For many people, the "escape from freedom" into nationalist ideology appears the simplest solution. As Erich Fromm argued, in a new form of submission the individual relieves himself of the burdens of individuality and freedom. Negative freedom, as Fromm describes the capitulation to totalitarianism, manifests itself when man "has been freed from traditional authorities and has become an 'individual,' but at the same time has become isolated, powerless, and an instrument of purposes outside of himself, alienated from himself and others; this condition undermines the self, weakens and frightens the individual, and makes the individual ready for submission to new kinds of bondage." In an authoritarian leader or an exclusive ideology, the individual injects meaning into an existence otherwise empty, an existence devoid of real human relationships and communities.

In one light, the adherents of extreme right ideologies, especially young people, could be seen as victims of larger processes over which they have no control. Ideology is a means of escape from postmodern anomie, violence a protest against the system's injustice. Who can blame the Hellersdorf teenagers for their situations, ask some. Don't gangs exist everywhere? Victims they may also be, but their protests are not empty expressions of frustration and boredom. They endorse racial prejudices and often act upon them with violence. Even the teenage radicals are organized, parts of national and international networks with specific political goals. The actions of the most primitive of these right-wing elements are inherently political, indeed fascistic, and must be treated as such.

Eastern Europe's slide into a black hole of right-wing autocracy and convulsive territorial wars is by no means prewritten history. Every former communist country stands at a crossroads of democracy and proto-dictatorship. Burdened with history and the enormous obstacles of transition, the countries of Eastern Europe can hardly be expected to reproduce the achievements of Western democracy at once. For some time, at least, the vast territory that communism once ruled will be one of turmoil and armed conflict, revolutions and putsches, crises and poverty. Radical nationalism and right-wing extremism are already part of every country's political landscape, and they will continue to exert their influences in the future. The case of former Yugoslavia shows us how quickly radical extremists can fan the flames of ethnic hatred, plunging whole populations into wars that will set their countries back by decades. Tragically, these spirits take immeasurably longer to exorcise than they do to awaken.

Since radical nationalisms and extremist rights are realities of Europe's new order, they must be understood in order to be checked. Dormant for so long, their dynamics, their aspirations and their precedents are obscure to most outsiders. Although the parallels to past eras are unmistakable, the new fascisms have resurfaced under a unique set of historical conditions, with characteristics specific to these conditions. This book provides a first, by no means exhaustive, look at these movements in five countries. Since they are new phenomena, the leading figures, party names, and the political relevance of these movements will change, but their essential logic will continue to guide whatever new formations take their place.

As much as the West would like to close its eyes to Eastern Europe's problems, its own future is inextricably bound with that of "the other Europe." The conflicts in the Balkans have already prompted Western intervention, and more than one potential conflagration could easily spread to NATO territory. The exodus of political and economic refugees from the East has put recession-strapped economies in the West under additional strain, as well as fueling the fortunes of Western Europe's own ultra-right progeny. Try as it might to throw up new walls and barriers to keep the East Europeans and their hatreds at bay, a new Iron Curtain is not at Western Europe's disposal. And, as communism illustrated, fascism is not something that walls protect against. The resurgent far right in Western Europe dispels any illusion that it is somehow immune to right wing radicalism. Today, the economic prosperity that accounts for a good measure of Western Europe's postwar stability seems no longer the given that it once was. As foreboding as the scenario for Eastern Europe may look, options remain open to encourage democracy and implement civil solutions in crisis flashpoints. The West and progressive forces need not look on helplessly as the nascent New Order disintegrates into lawless chaos.

Chapter 1

GERMANY
ONE PEOPLE, ONE RIGHT

Until late September 1991, one year to the week after the unification of the two Germanies, Hoyerswerda slumbered in the same listless anonymity as its many equivalents across former East Germany. Twenty miles from the Polish border, in the southeastern state of Saxony, the lonely sign on the city's outskirts greets visitors "Willkommen in Hoyerswerda."

German Democratic Republic (GDR) planners threw up the drab, uniform rows of concrete high rises in the late 1960s and early 1970s, transforming the rural village of 7000 into an industrial barracks of 70,000 in a matter of years. Like all of the GDR's self-contained *Neubau* cities, Hoyerswerda owed its existence to its local industry: the nearby brown coal mines and the "Black Pumps" electric power plant. The state enticed workers into the cultural no-man's land with the promise of modern apartments and higher-than-average wages. The relative splendor attracted a homogeneous, party-loyal population that was content to live in the cement towers, amidst the sulfur dioxide-fouled air, in exchange for minor material privileges. The Neubau settlement was completely devoid of social infrastructure and cultural opportunities, of pluralism and dissent—and, until the 1980s, of foreigners too.

Along with the majority of foreign workers from the GDR's "socialist brother countries," the first Mozambicans, Angolans, and Vietnamese arrived in Hoyerswerda in the early 1980s. In order to compensate for a short-handed labor force, the foreign workers took over the menial labor at the Black Pumps. In their *Ausländerwohnheime,* the designated dormitories for foreigners, there was little in the way of social or family life for the imported workers. On the weekends, before curfew, the men might have dropped in at the complex's local disco or youth club. If they danced with a German woman in Hoyerswerda, they could expect an angry rebuke at least. "My sister and I weren't allowed to go to the disco if Poles or Mozambicans were there," says Claudia, twenty-one, a Berlin biology student from Hoyerswerda. "My father worked with the Poles, but he warned us about them. Like everybody, he said 'ah, the Pollacks, they're dirty, they booze all the time and whore around.' " The usual wild rumors circulated about the foreign workers: They earn hard currency, they have better apartments, they don't pay rent, they buy all of our goods. "The state blows sugar right up those foreigners' assholes," griped the GDR Germans among themselves, repeating the common adage that the foreigners enjoyed privileges that they could only dream of. But as long as the police state enforced "solidarity" from above, racial discrimination was restricted mostly to insults, nasty looks, and social isolation.

The collapse of the GDR, the introduction of the "free-market economy" (formerly known as monopoly capitalism) and the onset of the unification process ended the Hoyerswerdians' staid life of security and comfort. The GDR's crash conversion to market competitiveness forced the closing of factory after factory in the East. In Hoyerswerda, fear set in as lay-offs began at the Black Pumps, and unemployment shot up from zero to seven percent. The FRG's new citizens, however, declined to direct their wrath at the ruling Christian Democratic Union's (CDU) full-speed-ahead economic transition policies, which had received the conservative Saxons' overwhelming support at the polls a year before. Instead, they targeted the 400 foreign workers, all of whom were scheduled to leave when their contracts expired at the end of the year. Federal authorities added to the locals' unhappiness by sending Hoyerswerda 230 applicants for political asylum from Romania, Cameroon, Turkey, Yugoslavia, Senegal, and Ghana. There, in the twelve-story Residential Complex IX on Thomas Müntzer Street, the refugees waited, unemployed and bored, as the state bureaucracy processed their applications for asylum.

The animosity that had accumulated during the years of marshalled goodwill poured forth. Complaints abounded that "the foreigners" played loud music and "the foreigners" threw garbage in the streets. Confronted now with the West Germans' significantly higher standard of living, and the new possibility of a decline in their own, the Hoyerswerdians' petty bourgeois indignation exploded against their unloved and now unneeded guests. "The niggers have incredible blue-tiled bathrooms," ranted one man to a German reporter "Do you understand, the niggers! And me, all I have is painted wallpaper!" The harassment of the foreign workers and refugees escalated until the foreign nationals no longer trusted themselves on the streets. "We learned right away that the people in Hoyerswerda were against us," recounts Pierre, a Cameroonian refugee. "Whenever you did something alone, like try to make a telephone call or go shopping, you'd be cursed or spit upon. We all hated it there. It was no life for us at all. We complained to the authorities, to the social workers, to the police, but they did nothing. From the very beginning they made no effort to protect us." Their response, he says, was always the same: "Kein Problem, kein Problem" (No problem, no problem).

Early in the week, September 17 and 18, 1991, came and went like most other hazy, overcast days in Hoyerswerda. In the central market place, eight adolescents with shaved heads, bomber jackets and big black boots smashed the street-side stands of the Vietnamese merchants, knocking the smaller men to the ground and kicking them. The police eventually dispersed the Skinhead gang, but, as usual, made no arrests. On their way home from school, some local kids shattered a few window panes of the Vietnamese and African workers' dormitory, and continued along their way. On the afternoon of Thursday the 19th, a crowd no longer confined to teenagers gathered outside the foreign workers' apartment block on Albert Schweitzer Street. The adults egged the youth on as they pelted the tower with rocks and empty bottles. About fifty local Skinheads and neo-Nazi types appeared on the scene, contributing their expertise to the action. The police were nowhere to be seen.

The following day there was no mistaking that a lynching was in the air. "The whole city knew what was going to happen," explained one Croatian refugee. "It seemed like it had all been planned well in advance, prepared by the whole population. The social workers came and warned us: 'Today there will be an attack, so be prepared, don't sleep, shut the windows, keep the lights out. They're coming to get you.' " Friday evening, after the shops had shut their doors, the Skinheads mustered again behind the Albert Schweitzer Street project and the pogrom commenced. "Foreigners out!" and "You nigger dogs, fuck off!" shouted the fifty-odd teenagers and young men, beer bottles in hand as if they were at a picnic. A crowd of voyeuristic onlookers, some with small children in their arms, gathered around the assailants. The Mozambican and Vietnamese workers crouched in their bathrooms as stones, fireworks, and finally flaming molotov cocktails pounded their walls. Some fled into the streets, wailing at the top of their lungs, "Yooouu faaasciiists!" Those that the crowd got a hold of were beaten bloody. Only hours later, police cordoned off the building, scuffling with the mob as it tried to break through to its quarry. From their uniform balconies, the Hoyerswerdians simply looked on—or away. Not a single person took action against the terror.

The workers were evacuated early the next day, but the crowd had yet to satiate its anger. News of the action spread through right-wing circles across Saxony. Organized neo-Nazi and Skinhead groups such as the *Gubner Front* from Guben and the *Deutsche Alternative* from Dresden and Leipzig mobilized their troops, descending upon Hoyerswerda by the carload. The site of the pogrom shifted to the political refugees' quarters at the other end of the city. In their new Volkswagens and once-prized Trabants, the mob and its cheerleaders sped to Thomas Müntzer Street, arriving, once again, before the police. By now the character of the manhunt was overtly fascist. Over 120 Nazis waved Third Reich flags, shouted "Sieg Heil!" and thrust out their right arms in the Nazi salute. The mood on the street was both festive and aggressive, like that in a beer hall or a soccer stadium. With their arms around one another, the racists sang old *Wehrmacht* songs and indulged in their common sport. Projectiles rained on the building until not a single pane of glass stood below the fifth story. "The social workers forbid us to answer the attacks, to defend ourselves," says Pierre. "We had nothing but our tables and our beds. We had no other choice but to hide ourselves as best as possible. If they had ever broken through, they could have killed us." Helicopters buzzed overhead and ambulances' sirens screamed as pitched street battles between the assailants and the police raged into the night. By dawn, the final tally was in: eighty-three persons detained, thirty-two arrested, twenty-nine wounded, four badly injured, three imprisoned.

Not until the morning of Monday, September 23, six days after the first stones flew, did former GDR army vehicles arrive to evacuate the refugees. Neighborhood locals stood across the rock-strewn street, cheering and shouting insults as the refugees picked their way through the splintered glass to the buses. "You goddamn niggers, we'll kill you all!" jeered one onlooker. Others expressed a kind of shame: "For years the foreigners did the dirtiest jobs for us down in the coal pits," said one worker. "They have to go now, but they should be allowed to go in peace." One mother admitted how happy she was that it was all finally over. "It was terrible," she said, "because of the noise the kids haven't had a decent night's sleep all week." While most distanced themselves from the violence of Skinheads and neo-Nazis, few were able to renounce the xenophobia that had gripped the whole community. The final rocks thudded against the buses as they lumbered off to an unspecified location. Hoyerswerda, the fascists rejoiced, was finally an *ausländerfreie Stadt*. Nazi policies during WWII had made Hoyerswerda *judenfrei* (Jew-free), now it was a foreigner-free city too. The state had capitulated to the mob.

As chilling as it was, the spectacle was neither the first nor the last of its kind in the united Germany. The brutality of Hoyerswerda differed only in degree from similar lynch mob actions that year that jolted former GDR cities such as Saarlouis, Zittau, Halle, Greifswald, Hünxe, and Cottbus from their postwar malaise. The pogrom was the first climax in a wave of racial aggression that had mounted steadily since the fall of the Berlin Wall. In cities on both sides of the newly united Federal Republic, right-wing violence had become an everyday fact of life for people of color. During 1991, the united Germany's first full year of existence, the number of assaults against foreign nationals shot up ten-fold over the combined figure in the two Germanies during the previous year, including 338 arson attacks. Although concentrated against foreigners with darker skin hues, the aggression was by no means restricted to non-Germans or people of color. Jews, leftists, Roma, the mentally handicapped, and homosexuals—the victims of Nazi persecution, and also of proto-fascist gangs in the GDR and West Germany—found themselves the victims of popular hatred once again in the united Germany.

The dramatic eruption of right-wing violence raised the gravest questions as to just what kind of Germany had emerged from the occupied country's postwar division. The Western powers' acquiescence to German unification rested on the assumption that the first Federal Republic had firmly anchored itself in the tradition of Western democracy. The FRG had distinguished itself as the motor of European integration, as well as its financier, and as a self-conscious voice of moderation in the Western military alliance. Despite the uneasiness of such close neighbors as France and Poland, nearly four decades of economic prosperity and obedient participation in NATO had assuaged the worst fears of the reemergence of an aggressive German chauvinism in the center of Europe. In the wake of the Eastern bloc's dissolution, the economic might of the old federal states seemed adequate to guarantee the new German states' integration into the European mainstream—a position of privilege unique among the post-communist countries. Even the spate of racial terror appeared not to jeopardize the FRG's status as a Western democracy. In principle, at least, the modern Rechtsstaat could and would endure the existence of violent racism and an active ultra-right movement within its borders.

The "good Germans," the non-rock-throwing majority, sincerely hoped that the brown flotsam would disappear down the same drain that had spit it up. Many wrote off Hoyerswerda as an extreme, exceptional symptom of post-totalitarian society in transition, a bug that would be worked out in time. The daily terror, however—vandalism, assaults, beatings, arson attacks, and even killings—continued to climb throughout 1992. In fact, by the end of the year the number of right-wing related assaults (2285), including 701 arson attacks and seventeen fatalities, had doubled from 1991.[1] But after a few months Hoyerswerda seemed to fade away, and the violence received ever smaller corners of the press. Until Rostock, that was, and then Mölln and Solingen, when images that made Hoyerswerda look like a picnic indeed were transmitted around the world.

The August 1992 violence in Rostock-Lichtenhagen, like Hoyerswerda, was also a pogrom, only bigger. Like Hoyerswerda, Rostock began with a group of local Skinheads and hooligan pals bombarding an asylum shelter with stones and beer bottles. It ended, five days later, with 600 assorted racists battling 1600 riot police. Although, like Hoyerswerda, partially spontaneous, the ground had also been prepared beforehand in the Hanseatic port city. Ultra-right groups had circulated anti-foreigner leaflets that called for "Rostock will stay German" actions. "It starts with one asylum hostel—and Rostock is already multicultural," said one piece of propaganda. The day before the violence, the local *Ostsee Zeitung* as much as announced what was in the works.

As if rehearsed, the Rostock-Lichtenhagen locals joined in to aid the teenage Nazis. Crowds of as many as two thousand gathered to urge them on and within twenty-four hours right-wing extremists from as far away as Hamburg, Berlin, and Dresden were on the scene with walkie-talkies and radio-jamming devices. The evening after the authorities evacuated the 200 Romanian Roma from the besieged shelter, the rioters encircled the building of the 120 Vietnamese workers living next door. Eyewitnesses report that as many as 500 police and well-equipped border guards stood in front of the building or in its vicinity. "The atmosphere was not tense," one television cameraman told the U.S.-based human rights group Helsinki Watch. "The police were talking to the demonstrators when we went into the house to do some interviews. When I looked out of the window, I saw to my shock that the police had withdrawn to a nearby hill top. The Skinheads were throwing molotov cocktails and storming the building." The police clearly had orders not to intervene. The assailants set fire to the building and chased the foreigners up the stairwell until they finally escaped across the roof to safety hours later. It was sheer accident that no one was killed.

The state interior minister, denying a failure on the part of the police, said that the force was "exhausted" and badly needed a rest at the time. Nor, he said, did they know for certain that Vietnamese were living there. Why the police had been in constant walkie-talkie contact with the hoodlums, he wouldn't explain. When Rostock's CDU mayor blamed the explosion on the "uncontrolled influx of foreigners" into Germany, he was simply reiterating the line of his more experienced colleagues in Bonn. "What the chorus of approval in Rostock expressed," said Federal Interior Minister Dieter Heckelmann, the chief of all police in the FRG, "was not right-wing extremism, anti-foreigner sentiment or racism, but rather justified unhappiness over the abuse of the right to asylum." The Rostockers from the Lichtenhagen Neubau projects echoed the sentiments of their counterparts in Hoyerswerda. "These aren't Nazis," one woman told the Berlin *Tageszeitung*. "These are our children, normal Germans who weren't going to put up with these foreigners here any longer." One television report after another showed beer-bellied men praising their childrens' actions. "The foreigners had it coming," said one man. "I would have done it myself too. They come here, destroy the buildings and use the gardens as toilets. Nobody felt safe with all those Gypsies around. Something had to be done."

The pictures of the Rostock youths hurling blazing *Mollies* at the foreigners' hostels sent shock waves around the world. In Germany, the Rostock events set off a storm of new attacks. Day after day the right wingers ambushed asylum shelters and foreigners in major cities as well as places with names that most Germans had never heard of: Stendal, Oscherleben, Lübbenau, Potsdam-Babelsberg, Quedlinburg, Eisenhüttenstadt, Dessau, Wittenberge, Cottbus, Greifswald, Schwerin, Wismar, Zielitz, Bad Lautenberg, and Holzhausen. "Rostock is everywhere!" read one headline. The state looked completely paralyzed, unable to move effectively against the terror spree. "What 1968 was to the left, 1992 is to the right," remarked one veteran leftist. Was a Fourth Reich really emerging in the united Germany? Was the state as powerless as it looked against the right? How to explain the complicity of population, police, and even the politicans in such primitive displays of hatred? And why did Chancellor Helmut Kohl wait until the December 1992 deaths of two Turkish women and a child in a firebomb attack in Mölln to openly condemn the violence?

Coming from German streets, the cries of "Heil Hitler!" and the sight of burning buildings and bloodied foreigners naturally set off alarms everywhere. Yet, hysterical predictions of an ultra-rightist takeover or a new Nazi state were premature. Forty years of allied supervision and material prosperity had ingrained a commitment to liberal democracy into most West Germans that would not be undermined overnight. Even if the Federal Republic had stopped short of the demands of the 1960s student movement, it had undergone a confrontation with the Nazi past that had at least discredited and delegitimized fascist ideology for the overwhelming majority of citizens. Racist, authoritarian, and fascistic attitudes still persist, and not always that far below the surface. They have their political manifestations too, in both traditional conservative parties and far right political parties. Under present circumstances, however, the far right parties remain small and isolated, with no possibility of coming directly to power.

Even in the untested political waters of former East Germany, a popular neo-fascist movement is unlikely to attract any more than a fraction of the population. As angry and as racist as some may get, the majority of Germans—East and West—know well that their welfare is ultimately tied to Germany's stability, to Western Europe, and to democracy. Yet, it was no coincidence that Hoyerswerda and Rostock lay in the former GDR. The conditions of frustration, disillusionment, and anxiety provided an explosive combination, particularly among a people inexperienced in living in a multi-ethnic society. The uncertainties of transition on top of forty years of communist socialization have produced an atmosphere particularly susceptible to social and racist demagoguery.

However far it may be from power, the resurgence of a potent ultra-right has enormous implications for the nature of the united Germany, for the state, for society and for democracy. As any victim will testify, the ultra-right poses a real threat to those unfortunate enough to be on its long hate list. The danger that the new level of right-wing violence becomes the status quo, an accepted part of the united Europe, would implicitly turn Germany and its neighbors into Rechtsstaaten in name only, states unable—or unprepared—to insure the safety and rights of certain peoples. The rhetoric of the right clearly has an appeal, which forces other political parties to respond and often take positions closer to theirs. Progressives already see many of their victories from previous decades being rolled back, and a new conservatism filling the vacuum. Now the goals of democrats are simply to protect what was, to control the damage in a society battling the influence of violence and right-wing beliefs on its political culture. Like in the Weimar Republic, the explosion of violence has put the right on the offensive, and the democrats on the defensive.

As a new international power, the united Germany finds itself under intense scrutiny as the New World and European Orders take shape. Horror stories such as Hoyerswerda and Rostock in the East and Mölln and Solingen in the West cast doubt upon the credibility of a sovereign Germany, and have therefore provoked concerns high in Germany's corridors of power. The state has responded to racial violence only when it has sensed its reputation abroad at stake, and then primarily against the "flood of foreigners" or the asylum law and not against the far right itself. Business interests too have taken great pains to keep Germany's clean-cut image unsullied. Unlike during the 1930s, big business has nothing to gain in having the extreme right flourish or come to office. Rather, Germany's financial society sees its interests best served in a conservative democratic state, kept on course by the same bureaucratic parties that have ruled the FRG since 1949. The political establishment and media from former West Germany have pointed accusing fingers at their Eastern countrymen for tarnishing the Federal Republic's postwar record, for undermining its painstaking effort to "return" to the fold of political normalcy. Statistics however show that racist aggression has skyrocketed on both sides of the dismantled border, with organized ultra-right forces from West Germany at the forefront of the crusade.

The West German establishment's attempt to blame the East alone for the racist violence conceals its own cynical complicity in the aggression toward foreign nationals in the new states. Unification transformed German racism and the activities of the two Germanies' ultra-rights into a single all-German problem. "One year after unification," commented the weekly *Die Zeit* after Hoyerswerda, "it appears that the Germans in East and West have at least found a common slogan again: foreigners out." The GDR's incorporation into the second Federal Republic (1990–   ) brought the easterners into an unfamiliar political discourse long pregnant with racism. Bonn, unable to provide the ex-GDR economy with the quick fix that it had promised, shifted responsibility for the country's economic pains onto Germany's liberal asylum law. Under the constitutionally enshrined right to political asylum, people at Germany's borders need only to utter the word "asylum" to be admitted, fed and housed until their case comes up before a tribunal—sometimes years later. Even supporters of the asylum statute agree that new laws are necessary to control immigration, but the conservatives (aided by just about the entire media) have unscrupulously used "the foreigner problem" to account for Germany's every woe. Since all of the political parties lack credible alternative policies to accommodate unification's enormous price tag, the Social Democrats as well as the ultra-right Republican Party have endorsed the CDU rationale.

In times of crisis, the German leadership inevitably falls back on the asylum law. First expressing his disgust at the events in Hoyerswerda, CDU Interior Minister Wolfgang Schäuble then underscored Germans' legitimate fears of being "swamped" by incoming foreigners. "Large parts of the population are worried about the massive influx of asylum applicants," said Schäuble. The real problem was the "misuse of the asylum statute." "Why," asked Schäuble, "should we demand that our citizens accommodate hundreds of thousands of asylum applicants at the tremendous expense of our taxpayers?" Such logic, often and skillfully used by the Bonn elite, effectively excused the perpetrators and blamed the victims. In response to Rostock, Chancellor Kohl could find no words of condolence for the people who had suffered the siege. Even more callous, he refused to attend the funerals of the Turks murdered in Mölln and Solingen. Kohl too stressed that the real problem was the number of foreigners in Germany. Remove the foreigners, and racism (the more polite terms used in Germany are *Ausländerfeindlichkeit* [animosity toward foreigners] or *Fremdenhass* [xenophobia]) will disappear. After Rostock, the major political parties obediently stepped up the campaign to change the asylum provision, reinforcing the consensus that the foreigners, the new Germany's ersatz Jews, were the ones to blame.

The West's tendency to pin Germany's right-wing extremism on the East Germans is undeserved. The far right political parties, for example, such as the Republican Party, have consistently racked up electoral victories in the old federal states, while winning only negligible percentages of the vote in the new states. At the same time, racial aggression on the territory of the former GDR has proved qualitatively nastier and proportionally greater than that on the other side of the dismantled border. The young, male militants often act with impunity, if not unabashed popular support. Understaffed and, in some cases, openly right-wing police forces have shown themselves either unable or unwilling to protect resident foreign nationals. Opinion polls consistently show higher levels of racism and intolerance among the former East Germans. Accustomed to a near-racially homogeneous society, the GDR Germans were taken by surprise by Bonn's distribution of asylum applicants through the new federal states, no matter how small their number. The federal government had made no effort to prepare its new citizens for coexistence with the foreigners. Just the opposite, the tenor of the asylum debate had all but guaranteed a welcome party like Hoyerswerda.

What conjured up images of the 1930s, what has made the names of Hoyerswerda and Rostock synonymous with racial hatred in the "New Germany," was the reaction of its average citizens. The overwhelming majority of the citizens didn't raise a hand against the foreign nationals—nor did they raise a hand to protest. In fact, they applauded. Even the police and their bosses watched on complicitly. It was clear where their sympathies lay, and without their tacit backing the first all-out pogroms in Germany since the Nazi era would never have been possible. Four constitutive components enabled the racists in Hoyerswerda and Rostock their "victories": the climate of hatred, the fascist shock troops, the laxity of the police, and the consenting majority. The future of the German ultra-right, as its leaders know, exists in reproducing those conditions.

RACISM IN THE GDR

Resident foreign nationals agree that racism was nothing new in the GDR. The communist regime had long overlooked the daily insults directed against the Vietnamese *"Fidschis"* or African *"Kohlen"* (coals). "It was something that we felt everyday," explains Stephen, an Ethiopian engineering student in East Berlin. "At the university or at work most of us didn't have any big problems. But usually we experienced it when we were shopping or at public places such as restaurants. It was obvious to us that many Germans didn't want us as part of their private society." One 1990 study showed that every fifth foreigner in the GDR had experienced being refused service in a restaurant. One out of five foreign nationals also admitted that they had experienced some form of physical violence in the GDR. The authorities went to great lengths to cover up the mounting violence directed against foreign nationals in the late 1980s.

The communist regime's short-sighted policies and institutional racism could hardly have bred anything other than xenophobic attitudes in the population. The state insured that the average GDR citizen's Weltanschauung remained profoundly Eurocentric, with the superlative socialist GDR itself at the very center. Pupils in the homogeneously white GDR schools came into little contact with material about other cultures or even with world literature, except when it served as propaganda. Many GDR burghers found it difficult to stretch their imaginations far beyond the confines of their own little nests. Travel restrictions reinforced the provincialism that the system engendered. Travel to the West was forbidden to all but an exceptional few; the single country that GDR citizens could travel to without a visa was Czechoslovakia. When abroad, the GDR Germans with their weak East marks were often treated as "second-class Germans," fueling a resentment that many then passed on to foreigners in their own country.

Wolfgang Thierse, a leading Social Democrat today in the federal parliament, argues that racism in the GDR reflected a continuity in the traditional German consciousness, one which "real existing socialism" only perpetuated. "The SED (Socialist Unity Party) leadership swept the GDR-specific intolerance toward foreigners under the carpet, and worse, from time to time instrumentalized it," explains Thierse. "The GDR-specific intolerance was and is an expression of our 'hospitalization.' We simply didn't learn how to relate to 'others,' to people from foreign countries. And how could we have, when we couldn't experience foreign countries for forty years! We were forcefully confined and now react accordingly, like hospitalized children: autistic, scared, uncertain, skittish, and aggressive." Not only couldn't the GDR Germans travel, says Thierse, but they also rarely came into contact with foreigners residing in the GDR. "The Vietnamese, the Poles, the Afganistans, the Angolans, who came here as 'guest workers'—although the state, of course, wouldn't use that term—lived and worked separate from us: in separate factories, in separate barrack-like living quarters. In truth, GDR socialism developed something quite similar to its own form of apartheid. There were few GDR Germans who were able to surmount these formidable barriers."[2]

It was no coincidence that the post-Wall racism directed itself most virulently against the very peoples whom the state accommodated under the name of "proletarian internationalism" and "international solidarity." In addition to the Warsaw Pact countries, the GDR's special "friendship with other peoples" extended to Ethiopia, Angola, Cuba, Vietnam, and Mozambique, which were bound with the GDR in the "the fight against imperialism, colonialism, neo-colonialism, racism, and apartheid." The state invited the majority of the 191,000 foreigners (1989 figure) to the GDR on four- and five-year contracts to compensate for the short-handed labor force. The largest group, the 60,067 Vietnamese, worked predominantly in the textile industry, the 15,483 Mozambicans in heavy industry. Poles constituted the second largest group of guest workers with 51,483 people. The total percentage of foreigners in the GDR only amounted to 1.2 percent of the nearly seventeen million population, a figure markedly lower than in the FRG, for example, where foreign nationals constituted 7.3 percent of the sixty-two-million-strong populace.

During their stay in the GDR, the guest workers lived as second-class citizens. As historian Irene Runge documented in her 1990 study of foreigners in the GDR, *Fremdenhass: Ausland DDR* (Xenophobia: Abroad in the GDR), their detailed work contracts stated expressly what they could and could not do, who could visit the dormitories and when, how many bicycles they could buy, etc. Seventy percent of the foreign workers and students were male, most between the ages of twenty and forty. The contracts of women workers from Vietnam and Mozambique forbade them to have children during their stay. Cuban women who became pregnant in the GDR found themselves on the next plane home. The contracts granted parents two months in five years to visit children who remained behind in their native countries. The GDR employed many of the guest workers below their level of qualification, most in the bottom-of-the-barrel jobs that the Germans didn't want. Vietnamese workers say that they were routinely given the lowliest and most dangerous tasks. If they had refused, they could have been expelled from the country upon the recommendation of the factory director. Most of the foreign nationals were placed in the lowest wage bracket, and then, in the case of the Cubans, sixty percent of their salaries were transferred directly to their bank accounts in Cuba. The state also regulated the type and amount of goods that foreigners could buy and send back to their families. The authorities, however, took no action to dispel the popular myths that "the foreigners buy up all of our goods." Such "common knowledge" proved as useful to the East Berlin regime as it does today for Bonn: It conveniently transferred responsibility for economic mismanagement away from the state, and on to someone else.

Nor did the state make an effort to integrate foreign nationals into German social life, a move that would also have helped bridge its own people's cultural isolation. One of the few places for foreign nationals to meet and socialize with GDR Germans was the Café Cabana in the basement of the East Berlin St. George's Church parish. Initiated in 1988, the project gave foreign nationals a weekly forum and GDR citizens the opportunity to share a bit of their foreign counterparts' culture. Even today on a Tuesday evening, you can still find the familiar face of the former dissident, Pastor Almuth Berger, at one of the candlelit tables, chatting with a handful of the Cabana regulars. "When we first proposed the café project the authorities naturally didn't like the idea," says Berger over a bowl of the Cabana's famous sauerkraut soup. Across the table a handsome Angolan student nods in agreement.

His German girlfriend stares blankly ahead. "The authorities looked at me as if I were mad when I talked about racism and anti-foreigner sentiment in the GDR," explains the outspoken Lutheran pastor, who now heads up the state of Brandenburg's Office for Foreign Nationals. " 'We don't know what you're talking about, Frau Berger,' they'd say to me. 'In the GDR there is no racism, only solidarity.' "

Typically, the GDR regime understood racism solely as a product of capitalism, to which "socialist" countries were by nature immune. As a communist state, the GDR and its citizens were biologically aligned with the world's oppressed. The state's official "anti-fascist" propaganda circumnavigated the centrality of Nazi racial policies to National Socialism, and addressed Germany's fascist legacy only in terms of its continuity in the Federal Republic. "Just because racism and anti-Semitism weren't spoken about doesn't mean that these ideas weren't still in the heads of many parents and grandparents in the GDR," says Berger. "Those years didn't go by without leaving a trace. They were passed down from generation to generation."

Studies show the GDR Germans' "international solidarity" with third world liberation movements and their "socialist brother states" at a high point in the 1960s, falling off precipitously in the 1970s and 1980s. By and large, people participated in the Day of Anti-Racism marches or fundraising campaigns for Ethiopia on the same opportunist grounds that they paid their party dues. Yet, argues Berger, there were also those who had a genuine human commitment to the campaigns to collect toys for children in Nicaragua or school books for Mozambique. Even so, "the GDR's collapse and the outright rejection of all that it stood for and presided over also discredited any of its positive aspects," explains Berger. "Many people, who expressed real solidarity with third world countries before, today will have nothing to do with it. It's impossible even to use the word 'solidarity' today, so negative are its connotations."

The third world peoples weren't the only ones to experience the GDR Germans' lack of camaraderie. As post-Wall violence against Polish citizens in Germany showed, the chauvinism of many Germans towards their Slavic neighbors is still frightfully intense. The lyrics of a GDR pop song underlined the East German's oft-heard charge against the *"Pollacks"*: "I came from the central department store, and I must tell you, the shelves are bare. Everywhere on the terraces and ledges sat the Poles with their relatives." The hostile tone echoed that of the GDR regime's propaganda campaign against Poland's independent Solidarity trade union movement in the early 1980s. In order to preempt the possible spread of the worker-led democracy movement to the GDR, the media depicted the Poles as a disorderly, lazy people, who would rather strike than work. The message sank in, as a December 1989 letter in the East Berlin daily *Die Berliner Zeitung* illustrates: "Everyone knows the mentality of the Poles. The majority of them are lazy and often earn their money by dishonest means. . . . It's astounding that we have to tolerate their streetside trade and outrageous prices. And the authorities do nothing to prevent it—incredible!"

Study after study in the new federal states attests to high levels of xenophobia, particularly racism, in the population. In 1991, the Leipzig-based German Youth Institute found that half of eastern Germany's young people felt that there were too many foreigners in the new states. Twelve percent of all those asked and twenty percent of vocational students stated that "every foreigner in Germany is one too many." The survey's authors noted that "the young peoples' aversion to foreigners is particularly significant" in light of the small percentage of foreigners in the total population in eastern Germany. The Leipzig social pedagogues observed that young people in West European countries with markedly higher percentages of foreigners "show much more tolerance." The youth formulated their prejudices largely along racial lines, expressing the greatest hostility toward Roma, Turks, Vietnamese, and black Africans, as well as toward Poles. Jews were near the bottom of the list. Although the degree of intolerance increased among those from families with less formal education, there emerged no direct correlation between racism and economic status. The intolerance toward foreigners, concluded the researchers just a few months before Hoyerswerda, "has increased drastically since 1989–90. According to our results, the present situation is clearly critical. There is a lot that points toward a further, perhaps even drastic, increase in anti-foreigner sentiment in the new federal states."

A 1991 Humboldt University study of (east) Berlin youth between the ages of fifteen and twenty-five yielded similar results. Over half of those polled agreed with the statement that "when a shortage of jobs exists, foreigners should be sent back to their native countries." A third of the young people admitted that they could not trust foreigners the way that they could Germans. The study showed little sympathy for the development of a multicultural society in eastern Berlin. Over half of the young people agreed that "foreigners in Germany had better adjust their life-style to that of the Germans." A quarter of the participants admitted that "countries like Poland and Bulgaria could never reach Germany's cultural niveau because of the genetic laziness and backwardness of the Slavs."

LEIPZIG AWAKENS

By the late 1980s, the growing resentment toward foreign nationals in the GDR had come plainly to the surface, finding its clearest expression in the GDR's underground Skinhead and neo-Nazi movements. From 1983 to 1988, the yearly number of criminal acts with right-wing political motives had more than quintupled, with assaults against foreign nationals comprising one category of that violence. Foreign nationals reported that the dirty looks had increasingly turned into physical aggression. Yet, the proliferation of racist assaults and right-wing activity in the GDR coincided with other developments in 1989, which, for a time at least, would overshadow the ascent of the right in the GDR.

As summer turned to fall in 1989, the snowballing exodus of thousands of GDR Germans through the newly opened border in Hungary brought the acute crisis in the GDR state to a head. Deep in Saxony, just over 100 kilometers from Hoyerswerda, the "democratic revolution" began to stir. The Monday evening peace vigils in Leipzig's Nikolai Church steadily drew crowds ever larger than their standard core of democratic intellectuals, environmental activists, and Christian pacifists. The more stubbornly the regime resisted change or compromise, the larger the Nikolai Church vigils grew until they spilled over onto the parish's cobbled square. By October, the vigils had evolved into full-scale demonstrations, the size of the marches doubling and tripling from week to week. The protests swelled until over 350,000 of the industrial city's half million residents took to the streets. The peaceful, candlelit processions through central Leipzig set the original tone of East Germany's "democratic revolution." The rallying cry that became the trademark of the Leipzig demos, "Wir sind das Volk!" (We are the people!), resonated off the gray, soot-scarred buildings. The single expression of hostility came when the procession passed the heavily armed headquarters of the Ministry of State Security, the home of the *Stasi*, the secret police. The air buzzed with long, shrill hisses, while high-school girls lit candles at the feet of the poised anti-riot forces, plexiglass helmets strapped on tight, Kalishnikovs at the ready.

With arms locked in solidarity, Saxons young and old belted out the lyrics of the Internationale and chanted "Neues Forum! Neues Forum!", the name of the newly formed illegal human rights and democracy movement group. At the forefront of the demonstrations, many of New Forum's intellectuals and longtime dissidents touted their vision of an independent democratic GDR, an alternative to the dictatorship as well as to the Federal Republic. In her fourth story apartment overlooking the jammed Karl Marx Square, New Forum's Leipzig spokesperson, writer Petra Lux, spoke enthusiastically about a progressive form of socialism, one based upon broad notions of civil society, pluralism and community. "But that's something that the people will decide upon," said the thirty-six-year-old dissident. "There is no political ideology attached to the demonstrations. We're simply demanding basic rights such as freedom of expression, free elections, and the right to travel." She underlined the centrality of nonviolence to the protests. "For forty years we've been subjected to the violence and repression of the police state. Since we're demanding an end to that repression, we've agreed to counter the violence of the state with nonviolence."

On November 9, 1989, the Berlin Wall fell. The course of the revolution, however, had changed direction even before the legalized democracy movement groups and the reform communist leadership had sat down to chart the GDR's transition. Although GDR legislation continued to ban the activities of neo-fascist political organizations, the chaos of the moment gave the right the room that it needed. A general amnesty for 2600 political prisoners in the GDR put hundreds of right-wing militants back on to the streets. GDR Skinhead, neo-Nazi, and fascist groups teamed up with their western associates, setting joint strategies into motion at full speed. Whatever illusions the democratic intellectuals harbored about a "new GDR," the right suddenly saw its years-long goal at the top of the popular agenda: the overthrow of the GDR and the unification of East and West Germany. Their unexpected "success," in fact, caught the still small, locally organized right-wing groups in the GDR off-guard. But the fallout from the dramatic changes underway played into their hands as neatly as they could ever have imagined.

The burst of democratic exuberance was short-lived. Democracy movement leaders looked on aghast as the Monday evening vigils in Leipzig turned into grotesque celebrations of German nationalism. By the year's end, the demonstrations' leitmotif had changed from "We are the people!" to "We are one people!", and nationalism reverberated throughout the Democratic Republic. The Saxon city echoed with shouts of "One Germany!", "Down with the Left!", and "Germany to the Germans!" The spirit as well as the composition of the demonstrations changed: less women and fewer older people, students, and foreign nationals appeared on the streets. When the initiators of the Nikolai Church vigils stood up to urge tolerance, they were drowned out by boos and whistles. Foreign students addressing the crowd were hit with beer bottles. Ordinary citizens who had chanted "Neues Forum!" two months before, now waved huge black, red, and gold German flags, singing "Deutschland, Deutschland über Alles" and "Deutschland einig Vaterland."

In mid-November Petra Lux took a visiting contingent from Leipzig's International Documentary Film Week to the central square. "It was clear to me only then that things had taken a sharp turn to the right," says Lux. "From what I had told them and from what they had heard, our guests from Eastern Europe, Africa, and Latin America expected to see something really great. But the racist, anti-foreigner sentiment was unmistakable. They were afraid and I was incredibly, incredibly ashamed. That was the last time that I ever went to a Monday demo. People with left-wing ideas knew that it was dangerous to show up there."

Behind the German flags stood an ugly ultra-nationalism, whose fires West German agitators tactically stoked in subzero Leipzig. The Monday demonstrations, the birthplace of the nonviolent revolution, witnessed the debut of over a dozen of West Germany's radical right-wing parties in the GDR. Leading chants of "Greater Germany!" and "Jews Out!", their demands clearly went a step beyond the average German's newfound longing for unification. The ultra-right Republican Party maintained a dominant profile at the actions, distributing reams of propaganda that it had smuggled through the porous borders. Young men above all eagerly snatched up the party's leaflets, bumper stickers, and lighters. Neo-Nazi and Skinhead groups marched through the icy streets with their arms extended in the Nazi salute and German Reich flags draped over their shoulders.

The warm welcome that greeted the West German right in Leipzig stirred new hopes among the established FRG extremist parties. Although the West German ultra-right had cultivated contacts with GDR neo-Nazi and fascist groups before 1989, the situation in the GDR opened an entirely new set of opportunities. The right's publications made it clear that "Middle Germany," as they referred to the GDR, was the new frontline of their campaigns. In an internal report, the Republican Party's Bavarian Campaign Manager, Reinhard Rade, glowed over their reception on Karl Marx Square in Leipzig: "Ninety-five percent of the demonstrators showed an interest in our propaganda, and within half an hour all of the 25,000 pamphlets were gone. A few West Germans(!) and Stasi informants tried to agitate against us, but the crowd silenced them."[3] Should they be allowed to run, Rade predicted a fifteen-to-thirty percent turnout for the Republicans in the first GDR election. He concluded his report: "This is the hour of the Republicans!" During a January 1990 visit to Thuringia, the West German neo-Nazi leader Michael Kühnen claimed that he was "simply swamped" with admirers. The initial enthusiasm seemed to extend beyond the core support of Skinheads and soccer fans. With the communist regime in ruin, many of its fair-weather supporters showed their true colors, relocating to the ranks of the ultra-right.

The ground swell of German nationalism put an abrupt end to the long-term possibility of a sovereign GDR. The collapse of the dictatorship dealt the final blow to the fragile GDR identity, to which the democracy-movement intellectuals had hoped to give new meaning. For a depoliticized people confronted overnight with an identity crisis, nationalism offered the most convenient and palpable option. The lives of the GDR citizens had taken an unexpected turn toward the unknown, an unknown they themselves were to decide upon for the first time. And now, those decisions would have to be made on the basis of an ostensibly new value system. As pleased as the average, law-abiding citizen may have been to see the state and its ethic dethroned, he had hoped for a change more in the form of a present than a struggle. The call of the democracy movement parties to build a civic society with participatory forms of democracy fell on deaf ears.

German nationalism offered the GDR citizenry a quick ersatz ideology, which, in the form of unification, also provided a paternal, ostensibly all-encompassing solution to their plight. The prospect of unification with the Federal Republic offered stability, financial security and a ready-made new ethic. The flat-out denial of the discredited communist state, as well as their role in the system, put the GDR Germans on the side of the "victors of history" once again. As GDR citizens they had been the conquerors of fascism, as FRG citizens they became the victors over communism. Anetta Kahane, Director of the Regional Office for Questions concerning Foreign Nationals in Berlin, argues that the GDR Germans' swift conversion failed to alter their essential convictions. Although the GDR state had played down national identification, explains Kahane, it simultaneously "de-emphasized the role of the individual and encouraged a Weltanschauung that was oriented toward quiet, order, security, cleanliness, and discipline. Even in their rejection of the state, the people did not alter this fundamental consensus. In fact, they rejected whoever called those values into question. The pettiness and brutality with which this popular repression occurred was indeed astounding."[4]

For the right, the developments in Leipzig signalled that the taboos of the police state were no longer in force. The months following the Wall's opening witnessed a chilling escalation of racist and right-wing activity in the GDR. No sooner did police scrub graffiti such as "Greater Germany awake!", "No recognition of the Oder-Neisse border!" and "Foreigners Out—We need Lebensraum!" off the walls, than more appeared the next day. The violence came largely from Skinhead and neo-Nazi groups, which had strengthened their existing structures with weaponry, propaganda, and tactical advice from the West. Soon the Skinhead and neo-Nazi gangs presided over arsenals of gas pistols, switchblades, and baseball bats—the standard weaponry of their Western counterparts. In the looming power vacuum, uncertain police units stood by as Skinhead violence against foreigners, punks, and representatives of the communist system exploded on an unprecedented level. The 1990 Federal Office for the Protection of the Constitution report described a "dramatic increase in right-extreme violence of eastern German Skinheads," particularly in Saxony, Brandenburg, and (east) Berlin. The report noted the GDR militants' particularly strong behavior patterns and their ability to amass large numbers of supporters on a given day. Experts estimated that the number of militant neo-fascists in the GDR ranged anywhere from 2000 to 3000 persons, with an unknown—and untapped—number of sympathizers.

Assaults against foreign nationals also increased and graffiti such as "Turks Out!", "Jews Out!", and "Ruskies up against the Wall!" proliferated. The first wave of post-Wall violence, however, primarily targeted the police, left-wing house squatters, and communist monuments—all, in the right's eyes, representatives of the system. Until the reform communist leadership and democracy movement parties were out of the way for good, "the left" remained Public Enemy Number One. In East Berlin, Leipzig, and Dresden, marauding Skin gangs launched nightly raids on the decrepit brick buildings that anarchist punks had occupied and turned into squatter communes. After soccer games, the GDR *Volkspolizei* ringed the colorfully muralled houses of the former "counter-revolutionaries," as the state had deemed anarchists, with riot vehicles and special anti-terrorist units to protect the squatters.

Even in smaller cities and towns, groups of fifty to sixty neo-fascist youths routinely wreaked havoc in train stations and on the streets, often directly attacking the outnumbered police forces. The early violence peaked on April 20, 1990, the 101st birthday of Adolf Hitler. After a soccer match in the East Berlin Cantian Stadium, 500 to 600 Nazi-Skins and assorted hooligans marched on the Schönhauser Allee Square, shouting "Reds out!" and "Heil Hitler!" Riot police skirmished with the intoxicated radicals, driving them toward the central Alexanderplatz where full-scale battles broke out between the celebrating Skinheads and 600 police.

THE RISE OF THE NEW RIGHT

The entrance of the West German ultra-right parties into the GDR marked a critical turning point for the GDR ultra-right. The West Germans lost no time transferring their structures onto the local, loosely organized cliques in the East. The more sophisticated, conspiratorial neo-fascist groups in the GDR quickly integrated themselves into the West German ultra-right parties. By early 1990, nearly all of the West parties had formed GDR sister organizations. The Skinheads, too, although they remained fragmented and unruly, received key support and guidance from the FRG parties. The first signs that a right-wing radicalism specific to the GDR would develop diminished from month to month. Time and again the recipe for terror proved to be brain power from the West and muscle from the East. "Around the middle of 1990," argues Berlin political scientist Norbert Madloch, "it was clear that in light of the strong 'comradely' aid from the West the organizational model of the FRG parties would dominate. The specific nature of the GDR right extremists was that they came forward as much more radical and militant than their counterparts in the West. Although they were ready to try out new courses of action, they were still intellectually and programmatically far behind their mother organizations."[5] According to Madloch, the potential for violence as well as the pace at which the East militants were arming themselves exceeded that in the West. Even at the primary school level, young radicals were armed and active in violent right-wing gangs.

The incorporation of the diffuse GDR right into the West German neo-fascist movement brought with it the strategies and ideological developments that had matured over several decades in the FRG. Since the early 1950s, ultra-right parties operated legally in the Federal Republic, as long as they refrained from using openly fascist language or symbols. The pre-1980s pinnacle of the ultra-right's electoral efforts was the 1964 federal vote, when the German National Democratic Party (Nationaldemokratische Partei Deutschlands), or NPD, captured 4.3 percent of the popular vote, just a fraction short of the five percent necessary to win parliamentary seats. The majority of nationalist conservative and ultra-right elements, however, made their homes in the right wings of one of the conservative mainstream parties, the CDU and its Bavarian sister-party, the Christian Social Union (CSU). But the CDU/CSU's early 1980s *Ostpolitik* of rapprochement with the GDR proved more than the conservative's right-wing could stomach. The time was finally ripe, they decided, to strike out on their own.

In the early 1980s, the arrival of the *Neue Rechte* in West Germany, along with the New Right in England, the *Nouvelle Droite* in France, and others throughout Western Europe opened a new chapter in the history of the European Right.[6] The stated goal of West Germany's early New Right thinkers was to bring the German Right "out from the shadow of Auschwitz," to distance the far right movement from the damning stigma of its Nazi past. The strategy of the like-minded discussion circles, publications, and organizations contained two major elements. First, the right-wing intellectuals sought to influence the postwar political culture in a way that would destigmatize the fascist ideas that fell outside of the liberal consensus. They argued that an ultra-right political movement could be possible only when its language and assumptions had first become an accepted part of political discourse. Through a right-wing "cultural revolution," the modern neo-fascists set out to create a social and political climate that would once again be receptive to fascist ideas.

U.S. President Ronald Reagan's 1985 visit to a German military cemetery in Bitburg, West Germany, and the Historians' Debate a year later were exactly what the New Right thinkers had in mind. Despite international outcry, Reagan agreed to participate in a May 8 service in Bitburg commemorating the fortieth anniversary of the end of

WWII and the capitulation of the Nazi dictatorship. The source of the protest stemmed not from the commemoration itself but from the world leaders' choice of the site: a cemetery that contained the graves of fallen WWI and WWII German soldiers, including those of former SS officers. In bowing his head with Chancellor Kohl, the President's minute of silence implicitly placed the deaths of the fallen German Nazis on the same moral plane as the deaths of all of those who had lost their lives at Nazi hands in the World War and the Holocaust. The implication was that all of those who perished in WWII were victims—Jews and Germans, Nazis and the Allies. The Bitburg ceremony went another step toward "normalizing" the Nazi legacy, toward relieving the German people of their historical burden.

On the heels of the Bitburg scandal followed the Historians' Debate. The apologetic interpretations of the Nazi era by a contingent of respected conservative historians ignited a stormy controversy in academic and public circles. Among other points, the revisionists equated National Socialism with the crimes of Stalinism, effectively playing down the singularity and particular evil of Nazi atrocities. Even though the academy roundly criticized the conservatives, the public controversy implicitly gave their ideas a new legitimacy. The ideas of the New Right were out in the open; new ground had been broken.

The New Right's second front was the construction of a modern image for the movement, one which could appeal to a broad, mainstream following. The movement replaced the brown shirts and swastikas of the past with a professional, young veneer. They dropped terminology such as "Aryan supremacy" and "Blut und Boden" society for their own racist versions of "European unity" and "environmental protection." The language was decisively less threatening, but the content no less reactionary. In order to free neo-fascism from the ballast of Nazism, the New Right sacrificed Adolf Hitler. The clear aim of their guarded critique of National Socialism was to excuse German fascism from the Nazi regime's two most ignominious crimes: the Holocaust and the World War. In order to circumvent National Socialism's darkest spots, the New Right theorists latched onto figures associated with the Third Reich's 1933–37 period like the Night of the Long Knives victim, SA Captain Ernst Röhm, and the pre-fascist thinkers of the Weimar Republic, such as the Strasser brothers, Gregor and Otto. In exchange for the Nazis' overtly racial theories, the New Rightists embraced cosmetic theories of "national identity" and "ethnic specificity," which distinguished a similar hierarchy of peoples. The product was slogans such as "Germans be proud to be Germans, Turks be proud to be Turks—united against Communism and Racial Mixing."

The core theoretical category that underpins New Right ideology is the *Volksgemeinschaft*, a concept at the heart of early Nazi theory and central to all ethnic nationalist ideologies. According to the New Rightists, all Germans, simply by being German, belong to the Germanic Volksgemeinschaft, a closed ethnic community based on common national culture and values. Within this "natural" community, all members are theoretically equal and superior to those outside of it. The New Right offers the Volksgemeinschaft as an alternative to the meaning that eludes people in modern postindustrial society. They argue that modernity has "uprooted" the human being, cast him as an atomized individual into an alienating, high-tech world. Yet rather than confront the dilemma of modernization with bonding forms of society and social community, the New Right retreats into the realm of tradition, family, and nation.

The Republican Party's (REP) meteoric rise in the late 1980s formally announced the New Right's arrival in the FRG. Founded in a Bavarian tavern in 1983, the new party rallied behind the sixty-year-old local radio journalist and former *Waffen SS* man Franz Schönhuber. Schönhuber presented the New Right's image with deft skill. He maneuvered around the category of the "old Nazi," while making plain that not only was he proud to have been in the Waffen SS, but that there was indeed something worthwhile that Germans could salvage from the Nazi era. The notion of the Volksgemeinschaft informed his two central slogans: "I'm proud to be a German" and "We want to stay German."

At first to receptive crowds in Bavarian beer halls, and then across the Federal Republic, Schönhuber peddled his national populist message with vigor. He stridently argued that German history be "decriminalized" so that Germans could once again take rightful pride in their national symbols and traditional values. Schönhuber posed the German petty bourgeoisie as the real losers in modern postindustrial society. The traditional German family's sense of security and closeness had been lost, not least because of "left" influences such as the women's movement. In tirades against the Federal Republic's "liberal" immigration and political asylum statutes, the Republicans tapped a potent combination of nationalism, racism, and social frustration. Only drastic curbs on foreigners in Germany would "prevent the misuse and injury of German citizens, their safety and their communal essence." Perhaps most maverick of all at the time, the Republicans called for the fall of the GDR and the immediate unification of East and West Germany. Unlike the other "Old Right" parties, the Republicans kept diplomatically silent about the "lost German territories" east of the Oder-Neisse border.

The REP's spectacular rise occurred within the space of one year. In January 1989, the party captured a shocking 7.5 percent of the vote in West Berlin municipal elections. Some working-class districts delivered the extremists twenty percent of their support, and similar successes followed. In June of that year, two million West Germans voted for the REP in the European Parliament elections, sending Schönhuber and five colleagues to the Strassburg parliament. Analyses of voting patterns revealed that it was primarily the racist demagoguery directed against foreign nationals living in West Germany that accounted for the party's victories. Ninety-seven percent of REP voters admitted that they were not prepared to recognize foreign nationals living in the FRG as "fellow citizens." Over two-thirds said that "had it not been for the war and the Holocaust, Hitler would have been one of Germany's greatest statesman."

Remarkably, the backgrounds of the REP voters present a near mirror image of right-wing sympathizers in the communist GDR and now in the new federal states. Although the REP crassly linked the country's economic and social problems to the presence of foreigners in Germany, those districts that voted heavily for the REP had only minimal numbers of foreign residents. In other words, REP voters were not anti-foreigner because their neighbors were Turks. In fact, in city districts where high concentrations of foreigners resided, the turn-out for the REP sank below the average. Nor did the party rally large ranks of the unemployed or underprivileged. Just as the Hoyerswerdians, the average REP voter boasted a middle-class or higher standard of living. The small business people, bureaucrats, and wage earners who backed the REP did so out of fear of the future. Many had shifted their votes from the Social Democrats to the ultra-right. A disproportionately high percentage of REP voters were male (three times more than women), young (many between eighteen and twenty-three years old) and with lower levels of education than other voters. The REP also scored exceptionally well among people living in the urban "social housing projects," the Neubau complexes of the Hoyerwerda variety, which the Social Democratic government had erected in the sixties and seventies.

The New Right succeeded in charting a course between the old-school neo-fascists and the CDU/CSU, but failed to eliminate the array of openly radical factions from the far right scene. Unlike the National Front in France, the Republicans were unable to unite the spectrum of ultra-right forces under their banner. The Republicans represented a loose coalition of right-wing forces with different identities, conflicting goals and, most critically, rival leaders. Revamped New Right parties such as the NPD and the *Deutsche Volksunion* (German Peoples Union) also relied upon primarily electoral strategies, although not to the exclusion of courting Skinheads or expediting violence. Neo-Nazi organizations such as the Nationalist Front, the Liberal German Workers Party, and the *Deutsche Alternative* regularly employed violence and relied heavily upon Skinhead and hooligan groups. Despite their small numbers, even the fringe neo-Nazi groups have shown themselves capable of influencing public opinion and even political debate. Hoyerswerda and Rostock are cases in point.

A short sketch of the major neo-fascist groups gives a picture of the ultra-right to the right of the Republicans.[7]

GERMAN NATIONAL DEMOCRATIC PARTY
(*NATIONALDEMOKRATISCHE PARTEI DEUTSCHLANDS*), NPD

The oldest of the major neo-fascist parties, the NDP has never repeated the stunning performance that it delivered in the 1969 federal elections.

The "hardcore of the German right," however, as they describe themselves, has continued to pursue an electoral strategy, despite falling consistently below one percent of the vote totals. In contrast to the REP, the NPD demands the reinstatement of Nazi Germany's 1937 borders. As do all of the openly neo-fascist groups, the NPD insists upon the restoration of the German Reich's "lost territories," including the Alsace-Lorraine in France, as well as western Poland, the former Sudetenland in the Czech Republic, former East Prussia in the former Soviet Union, and Austria. According to the NPD, the unification of the two Germanies was only the first step in the resurrection of Germany's "true ethnic borders." The NPD's platform has long stressed "the asylum swindle" and Germany's "foreignization" (*Überfremdung*). The party's decline in recent years has led to internal discussions of participation in a broad right coalition.

GERMAN PEOPLES UNION (*DEUTSCHE VOLKSUNION*), DVU

With the arrival of the REP, the DVU dropped in numerical strength to second place among the ultra-right organizations in the FRG. An off-shoot of the NPD, the DVU's president and uncontested *Führer*, Dr. Gerhard Frey, founded the party in 1971. The DVU sees itself as a "supra-party movement," encompassing such groups as the "Popular Movement for a General Amnesty" (for Nazi war criminals) and the "Initiative to Restrict Foreigners." Behind its democratic lip service, the DVU promotes an aggressive xenophobia and caustic anti-Semitism. It calls for a sweeping reappraisal of the National Socialist dictatorship and German responsibility for the outbreak of WWII. Like the other neo-fascist parties, the DVU demands strong-arm "law and order" policies to halt "foreigner-inspired" crime.

The Republicans' success seemed certain to doom the DVU to electoral obscurity. Yet, local 1990 and 1992 elections in Bremen and Schleswig-Holstein (in which the REP did not participate) gave Frey and company unexpected triumphs. In 1990, the DVU doubled its 1987 Bremen showing with 6.6 percent of the total vote and over ten percent in the port city of Bremerhaven. Before and during the election run-up, the party maintained next to no profile in Bremen, running its multimillion mark media campaign from its Munich headquarters. The DVU's single theme: the FRG asylum policy.

LIBERAL GERMAN WORKERS PARTY
(FREIHEITLICHE DEUTSCHE ARBEITERPARTEI), FAP

The FAP had boasted the largest militant neo-Nazi membership in the country for years. Although the organization of less than a thousand members has no electoral prospects, it commands daunting violence. Under the helmsmanship of its sixty-two-year-old president, Friedhelm Busse, the group met startling success in recruiting Skinheads and soccer hooligans in the new federal states. Busse, no newcomer to the neo-Nazi scene, has spent the last few decades in West Germany in and out of jail for crimes including right-extreme agitation, incitement to riot, the celebration of violence, and the illegal possession of weapons. According to the federal Interior Ministry, FAP members stand behind a disproportionately high share of right-wing violence.

GERMAN ALTERNATIVE (DEUTSCHE ALTERNATIVE), DA
/NATIONALE ALTERNATIVE (NA)

The DA and the Berlin-based NA are two of the splinter parties associated with the late Michael Kühnen, until his 1991 death the controversial leader of the West German neo-Nazi movement. Between prison stints, Kühnen stood at the movement's forefront, founding a number of parties and groups, the FAP among them. The Kühnen organizations openly follow in the footsteps of the pre-1945 Nazi party, the National Socialist German Workers Party (Nationalsozialistische Deutsche Arbeiterpartei) or NSDAP, whose criminalization in the FRG the neo-Nazis have long lobbied to repeal. The neo-Nazis make no effort to disguise the racial theories that the Republicans try to mask. The "neos" greet each other with the Hitler salute and often sport brown shirts and swastika arm bands. The DA's honorary members include Adolf Hitler, Rudolf Hess, Ernst Röhm, and Joseph Goebbels. The DA/NA rally cry: "The Fourth Reich is coming!"

In February 1990, the East Berlin–based NA's occupation of a vacant building in the Berlin-Lichtenberg district stirred a furor in the postcommunist GDR. The address of Weitling Street 122 became the residence of the NA leadership, as well as the DA's "National Communication Center." Regular guests there included Kühnen and propaganda director of the NSDAP–International Development Branch, U.S.-citizen Gary Rex Lauck. After the April 20 melee on Alexanderplatz, police shut down the Weitling Street squat. The authorities confiscated an armory of weapons, piles of Nazi propaganda, and a computerized "List of Left Enemies."

By December 1992, when the Interior Ministry finally banned it, the DA had become the biggest neo-Nazi group in the new states with centers in Brandenburg and Saxony. Experts put the membership nationwide at over 1000 people. The DA's success was largely due to its chairman, the twenty-eight-year-old Frank Hübner, hailed by many as Kühnen's heir. In fact, Kühnen handpicked the clean-cut, articulate Hübner, a Cottbus native, to put his "Blueprint East" into practice. Although banned, the DA members have regrouped under other DA-related parties such as the NA, the Hamburg "National List," the Dresden "National Offensive," and the Thuringia "German National Party." As Hübner said after the police raided his apartment: "You can ban a party, but not the people behind it."

NATIONALISTIC FRONT (*NATIONALISTISCHE FRONT*), NF

The NF, also outlawed in 1992, considers itself the successor to the SA Nazi shock troops of the 1930s. The militant "national revolutionaries" say that their aim is to "make life for foreigners in Germany as uncomfortable as possible." The organization's literature appeals to the Skinhead and soccer hooligan scene with crude caricatures of Skinheads in huge boots squashing Turks. The NF is organized in conspiratorial "cells" which often join forces with other neo-Nazi groups, such as the Ku Klux Klan, for raids and cross-burnings. They endorse an anti-imperialist and anti-capitalist "folkish socialism."

The West German right's blitz into the GDR and cozy reception on the streets of Leipzig prompted hysterical forecasts that a radical right-wing backlash would grip the country. GDR sociologists who had dealt with pre-1989 right-wing extremism predicted a massive right-wing surge among the youth. The reform communist party posed the "threat from the right" as a justification for a "new" secret police. Anti-fascist demonstrations in East Berlin brought together an unlikely coalition of hard-line communists, democratic socialists, anarchists, and the militant-left West German *Autonomen*. Ironically, some of the democracy movement leaders, the first people in the GDR to address the danger of neo-fascist currents in East German youth, played down the phenomenon at first. They argued that, as in the West, a marginal ultra-right constituted a normal part of a pluralistic democratic spectrum.

Studies conducted in the early post-Wall period did nothing to dampen those initial fears. And while the right-wing backlash failed to materialize in the proportions that some observers had first predicted, the statistics were hardly encouraging. The Leipzig German Youth Institute revealed an extraordinarily high right-wing potential in the GDR youth, which, the researchers underlined, was closely connected with negative attitudes toward foreigners. A third of those polled admitted that they would prefer the security of an authoritarian state to the uncertain chaos of the transition underway. Thirty-three percent of the youth agreed that "the most important thing today is upholding law and order, with violence if necessary." Only eighteen percent unequivocally disagreed with the statement. And while seventeen percent felt that "the Germans should have a strong-arm ruler again," just over half categorically rejected the statement.

Large percentages of the youth agreed with the standard slogans of right-wing groups, even though only a fraction of those polled actually identified with a specific political party or group. Forty-seven percent of all those asked, and two-thirds of vocational students, endorsed the slogan "Germany to the Germans!" Among members of extreme right-wing organizations, 100 percent agreed that youth were attracted to right-extreme groups because "they were against foreigners." The sociologists discovered a close correlation between nationalist identification and authoritarian, intolerant attitudes. Fifteen to twenty percent of all youth, they concluded, exhibit "authoritarian, nationalistic, and xenophobic" orientations, with a much higher percentage who showed antagonistic feelings toward people who thought or lived differently.

A summer 1990 study that compared the attitudes of eastern and western German youth showed a somewhat higher propensity to right-extreme views in the easterners. In comparison to seven percent in the FRG, sixteen percent of GDR youth said that they wanted to have another Führer (leader) who "rules Germany with a strong hand for the good of all." One result that surely pleased the New Right movement: Over a third of both the East and West Germans claimed that "people of their age need not be ashamed of the legacy of German fascism." The Munich and Leipzig sociologists found that eleven percent of the GDR youth and thirteen percent of the FRG young people saw fascism as a "good thing" that was "only poorly implemented." Their feelings toward foreigners yielded the greatest contrast, although the numbers spoke highly of neither group. Forty-two percent of GDR youth (compared to twenty-six percent in West Germany) admitted that the number of foreigners in Germany disturbed them.

In the 1990 federal and state elections, however, history temporarily overtook the electorally oriented New Right parties, delivering them pounding defeats. The theme that the right alone had embraced for years—German unification—had become official state policy. Chancellor Kohl's January 1990 10 Point Plan for Unification, Schönhuber protested, was identical to the Republicans' earlier proposal. In the late 1989 and 1990 West German elections for the state legislatures, the REP's support sank beneath the five percent hurdle necessary for parliamentary representation. In the East, Kohl and the CDU rode the wave of nationalist euphoria against a backdrop of billowing red, black, and gold flags. The "Unification Chancellor's" grand promises of economic prosperity and security for the soon-to-be new federal states were simply too idyllic for the East Germans to pass up. The dizzying speed of events in Germany had left the Right temporarily empty-handed. In the October 1990 elections for the GDR state legislature, the combined total of REP and NPD votes fell below the one percent mark. Two months later in the first all-German federal elections, the REP tripled its showing in the eastern states, but garnered only 115,496 votes, or 1.5 percent.

On neither side of the former border did right-wing sympathies just disappear. The CDU/CSU simply succeeded in winning back the right-wing vote that it had had in its grip until the REP came along. Unfamiliar with the West German political spectrum, the uncertain GDR electorate showed themselves more inclined to wait and see which party could offer them optimal security. The "Leipzig phenomenon" characterized the disorientation of a depoliticized people, unpredictable and susceptible to abrupt changes in allegiance. One factor that would typically distinguish the electorates in the old and new federal states was the former GDR Germans' reluctance to join or identify with political parties. The population in the new federal states has proved easier to rally for a short time around emotional, immediate issues than to organize into coherent structures. The inability of the New Right parties to amass substantial memberships in eastern Germany in no way spelled their demise. In fact, after the December 1990 elections several analysts pointed out the New Right parties' impressive accumulation of over 150,000 combined votes in the new federal states, considering that they ran with virtually no organizational structures or publicity.

The issues that had buoyed the Republicans' fortunes in 1989 soon resurfaced once the national ecstasy over unification receded, and the ultra-right parties struck back with more strength than ever. In the 1992 and 1993 local elections in several former West German states, the Republicans and the DVU scored record victories, capturing between six and eleven percent of the vote where they had next to nothing four years before. On the heels of the National Front's successes in France and the triumphs of similar parties in Belgium, Austria, Italy, and Sweden in 1992, the comeback of the German right should hardly have registered the shock that it did. The mainstream parties had kept the issues so important to the ultra-right on the front burner. The Republicans took the Bonn establishment's logic on the asylum issue one step further and cashed in on the growing disillusionment with the major parties' inability to address the burdensome problems of unification. The ultra-right, it seemed, had become part of the German political landscape that was there to stay.

DRESDEN—CAPITAL OF THE RIGHT

The initial benefactors of the CDU's early electoral rout of the New Right in the East were the neo-Nazi groups. Just as some critics had feared, the movement went underground again, where it was more difficult to observe, control, or predict. The unofficial headquarters of the neo-Nazi scene shifted from Berlin, the future capital of the united Germany, to Dresden, the capital of Saxony. The ultra-right mobilized with virtual impunity in the traditionally conservative region, gaining tacit if not open support from the population and police forces. In Dresden, as well as in Cottbus, Leipzig, Halle, and Hoyerswerda, the threat of racist violence became an everyday reality for the foreign nationals there. The reigning political climate was one that enabled the right-wing British revisionist historian David Irving to propagate in university halls his thesis that the Holocaust was a myth invented by the Allies. In the dark passageways of the Hauptbahnhof train station, the DVU's daily *Die Deutsche National Zeitung* sells for one German mark.

Outside of the historic city center, most Dresdeners live in one of the many sprawling Neubau settlements, testament to the Allies' merciless 1945 bombing of Saxony's "Baroque pearl on the Elbe," which reduced ninety percent of the city to rubble. One streetcar stop beyond the Square of the Construction Workers begins Dresden's largest housing project, Gorbitz. On an early winter evening, the blue-purple flicker of television sets illuminates the cloned towers. Below, the empty maze-like pathways weave their way through the self-contained cement city: the uniform GDR supermarket, the uniform GDR barber shop, the uniform GDR playground. A mobile sausage stand shows the only sign of life. Four men in bulky winter jackets huddle around the warm, acrid fumes of frying *Bratwurst*, beer cans gripped in their gloveless hands. Up a muddy incline sits a flat, single-story building—the uniform

GDR youth club. The graffiti covering the Espe Club's walls shows that Gorbitz has earned its reputation as the stronghold of Dresden's hardcore neo-Nazi scene. It reads: "Foreigners Out!", "Third Reich Again!", and "Hoyerswerda—Foreigner Free!"

On a quiet Monday evening, a handful of plainly dressed teenagers hang out listlessly, playing ping-pong in the bright neon-lit room. The only evidence of the GDR's collapse is the video rental booth that stands in a converted broom closet. A poster on the open door advertises *Rambo III*. The Gorbitz Brotherhood had met weekly at the Espe until the loose neo-Nazi alliance broke apart, again scattering the 100 to 150 violent right-wing youth that Dresden police estimate live in Gorbitz. Three to four times that number are active in all of Dresden, as well as several thousand sympathizers of varying degrees of commitment. Elementary school teachers in Gorbitz say that eighty percent of their pupils boast of being "right-radical." In class elections, it is the right-wing gang leaders who consistently top the school ballots.

Nervous and obviously out of place, I drift over to two young guys, perched on bar stools at the closed soda bar. I tell them that I'm doing a story on "youth culture" in Dresden and that I've already been to talk with the "lefties" across the river. The bigger one laughs. "Culture? In Gorbitz? Well, you aren't gonna have much to write about." His friend laughs too. But they don't have anything better to do than talk with me, so why not. "Yeah, we're all right-wing here," says Jörg, eighteen, in a rough, working-class Saxon accent. Tall and muscular, with short-cropped brown hair and flashing dark eyes, Jörg also says that he's a member of the Ku Klux Klan (KKK). Although he's never met another Klan member, he has their translated literature. The KKK, which has long had links with West German neo-Nazis, first began recruiting its own membership in the new federal states in early winter 1991. Jörg knows that the U.S. KKK leader Dennis Mahon and German colleagues initiated the KKK campaign with a cross burning outside of Berlin. "The Klan takes the strongest stand against the niggers and the fidschies," he scowls defiantly, "those who take away our jobs and flats." He hesitates for a moment, adding "yeah, and of course against the lefties, too."

Jörg and his pal Gerd are both apprentice bakers. That Gerd belongs to the FAP doesn't faze his KKK-loyal friend. "We're both National Socialists, and that's what counts," says Jörg. The shorter, wiry Gerd nods respectfully. Lisping slightly, Gerd says that he's a member of the FAP because "they got the best program." That program he summarizes in two words: "Stop foreigners." A black winter cap pulled down over his crew cut, he isn't forthcoming with more information. Basically, he admits, it's that the Gorbitz FAP has the "best guys" that prompted him to join up six months ago. The group of about thirty neo-Nazis maintain regular contact with the movement's leadership in the West.

Two young ladies in bright baseball jackets and tight-fitting stone-washed jeans appear on the scene, one sliding her arm through Jörg's. Ute says that she will join the Aryan-supremacist *Wiking Jugend* (Viking Youth) as soon as she turns eighteen next year. "The WJ just wants to restore traditional German values and Germany's real borders," she says, accurately repeating the neo-Nazi group's platform. Modelled upon the Hitler Youth and its sister organization, the Union of German Girls, the WJ stresses the revival of folkish German customs and culture. How willingly Ute would trade her "Kansas City Stars" jacket for a Bavarian dirndl, she doesn't say. But the prim, shapely teenager would sign up with the WJ immediately, if her parents would only give her permission as a minor. "In principle, my parents agree with a lot that the WJ stands for," she says, "but they're your typical *Mitläufer*, the followers, the worst of the whole lot." The others nod with disgust. "First they were communists, now they vote CDU," she says, her high voice rising higher. "And we're the ones who pay!"

A few thirteen- or fourteen-year-old "Baby Skins" peek inside the club to see what's happening. Gerd shoots them a reproachful look. He says that the "Skins ain't real Nazis. They think that just because you knock someone's head in that that makes you a man." Jörg snorts disparagingly. On most issues, there is a consensus among the foursome. They agree that Germany's 1937 borders must be "restored." They agree that the Federal Republic is a U.S.-imposed creation, not to be confused with "Germany." Above all, they agree that unification has brought them nothing save more problems. The topic of the Holocaust, however, raises differences of opinion. "The extermination of the Jews was inhumane," Ute shakes her head. "I couldn't go along with that."

Jörg grins maliciously, shrugging his shoulders. He's not so sure. "This whole Holocaust thing has been exaggerated anyway," says Jörg. "Whatever the case, the Jews aren't the problem today. There are other things now which are much more important."

The Espe crew makes it plain that what is most important is the "foreigner problem." "We don't hate foreigners," explains Jörg even-handedly, "just as long as they stay in their own countries. Vietnamese in Vietnam, Africans in Africa, Germans in Germany. That's only normal." For the Gorbitz youth, as for the entire German right, the evacuation of Hoyerswerda constituted a landmark victory. Jörg grins. "Hoyerswerda showed what we can do. Lots of foreigners have already left. And they're the smart ones, because Hoyerswerda's gonna happen again and again and again." He gestures over his shoulder in the direction of a certain apartment block, "until they all leave."

After a while, a short, stocky man with thick plastic glasses emerges from behind the bar. He presents himself as the manager of the Espe and demands to know what I'm doing there. I tell him and dig out a U.S. press card that he looks over and pretends to read. "These are good kids," he says in a loud voice. "I know what you journalists write about them and it's all lies. Lies!" My new acquaintances look at me. Had I been trying to dupe them? Listen, I say with feigned nonchalance, I'm not going to print any lies, and maybe not anything at all. We're just having a friendly little chat. Though not convinced, he disappears again behind the bar. The time to leave, however, has clearly come and I don't feel like pressing my luck. As I begin to put on my coat a few minutes later, I see one of the girls surreptitiously eye Jörg, make a fist, and nod in my direction. I swallow hard and pretend not to have seen. Jörg gives me a quick glance and looks back in the direction of the girl. He shakes his head meaningfully—no. The twenty dark yards from the Espe to the streetcar were the longest that I ever care to experience.

As the Gorbitz militants readily admit, the neo-Nazi scene in Dresden had fragmented since the movement's loss of its central figure, Rainer Sonntag. Sonntag had worked closely with the Kühnen movement in West Germany since he left the GDR in 1987 under "unclear circumstances." Shortly after the communist regime's collapse, Sonntag returned to his native Dresden with a mission: the organization of the Saxon right. The charismatic thirty-six-year-old quickly took charge of Saxony's neo-Nazi scene, founding an array of militant groups such as SS-East, the Union of Saxon Werewolves, and *Nationaler Widerstand Deutschlands* (National Opposition of Germany), or NWD. With his German shepherd at his side, the pudgy, brown-haired Sonntag was a common sight in central Dresden, often surrounded by a contingent of young Skinheads and neo-Nazis. Sonntag groomed his troops in the tradition of the SA, as elite vigilante squads to combat unemployment, drugs, the sex industry, and crime. "Only united are we strong," Sonntag preached to the ranks, "regardless of whether you come from [the Dresden districts of] Johannstadt, Gorbitz or Hauptbahnhof, whether you are faschos, Skins, or hooligans: Clean the scum off of Dresden's streets!" The NWD formed the movement's political wing, a party "against the dismantlement of state social services" and for "popular law and order."

The Elbe city's half-million population watched as the neo-Nazi militants raided the city's left-alternative cafés and ransacked the cardboard booths of Vietnamese street merchants. Nor did the police take action against the vigilantes' "citizens' initiatives." The Nazis' "clean-up actions" shut down several bordellos and sex shops, as well as putting an end to the Hungarians' street-corner gambling operations. Even the neo-Nazis' demands for Mafia-style "protection fees" from local businesses failed to provoke a reaction from the authorities. Saxony's President Kurt Biedenkopf (CDU) played down the right-wing underworld as a "marginal phenomenon of the changes," which the press had blown out of proportion.

On May 31, 1990, Sonntag fell victim to the cycle of violence that he had helped set in motion. Just before midnight that Saturday evening, Sonntag and sixty of his followers mustered for a raid across from the new "Sex Shopping Center." Earlier in the day, a few of Sonntag's henchmen had paid the sex shop's West German owners a visit and demanded 50,000 marks. The two proprietors, Nikolas Simeonidis, twenty-four, and Ronny Matz, twenty-five, refused and proceeded to barricade the shop in anticipation of the promised attack. As the neo-Nazis gathered, Simeonidis and Matz went out to negotiate with Sonntag. In a black Mercedes coup they pulled up next to the Nazi leader and heated words were exchanged. When Simeonidis reached for his shotgun, all the Nazis except for Sonntag scattered. Sonntag put his hands in the air and kept talking. A loud crack then pierced the air as Simeonidis fired a single bullet into Sonntag's face. Before the Nazi leader's bodyguards could react, the vehicle had sped away. The militants wrapped their Führer's blood-spattered corpse in a Third Reich flag, shouting "Sieg Heil!" and "We'll fight the lot of you!" Days later the police arrested the two men in the Red Light district, charging them with Sonntag's slaying.

Sonntag's funeral procession drew the largest single mass of neofascists in postwar German history. Nearly 2000 assorted ultra-rightists accompanied Sonntag's Nazi flag-draped casket through the streets of Dresden. Some with shaved heads and black flight jackets, others in SA uniforms, and the majority indistinguishable from the average citizen, the procession snaked through the city to cries of "Sieg Heil!", "Rainer Sonntag—Martyr of the Reich!" and "Revenge!" At the front of the march walked the Who's Who of the German right, with the notable exception of Kühnen, whom the cause had lost to an AIDS related virus a month earlier. At Sonntag's grave, neo-Nazi leader Heinz Reisz mourned the murder of his "partner in the struggle against the Bonn Republic." "Sonntag died like a soldier. Treacherous assassins slaughtered Sonntag, just as the allies bombed Dresden!" he bellowed. "Fight the chaos that stands at our door!", he concluded the ceremony, turning to a police officer in the crowd: "And for that we need you, too!" The Dresden authorities admitted that they permitted the gathering with a "heavy heart," but saw no other alternative.

Sonntag's death dashed neo-Nazi leaders' hopes of a united movement in southeastern Germany. The fragile coalition around Sonntag fractured, although not to the exclusion of reaping the revenge that it had sworn. Violence escalated across Saxony. The molotov cocktail bombings of the apartment blocks of foreign nationals represented a qualitatively new degree of terror. In April 1991, six Dresden Skinheads threw twenty-eight-year-old Mozambican student Jorge Gomondai to his death from a streetcar. Even though the neo-Nazis operated in small, local groups, evidence clearly pointed to the hand of the nationwide parties in whipping up hatred and provoking violence. Police records show West German neo-fascists present at almost every major action. One of the strategic goals behind the wave of racist aggression was to normalize the level of violence in society, to create an atmosphere in which society tolerated the new degree of right-wing terror. The climate legitimized the use of violence among those who harbored passive sympathies, while extending the outermost limit of what the majority of society would accept before actively responding.

In the restored Baroque city center, at the Dresden Office for Foreign Nationals, lawyer Stefan Tranberg disputes his superiors' claim that racial aggression is a "marginal phenomenon" in Saxony. "Of course, racism existed in the days of the GDR, too," says the forty-one-year-old Swede, working on a two-year special assignment for the city. Outside his office, the unheated waiting room is packed with foreign nationals, collectively trying to decipher the official paperwork required from them. "But now people of color in Dresden are scared to walk the streets alone. You won't see any third world peoples out after dark." Tranberg maintains that the intolerance extends far beyond Nazi youth gangs. "There exists a deep anti-foreigner sentiment in this city, which ranges from casual to extreme. Many people here feel that both communism and capitalism have betrayed them. They see the West Germans as colonial lords. The dreadful economic situation and the psychological toll of the changes has simply been too much for many people." The reaction of many, he explains, has been to turn on the foreigners, the most convenient scapegoats for their frustration.

The city of 500,000 has only 10,000 foreign inhabitants, among them just twenty-seven asylum applicants. Most of the former Soviet Union citizens, Vietnamese, Hungarian, and other peoples from former socialist countries have work contracts that the FRG has agreed to honor. According to Tranberg, the number of foreigners in Dresden will increase drastically as the new federal states take on their share of the FRG's immigration flow. Over the coming years, the number of foreigners in Dresden is likely to triple and quadruple. "When the economy picks up, they will be needed, too," hopes Tranberg, "but the state must do something to prepare the population for life in a more multicultural society. At the moment there is no policy at all. There is nothing to prevent another Hoyerswerda."

Across the coal-blackened George Dimitrov Bridge lies the Neustadt district, the home of the Dresden's left-alternative scene. One of the few historical quarters that emerged relatively unscathed from the WWII bombardment, the turn-of-the-century workers' district fell into disrepair during the communist decades. In the early 1980s, an informal community of writers, painters, and musicians set up house in the abandoned buildings and their small, coal-heated apartments. With the political transition, a vibrant alternative subculture blossomed in the formerly condemned quarter—which both the right-wingers and the police were quick to persecute. Neo-Nazi attacks on the cafés and night clubs are a matter of course in Neustadt. The police, the Neustadters say, turn a blind eye to the violence, arriving on the scene hours later, if they appear at all. In the early morning of New Year's Day, 1991, the Bronxx Club on Alaun Street went up in flames. The arsonists, like the murderers of Jorge Gomondai, were never brought to justice. When it came to shutting down Neustadt's handful of anarchist squats, however, the police force showed no shortage of determination. Typically, when the squatters responded to a Skinhead raid with molotov cocktails of their own, the police, arriving after the Nazis had fled, arrested the squatters.

In Saxony, responsibility for "combatting political extremism" has been left in the hands of the police force. The authorities throw "left radicalism" (the Neustadt anarchists) and "right radicalism" into the same pot, a lack of distinction that relativizes both the right's violence and political potential. "It doesn't matter to us if somebody beats somebody up just to take his money or for ideological reasons," admits a senior officer at the Dresden police department. "We handle it the same way." With a key from his belt ring, the good-natured, barrel-chested cop unlocks the cabinet containing confiscated weapons. "You know, after the Wall came down some shops began carrying baseball bats, and they sold like hot cakes," he says, pulling a three-quarter size pink bat from a macabre pile of Ninja stars, switchblades, brass knuckles, gas pistols, and other instruments of violence. "But, you know," he shakes his head, slapping the bat in the palm of his meaty hand, "there's no one in Dresden who knows how to play baseball."

The Saxon authorities' assessment of the neo-Nazi movement there raises serious questions about their ability to respond to the far right. Just as the GDR leadership had done, the federal states on both sides of the former border address right-wing extremism primarily in criminal, rather than in political terms. Despite the clear ideological nature of the neo-Nazis' assaults, experts at the Saxony Interior Ministry describe the militants simply as "frustrated, criminally-oriented youth," basically just juvenile delinquents. They point to the perpetrators' shaky grasp of fascist theory, their limited numbers, and the splintered scene as grounds not to address the violence in political terms or to unduly overestimate its potential. At the same time, they concede that they are unable to guarantee the safety of foreign nationals in Dresden. The special West-trained anti-terrorist units now in Saxony will prevent another Hoyerswerda from escalating out of control, they say. "Nothing like Hoyerswerda could happen again," the chief of the Special Commission for Right-wing Radicalism in Dresden told me six months before Rostock.

Critics insist that the authorities' emphasis on the neo-Nazis' ideological weakness skirts the fundamental issues. According to New Forum's Andreas Meinel, a deputy in the Saxony legislature, the real danger is that the ultra-right's propaganda strikes a sensitive nerve in the region. "These groups and parties employ all of the usual social language of the left—jobs, flats, kindergartens, etc.," says the thirty-five-year-old social worker. "At the same time, they appeal to the people with the traditional nationalist rhetoric of the right. If the democratic parties don't respond to the economic and social crisis here," he warns, "the right alone will occupy this ground. This is exactly what's been happening." Meinel argues that the right stands a real chance in Saxony if it succeeds in making contact with the average citizen.

In word, at least, the explosion of right-wing violence provoked condemnation from across the German political spectrum, including the Republicans. After Hoyerswerda, multimillion mark state- and party-funded advertising campaigns plastered German bus stops and shopping centers with posters urging tolerance. "Abroad we're all foreigners," say tennis star Steffi Graf, playwright Heiner Müller, and the rockband Die Toten Hosen. Demonstrations in both the old and the new federal states drew crowds far in excess of anything that the ultra-right could ever hope to amass. In November 1991, a politically diverse alliance of over 100,000 people marched against racism in Berlin. But not until the Mölln murders in December 1992, however, did the entire country really begin to take the terror of the right seriously. Kohl dragged his feet until then to directly address "right-wing radicalism in Germany" before the parliament, and even then continued to equate the threat of "the extreme right" with that of "the extreme left." On chill winter nights, hundreds of thousands of "good Germans" across the country marched in candlelit processions against the violence and xenophobia. The outpouring of protest was truly remarkable, and the numbers probably exceeded anything that any other European country could hope to duplicate.

The Germans' rejection of racial violence and the far right was also sincere. But just how far the sympathy extends is another question. There is little evidence to show that the Rostockers and Hoyerswerdians have changed their minds about having Asians and Roma as neighbors. Only the Greens and the reform East German communist party used the Christmas demonstrations to lobby for the preservation of the right to political asylum in the Federal Constitution. Even after the barrage of condemnation and outrage in the aftermath of Rostock and Mölln, the Republicans received eight percent of the vote in the state of Hessen's March 1993 elections.

On the left, the face of neo-fascism brought together anti-fascist coalitions of church groups, left parties, foreign national groups, radical Autonomen, and the old GDR anti-fascists. But despite their general anti-fascist consensus, they remained deeply divided over strategy. Church groups and social workers insist that they have met encouraging success in working directly with right-wing youth, trying to integrate them into society through job and recreational programs. The treatment of neo-fascist youth as "social victims," however, raises protests from other corners. Some critics counter that only radical changes in the nature of capitalist postindustrial society will terminate neo-fascist tendencies at their source. Others argue that the solution lies in the development of a broadly democratic multicultural society, in which the values of tolerance, solidarity, and community replace those of intolerance and authoritarianism.

The inability of progressive forces to make headway in the East has left plenty of opportunity for the all-German ultra-right to turn racism and social discontent into active support. Despite the uproar over Hoyerswerda and Rostock, the basic constitutive elements of the pogroms remain in place throughout the new federal states. Neither has the former GDR economy begun to rebound as promised, nor have the political parties altered the discourse surrounding immigration and political asylum. If the Republicans or other national populist alternatives manage to wage effective campaigns in the East, they could well take big chunks of the vote from the mainstream parties there in the 1994 local and federal elections. But for those peoples whom the right considers undesirable in the New Germany, the rule of the mob is already a fact—whether it sits in parliament or not.

Chapter 2

EAST GERMANY
FASCISM IN THE
ANTI-FASCIST STATE

The German Democratic Republic (GDR), true to the interests of its people and international responsibilities, has extinguished German militarism and Nazism on its territory.

Even before the GDR officially enshrined its anti-fascist credo in the 1968 constitution, the state had long claimed to have "expunged all roots and traces" of German fascism from communist East Germany. But almost a decade before Hoyerswerda and Rostock, the reemergence of neo-fascistic currents in its youngest generation plainly contradicted the state's proclamation. By the mid-1980s, the writing was spray-painted on the walls for all to see: "Jews Out!", "Sieg Heil!", and "Third Reich Again!" The desecrated Jewish cemeteries, vandalized Soviet war memorials, and escalating violence of neo-Nazi Skinhead gangs attested to the fact that something had gone terribly awry in the orthodox East bloc state. In East Germany, as well as Czechoslovakia, Poland, and Hungary, the regimes attributed the existence of ultra-right currents to "Western inspiration" and locked up their adherents as "rowdies" or social deviants.

For the communist leaderships, it was inconceivable that fascist youth cultures could be indigenous products of their states. In the GDR, many of the top Politburo members, among them GDR President and Party General Secretary Erich Honecker, had spent the war years in Nazi prison camps as political prisoners. The GDR based its very legitimacy as a state—a second German state—on its identity as an "anti-fascist state of workers and farmers." Honecker and company adhered to the classic communist definition of fascism as a strictly economic phenomenon, namely as the most reactionary form of monopoly capitalism. Accordingly, fascism could not possibly persist or reemerge in a socialist state. And since, in the eyes of the GDR, the capitalist Federal Republic constituted the "successor state to the Third Reich," the Old Guard reflexively attributed such abnormalities in the GDR to West German influence. The "opposition" of the right-wing youth, however, which both the state and the Skinheads perceived as the highest form of anti-communist rebellion, bore the unmistakable imprint of the GDR. The ethic that fascinated the young radicals had roots deep in German history, stretching from early Prussia, through the Nazi regime, to the neo-Stalinist GDR. Though the young neo-fascists revolted against the system, they were unable to break with its totalitarian assumptions; the dictatorship had succeeded in imbuing at least one part of the masses with its values, if not its ideological convictions.

Documentation of the full extent of neo-Nazi activity in the GDR still lies buried deep in Stasi files. Right-wing nationalist and neo-fascist cliques existed in the GDR from its inception, both inside and outside of the official structures. The first assaults against foreign nationals happened in the 1960s, when the GDR began to accept limited numbers of politically persecuted persons into the country. Chileans who had fled the terror of the 1976 military coup in Chile report that they woke up to swastikas scrawled on their doors. During the 1970s, vandals desecrated Jewish cemeteries in Zittau, Potsdam, and Dresden. "There was always a latent affinity to fascism in the GDR, even in the party," explains Thomas Krüger, a former democratic activist in the GDR and today the Senator for Youth Issues in Berlin.[1] "I remember once in 1978 when I went to Poland with some local factory directors. No sooner were we over the border than the party comrades and union bureaucrats began to sing old Nazi songs. These were the types who would get drunk and hum the Horst Wessel song as they took a piss alongside the road." In one form or another, most GDR Germans can tell a similar story, be it of the boastful construction site foreman with the SS tatoo or the downstairs neighbors who sang old Wehrmacht songs during late-night drinking sessions. Witnesses report that by the mid-1970s isolated neo-fascist cliques had formed within regional police reserve units around Berlin and Leipzig. When it could, the GDR unloaded its unwanted "brown spots" on the FRG. Throughout the 1970s and 1980s, the GDR released a variety of politically undesirable people, both right and left, to the Federal Republic in exchange for hard currency payment.

The right's earliest public arenas were the soccer stadiums, which became the breeding grounds for the GDR's teenage fascists. Already in the 1970s, drunken brawls and neo-fascist jeers from fans were part-and-parcel of the Saturday afternoon outing, just as they were in Western Europe. The police squads patrolling the games overlooked taunts of "Jews Out!" directed at the referees or opposing teams. Nasty clashes regularly broke out between fan clubs, particularly when regional north-south rivalries were on the program. The authorities went remarkably easy on the fan club hooligans, especially those from Dynamo Berlin, the Stasi's pet team.

The 1980s also witnessed the evolution of a number of fringe subcultures in the GDR. In that decade, a new generation came of age, the offspring of the first generation of GDR children who were born after WWII. Born roughly between 1964 and 1975, the second generation's relationship to the GDR differed significantly from that of their parents'. Although the state had tempered the Stalinist orthodoxy of the first postwar decades, the rigid system appeared ever more anachronistic to the GDR's young people. Thirty-five years after WWII, the communist slogans and ideological rhetoric that might have seemed credible in the 1950s rang pitifully hollow in the 1980s. No longer could the regime's high-handed tirades against "Western imperialism" excuse the blatant hypocrisy of its own actions. Economically, the energy crisis and high world market prices for raw materials dealt the final blow to the GDR's losing battle to keep pace with the West. The prospects of the majority of GDR youth looked bleaker than ever before.

Opinion polls conducted in the late 1980s attest to the youth's disillusionment. Even sociologists from the state-sanctioned Leipzig Central Institute for Youth Research admitted that in contrast to the past decade "decisively fewer older pupils and apprentices identify unconditionally with socialism" and even fewer "identify with the socialist Fatherland." The studies showed that official political activism had dropped to an unprecedented low. In 1985, only nine percent of those youths polled considered themselves "unconditionally a communist." A decade before the figure was twenty-two percent. Only half of the young people thought of the GDR as their "Fatherland," while ninety percent considered themselves simply "German."

The studies underlined the deep identity crisis that had infected young East Germans. The unique GDR identity that the state had tried so painstakingly to cultivate simply didn't take hold in the new generation. The GDR rested its legitimacy as a state not upon its national credentials, i.e., as a *German* state, but upon its political identity, as a *socialist* state. Two German states could only be justified if they were politically opposed—one communist, one capitalist; one the anti-fascist state, one the "successor to fascism." Thus, the GDR attempted to supplant a German national identity with the identity of a "socialist nation" that the East Germans could call their own. But perhaps even more pressing for the state than the underpinning of its political sovereignty, which Soviet missiles ultimately insured, was the regime's hope that the GDR identity would dam the flood of emigration to the FRG. Yet, as the legitimacy of communist ideology across East Europe deteriorated, so the foundations of the GDR identity crumbled from beneath the state. The youth drifted either into a defeated "zero identity" or toward other alternatives.

The GDR's malaise sowed the seeds for the growth of subcultures that offered something different from the status quo. In the early 1980s, illegal fashions reflecting trends in the West European music scene began to crop up. Refracted through the images of West German television, the outlandish attire and wild multicolor hair styles of the GDR punks mocked the culture of the punk rock explosion in England. Soon after the punks came others, such as Goths, Skinheads, New Wavers, Heavy Metals, New Romantics, and Psycho-Billys.[2] In its early stage, the tiny underground scene was "wild," as one Dresdener put it. The groups were mixed, styles undefined, and people shifted cliques from week to week. The common denominator was dissatisfaction with the official youth culture. One of the punks' first slogans was simply "*Spass haben!*" (Have fun!) The frowned-upon styles represented a contemptuous break with the passive conformity of their parents' generation, as well as that of most of their peers. Through music, dress, make-up, haircuts and symbols, the malcontents vented the feelings that the system repressed.

Par for the course, the state condemned the fashions as "manifestations of the capitalist culture industry." Shut out of the youth clubs and discos, often arrested for "unacceptable" hair styles or clothing, the scene retreated into private niches, where it diversified and flourished, although still among a minute fraction of young people. What first appeared as style, gradually began to crystallize into defined, in some cases political, identities. The different subcultures evolved along the general lines of their Western counterparts, but in each case with a flavor unique to the youths' GDR experiences.

One strain of punk gravitated toward the West European punk culture. But whereas the English punk movement responded to an industrial capitalist order whose production processes could not provide them employment, the GDR punks reacted to a command economy that forced them to work, on the one hand, and criminalized them, on the other. The punks felt that if society was going to reject them, then so be it. With tattered clothes and down-and-out life-styles, they proudly accepted their status as the refuse of a morally bankrupt society. Their anarchistic inclinations rejected the state's hierarchical structures for a communal notion of anti-order that emphasized spontaneity and nonchalance as a conscious protest against the system's structured uniformity. The new youth movement replaced the communist work ethic of productivity at all costs with a self-fulfilling concept of creativity. In the confines of the Lutheran churches, many punks contributed to the *verboten* democracy and environmental movements. Socialism remained their ideal, but a humanistic socialism very much at odds with that in the GDR.

SKINHEADS COME OUT

The original GDR Skinheads were as overtly apolitical as the early punks, although their subculture too contained distinct political implications. Most of the Skins came from the ranks of the early punks, the Goths[3] and other groups. Their external trade marks mirrored those of Skinheads in the West—bulky green "bomber" jackets, shaved heads, jeans rolled up at the ankles, and heavy, hightop black boots. Their style also mimicked one current of London subculture, which by the late 1970s had made its way to West Germany. The British Skinhead movement emerged from working-class districts of East London that had been hard hit by unemployment. For the out-of-work young men, the proletarian garb and Spartan, masculine image provided an ersatz identity for the one that they had lost with their factory jobs. At soccer matches or on the streets, they won reputations as hard-nosed brawlers, their hair cut so short that opponents had nothing to grab on to. As aggressive as they were, the original London Skin gangs were not right-wing. As Great Britain's economic crisis sharpened, however, the over-whelmingly white, displaced men directed their resentment against black and Asian immigrants. Racist "Oi-Skin" bands stirred the hatred that the National Front party formulated in political terms.

In the GDR, the split between punks and a right-wing strain of Skins came into the open as the groups' cultural philosophies matured. "We always used to hang out together, dance to punk and drink," says Holger, twenty-six, one of the punk scene's original members. Today Holger, who sports a bright red "Iro" or "Mohican" down the center of his head, lives in one of East Berlin's leftist squats. "But there were always some people, punks too, who wanted a leader and structures. That wasn't for us. We felt you should be able to do your own thing, whatever it was. The others went their own way and became Skins."

More than anything, the personal values of the early subcultures' members informed the underground's metamorphosis. Before fascist ideology had come to the surface, the Skinhead subculture possessed distinct fascistic inclinations. The young men that moved toward a Skinhead identity disapproved of the punks' dress-down attire and un-kempt personal appearance. The punks, they said, were dirty and smelly. The orderly uniform of flight jackets and combat boots, as well as the antiseptic look of shiny shaved heads, suited them better. They scorned the punks' pacifism, opting instead for a militaristic code and macho aggressiveness. The Skinheads were typical "young bulls"—

harder, angrier types in contrast to the more thoughtful or artistic punks. Instead of creating something new or better, the Skins said "Wo Worter nicht helfen, überzeugt die Faust." (When words don't help, the fist will).

The Skinheads prided themselves on their ability to keep their noses to the grindstone and follow orders. The charge that the right-wingers leveled at the regime was not that they objected to its Prussian work ethic, but, just the opposite, that the state was too lax in enforcing it. As one Skinhead criminal offender, J. from Potsdam, eighteen, stated in legal testimony: "I go to work regularly and I think that I work well and efficiently. That's the thing that shows a good Skin. All my buddies are really industrious, too. We can't stand people who slough off. We want to accomplish something, and to do this there must be discipline and order." Skinheads felt comfortable in the atmosphere of order, discipline, and punctuality. They were reliable, hard workers, who, when facing trial, never had trouble getting their foreman or factory director to testify that they were stellar workers. In the trial of P., a twenty-six-year-old Skin from East Berlin, his gastronomy collective testified that: "P. immersed himself positively in the collective, had good relations with everyone and, in his work, was held up as a model for others. He commands excellent professional skills and is universally deployable. He was also always prepared to take over extra shifts. We don't believe that colleague P. committed this crime. There must be some kind of error here. He has enjoyed our trust for years."

The earliest, top-secret studies of GDR Skinheads produced results so damning that the state immediately confiscated the documentation and ruled the topic off limits for independent researchers. The surveys, conducted from police records and trial material at the state's request, showed that most of the Skinhead offenders in the "socialist workers' state" were young male workers from socially secure families.[4] Nothing less than the state's skilled workers, had turned so vehemently on the ideology that claimed to embody their interests above all others. The statistics revealed that though the offenders were mostly workers, their parents came from the entire professional spectrum that existed in the GDR. Yet, the research also showed that a disproportionately high percentage of the offenders' parents were in some way related to the state apparatus—as bureaucrat, party apparatchik, Stasi, or military personnel. The teenagers most inclined to criminal acts with right-wing motives were those who had been most thoroughly imbued with the values of the state.

According to Professor Loni Niederländer, a sociologist at the East Berlin Humboldt University and author of the study, eighty percent of the criminal offenders with political orientation were vocational students or young workers. Over three-quarters of those examined in her study were between seventeen and twenty-two years of age. "Many of these cases were children from orthodox communist families, families that tended to be the strictest and most authoritarian with their children," she says. "The state authorities simply didn't know how to respond, so they steered me away from the topic by further restricting my already restricted access to information." Neither social scientists nor the police ever studied the bulk of the information that the Stasi kept under lock and key.

The cultural emphases that initially split the underground scene between Skins and punks quickly took on a political character. The first openly political object of dispute that arose between the future arch enemies was the Berlin Wall. They agreed that the communist state was completely bankrupt and that "the Wall must fall." The punks, however, criticized the system's structural violence, its means of indoctrination, and its undemocratic structures. The Skins, on the other hand, embraced nationalism as the answer to communism, replacing the manufactured state identity with that of being German. In the soccer stadiums, the Skinheads bellowed "I'm proud to be German!" While the state discouraged nationalist identification, even it described itself as the "socialist German nation." For both the Skins and the state, being German meant being productive, orderly, clean, superior, and strong.

By 1985–86, the Skins took the inevitable next step in their nationalist logic, and the cry "One Germany!" could be heard loud and clear. The call for German unification was tantamount to treason, even though the Skins rejected the Federal Republic as a model for a united Germany. They argued that both East and West Germany had suffered the humiliation of postwar occupation forces on their soil, which limited the German nation's sovereignty and national aspirations. "We just want Germany to be great again. Germany should just be Germany, not ruled over by the Soviet Union or America," they said. The question of the two Germanies also provided the Skins with additional ammunition against the "leftist" punks, as well as opposition democrats. For the purposes of the rabidly anti-communist Skinheads, the punks' anarcho-Marxist critique of capitalism and the democracy movement's vision of an alternative GDR state placed them both in the same boat with the SED: As "leftists" their opposition to the state amounted to *Scheinopposition*, or symbolic opposition.

The Skinheads coalesced into ever more structured groups, usually of between seven and fifteen persons. Initially in Berlin, Leipzig, and Dresden, bands of a dozen or so at a time could be spotted on the streets. In discos or pubs, the neighborhood or district-based groups met regularly. At the soccer stadium they made contacts with other Skin gangs. The groups that stayed together over time were centered around strong, charismatic leaders, who commanded the gangs' unequivocal allegiance. When the leader left, the gangs fragmented. The total identification with the troop was a prerequisite, and the Skins gave freely to the group the loyalty that they denied the state. "In Karl Marx City I was a *Stino* ("stinking normal person")," said B., a Skinhead from Berlin, in 1988 testimony to the GDR police. "Then here in Berlin I was first a Heavy Metal, then a Skin. The feeling of togetherness is strong among us. We all stick together. Amongst the Skins I found support and security. Everyone helps everyone." In testimony and interviews, the Skinhead youth underlined, above all, the security, identity, and community that they found in the group.

Until 1987, the official press maintained an official silence on the uncomfortable new developments in the GDR. The Stasi and the police turned a blind eye to violence within the alternative scene itself, refusing to respond to reports of Skinhead attacks against punks, hippies, and others. Nor did the Skinhead phenomenon turn the heads of average citizens. On the streets and on the shop floor, the diligent, clean-cut Skins received a much warmer reception than the far-out Goths or ragtag punks. The state apparatus, however, knew well that something nasty was brewing as the number of violent and criminal acts perpetrated by Skinhead gangs rose from year to year. Yet, even when the police decided to apprehend the aggressors, the courts addressed their offenses under strictly criminal headings such as "rowdiness" or "disorderly conduct." Their sentences were light, especially when their apparatchik fathers pulled a few strings. The state kept mum about the maturing political direction of the assaults and the content of the graffiti.

CHURCH UNDER SIEGE

The evening of October 17, 1987, put an end to the state's silence overnight when a Skinhead raid on a punk concert in the East Berlin *Zionskirche* (Church of Zion) catapulted the Skinhead issue into the public spotlight. That Saturday afternoon, the soccer match between the rival clubs Berlin Union and Leipzig in East Berlin attracted the largest single mass of Skinheads and like-minded hooligans to date. According to Speicher, a punk and long-time Union fan, somewhere between 400 and 500 "Nazis" attended the game. "I went to the soccer games every weekend and I had never seen so many at once in my life," he recounts. "Every fascist in Berlin must have been there. All hell broke loose, and the police had no control over it." The atmosphere in the stadium bristled with hostility. From the Berlin side, shouts of "I'm proud to be German!" or "I'm proud to be a Berliner!" rang out against the "stupid" Leipzigers from southern Saxony. Even before the game, the East Berlin police sensed that tension was reaching a tearing point. Police vans met the Leipzig fans' train in Potsdam, outside of Berlin, and brought the Leipzigers directly to the stadium in order to circumvent the Union fans, who lay in wait at Berlin's Lichtenberg station.

That evening was a wild one in East Berlin. Several Skin groups, already well-inebriated from the afternoon game, continued their celebrations at various parties across the city. In the Sputnik tavern on Greifswalder Street, eighty Skinheads from both East and West Berlin held a send-off party for one of their favorite comrades who was about to begin a voluntary ten-year stint in the *National Volksarmee* (NVA).

Word was in the air that the "stinky red punks" were going to get their comeuppance later that night.

Among the troops there, the *Lichtenberg Front*, the East Berlin Skinhead gang founded in 1986, maintained a prominent profile. The night of October 17 was neither the first nor the last that would be dominated by the Front and its leaders, such as Ingo Hasselbach and his friend André Riechert. Riechert, the son of a high-ranking Stasi officer, would found the neo-Nazi group "The January 30 Movement" less than a year later. After the Wall's dismantlement, the duo would head up the Nationale Alternative, the Berlin-based GDR sister organization of the West German neo-Nazi party, the Deutsche Alternative. The Skinhead leader Jens-Uwe Vogt would go another route after 1989, taking command of the "BFC Hooligans," the racist fan club of Berlin's biggest soccer team. Even more interesting, the 1991 opening of the Stasi files would disclose Vogt's years-long cooperation with State Security Section XX/2, the department responsible for the observation of domestic opposition.[5] Vogt's role as an inside informant means that the secret police probably knew all along about the Front's plans to raid the Zionskirche, as well as other Skinhead actions. Long before Vogt's collaboration came to light, speculation was rife that the Stasi sought to instigate violence within the underground scene.

Not far away from the Sputnik tavern, organizers from the *Kirche von Unten* (Church From Below) and other opposition groups were preparing for a concert in the Zionskirche. By 1987, a hodge-podge of Christian groups, peace and ecological activists, and political dissidents had secured a measure of independence under the protective wing of the Lutheran Church. The musty cellar of the dilapidated brick church housed the single-room "office" of the *Umweltbibliothek* (Environmental Library), an illegal group responsible for the samizdat publication *Umweltblätter* (Environmental Pages). Within the church's confines, rock groups that had been banned from the official youth clubs for their subversive lyrics performed regularly. East Berlin's most popular punk band, *Die Firma* (The Firm), and the West Berlin rock band Element of Crime were scheduled for the altar that evening. According to Kirche von Unten organizer Silvio Meier,[6] by then many people in the scene had had run-ins with Skinheads and recognized a raid as a distinct possibility. "By the time of the Zionskirche, Skinhead attacks against punks were nothing new. We had even discussed what to do in the event of an attack that night. But while most of those at the concert had heard about Skin violence, it hadn't really sunk in because they had never encountered it firsthand."

The crowd of about 1000 people in the Zionskirche had thinned out after Die Firma's final encore. As Element of Crime prepared the stage, forty to fifty Skins from the Sputnik, including the nucleus of the Lichtenberg Front, reached the Dimitrov Street subway stop. En route to the church, the mob jumped passers-by, pushing them around or kicking them to the ground. The police surveillance units in the six squad cars stationed around the corner watched as the Skins approached the church entrance. Then, at 10:15 PM, half of the troop stormed the concert. Yelling "Sieg Heil!", "Jewish Pigs!", and "Jews Out of the German Church!", the Skins rushed the stunned crowd with bottles and bicycle chains. Blood flowed, bodies fell, and the crowd panicked. The blitz lasted only minutes before some of the punk scene veterans responded, beating the outnumbered Skins back out of the church. The cops stayed put until after the Skinheads fled, tailing them from a distance as they continued on to the Schoppenstube bar, where they then beat up a handful of suspected homosexuals.

The violence of the spectacle proved too dramatic for the state to ignore. Four days later, the police rounded up all of the Skinhead assailants. The police surveillance teams, it seems, had managed to photograph all of the Skins before and after the raid. While their West Berlin accomplices were left to the justice system across the Wall, the GDR Skinheads were put on trial a month later in East Berlin. The hastily prepared show trial of the first four accused brought prison sentences of between one and two years for "rowdiness," as well as for "public expressions of a fascist, racist, or militaristic character." But the verdict didn't suit the state. Responding to the protest of the Prosecuting Attorney's office, two weeks later the court upped the sentences to one-and-a-half to four years. Twelve more Skins were tried on similar charges and sentenced accordingly.

The Zionskirche trial marked the first mention of Skinheads in the GDR press. (The Western press was banned from the proceedings.)

Under the headline "Trial Opens in Berlin" on page two of the Nov. 27, 1987, *Junge Welt*, the editors of the party youth organ wrote that the offenders had perpetrated "riotous and violent acts." The twenty-line snippet continued: "During their riotous acts, the rowdies used slogans from the Nazi period, which is against the law in the GDR, where fascism and all of its roots have been purged." Subsequent reports characterized the youths as "Skinhead rowdies" rather than just as "rowdies." The press response furnished evidence that the state indeed had its all-encompassing cyc on developments, as well as its hand on the press. Yet, while the state had obviously taken pains to formulate some kind of line on the issue, its position was riddled with contradictions. Such fascist phenomena had no basis in the GDR, the statements claimed, but if they did appear, then they would be dealt with severely. The alteration of the first four offenders' sentences, however, revealed that even in a publicized show-trial, the degree of severity with which they would be punished was open to dispute. The lenient initial sentences could well have been the work of the Stasi, in an effort to aid their man Vogt and Stasi-son Riechert. The trial and press coverage also emphasized that Skinhead violence was and would be treated as common criminality and not as a political phenomenon. The use of fascist slogans and symbols from the Third Reich period, however, was attributed to the "export of Western ideology." Thus, the state acknowledged an ideological content to the acts, while it continued to treat Skinhead violence as an apolitical, criminal offense.

According to the former director of the East Berlin police section responsible for combatting political extremism, Bernd Wagner, discussion over neo-fascist activity in the GDR only revolved around the best way to manage the problem and play it down. "What the Central Committee and the Stasi discussed was how best to activate the state mechanisms, such as the schools, the youth organizations, and the police in order to suppress the expression of right-wing ideas. They wanted to put a lid on the issue as quickly as possible in order to avoid international embarrassment." The state felt that the tried-and-true recipe of a few quick show trials and a propaganda campaign would do the trick. When Wagner attempted to initiate a substantive debate about its sources, he found himself transferred to another section.

By the time of the Zionskirche raid, many Skin gangs had adopted Nazi symbols and slogans. At first, the graffiti and soccer match heckling of "Sieg Heil!", "Third Reich!", and "Communists Against the Wall!" rarely bore a direct connection with an ideological program. Rather, many of the young antagonists knew that the public display of Nazi symbols violated the anti-fascist state's most sacred taboo. Nothing, for example, would turn the whole high school upside down like a swastika scrawled on the black board. What spurred some of the boys on was simply the desired shock effect that they were certain to elicit. At the same time, a peace sign or a circled anarchist "A" were also symbols with oppositional content, which they consciously or unconsciously opted not to use. Among the perpetrators, there were those who knew very well what they were up to. They employed fascist symbolism as a tactic to influence their peers, to demonstrate that fascist ideas posed a real alternative to those of the state and the democratic opposition.

As their growing assortment of "un-German" enemies gave the Skinhead groups a sense of direction above and beyond simple brawling, they shifted the stage of confrontation from the soccer stadium to the streets. The first isolated attacks in 1985, and then the more frequent in 1986, targeted the punks. On the way back from soccer matches, Skin gangs beat up punks and Goths with increasing regularity and brutality. Some of the Skin gangs expanded their hate lists to include foreigners and gays. Outside East Berlin's reputed gay hang-out, the Schoppenstube bar on Chaussee Street, they jumped and beat up men considered to be gay. The onset of assaults against third world "guest workers" and students marked another stage in the Skinhead movement's progression toward full-fledged fascist ideology.

In keeping with the Skins' warrior code, girlfriends stayed on the sidelines, as idols to protect and to win glory for. Hard-core soccer fans, they held the ritual of physical contest in the highest esteem. Violence also served as a group action that cemented bonds within the gang. The "Skinhead personality type" coveted the thrill of weaponry and battle. And in the GDR, there were plenty of opportunities for young men to hone their fighting skills. Many of the Skins voluntarily signed up for extended and career terms of service in the army, which, studies confirm, served as prime recruitment territory for right-wing extremists. The state encouraged young men to take courses in judo, boxing, and karate, as well as shooting and motorcycle driving at the local *Gesellschaft für Sport und Technik* (GST). The GST, a kind of paramilitary preparatory school for armed service, was an ideal training camp for the Skinheads. And they took advantage of it. At the GST centers, the groups met, trained and made contacts.

Many of the extremists also found themselves right at home in the elitist sections of the communist youth organization, the *Freie Deutsche Jugend* (FDJ). As journalist Bernd Siegler argues in his excellent book *Auferstanden aus Ruinen: Rechtsradikalismus in der DDR* (Out of the Ruins: Right-wing Extremism in the GDR), it was no coincidence that an extraordinarily high number of right-wing criminal youth offenders belonged to the GST and FDJ *Ordner* groups. The function of the exclusive Ordner groups, selected from those young comrades who best exhibited the qualities of "patriotism, military readiness, discipline, and state loyalty," fell somewhere between that of security guards and bouncers. Their stated duty was to insure a "clean atmosphere of order, discipline, and security" at SED and FDJ events. Another responsibility of the young cadre units, in which neo-fascist nuclei had formed, included waking "hate and repulsion in the youth against fascism." One of the tasks that the Ordner carried out with relish was cleansing the streets of punks and other public eyesores. A 1989 study showed that nearly a quarter of the right-wing criminal youth offenders surveyed had been members of FDJ Ordner squads.

In the aftermath of the Zionskirche, the maturing neo-fascist character of the Skins became decisively more pronounced. Scene leaders such as Riechert and Hasselbach pushed the Skinheads toward more tightly organized structures with expressly political content. As one member recounted his own personal development: "It first became political for me after the Zionskirche. The Zionskirche thing wasn't political. It was simply directed against the punks 'cause they were our enemies. But then we noticed that the Zionskirche did us more damage than anything else. Then I saw that we had to work politically."[7]

The state clamped down all the harder as Skinhead violence soared dramatically. Between November 1987 and February 1988, radicals vandalized the Jewish cemetery in East Berlin's Prenzlauerberg district five times. On one occasion, a group of Skins knocked over 222 gravestones. One Skinhead gang was apprehended in Oranienburg, the location of the WWII Sachsenhausen concentration camp memorial, for harassing visitors and painting fascist graffiti on the former camp walls. In the southern city of Halle, police arrested four Skinhead youths for vandalizing Jewish gravestones and sentenced them to between two-and-one-half and five years imprisonment. Youths in both Halle and Dresden were put on trial for physically assaulting African guest workers on the streets. Between late November 1987 and July 1988, the GDR courts prosecuted at least nine Skinheads cases, involving forty-nine persons between the ages of sixteen and twenty-five years old.[8]

The sociological research that began after the Zionskirche melee also documented an increasing role of women in Skinhead groups. Although the female group members were rarely involved in criminal acts, they had become integral parts of some Skinhead gangs. They supported the groups and served as witnesses on behalf of the accused at their trials. Some even donned green flight jackets and combat boots. According to the Niederländer study, in contrast to 1987, 1988 "showed a new tendency of self-consciousness and independence of female Skinhead followers, which could develop into smaller right-wing womens' groups in the future."

The state's heavy-handed response to opposition of all kinds only drew the battle lines more clearly. By 1987, the GDR leadership was resisting the liberalizing influences of glasnost in the Soviet Union with all of its energy. The general disillusionment was palpable, and the opposition peace and democracy movement had also increased their pressure on the regime. Sociologists and church leaders estimated that the number of hardcore Skinheads and neo-fascist youth in the GDR in 1988 had swelled to somewhere between 1000 and 1800, with a concentration of 450–600 in East Berlin. These numbers included neither casual sympathizers nor right-wing soccer hooligans. Although the actual number of active neo-fascist youth in a country of seventeen million remained small, opinion polls revealed that the Skinheads dared to express sentiments of many of their peers. A 1989 Leipzig Central Institute for Youth Research poll of 3000 young people in the GDR showed thirty percent "in general agreement" with the activities of the Skinheads. Four percent considered themselves "sympathizers" of the Skins and another one percent "members."

As certain groups began to take their politics seriously, emergent *"Nazi-Skins"* distanced themselves from other less political varieties, such as *"Mode-Skins," "Oi Skins," "Edel-Skins,"* and *"Schmuddel-Skins."* At meetings held several times a week, the groups discussed a wide range of issues, from foreigners in the GDR and the environment, to the history of National Socialism and the economy. The group members pumped their grandparents for information about the Nazi years. They dug out old Nazi propaganda from attics and cellars. When read against the grain, the state's official "anti-fascist" literature contained plenty of information about fascism. Since photocopy machines were scarce, the groups copied material by hand or typewriter, and recorded information onto cassettes which were then recopied and distributed. In the army, the GST, and the prisons, contacts with other groups were made and ideology dispersed. The prisons, where the state lumped right-wing offenders together, became such a renowned source of schooling that they were nicknamed "the academy" for the right. Trial after trial landed the perpetrators behind bars, only to release them angrier and better indoctrinated a year or so later.

FROM SKIN TO FASCHO

As the subculture matured, an ever more advanced form of neo-fascist ideology took shape. For the Skinheads, fascist theory provided a new legitimacy to the values and prejudices of their street code. However rudimentarily most of the young, working-class Skinheads may have grasped Nazi ideology, they began to see themselves as a political movement, and their practices justified as political acts. The Skins' initial expression of German identity transformed itself into an extreme nationalism, complete with Nazi convictions of German and Aryan racial supremacy. The "laziness" of third world guest workers, for example, could now be explained as a characteristic of their inferior race, and Skinhead attacks on the foreigners seen as actions to purify German society. Punks and homosexuals were "deviants" who contaminated the purity of the German nation. The Skins' hatred of the communists, of course, fit neatly into fascist ideology. At the same time, fascism promised the youth a state form with the order and security that they coveted and a new dictator for them to serve. The desire for German unification also found an echo in the Nazis' drive to unite all Germans in one German Reich. Nazi Germany, the young fascists argued, must rise again in order to restore the German nation to its proper place as a world superpower.

The introduction of fascist theory, together with the worsening political and economic situation in the GDR, brought about new, more advanced fascist formations. Among a somewhat older category of young men, "neo-Nazi" and "fascho" groups appeared. The more educated and socially diverse fascists drew selectively from the ranks of experienced Nazi Skins, as well as from mainstream society. The new groups signaled the movement of right-wing ideology from the realms of youth subculture to the center of society. In contrast to the more primitive Skinheads, the neo-Nazis and faschos saw their project in explicitly political terms—namely, in the building of a fascist movement that would overthrow the GDR, as well as the Federal Republic. Their goal was the resurrection of National Socialism and the creation of a Fourth Reich modeled upon Hitler's Germany of 1933–1939. The Skinheads never sought, nor could they hope, to attract a broad spectrum of the population to their cause. The neo-Nazis and faschos, however, had something much different in mind.

The neo-Nazis fell between the Skinheads and the higher-caliber faschos, although the different categories were by no means strictly defined and membership often overlapped. Many neo-Nazis had graduated from the leagues of the Nazi-Skins. Riechert, for example, released early for good behavior from the two-year prison sentence that he earned from the Zionskirche attack, left the Lichtenberg Front in 1988 to found the neo-Nazi "January 30th Movement." (On January 30, 1933, Hitler formally became the Chancellor of Germany.) In conspiratorial structures, the fascho and neo-Nazi groups remained locally organized and restricted in number to committed and loyal fascists. Usually between twenty and thirty years old, the new fascists either dressed inconspicuously or sported short-cropped haircuts and straight, short mustaches, imitating the style of Hitler or the Hitler Youth. Some groups wore the brown shirts and black ties of their historical mentors. The neo-Nazis maintained a close relationship to violence, but usually exercised it tactically, to accomplish specific goals. Studies show that while connections between groups criss-crossed the country, rarely did substantive joint actions get off the ground. The movement remained splintered and small in number.

Many neo-Nazi groups, such as that of Uli K. from East Berlin, stayed near to the Nazi-Skinhead scene. "Yeah, me and my buddies, we used to run around as Skins," explains the twenty-two-year-old window washer in a heavy Berlin accent. His brown hair is trimmed short on the sides with a longer shock on top parted to the right. His smooth, boyish face seems incapable of cultivating the mustache of his self-acclaimed mentor, who Uli refers to simply as "Adolf." "The real Nazi-Skins, not those who just go around in bombers and boots, they're OK. But the Skins can be young and dumb, and as a Skin you get singled out. You're just asking for trouble. That's why we changed. People respect us more now," he says, dressed in a snappy, colorful track suit and a pair of brand-new white basketball shoes. "The whole situation here is shit, with the reds and all," he explains, shortly after the opening of the Wall. "We realized a while ago that we got to get serious if we really want to change things in the GDR."

When Uli first joined a Skinhead clique in 1986, his mother's only fear was that he would be arrested. His father had spent most of his son's childhood in jail, "a total *Asi*" as Uli describes him, using the state slang for an "asocial person." The Skinheads, he says, gave him the chance to make something out of his life. Uli first learned the "truth" about National Socialism from his grandfather. A pilot in the *Luftwaffe*, his grandfather stashed away some Nazi books and propaganda after the war, which he later passed on to Uli. "My *Opa* told me that he lived better then than now, earned more for his work. The Nazis built the *Autobahn* and schools. They took the unemployed off the streets and there wasn't any problem then with niggers and foreigners."

Uli, like one strain of neo-Nazis, maintains a critical distance from the Final Solution policies. "It was bad that Adolf gassed the Jews. That's inhumane. He should have just sent them away," explains Uli in the rational tone of someone who has given the matter a good deal of thought. Although his knee bobs nervously up and down as he talks, he exudes an air of self-confidence and purpose. I had arranged to meet Uli through a mutual acquaintance, a young punk who knew Uli from high school. Uli agreed to meet me, the acquaintance having been a neighbor for years and not such a bad guy, even if he was a punk and drank too much, according to Uli. "What was good was that Hitler wanted to rule the whole world," he says. "If Germany had the power again, everybody would live better. We just want the end of communism so that Germany can be powerful and great again." The Führer of the Third Reich remains the young neo-Nazi's personal idol. "Adolf said what he wanted and put it into action. In our age people just talk and talk and nothing happens. The Nazis did something."

Uli's group fluctuates between ten and fifteen members who have known each other from their school days. "We discuss everything, even what we read," says Uli, who has read his grandfather's copy of *Mein Kampf.* "Unlike the punks, we know that there can't be anarchy. There has to be someone to say how things will be done. If there's total freedom, then no one will work. And there must be work and order." When Uli's gang wasn't talking, it put its words into action. At weekend discos, they stormed across dance floors with their fists raised in the air, shouting fascist slogans. Graffiti was another means to "show people that the communists aren't the only ones with power here." A hidden arsenal contains the group's clubs, chains, and a gas pistol that a West Berlin buddy had smuggled into the East before the Wall came down. "We don't need foreigners to build a new Germany," says Uli. "If the Turks start coming over here from the West, we're ready."

Contacts with neo-Nazi movements in the West bolstered the GDR fascist groups' ideological foundations. As early as 1986, GDR Skinheads were in touch with counterparts from Hungary, the Netherlands, Switzerland, West Germany, Austria, and England. The first known contacts with foreign Skinheads were with the radical "Pannonia Skins" from Budapest, whose 1986 ransacking of several East Berlin bars set precedent for the East Germans. Shortly thereafter, the West German ultra-right political parties gradually began cultivating connections and funneling propaganda into the East. For the most part, the pre-1989 influence of the West German far right parties in the GDR was restricted to propaganda and consultation.

The faschos were the most sophisticated and potentially most dangerous of the neo-fascist tendencies in the GDR. The average fascho tended to be older than the neo-Nazis. While the faschos belonged to a wide range of professional categories, as a rule they came from a qualitatively higher social strata than the Skinheads or the neo-Nazis, often from the respected service industry or the lower technical professions. Older men from the Nazi period and the likes of army and police officers also contributed to the fascist groups' secretive, exclusive meetings and study sessions.

Since the faschos abstained from the street violence of the Skinhead sort, less information about the groups wound up in police records, thus restricting knowledge of their activities. Yet, violence also played a central role for the faschos. For one, they ultimately envisioned the violent overthrow of the state. Victims also reported that the groups employed force to protect the clique from exposure or to pressure members to adhere to the group's ideals. The fascho code was strict—those who failed to live up to their ethic found themselves either expelled from the group or the victim of brutal disciplinary actions. But despite the scarcity of information, the names of various suspected fascho leaders surfaced again and again in the testimony of Skinhead and neo-Nazi offenders. Some of the organized faschos obviously maintained links with select neo-Nazi and Nazi-Skinhead gangs, providing them with councel and direction, as well as tapping their ranks. "Some of the faschos and experienced neo-Nazis tried to discipline the periphery," says Niederländer. "The Skinhead scene was unruly and mixed in with soccer hooligans and all kinds of other types. The older radicals who had been in the Nazi-Skin scene for years laid it on the line—either you act like an upstanding German, ascribe to certain values and work hard, or you're out."

The faschos and neo-Nazis insisted that they were not the "scum of society," but the "elite." According to police specialist Wagner, by

1987–88 many of the neo-fascist types opted to stay in the GDR and confront the state, rather than apply for exit visas to emigrate to the West. "Often highly educated, these people could see that the economy here was going down the tubes. Their strategy lay not just in accelerating the state's demise, but also in positioning themselves well in society, in order to influence the state's present direction and to lay the groundwork for a new society," says Wagner. "The question of military service, for example, was also posed anew. Before they had joined the army out of a love of weaponry and military discipline. But later military duty became a conscious tactic to prepare for the overthrow of the state."

MADE IN THE GDR

The first efforts to probe beyond the state's diagnosis of neo-fascism in the GDR as a "Western import" came from a corner of the GDR's dissident intellectuals. Leading regime critics such as author Christa Wolf, theater director Freya Klier, and film directors Konrad Weiss and Roland Steiner were the first to look for the origins of the young peoples' affinity to right-wing ideas in the GDR itself. In a controversial 1988 article in the samizdat publication *Kontext*, Weiss asked how it was that ideas clearly bound to Nazi Germany could find such fertile soil in an anti-fascist, socialist state. His analysis, still hotly debated today, contends that the explanation for ultra-rightism in the GDR lay both in the Nazi past and the communist present.

Whatever the grandiose claims of the GDR, argued Weiss, the substance of the ideas that spellbound the majority of Germans during the Nazi era had never been directly confronted, much less overcome in the GDR. "After the war, the Germans in this country adopted the agenda of a new order too quickly," wrote Weiss. People had no opportunity to feel shame and remorse for what had happened during the war. "Many of those who openly cried 'mea culpa' changed their flags, uniforms, and party books, but inside they stayed the same. Most of the people, the Mitläufer and the silent majority, felt misled and used by National Socialism. It was so awful and horrible that they suppressed it. The superhuman amount of guilt, as well as shame, hindered any real coming to grips with the past." Their values remained more or less intact, latent, waiting for the right conditions to reappear. They passed many of the underlying prejudices and assumptions of National Socialism on from generation to generation. "On the surface," wrote Weiss, these people "lived for forty years as seemingly adjusted, politically indifferent or well-behaved socialist citizens. It is they, I think, who waited patiently for their hour and now pass on the brown baton to their grandchildren."

Weiss went on to argue that the GDR itself failed to replace fascism with a qualitatively new, democratic political culture. "Even for those people who honestly turned over a new leaf, there remained unconscious and subconscious traces of the Third Reich," wrote Weiss. Under a new mantle, the communists utilized many of the psychological and ideological mechanisms that the Nazi regime had relied upon. "Our everyday culture (*Alltagskultur*) was never fully de-Nazified. It is not the individual and the particular that are highest on the socialist scale of values, but the collective and the general. It is not originality and innovation that are praised, but subordination and convention. It is not contradiction and critique that are produced, but conformism and moral cowardice." With the formation of a Stalinist dictatorship of the proletariat, he argued, the GDR bypassed the chance to link itself with the democratic traditions of the 1848 revolution or the Weimar Republic. The communist state rejected liberal democracy for a system of new privileges, hero worship, and party discipline.

As Weiss and others note, the ethic of the GDR's right-wing youth, thoroughly petty bourgeois despite its fanaticism, reflected the essential values of a socialization process which they had been subjected to from their earliest days. In his 1990 study, *Der Gefühlstau: Ein Psychogramm der DDR* (Pent-up Emotions: A Psychogram of the GDR), GDR psychologist Hans-Joachim Maaz argues that the state drilled qualities such as punctuality, discipline, cleanliness, and politeness into children at every possible occasion. "One was forced to subordinate oneself to a collective and to collective norms at the expense of individual particularities, possibilities, and potentials. The foremost virtues and duties of every child included: sitting still, controlling oneself, pushing oneself in order to accomplish something, practicing obedience, and acknowledging the leadership role of adults gratefully and without contradiction," writes Maaz. "One can summarize the goal of the state educational processes in one line: to curb individuality and break the individual will! This principle was ruthlessly applied at every level of a child's education."

The GDR "learning factories," as one student described the schools, discouraged the development of facilities for critical thinking. Children were treated as blank slates upon which the state etched its program. The educational processes denied children the chance to develop the self-confidence necessary for original thought, much less to challenge a single, all-knowing authority. In the school curricula, the authorities pushed science and technological subjects at the expense of the liberal and creative arts. The unleashing of critical or creative energy represented an implicit threat to the state's monopoly on information and truth. As much as the citizens may have resented the party dictatorship and the Kafkaesque security apparatus, many had come to rely upon the existence of a strong, paternalistic force in their lives. If pedantic school teachers treated children as mindless sheep, then the all-powerful state treated adults as children. The authorities assured their charges that "We know what is best for you; we'll tell you what to do, what to feel and what to like; we will take care of you."

The system's structural violence also molded the GDR psyche. The GDR was a police state that relied upon the classic totalitarian mechanisms of intimidation: informant networks, the breach of personal privacy, and psychological terror. The Stasi not only rooted out opposition where it existed, but also struck an ever-present fear into the most loyal citizen. So all-encompassing was the Stasi network that even if one wasn't under surveillance, one suspected or feared that it might be the case. The general character type that the system shaped was not that of a risk taker, but one that craved security. Whether the GDR's young people bought the content of the state's ideology or not, they mastered the rules of the game. They knew what they had to say and what organizations they must belong to in order to climb in the social hierarchy.

In many cases, although not all, relations within the family reflected those between the state and its subjects. Parents were often strict and authoritarian, quick to discipline children for spontaneous expressions of emotion or noise. As Maaz writes, the best child was the "little adult." "During childhood there was always great stress laid on the importance of doing things regularly, always being punctual, and fulfilling one's duty before play or fun. A foremost principle of child raising was to teach children to hold back and to conquer their emotions. The repression of emotions was the absolute norm: self-control, courage, hardness, and obedience to authority were the ordained values."

Militarism permeated the educational processes and youth propaganda. The state portrayed socialism in terms of a life-or-death "class struggle" against the "imperialist enemy" in the West. On the frontline of the East-West conflict, the battle was one that the younger generations had to prepare for and eventually take over from their parents. In periods of crisis, the state stepped up its propaganda campaigns. Although the requirement of military duty from all young men hardly stood out as unique in the world, what was more unusual was the training of both boys and girls starting even before their entry at age six into the Pioneers, the first of the official party youth organizations. Already in the nurseries, children had been systematically confronted with "enemy images" and taught paramilitary games and songs. The Pioneer organization came complete with all of the trappings of a military force: uniforms, a regimented hierarchy, drills, medals, roll call, distinctions, etc. "At the ready for socialism and freedom!" the Pioneer director addressed the young cadre. "Always ready!", responded the brave little Pioneers. A career in the NVA was held up to the boys as the highest possible honor and expression of patriotism and manliness.

While the GDR's repressive culture appeared to succeed in molding a tractable, subservient population, psychiatric experts note that frustration and anger only accumulated, releasing itself in self-destructive forms. The GDR, for example, had exceptionally high rates of alcoholism, suicide, and divorce. According to GDR psychologists, the manner in which the right-wing youth vented their pent-up aggression differentiated them from their conformist peers. Rather than internalize their anger, the young radicals externalized it—against their parents, against society, and against the system. The violence and intolerance to which they had been subjected was turned against others, most often against those one notch lower on the social ladder. In a society that offered no alternatives, they struck out in the most vengeful, destructive manner possible. The feelings of inferiority and insecurity that had been impressed upon them they countered with a newfound sense of elitism and the power of physical violence.

HISTORY'S BALLAST

When the young radicals struck out, the direction of their protest was hardly random. As Weiss argued, many of the assumptions of the National Socialist era lay close to the surface in the GDR. During the postwar decades, the GDR was as remiss as the Federal Republic in addressing the legacy of Germany's Nazi past. On both sides of the border, the young states brushed aside the truth of its citizens' participation in the Third Reich in order to get on with the building of the new states. The West tried to bury the legacy of fascism under its economic successes. In the East, the state's distortion of history formed the bulwark of its legitimization. The reductive economic explanation of Nazism preempted any real discussion over the moral, historical, psychological and social sources of German fascism. While the cover-ups expediently enabled the states to proceed in the present, the issue of the past lingered unaddressed in many peoples' memories and consciences. In most households, parents or grandparents rarely broached the subject of their role during the National Socialist regime. Many of the young right-wing extremists in the former GDR today say that their grandparents either said nothing to them about National Socialism or spoke of those years in uncritical, somewhat nostalgic terms, claiming that "well, some things about it weren't so bad."

From the earliest days after Nazi Germany's capitulation, the issue of occupied Germany's relationship to fascism took different directions in the eastern and western zones. After the August 1945 Potsdam Conference, the four allied occupation powers in Germany embarked upon similar processes of purging all "more than nominal" former National

Socialist German Workers Party (NSDAP), or Nazi party, members from public institutions and bringing Nazi war criminals to trial. At first, the authorities executed the Potsdam decree with markedly more vigor in the eastern Soviet-occupied zone, the territory that would soon become the GDR. In contrast to the West zones, for example, the Soviets removed all teachers who had been Nazi party members from their positions. By 1948, 520,000 former NSDAP members had been expelled from their posts and two years later a total of 12,147 war criminals had been sentenced in the by-then GDR.

"De-Nazification" in the eastern zone however proceeded in a manner that would soon change. After the war, communist, social democratic, and Christian opponents of the Nazi regime returned to Germany from detention camps or exile to join in the country's physical and spiritual reconstruction. The mixed bag of exiles conceived the original de-Nazification program as a broad process of social re-education that would replace the values of National Socialism with humanistic, democratic anti-fascist values. As the eastern and western zones of occupation rapidly consolidated into opposing camps, however, the Soviet-backed SED, the newly-formed communist party, moved to monopolize the anti-fascist effort in the East. Less than three years after the re-education campaign had begun, the communist hardliners, fresh from wartime exile in Moscow, transplanted the ideals of the French Revolution with those of Stalinism. The brief period of democratic experimentation in the schools and universities ended, and anti-fascists with political convictions other than those of the SED cadre were either marginalized or purged.

The treatment of former NSDAP members and regime collaborators in the eastern zone also changed as the frontline of the Cold War hardened. Since only a tiny fraction of Germans had actively resisted Nazism and an even smaller number as communists, the SED lacked a mass base upon which to legitimize its bid for power. The SED leadership feared that pursuing the issue of the past too forcefully would risk alienating large parts of the population, as the Austrian Communist Party had done. In 1946, the SED was the first of the political parties in the Soviet-occupied zone that began to court the allegiance of the "little Nazis," those who had been party members but not war criminals. Party membership swelled as it became clear that it was no longer the past that mattered, as Freya Klier writes in *Lüg Vaterland: Erziehung in der DDR* (Fatherland of Lies: Growing Up in the GDR), but where one placed one's loyalty in the present: "The ranks of the party were filled with 'responsible' comrades. Most of the new members were young, naive cadre, but there were also Mitläufer from the Nazi days among them. The criteria for 'responsible' was not the political past, but rather the solidity with which one then stood on the 'right' side. . . . That meant that whoever was a Nazi, but not really such a nasty beast, could from one week to the other stand on the 'right' side and be a 'communist.' . . . The paradox couldn't have been greater: while anti-fascists who had suffered [under the Hitler dictatorship] were shuffled out of positions of importance, fascist collaborators found a new model of order in the SED."

Almost overnight, a nation of collaborators was hoisted onto the pedestal of the "victors of history," the conquerers of fascism. In 1948, the SED officially concluded the process of de-Nazification and set the construction of the workers' state in full forward motion. The GDR leadership heaped praise upon the East German people as the flagbearers of the "anti-fascist resistance tradition," while blasting the Germans in the West as unrepentant Nazis. In the FRG, former high-ranking Nazis' occupation of top positions in government and industry was no secret. But neither did many former lower-level Nazis and SS members in the GDR find it difficult to scale the communist hierarchy. A 1981 West German study identified 900 former NSDAP members in official posts in the GDR.

In the GDR propaganda sections former Nazis cliques reestablished themselves nearly intact. Some of the former fascist propagandists won leading positions in the GDR media, where they continued to use anti-Semitic terminology nearly identical to the wording that they employed under National Socialism. The GDR not only showed little sensitivity to the WWII persecution of the Jews in Germany, but actually perpetuated anti-Semitism with crass tirades against Zionism that implicitly stigmatized all Jews as "counter-revolutionaries" and "imperialist agents." A 1968 report written by Simon Wiesenthal, Director of the

Documentation Center of the Union of Jews Persecuted Under the Nazi Regime, analyzed the tone of the East German propaganda toward Israel, Zionism, and Jews. "When one replaces the word 'Israeli' with 'Jew' and 'progressive forces' with 'National Socialism,' you would think that you had before you a piece of propaganda straight out of Goebbel's Propaganda Ministry," wrote Wiesenthal about the GDR press. "The similarities of the thoughts and concepts are revealed the other way around too, when one substitutes articles from the Nazi period with GDR vocabulary."

After the initial period of de-Nazification, the GDR leadership transformed "anti-fascism" into a blunt instrument of propaganda and indoctrination. Right up until the Wall came down, the state subjected the GDR youth to what it termed an "anti-fascist upbringing." The particular brand of anti-fascism, however, may have done more harm than good. History courses and school books dealt with fascism and the German people's relationship to National Socialism briefly and abstractly. The center piece of institutional anti-fascism was lectures that former "anti-fascist resistance fighters" gave to students once, or maybe twice, during the entirety of their school education. Every student was required to visit a concentration camp memorial once.

According to historian Annette Leo from former East Berlin, the state-ordained anti-fascism simply didn't penetrate the consciousness of the youth of the 1980s. In contrast to the 1950s, she explains, when there was still some vitality and sense of immediacy to the official anti-fascist program, the lectures and trips had become rote. The pupils showed little interest in the often elderly, old-school communist "anti-fascist" representatives from the GDR's official organization, the Committee of Anti-Fascist Resistance Fighters. "The old anti-fascists spoke in terminology and clichés that the kids couldn't relate to," says Leo. "They saw through it immediately for the propaganda that it was. Rather than tell the children about their real and naturally very moving experiences during the war, they just repeated the standard lines that everybody had heard a million times. The kids would just laugh at them when they'd say things like 'Oh, you kids, you don't know how lucky you are to live today in the GDR.' "

In early 1990, a friend and I took the convenient half-hour train trip from Berlin to Oranienburg, the site of the Sachsenhausen concentration camp memorial. Had it not been for its proximity to the former German capital, Oranienburg would blend in inconspicuously with countless other East German towns. But in 1936, while the world celebrated the Olypmic games with the leaders of the Third Reich, the construction of the camp was already well underway. During Nazi rule, the people of Oranienburg would watch 200,000 people transported there from Berlin, only half of whom would ever leave Sachsenhausen's barbed-wire confines.

On a bright, sub-zero winter's afternoon, only a handful of Western tourists inspect the barracks and watchtowers that still stand on its stark, windswept grounds. The visits of GDR school groups are no longer mandatory. Within the long cement walls of the triangle-shaped camp, the brutality of Sachsenhausen's SS commanders comes vividly to life. Black-and-white photos in the camp museum show emaciated prisoners crammed in straw-padded bunks, stacks of mutilated corpses and rooms filled with body limbs, jaw bones and hair. Outside, the outlines of the "shoe-testing track" are discernable under the freshly fallen snow. There rag-clad prisoners were forced to carry sand bags for twenty-five miles at a time to test new shoe soles. A stone's throw from the former barracks stands a monument to Station Z, the camp's execution site. At its base is a withered wreath from the former official GDR trade union, dedicated to the station's victims. Until 1940, prisoners were bound to a single wooden post and shot. By 1943, four crematoriums and a gas chamber had been added to expedite the killing.

As it stands, Sachsenhausen is as much as relic of the GDR as it is of the Third Reich. At the camp's entrance, next to a grove of snow-laced pines, is the Museum of the Anti-Fascist Freedom Struggle of the Peoples of Europe. In turgid GDR jargon, the country-by-country exhibit documents the heroic struggle of the "class-conscious nucleus of the international resistance—the communists." With a quasi-religious, almost cultist aura, the propaganda sensationalizes the persecution of communists, portraying them as the greatest martyrs of "fascist barbarism." The magnitude of the persecution of Jews, homosexuals, social democrats, Roma, and the mentally ill, as well as the diverse nature of international anti-fascist resistance, is obscured, when alluded to at all.

Since the citizens of the GDR (and their "brothers" in the Soviet Union) were communists, 1945 marked their "victory" over fascism rather than the "defeat" of the German people. The exhibits portray fascism either as a mystical evil that "swept over" the German people, or as a form of capitalism, which implicitly or explicitly linked the West with fascism. The picture is black-and-white: Being an anti-fascist means being a communist, and being anti-communist means being fascist. For those people in the GDR who didn't consider themselves communists, the state was telling them that they were fascists.

At every turn, the memorial's displays and literature attempt to unload the burden of German fascism onto the West. Unlike the mass extermination camps at Auschwitz or Treblinka, Sachsenhausen also served as a work camp, where giant profits were made from hiring out prisoners to local armament factories. "German Monopoly Capital— They Gave the Orders" reads one display above the photographs of such Nazi industrial magnates as Friedrich Flick and Gustav Krupp, family names of firms that still operate in West Germany. Below the capitalists are the photos of Sachsenhausen's SS officers with the caption: "The Executioners and the Hangmen—They Carried out the Murders." "Many of the murders," states the brochure, "known and unknown, are still alive in West Germany today." The displays tend to demonize the "SS perpetrators" and the "SS terror," creating an exaggerated distance between the inhuman acts of "the Nazi butchers" and the complicity of the average German.

At the base of the camp's triangle in Tower A, Johann Hirthhammer, Sachsenhausen director since 1986, sits in the same office where his notorious predecessors once sat. From a broad picture window, Hirthhammer looks out over the camp's eerie grounds. He says that changes in the memorial's conception are already underway. "As it is, the presentation is much too reductive," admits the kindly, seventyish man, who had worked in the communist underground during the war years. Most of the displays were conceptualized in the early sixties, he says, at the height of Stalinist orthodoxy in the GDR, and hadn't been reworked since. "There was too much emphasis on the communist resistance and the SS terror," he says. "The victims of the Nazi racial ideology must be portrayed more realistically, and each in their own identity. And the whole spectrum of the resistance, such as Christians and social democrats, also have to be documented more objectively." The first change will be the addition of documentation on Special Camp No. 7 to the exhibit, which from 1945 to 1950 functioned as an intern camp for Nazi war criminals, as well as for other political opponents of the Soviet occupation power.

Since fascism had supposedly been extinguished once and for all in the GDR, the institutional anti-fascism didn't even claim to counter remnants of or affinities for fascism in the GDR population. Rather, the purpose of even the concentration camp memorials was to "engender patriotism" and to establish the "authority and leading role of the party in the GDR." Some of the anti-fascist programs expressly sought to encourage young men to choose a career in the military. In displays and exhibits, the depiction of the "the fight against fascism," which claimed in the same breath to be "the fight against militarism," was heavily laden with militaristic language and imagery. The stated ideals that the exhibits sought to transmit have a familiar ring: male camaraderie, discipline, subordination, and military heroism.

Studies that the Leipzig Central Institute conducted in 1988 and 1989 exposed the implications of anti-fascist upbringing for the historical consciousness of GDR youth. Less than half of the youth questioned, and only a third of secondary school pupils, expressed a strong interest in "the history of their fatherland." Thirty-seven percent of the pupils stated that they "had already heard enough about WWII." About a quarter of the youth showed a complete lack of concern about the fascist past, agreeing with the statements: "The fascist era doesn't mean anything to me anymore" and "I don't want to hear any more about fascism." A survey of young visitors on mandatory class trips to the Buchenwald concentration camp memorial found that eleven percent of all youth and fifteen percent of vocational students from cities acknowledged that "fascism also had its good sides." They pointed to the orderly highways, the variety of motorcycles and trucks available, and the reduction of unemployment. Six percent of all of those asked and eleven percent of vocational students believed that "Adolf Hitler only wanted the best for the German people." Only fifty-seven percent would do everything in their power to prevent the revival of fascism.

Asked how they would judge their grandfathers had they been NSDAP members, one response was: "He would have done it for the same reasons that a cadre today joins the SED, because he wanted to improve his position in society."

In the debate over the sources of right-wing extremism, the original "Weiss thesis" is just one of several attempts to explain the phenomenon. Those who accept the general sociohistorical direction of Weiss's inquiry tend to look to the kind of society and political culture in a given country, as well as its relationship to its past, to explain undemocratic, right-wing trends. But why, ask critics, if right-wing extremism in the GDR was a product of the system and German history, does it look so similar throughout Western Europe? How is it that Skinheads, identical in appearance, in former East Germany, former West Germany, England, and Sweden all say roughly the same thing? And, ask others, if the communist GDR was such a hotbed of reaction, then why haven't the ultra-right parties cashed in on the potential? In fact, the far right parties such as the Republicans seem to have signif icantly more support in West Germany.

One of the most popular current theses in Germany is the "alienation" or "modernization" explanation. For theorists such as Bielefeld Professor Wilhelm Heitmeyer, the problem is not so much one of "racism" or "right-wing extremism" as it is *Fremdenfeindlichkeit*, best translated as "xenophobia."[9] The source of xenophobia, Heitmeyer and others argue, is the estrangement and powerlessness of the individual in an increasingly modernized, impersonal society. The individual today is thrown into an atomized world in which people are no longer unified as they once were through the bonds of family, class, etc. "The individual today," writes Heitmeyer, "not only can, but he must, increasingly shape his life by himself. In the final analysis, it is he alone who must bear the risks of failure. Anxiety caused by the risk of failure and isolation as consequences of harsher individual competition are major sources for feelings of estrangement." Problems such as housing shortages and unemployment, as well as the influx of foreigners, exacerbates these feelings of uncertainty. Young people attempt to compensate for their estrangement by searching for certainties in "natural" communities, symbols, and powerful organizations. Violence is another means of overcoming powerlessness and "creating clarity in unclear situations."

Since most of Europe is subject to the same processes of modernization, the Heitmeyer thesis explains how xenophobia can look so similar from country to country. For Heitmeyer, even foreigners are subject to fallout of "individualization" and thus xenophobia and reciprocal violence too. Critics, however, argue that the modernization theorists depoliticize right-wing extremism, turning racist, neo-fascist phenomena into the empty protests of frustrated kids. The young radicals and their victims are thrown into the same pot, all the helpless victims of a social alienation for which they themselves can hardly be blamed. The modernization approach tends to downplay the neo-fascist nature of the Skinheads, neo-Nazis, and certain political parties, as well as their political potential in society. The analysis of Heitmeyer and his colleagues is the same as that which enables the German political establishment today to explain the actions of right-wing extremists as those of "individual, social deliquents" and not of neo-fascists connected to a much larger ultra-right network. While even critics of the modernization approach admit that estrangement, anxiety, and frustration bolster ultra-rightist activity, they argue that the roots of the problem, be it in former East Germany or Sweden, must be sought first and foremost in the racist and authoritarian aspects of the political culture. Simply because Sweden or the FRG are bourgeois democracies doesn't mean that racist and undemocratic tendencies don't persist in their societies too, just as in the GDR or other systems.

My analysis of right-wing extremism in all of the post-communist countries tends to side with the critics of the modernization theories. In the GDR, the anger that the Skinheads vented in seemingly wanton acts of violence had a specific political character, with roots that extended deep into the mainstream of East German society. It was not by chance that one segment of the youth gravitated toward fascist ideology. The fascistic direction of their initial impulses, well before the introduction of an explicitly political ideology, attests to the fertile ground that Stalinist political culture provided for the growth of right-wing and neo-fascist ideas. The Skinhead phenomenon constituted neither the blind expression of frustration nor the protest of an economically deprived group. Rather, the youth movement represented an active, albeit extreme extension of the authoritarian, petty bourgeois mindset that the state had nurtured. Although only a fraction of the youth, much less the total population, openly identified with some form of fascist ideology, the opinion polls conducted before 1989, as well as those done afterwards, clearly show a propensity to undemocratic ideas in a shockingly large percentage of the population. The structures that the people resented and simultaneously tolerated had become part of many of their individual consciousnesses. The 1989 "democratic revolution" created the myth that the people of the GDR had always been democrats, straining at the yoke to burst out of the system and assert their true nature. But the extent of genuinely democratic opposition in the GDR before the walls began to crumble tells another story. In 1989, the very same mentality that had kept the GDR and most of its East bloc counterparts afloat finally turned on its creator. Only the minuscule underground democracy movement tried to make a real break with the essence of the system's values. The reality that the regime chose to ignore boded ill for the day when the people of GDR finally found their voice. As the tumultuous collapse of the GDR and the painful process of unification took its course, Germans on both sides of the dismantled wall would begin to learn what four decades of repression had made of a society.

Chapter 3

HUNGARY
THE GHOSTS OF
CONSERVATISM PAST

By early 1990, pluralistic forces had removed the last formal
barriers to closing the era of communist rule in Hungary. Along
the eastern bank of the Danube, in Budapest's back-street beer
bars and corner cafés, there was something distinctly fresh in the air,
something that defied the stereotype of the pessimistic, darkly prophetic
Magyars. As the March 20 election approached, the first free multi-
party vote since 1947, Hungary radiated an unfamiliar sense of hope.
In contrast to the bloody revolution in Romania or the mass demonstrations in Czechoslovakia and East Germany, the Hungarians were
eagerly preparing to vote the reform communist party, recently renamed the Hungarian Socialist Party (HSP), out of office.

Even though the dark, narrow streets at the base of the Erzsébet
Bridge are awash with vibrant campaign posters, in my corner local,
the Wernesgrüner in Sörház utca (Beer House Street), the effervescent
barroom chatter revolves little around political parties and economic
programs. Many of the regulars, mostly workers, have *kokárda* proudly
pinned on their lapels, decorative ribbons with the red, white and green
national colors. For most people, it is still too early to articulate one's
own politics, much less those of dozens of upstart parties. Certainly,

it's clear that the intellectual-led Alliance of Free Democrats (AFD), fresh from the opposition underground, emphasizes the country's "return to Europe" and the necessity of introducing a Western-style economy into Hungary with the utmost speed. On the fuliginous, bullet-pocked buildings, ubiquitous placards sport the bearded face of the dissident philosopher Gáspár Miklós Tamás, the Free Democrats' district candidate. The fact that a good part of the AFD's leadership is Jewish would be common knowledge even if the posters of Tamás and others hadn't been defaced with David Stars and graffiti such as "Jews Out!"

Across the street from the Wernesgrüner, the lights in the office of the Federation of Young Democrats (Fidesz) burn until well after even the hard-core beer drinkers have called it a night. The sassy new party is the brainchild of a handful of rebellious young Budapest law students, whose commitment to Western democracy reflects its mostly young, educated constituency. The maze-like streets and alleyways also display the campaign propaganda of the Hungarian Democratic Forum (HDF), the largest opposition party in Hungary, which sees itself as the architect of the country's national renaissance. One of their posters has a young, blond-haired, blue-eyed boy gazing expectantly into the distance. Another is a soft Klimtesque watercolor of a pregnant woman dozing dreamily. Underneath both read: "Toward a Hungarian Future." In addition to the standard language of Europe, anti-communism, and democracy, the Democratic Forum's representatives stress the priority of national renewal and the vast potential of the Hungarian spirit. All of the other parties, from the HSP to the Christian Democrats, also back Western Europe's apparently tried-and-true postwar recipe of "democracy" and "market economics." Among the Wernesgrüner crowd, too, the promised free-market panacea for the ailing economy enjoys a popular consensus.

At first glance, the six hundred or so foreign journalists that have descended upon Budapest for the historic vote are also a bit hard-pressed to discern real differences in the thicket of parties. The standard tags of "right" and "left," "conservative" and "liberal" seem to bear no apparent connection to their Western applications. The "left," clearly enough, refers to the HSP, although in fact its reform-minded leadership has backed free-market reform policies for years, earning Hungary's mixed economy the dubious title of "goulash communism." At the same time, "left" also refers to the party of the communist regime's die-hard Stalinists, the likes of whom the Western press refers to as "conservative hardliners," and whom the HSP liberals booted out of the party at their recent congress. All of the parties insist that they are to some degree "liberal," in that they stand in the Western liberal tradition of market economics, the rule of law, and political pluralism. Except for the insignificant Stalinists and the HSP reformers, all of the parties are equally adamant that they have nothing whatsoever to do with the "left" or "socialism." The two most explicitly Western, "liberal" parties, the AFD and Fidesz, endorse economic philosophies close to Thatcherism. Yet, from the corner of their main rivals in the HDF, the Free Democrats are routinely castigated as "leftist" or even "Bolshevik." Rather, it is the nationalist HDF and the Christian Democrats who qualify their credentials with the adjectives "conservative" or "center-right," even though they urge more cautious approaches to the market transition. Simply to add to the confusion, each of the nascent parties encompasses a diverse body of opinion within its own ranks. Many of the "right" and "left" wings, "conservative" and "liberal" currents within the parties have more in common with those same wings in other parties than they do with the polar end of the spectrum in their own parties.

As the media pack trudges from one press conference to another, some journalists gradually recognize the contours of several fundamentally divergent political cultures, traditions that in fact flesh out a political spectrum significantly broader than in most of Western Europe. Around the corner from the Free Democrats' neighborhood office and luncheonette, the forty-three-year-old philosopher Tamás introduces himself to the members of the fourth estate. To either side of him stand AFD chairman János Kis, also a philosopher, and the writer Miklós Haraszti. In a well-worn corduroy sport jacket, Tamás lifts his slender frame onto the edge of the table in front of the jam-packed room. With a devilish grin and a flick of his wrist, he has his audience's undivided attention. Shifting fluidly between Hungarian, English, German, French, and Romanian, the bespectacled professor laces his animated oratory with anecdotes, witty asides, and stinging jabs at the old regime. In a confident, boyishly charming style, he spellbinds the crowd as if he had been making public appearances for years. As a matter of fact, for all but two of the twelve years that Tamás has lived in Budapest since emigrating from his Transylvanian homeland in western Romania, he has been banned not only from the media but from all official academic positions as well. Tamás, like Kis and Haraszti, earned his living as a freelance translator and language teacher until the state conveniently rid itself of his presence, giving the critic permission to lecture abroad.

When Tamás first arrived in Budapest in 1978, he immediately fell in with Kis and other future leading figures of the Democratic Opposition, the illegal democracy movement. Many of the circle's core members had been pupils of the Marxist philosopher George Lukács, and the early opposition bore the marks of that heritage. In the late sixties and seventies, the Lukács School Marxists attacked the communist regime from the left, invoking the state's self-acclaimed ideology to expose it's hypocrisy and contradictions. But the rebels' scholarly polemics rebounded off the regime like dummy bullets. The intellectuals soon concluded that the socialism of the East bloc regimes was little more than an ideological facade to legitimate their monopoly on power. Expelled from the party in 1973, Kis and his allies grew increasingly skeptical about the value of Marxist analysis of any kind to explain society. The emergence of the Polish democratic underground, culminating in the Solidarity movement in 1980–81, prompted the Hungarian opposition's definitive break with even the most revisionist forms of Marxism. With the establishment of the samizdat journal *Beszélő* (Visiting Hours), the intellectual circle placed itself firmly in liberal, democratic opposition to the regime. At times jailed, regularly harassed, and under constant surveillance, the democratic opposition remained illegal until AFD's foundation in Fall 1989.

Although never a Marxist of any sort, during the seventies and eighties Tamás' politics also gravitated away from his early anarcho-leftist convictions. Today, Tamás considers himself a libertarian conservative, strongly influenced by the theories of Fredrich August von Hayek, James Madison, and Edmund Burke, among others. Within the

AFD, Tamás leads the "conservative liberal" wing, while Kis, before his resignation in 1991, headed up the more social liberal faction in his party. Before the journalists, Tamás argues that Hungary must privatize its state-owned factories completely and as quickly as possible. It is the forces of market competition, he says, not the decisions of state planners, that will determine the composition of a decentralized, deregulated Hungarian economy. His radical laissez-faire beliefs and deep prejudice against all forms of state intervention in society naturally rule out any state safety nets for the trying economic transition in store for the country. Tamás makes it plain that even the watered-down notions of the common good and the redistribution of wealth in Western European countries smack of communism's collectivist ideals. For Tamás and his allies within the Free Democrats, the essence of political liberty in liberal societies is the unhindered freedom of the individual—free to accumulate wealth, or free to perish, according to his own initiative.

At an afternoon press conference across the swollen Danube, the campaign's front-runner, the Democratic Forum, espouses a markedly different brand of political conservatism. The contrast in the two parties' styles and personalities alone is striking. Against the background of a banner heralding "A strong parliament, a strong government and a strong forint . . . !", sit four members of the Forum's executive, among them party chairman and Hungary's future Prime Minister, József Antall, and the populist playwright István Csurka. In their stiff brown suits the Forum representatives have a decidedly provincial, crusty quality about them. A bit awkwardly, one of the men clears his throat and, through an interpreter, greets "the esteemed ladies and gentlemen of the international press." Antall then elaborately excuses himself for not rising, but the television cameramen, he explains, unfairly focus upon his paunchy midsection, transmitting an unbecoming image across the airwaves. Silence. The first speaker resumes his wordy monologue, which sounds distinctly similar to the circuitous, self-important bureaucratic pomp that the communists had so relished. The HDF, he insists, is a modern democratic party. Yet the country's reintegration into the European consensus should not undermine the restoration of national values and national pride that the "Bolsheviks" neglected with such disastrous consequences.

Unlike the Free Democrats or Fidesz, the HDF's programs are broad and vague. Antall, who worked quietly and diligently as a school teacher, librarian, and finally museum director during the Kádár years, assumed the Forum's top post only in late 1989. His father, a top national-liberal minister during the final years of Admiral Miklós Horthy's 1920–1944 regency, bequeathed the young Antall an impeccable anti-communist pedigree, as well as a political education that would follow him into office. Upon taking the HDF's helm, Antall aspired to project a moderate, center-right, thoroughly anti-communist image for the party. His self-acclaimed role model: West Germany's postwar chancellor Konrad Adenauer. The task, however, required integrating the three general tendencies that had emerged within the HDF. Antall's views spanned the party's national-liberal wing, which advocated a relatively rapid transition to a market economy, and the Christian democratic wing, which emphasized the nation's moral regeneration. Simultaneously, although not without misgivings, he also won the backing of the national populist current, which saw its mission primarily in terms of the nation's spiritual rebirth.

The diverse elements within the HDF possessed a common vision of a traditional Hungary, composed of hard-working, pious residents of small towns and village communities. If elected, the party promised to break down the state agricultural co-operatives into private family farms, enabling the peasantry to reestablish itself. Although the historical precedents of the Democratic Forum's different factions varied, they all reached back to some aspect of Hungary's Christian Course of the 1920s and 1930s for their historical bearings. The thread that wove together the party's program was its understanding of the 1000-year Hungarian nation. Even in their economic program, the HDF refered to "the nation" again and again. The HDFers stressed a slower approach to privatization, one that would give priority to the formation of a strong Hungarian middle class. Their notion of a "socially conscious, mixed-market economy" would be based upon the "hitherto untapped human potential, imagination and innovative spirit of the Hungarian nation."

The nationalists spoke out with more conviction on the question of the ethnic Hungarian minorities in neighboring countries. The post-

WWI Treaty of Trianon, as any Hungarian will tell you, whittled Habsburg Hungary down to one-third of its former size and left ethnic Hungarians stranded in Romania (1.7 million), Slovakia (600,000), Serbia (400,000), the Ukraine (160,000), as well as Slovenia, Croatia, and Austria.[1] Trianon's injustice and demands for its revision served as the rallying points for all of Hungary's interwar nationalist movements, and the prospect of regaining parts of its lost territories encouraged a vacillating Hungary to join forces with Hitler Germany as one of the Axis powers. As a party, the Democratic Forum denied that it harbored ambitions to redraw the present borders. As unfair as it was, the HDF claimed that it accepted the size and shape of modern-day Hungary. What it would not accept, however, was the discrimination and persecution of the minorities. The self-appointed protectorate of all of the Hungarian minorities abroad (a figure the HDF put at five million), the Nationalists directed their protests mostly against Romania, where the Hungarians had suffered particular persecution during the Ceauşescu dictatorship, and interethnic violence had recently erupted again in the Transylvanian city of Tîrgu-Mureş.

Along with national issues, the HDF also called upon another familiar ghost from Hungary's historical chest. From its first days, an oblique anti-Semitism tainted the HDF's image. During the election campaign, the HDF's anti-Semitic undertones stemmed primarily from the Forum's presentation of itself as the nation's single true representative of Hungarian culture, the Hungarian spirit, and Hungarian tradition. The HDF's contention, the Free Democrats above all protested, drew a line between "real Hungarians" and those who supposedly maintained allegiances to "other," unidentified, non-Hungarian traditions. Read between the lines, the insinuation was that certain suspect forces (like the AFD leadership) were not trustworthy of administering Hungarian culture, much less of presiding over its rebirth.

An early showdown over anti-Semitism came to a head in February 1990, when a pamphlet entitled "Wake Up, Hungarians!" hit the streets in eastern Hungary. It's author, one of HDF's founding fathers, the poet-playwright Csurka, maintained that the "pursuit of self-interest" of an unspecified "dwarf minority" (*törpe kisebbség*) blocked Hungarians from realizing their true national essence. "Wake up, Hungarians!", the pamphlet read, "Terror. Soldiers. Blood and final collapse. Everything around us is crackling and crashing. War can start again at any moment with Romania. . . . The Hungarian people, drained of blood, confused in their souls and humiliated many times cannot afford another violent solution." The reference to the "dwarf minority," a barely concealed swipe at Hungarian Jews, provoked a thunder of protest from all of the other major parties—but to no avail. Even moderates within the HDF declined to either condemn the statement or distance themselves from Csurka.

Typical of the emergent conservative ideologies throughout freshly liberated Eastern Europe, an ethnic concept of the nation was the very cornerstone of the Democratic Forum's raison d'être. With few exceptions, such as thinkers like Tamás, communism effectively thwarted the evolution of a modern conservatism in Eastern Europe. Hence, in the vacuum of postcommunist politics, the recourse of most self-acclaimed conservatives was to the past, to political traditions with "Hungarian roots," to a policy of national and historical restoration. Unlike Western neo-conservatives, who for the most part seek to build upon twentieth century models of progress and rationality, the vision of many of Eastern Europe's national conservatives is regressive, harking back to a folkloric utopia that they claim existed sometime, somewhere in their country's noble and glorious past. While even the radical restorationists pragmatically acknowledge that a return to the last century is neither feasible nor wholly desirable, they romantically seek to revive the values and traditions that had flourished in Hungary before the rude interruption of communism and other "foreign" ideologies, such as liberalism.

In contrast to modern neo-conservatives' emphasis on the individual and the free market, traditionalist conservatives, such as HDF and its allies, stress the nation, family, religion and tradition.[2] Not all so different from the rationale of the communist regime, which subordinated the rights of the individual to the supposed collective interests of the working class, the ideology of the nationalist conservatives subsumes the role of the individual under the collective of the nation. In the atmosphere of newly post-communist Eastern Europe, where identification with any kind of left or social democratic position was tantamount to political suicide, the new constellations tilted the political spectrum dramatically to the right, defining a mainstream in which a party such as the Free Democrats stand on the center-left and the HDF on the center-right. Where the mainstream is so right-wing, it tends to encompass radical elements that in the West would normally find themselves on the outermost margins of political discourse. In Eastern Europe, such far right tendencies have a place solidly within the accepted boundaries of political discourse.

Alongside the HDF, the historical Independent Smallholder's Party and the Christian Democratic People's Party rode to victory with just over sixty percent of the vote, which enabled the three parties to form a conservative ruling coalition. Reemerging after a forty year hiatus with manifestos hardly more modern, the two "historical parties' " seemed so compatible with the HDF that they regarded one another as "natural allies." The Smallholders, Hungary's largest democratic party in the immediate postwar period, won an absolute majority of votes in the 1945 elections before the communists seized power three years later. During the 1930s, the rural-based party gained popularity as a defender of agrarian and small business interests. Today, the elderly party leadership remains fiercely patriotic, emphasizing their commitment to Hungarian national interests, independence, and Christian values. The party's sixty-year-old slogan remains "God, Family and Fatherland." The Smallholders' top pledge, and traditional base of support, the farmers, was the full restitution of all property confiscated by the communists after 1947.

The Christian Democrats, the successor to the prewar Democratic People's Party, also reemerged in 1989 with little more than its past to show for credentials. With nebulous slogans such as "A Christian Path toward Modern Europe" and "With God for the Fatherland and Freedom," the party promised the rejuvenation of Hungary's national and Christian values. Its program, based on the Ten Commandments, stressed a return to traditional education, the protection of the family and motherhood, and compassion toward the elderly, the poor and the handicapped.

POWER TO THE POPULISTS

The populist-urbanist split in postcommunist Hungarian politics runs
along fault lines that had put rural-oriented nationalists and westward-
looking intellectuals in Hungary on opposite sides since the turn-of-
the-century. The Democratic Forum's initiators, most notably poet Sán-
dor Csoóri and the playwright Csurka, represent the youngest generation of Hungary's *népi írók*, or folkish writers. The original népi writers
emerged during the turbulent interwar period as a rural cultural movement committed to the peasantry and as a political force with populist
goals. Although the movement arose in opposition to Trianon, for the
népi writers, the tragedy of modern Europe's intrusion upon Hungary
went beyond the country's territorial dismemberment—it penetrated to
the very depths of the Hungarian soul.

The népi movement articulated a protest against modernization's
erosion of the "true Hungarian consciousness," a process, they argued,
like Trianon, that was perpetrated by foreign protagonists, most notably
the Jews and the Germans. In their romantic vision of pure Hungarianism, the repository of the Hungarian soul lay in the traditional peasantry, in the small plot farms and the folkish way of life. Neither left
nor right, the népi movement's populism endorsed a "Third Way"
between socialism and capitalism, both of which it considered un-Hun-
garian ideologies. Only by elevating "the Hungarian people" from their
poverty and breathing new life into Hungary's weary spirit could the
populists rejuvenate the "vital energies" of the nation. While the movement progressively set itself against the big land-owning aristocracy
and promoted radical land reform, racism and anti-Semitism were the
dark underside of the most famous and talented *népi* writers. Although,
in word, the movement extolled grassroots forms of popular democracy,
its conception implicitly called for a strong leader to lift the peasantry
out of its poverty and lead the nation. The movement's amorphous
political categories enabled some of its proponents to take a fascist path
in the late 1930s (although the original népi writers themselves
staunchly opposed fascism), and others to espouse socialism.

The historical populist-urbanist cleft followed Hungary's postwar
intellectuals into the anti-communist opposition, determining the dif-

ferent courses that the two opposition currents would elect under President János Kádár's "soft dictatorship." At every opportunity, the HDFers stalwartly paraded their anti-communist credentials, rarely passing up the chance to point out the Free Democrats' origins in the communist party. Yet neither the form nor the content of the HDF leadership's protest under the old regime compared to the outspoken, democratic dissidence of Tamás, Kis, and company. As the Democratic Opposition consolidated itself in the late 1970s, the national populist intelligentsia around Csoóri and Csurka also saw that the time was ripe to put more pressure on the regime. For the populists, the tragedy of communism lay primarily in its ideological neglect of Hungarian nationalism, on the one hand, and the adverse impact of socialist modernization on "traditional Hungarian life," on the other. Through inroads to nationalist reform currents within the communist party, the national populist writers sought to win concessions from the regime, ranging from funding for their own journal to greater emphasis on national traditions in school curricula. While the state restricted nationalism, it strategically abstained from directly persecuting the nationalists as it did the Democratic Opposition. In return for concessions, the regime tacitly stipulated that the populists blunt their criticism of official policies: a quid pro quo that effectively incorporated potential critics into the system. ("Who's not against us is with us," as Kádár said.) Simultaneously, the compromise reinforced the split between the two major sources of opposition.

Indeed, the lines of confrontation had been drawn long before September 1987, when 150 representatives of Hungary's national, Christian, and populist intelligentsia met in the southeastern village of Lakitelek to found the Democratic Forum. The guest of honor at the first historic Lakitelek meeting was the secretary of the official National Patriotic Front, Politburo member Imre Pozsgay. At the time, Pozsgay was Hungary's most popular communist politician, a leading party reformer who had long cultivated contacts with the populists.[3]

The urban post-Marxists from the Democratic Opposition were conspicuously absent from the HDF charter meeting. "First, it would have been impossible for Pozsgay to attend if the likes of Kis had been there," explains sociologist Ferenc Miszlivetz, a former dissident close to the Democratic Opposition. "However, not only were we considered enemies of the state, a fact that surely would have spelled Pozsgay's expulsion from the party, but the HDF leadership clearly didn't want us there either. They let us know in no uncertain terms that we were unwanted." The nationalist reform-minded nomenklatura and the national populist intellectuals saw the reign of the Old Guard drawing to a close, and Lakitelek marked the cementing of an alliance that presaged some kind of power-sharing compromise when the hard-liners fell. For both sides, the Democratic Opposition's Jewish intellectuals were incompatible partners.

By the time of Lakitelek, tension between the national populists and the Democratic Opposition had already flared up. One of the central points of dispute was the opposition's approach to the ethnic Hungarian minority in Transylvania, a thorny issue that the regime handled with kid gloves in view of its special relationship with socialist brother country Romania. "The nationalists harped on what was indeed a terrible situation for the ethnic Hungarians in Romania. But at the same time they refused to make a connection between the rights of the Hungarian minority and the violation of human rights throughout the Soviet bloc," says Miszlivetz, one of many human rights activists who helped bring the plight of the Transylvanian Hungarians into the international spotlight. "Their general orientation was very nationalistic and backward-looking even then. They urged us not to be so openly critical of the regime, since Kádár was 'protecting us as best he could.' And, certainly, they were protected. Only the Transylvania issue enabled them to live the lie that they were opposition."

NATIONAL RESCUE

The silence of many of today's loudest anti-communist nationalists during communism left a yawning gap in their political philosophies that they were quick to fill with the only functional concept at their disposal—that of the nation. For the HDF, as their many counterparts throughout the region, the nation functions as the pivotal category from which all else flows: its internal cohesion, its inspiration, its political legitimation, its concept of democracy, and its popular appeal. In and of itself, the Democratic Forum's definition of the nation in ethnic terms, i.e., the *Hungarian* nation, appears unproblematic. Ethnicity is one of almost every nation's defining characteristics, and the nation a defining characteristic of most modern nation-states. Yet the nationalists go a step further by elevating the ethnic or national community to a position of importance above that of the state and citizenship. They view membership in the nation as the single most essential characteristic of every person, an innate, organic bond that also determines one's interests and values. The HDF's definition of Hungary as the *Hungarian* nation, in which all *Hungarians* are by nature equal and possess like interests, is essentially the same as the German right's notion of Volks- gemeinschaft, or folkish community. Although Hungary has never in its history been so Magyar, many ethnic and national minorities live within its borders. If the HDF represents the ethnic Hungarian citizens of Hungary, then who represents the Roma and the Jews, the German, Serb, Romanian, and other national minorities? And even if the HDF pays lip service to the equal rights of all of Hungary's citizens, which it does, there nevertheless exists an implicit hierarchy of peoples in its rationale, with blood-pure Magyars at the top.

Also, and with baffling candidness, the HDF doesn't hesitate to take the next step in the logic of the Volksgemeinschaft, asserting itself the representative of "all fifteen million Hungarians both inside and outside of Hungary." As the guardian of the ethnic Hungarians abroad, the HDF invokes a spiritual, supra-political concept of the nation that transcends state borders. Needless to say, the inherently irredentist claim is not one that sits well with Hungary's neighbors. Theoretically, at least, the ethnic Hungarian minorities in other countries thus enjoy Hungary's protection, which, according to nationalist thinking, cannot be guaranteed otherwise. This, however, puts the minorities in a pre- carious situation in that they find themselves represented by a govern- ment whose legal jurisdiction stops its own borders. The Hungarian minorities, of course, depend upon their home states for rights and legal protection, not Budapest, whose influence over their situations is limited to threats and appeals. The nationalist rationale, taken to its logical conclusion, also puts the minorities under the authority of a government in which they have no voice. The ethnic Hungarians in the Vojvodina vote in the Serbian, not in the Hungarian elections. But for parties such as the HDF, the contradiction is academic. A Hungarian national government automatically represents the interests of all Hungarians, simply on the basis of common ethnicity, whether those people voted for it or not.

The HDF's idea of democracy is closely tied to its conception of the nation. In terms of its own role, the Democratic Forum, like the interwar népi movement, imagines itself as "the voice of the nation," the mystical link between the people and the historical destiny of the Magyar nation. The notion of a fatalistic, spiritual mission implies recourse to a morality above such temporal matters as electoral mandates, state law, or economic policy. The element of ethnicity embedded in the HDF's operative logic turns it into a supra-political manifestation, one that could or could not take a political form. The HDF, for example, began in Lakitelek as a "movement," becoming a political party only in 1989. The very same rationale underlies other such national movements in neighboring countries, such as the Croatian Democratic Community, the Movement for Romania, the Movement for a Democratic Slovakia, and all of the early "peoples' front" organizations in the former Soviet Union. The concepts contained in their names alone—forum, community, movement, front—imply much broader, general grounds for membership than the constituencies of political parties. Such a concept of nation doesn't expressly state what the rights and privileges of its members are, simply that they are superior to those of people outside the ethnic community. It does, however, imply that all members owe an unspecified moral responsibility and spiritual allegiance to the nation. The individual's responsibility is not to his own interests, not to his fellow citizens, a class or a state, but to the nation, incarnated in its one and only legitimate representative.

Once in government, the Democratic Forum called upon nationalism not only to substantiate its ideological mission, but—more critically at the time—to legitimate its tenuous hold on power. The conservative coalition set about transforming "popular nationalism," a genuine national enthusiasm at a grassroots and oppositional level, into "official nationalism," namely, "a conscious self-protective policy . . .

emanating from the state and serving the state first and foremost."[4]
The distinction, which Benedict Anderson uses to explain the nation-
building methodology of new postcolonial states, is equally valid for
the nation "rebuilding" aims of the postcommunist states. The official
nationalisms of the new states, as Anderson describes, often exhibit a
"systematic, even Machiavellian, instilling of nationalist ideology
through the media, the educational system, administrative regulations,
and so forth."

For the conservative coalition in Hungary, facing a crisis situation
in 1990 that would have tied the hands of any government, the creation
of a consensus around the nation became nothing less than the pre-
condition for maintaining power. With an economy in steady decline,
a gargantuan (and mounting) foreign debt, and the eyes of the world's
financial institutions upon it, the new regime's first priority was to
insure its own stability. The IMF, which presided over the country's
debt-servicing schedule, quickly quashed any illusions of a "Third
Way" or "socially conscious" transition to a market economy. In their
social and political programs, however, where international scrutiny
was less severe, the nationalists managed to make a mark on the country's young democracy that was certain to outlive their numbered days
in office.

As Prime Minister, Antall bore the imprint of his father's political
class. Although Antall refrained from references to a "kingdom without
kings" and was hardly fit to carry off ceremonies atop a gleaming white
mare, his lordly, authoritarian manner invoked vivid images of the
Horthy regency. As the representative of the national soul, the HDF
handled itself as nothing less than the absolute embodiment of that
genius in power. In parliament, in public discourse, in the media, and
even within the government, hostility toward criticism of any kind
became the ruling party's trademark. Like a pedantic school teacher,
Antall ranted and raved when parliament or the media refused to follow
his "instructions." In parliamentary debate, HDF deputies treated the
opposition as personal enemies rather than legitimate political opposition, equating differences over government policy with slander of the
nation. For the first two years, until major splits developed within the
HDF in 1992, no scandal or gaff involving a party member was serious

enough to warrant self-critique. Whether the charge was anti-Semitism, racism, parliamentary misprocedure, or corruption, the HDF and the government refused to discipline or condemn any statements or actions if they came from within their leagues.

For the HDF, its electoral majority signified not only a mandate to govern, but also the position of the single executor of the nation's interests. "The HDF politicians see themselves as more than ordinary people who were elected as politicians," explains political scientist and Fidesz advisor, András Bozóki. "They behave as if they were ordained with the task of the nation's salvation from an authority much higher than the majority of voters. In parliament, they behave as if they simply can't understand why the opposition is there. They don't seem to understand that just because they received 1.5 million votes and the opposition 1.2 million, that they aren't free to exercise power as they please." The idea that the opposition would also participate in the political process, with a legitimate right to represent the interests of its constituents, contradicted the coalition's concept of national democracy.

The fact that the conservative coalition didn't preside over the nation's unequivocal support became increasingly evident as it waded into its four-year term. The HDF's popularity sank to all-time lows as the government stumbled from crisis to crisis, and the economy continued its slump. For a party so certain of its own mandate, the disparity between its understanding of the national consciousness, which *should* naturally support the nation's guardian through thick and thin, and the population's waning support for its program, sent shocks of indignation through its ranks. With a logic reminiscent of times supposedly past, the government set in motion an aggressive campaign to fortify its dwindling power base. The strategic centralization of power sought to eliminate, or at least soften, parliamentary as well as extra-parliamentary (such as the media, labor unions, civil society, etc.) checks on its power.

One critical element of the centralization campaign focused upon the use of political nepotism to lure "clients" into the government camp. In an economy in which four-fifths of all property still remained under state titles, the reward for loyalty could indeed be lucrative. At the expense of expertise, the price for positions in the bureaucracy, the media, or private sector became one's allegiance to the government. The campaign's centerpiece was the 1991 Zétényi-Takács bill, which would have enabled the government to purge from public institutions those people responsible for broadly defined acts of "treason, murder, and fatal injury" between 1944 and 1990. The constitutional court, however, struck down the controversial bill, which the socialist and liberal oppositions claimed would lay the ground for an "anti-communist witch-hunt."

Moreover, the government set out to raise the national consciousness to its "rightful" level, namely to a level at which it would recognize its "true" national interests. The institutionalization of national ideology, and thus of power, rested upon government domination of the machinery of idea and identity production—namely, the media. The HDF strategy targeted the state-owned electronic media, which, the nationalists charged, lay in former communist and opposition liberal hands. HDF fraction leader Imre Kónya minced no words in his 1991 address to a party assembly: "Change can only come if hostile journalists understand that the government coalition position during this process of transition is difficult, and if they recognize that they depend upon us for information. We have to give information to those who really report objectively. . . . I am convinced that a change in the Hungarian Radio and Television's political outlook and mentality is possible." The "media war," as it was called, dominated political debate in Hungary as no other issue. The tug-of-war between government and opposition finally ended when the appointed heads of radio and television, both respected independent academics, handed in their resignations. Upon stepping down, television president Elemér Hankiss admitted that victory had gone to the government.

In its policy toward and relationship to the three major churches, the Catholic, the Reformed (Calvinist), and the Lutheran, in that order of size, the coalition government's recruitment of loyal clients conveniently dovetailed with its restorational agenda. Positively, the withering away of the communist regime in Hungary saw the full reinstatement of believers to practice their faiths. Under the communist regime, the state presided over full control of the churches, confiscating the greater share of their property between 1948 and 1950. Religious instruction in schools, mandatory until 1948, was outlawed. Parents could register children in classes in the handful of church schools that continued to exist, but believers often paid for their faith through state harassment or limited access to higher education or professional promotion. The restrictions had a devastating effect on the churches, leaving contemporary Hungary secular as never before. By 1985, only four percent of school-age children attended religious instruction, the number of church-goers fell off drastically, and the internal structures of the churches deteriorated.[5] Moreover, unlike the churches in East Germany or Poland, none of the major Hungarian churches managed to maintain their flock under the banner of opposition. On the contrary, the church hierarchies emerged badly tainted from their years of collaboration under the Kádár regime.

Although a significant religious revival in Hungary has accompanied the change of regimes, the upsurge in believers scarcely justifies the proportions of the churches' (particularly the Catholic's) return to prominence. The state's relationship to the churches in no way compares to that of the state and the Catholic Church in Poland. Yet, more than once, as opposition critics protested, the new relationship has breached the principle of the separation of Church and state. The churches became one of the government's top "clients," and, naturally, also one of the its most faithful devotees. For one, the government pledged the restitution of all church property. The return of the decimated churches' massive holdings would leave the religious institutions almost wholly dependent on government aid to maintain thousands of rundown buildings. The opposition insisted that current social needs, not the status of property forty years ago, should guide the reallocation of property.

The reintroduction of religious instruction in the schools proved an even hotter item. While the government's proposal made such classes optional, it stipulated that the state would pay religious instructors' salaries. The proposal, however, came under heavy opposition fire and was eventually withdrawn. In the heat of the emotionally charged debate, one Smallholder deputy blurted out the unspoken thoughts of many of his colleagues. "Regrettably," he insisted, "religion is widely considered a personal issue" and that it was "reprehensible" that parents should have the final say in what ideology their children are educated under in the schools.

The opposition was less successful in blocking the church and coalition imposition of quotas on religious broadcasting on Hungarian Radio and Television. Citing the media's "deliberate religious persecution" and the "demand of the masses," the protagonists insisted that religious broadcasting be upped from 5000–6000 minutes a year to 30,000 and that the heads of the electronic media be sacked. Although the Christian Democrats charged a "serious imbalance between the proportion of believers and the amount of religious broadcasting," opinion polls revealed a questionable popular base for the move. An 1992 Gallup Institute survey showed that religion was "extremely important" for only sixteen percent of the respondents, "rather important" for twenty-six percent and either "not particularly important" or "unimportant" for fifty-five percent. Only thirteen percent of the poll's participants found Radio Kossuth's religious programming insufficient.

The interests of the churches, particularly the Catholic Church, and traditionalist political forces have merged nowhere more conspicuously than in questions relating to the family. Since even the populist radicals reluctantly concede that the days of the patriarchal, self-reliant peasant family are over, the nationalists have settled for its "modern version," namely the stable petty bourgeois nuclear family with tradition Hungarian values, modest aspirations, and a low level of education. "It's difficult for many Westerners to understand, but many of our traditional symbols, ways of life, and cultural values were destroyed under communism," explains HDF spokesperson Tünde Vajda, echoing the oft-heard "Westerners just don't understand" claim of nationalists. "Under the communists, most women and mothers were expected to hold full-time jobs. This led to a breakdown in family relations, and to the disintegration of extended families as well." If women choose to work, then that's their decision. But families should also have the choice to have full-time mothers in the home, explains Vajda.

In Hungary, as just about everywhere in post-communist Eastern Europe, conservatives have tried to restrict the liberal abortion laws of the communist era. Part of the raging debate sounds a lot like that in the West, setting women's right to choice and bodily integrity against the sanctity of human life and the moral imperative to preserve and protect it.[7] In Hungary, however, the imbroglio takes a uniquely Eastern European twist. What is at stake, say the nationalists, is nothing less than the fate of the Hungarian people. The birth rate in Hungary has been on the downswing for decades, and the population is shrinking at one of the fastest paces in the world. "In light of the population decline, it is clear why abortion is not merely a question of the right of the mother, but the survival of the Hungarian nation," explained the independent, conservative parliamentarian Ágnes Maczó.[6] "You're not only deciding what is happening to the fetus, but what is happening to the Hungarian nation. Abortion is a nation-destroying procedure." According to Maczó and her allies, the abortion policies of the communist regime amounted to state-sponsored genocide. And if the Hungarian population continues to recede, before long Hungarians will become "a minority in their own country." The fear of becoming a minority in their own country is one commonly spoken by ethnic nationalists. In fact, Romania's national communist dictator Ceauşescu used the same argument to outlaw abortion and contraception in Romania.

The national conservatives' puritanical, male-oriented attitude to women's issues and the family has sparked dissent even from within the coalition. Emese Ugrin, now a Smallholders deputy, broke with her original party, the Christian Democrats, and then with the ruling coalition over their outdated approach to questions of women and the family. Ugrin considers herself a "Christian conservative," but a modern "twentieth century conservative." "The coalition has an extremely stiff, conservative, basically nineteenth century attitude on most of these issues," says Ugrin, a leading member of the Smallholders' Women's Platform. Ugrin notes that very few women maintain prominent places in the overwhelmingly male HDF, and that the exceptional cases don't stay in place for long. "Finally we've succeeded in bringing down the communist system," she says, "but what the coalition wants to do is revive a sixty-year-old model which just doesn't fit society's needs or wishes." Ugrin and like-minded critics support a drive to bring sex education programs into the schools, a measure that has roused considerable opposition from her former coalition colleagues. "This kind of narrow-minded rigidity and prudery is the negative side of Hungarian conservatism," says Ugrin. "These are life and death issues and should be treated as such, not as parts of some self-serving ideological program."

PROPHETS OF THE PATRIA

The coalition's drive to bring public institutions under its direct control coincided with a pronounced rightward lurch within the HDF itself. Despite Antall's moderate leadership, the Democratic Forum's national-liberal and Christian-democratic wings steadily lost ground to the party's national populist radicals. At the head of the national populist, or *nép-nemzeti,* wing stood HDF Vice President Csurka, whose crass, thinly vieled anti-Semitic diatribes had become run-of-the-mill since his election-time scandal. Unlike Antall, who at times proved a skillful politician, the writer Csurka fit the classic mold of the intellectual ideologue. Son of a notoriously right-wing prewar writer, Csurka the younger embarked upon a highly acclaimed literary career after his participation in the 1956 revolution, which Soviet tanks eventually put down with brutal force. Under the self-procured mantle of the népi writers' movement, Csurka's witty, satirical short stories and plays subtly exposed the tragedy of the suppressed uprising for Hungarian society. Yet his work always tread a fine line, enabling his pieces to appear in Budapest's top theaters. The regime's favorite enfant terrible was twice awarded the official József Attila Prize for literature. He was also temporarily censored for two years in the early 1980s. During the sixties and seventies, Csurka met and played cards with a left-intellectual circle of writers, including the likes of Tibor Déry (a Jew) and István Örkény. But during prolonged drinking binges, he often flew into fierce anti-Semitic rages, resuming his contact again with Jewish friends after he had slept off the alcohol. In the mid-1980s, as the Kádár system began to buckle, he broke off relations with the leftist writers' circle altogether. Politically, he went the way of his father.

In his boxy office in the gray granite-block "White House," the former communist party headquarters and today the home of Hungary's parliamentarians, the hulking figure of the fifty-seven-year-old writer-turned-politician dwarfs all that is around him as if he is in a doll house. Everything about the man is of giant proportions—his thick, corpulent hands, his lion-sized head, his booming voice. He looks up from a toy-like plastic typewriter to peer out across the Danube, his deep, heavy breathing filling the little room. "At the time of the original népi movement, over half of all Hungarians lived on the land," he frowns, removing his brown plastic eyeglasses to wipe perspiration from his high forehead with a handkerchief. "Today it's only a fraction of that, twelve percent, but we've kept the popular ethos of the movement, such as the solidarity of the poor and the centrality of the question of nations. Now the movement is broader, inclusive of all of society, not just the peasantry," he explains. "That's why we refer to ourselves as *népi* (folkish) and *nemzeti* (national)."

Since his rise to political prominence, Csurka has become accustomed to Western critics "who just don't understand" the unique Magyar affinity to the népi traditions. "If the West questions our democratic traditions then it should do so sincerely, out of genuine sorrow, since the roots of the Hungarian nation's problem lies in Yalta and Potsdam. We are not in the position that we are today because Hungarians rejected democracy," he explains, pointing out that in 1945 the democratic parties won the free election with sixty percent of the vote. He looks up from a pile of papers and smiles disinterestedly. "Another thing that you American and Israeli journalists don't understand is that this tradition was opposed to fascism during WWII." The liberal opposition, he grumbles, staring out again over the Danube, "thinks that we have to learn everything from the West, that we should be European conformists. But because of communism now we have to relocate our national values and rejoin Europe simultaneously. That's Hungary's dilemma."

Actually, that's just one of Hungary's dilemmas. Equally confounding to the playwright is the question of the Hungarian minorities. Inside Hungary's (post-1919) "Trianon borders," says Csurka, there are "practically no minorities." And those that do exist, enjoy all of the rights of the state, he asserts. But the Hungarian minorities outside of Hungary, says Csurka, "suffer forced assimilation and persecution. Part of

our nation lives outside of our borders, and we want only to protect
them. People charge us with wanting to change the borders, but that's
a lie. We must accept the European status quo," he says, shaking his
head, "but as the leader of the nép-nemzeti wing of the HDF I will
also say that morally I will never accept this situation." He straightens
up in his overburdened desk chair and sighs, "practically yes, but morally no."

As our interview nears its end, there is a silence, and he looks at
me with his lips pursed, waiting. He knows that the question's going
to come just as sure as I'm sitting there. "I have never been an anti-
Semite, and my entire life work is proof of that," he responds as if he's
been forced to repeat those very same words a thousand times. "The
wind doesn't have to blow and the press around here calls me an anti-
Semite." His references to the influences of "foreign" and "alien"
elements on Hungarian culture, he insists, are directed at the Soviets,
and before them, the Germans. "During the Kádár era, the influences
of American culture and consumerism also became strong." He can
only smile, he says, when he hears that Soviet industrialization or American television represent modernization. "Even in a democracy, especially here where the masses are so unprotected from the influence of
charlatans, society must defend itself against this culture of waste, dirt
and drugs. If being modern means that I have to watch programs like
Dallas on TV, okay, then I'm a conservative."

Social critic and playwright István Eörsi, a former friend of Csurka's, claims that history has overtaken the goals of the original népi
writers to the extent that the contemporary movement is only a negative
apparition of what it calls back upon. "Even the labels 'népi' or 'populist'
are inaccurate for someone like Csurka," says Eörsi, one of Hungary's
most respected left literati. Eörsi points out that Csurka was born and
grew up in Budapest, his literary work "absolutely bourgeois," reflecting nothing of the népi tradition. "The interwar népi writers movement
had some very progressive aspirations, such as land reform and the
establishment of a new intellectual stratum from the working-class and
the peasantry. They fought against feudalism, against the aristocracy
and the Germans. But after 1945, the communists fulfilled most of the
movement's social demands. All that is left now is a romantic yearning

for some mythical 'Hungarian way of life' and the nostalgia for unifying all Hungarians," says Eörsi. "Now all that one sees are its negative sides, such as racism, revanchism, and anti-Semitism."

The HDF's népi-nemzeti forces spearheaded the government's all-out drive to bring the media under its control. Csurka and company refuse even to acknowledge the need for an independent media in Hungary. The stakes are too high. "We need to get hold of the media not because some of us want new jobs, but because there the fate of the Hungarian nation will be decided," Csurka rallies his devotees. Only those who "own the media have the potential of changing Hungarian society." In his rabble-rousing style, he claims that the government and the HDF must "take a whip" to a media that fills the public's head with "Marxism." In Csurka-speak, "Marxism," "communism," "Bolshevism," "cosmopolitanism," and "liberalism" are synonymous: foreign, anti-Hungarian ideologies. For most peoples' tastes, the air waves are already overloaded with interminable népi-nemzeti programming, such as religious shows, folk music specials, and endless documentaries about the Hungarian minorities. But Csurka and company demand more—much more.

In order to combat the influence of the major daily newspapers, the Democratic Forum has encouraged the proliferation of its own "government-friendly" publications. On the crowded Blaha Lujza Square, where the communist party's ten-story publishing house once brandished the names of its three dailies in big neon letters, now stand the illuminated logos of the HDF-oriented papers: *Magyar Fórum, Új Magyarország, Expressz,* and *Heti Magyarország.* In *Magyar Fórum* (with a 1993 press run of 50,000), the de facto nép-nemzeti mouthpiece, and in his Sunday morning radio spot, Csurka spares none of the niceties that he does before American and Israeli journalists. Hungarian politics is a knock-down-drag-out battle between the "sons of all peasants, plebeian professionals, and priests" and "the garrulous urban loud-mouths" of the liberal opposition and media who "bombard Hungarians with pseudo-questions and alien (*idegen*) points of view." In calls for a strong-arm government, Csurka blasts the media as "the enemy which basically doubts the electoral victory of the (HDF) rednecks. . . . It defends the interests of those who loved Kádárism. Only if the Christian-national coalition becomes stronger might it halt the middlemen devouring the vitality of the Hungarian nation."[8]

Although Antall has kept diplomatically tight-lipped about Hungary's frontiers, the tragedy of Trianon remains top on the national populists' list of grievances. The tone in *Magyar Fórum* often reaches hysterical pitch against both Serbia, where Hungarians are being "led to the slaughterhouses," and Romania, which aims to "complete Ceauşescu's 'homogenization' program." Hungarian nationalists have kept a close eye on the national fragmentation in the former Soviet Union and former Yugoslavia. As fiercely as they rail against the Serbs, the national populists simultaneously endorse the Serbs' greater state logic, namely that national minorities needn't stay "trapped" inside neighboring states.

If the ethnic Serbs can't live in Croatia, then why should ethnic Hungarians be forced to live in Serbia, Slovakia, or Romania? In a climate of changing borders, of decades-old injustices being redressed, Trianon should be renegotiated too. If the Romanians in the former Soviet Republic of Moldavia elect to rejoin Romania, then the Hungarians in Transylvania should also have the democratic option of rejoining Hungary. Characteristic of ethnic nationalists, Csurka sees Europe in terms of a "Europe of nations," in which states delineate nations' "proper" ethnic and historical borders. Since, of course, no two neighboring East European states concur on where those "proper" frontiers lie, "there must be quarrels, fights, local wars, and in the end there will be a big negotiation," writes Csurka frankly, "which will decide upon the *Lebensraum* of the European nations. . . . This process isn't merely a custom in Europe," he speculates, "it may even be a biological rule."[9]

Indeed, for ethnic nationalists, arguments inevitably boil down to science—to states of nature, organic essences, processes of evolution, and biological laws. The biological logic of "pure ethnicity" unmasks the racial component in such forms of nationalism that inform racist prejudices and discriminatory policies. The same claims of a sui generis Magyarism that led prewar nationalists in search of a "Hungarian gene" ultimately inform Csurka's anti-Semitism, as well as the general népnemzeti intolerance towards all less than "pure" Magyar citizens of

Hungary. It is exactly these racial convictions that enable the national populists to draw a direct line of continuity from the rise of Jews in Hungarian society at the end of the nineteenth century, to the appearance of liberalism in Hungary, to the Soviet Republic of 1919, to the post-WWII communist regime, to the present liberal opposition. The seemingly incongruous ideologies of Bolshevism and liberalism are interchangeable and intertwined curses because both are linked to the destructive trends of modernization and their supposedly Jewish flagbearers. The word that Csurka invokes again and again to single out "non-Hungarian" elements in Hungarian society is "idegen," or alien, a term whose racial implications are transparent to anyone familiar with Hungarian history or literature.

In one piece, par for the course in *Magyar Fórum*, Csurka condemns the lack of social mobility in Hungary, stretching the limits of his literary powers not to use the word "Jew":

> The same people ... are on a merry-go-round and these people are just the same alien-like (*idegen-szerű*) elements as during the last third of the century [during the introduction of capitalism, when Jews rose to positions of power] and immediately after WWI [a reference to the short-lived 1919 Hungarian Soviet Republic] ... [Hungarian writer] Dzeszö Szabó pointed out their alienness. Now, we don't speak about their racial alienness, as Szabó didn't only speak about that either. But today alien means an indifference toward fatal questions. Today, when there are flames on Hungary's borders and Hungarians live in peril, the most elementary need is to reach for power from the deepest depths, to an inner motion from within society. This new stratum must have power since only it would feel its own liberation and power, only it would sense the importance of what is at stake. That's why we need a *new authentic people* so that we can defend ourselves all the more passionately in order to save ourselves. The merry-go-round of elites has a most sad reputation on this account. This is when the eternal alien-like elite refuses to address the fatal questions. Instead it maintains its own inner motion, distributing power corruptly according to its own principle, namely liberalism *without nationalism.*"[10]

The references to the "inner motion" of ethnic groups, specific to each group and at odds with that of others, reflects the mysterious, primordial essence that ethnic nationalists see as the immutable determinate of their community's being and fate. As Anthony Smith argues in *Ethnic Origins of Nations*, "The folk assumptions of indigenous root-edness and native value . . . (inform) the idea that each community evolves according to its own inner rhythms and that its self-expressions and destinies are radically different, even unique. In the ethnic con-ception of the nation, 'history' becomes the counterpart of 'culture' in territorial [civic] conceptions of the nation. But not history-in-general, with its universal laws of human development, but separate histories of particular communities; only the latter can bind populations and fulfill the promise of progress."[11] The "laws" of history are specific to ethnic communities and eternal, rooted in naturalistic concepts of that community's origins. Thus, for Csurka, it is only "natural" that even assimilated Hungarian Jews beckon to inner calls of their own, and when in power take Hungarians of pristine Magyar blood down paths of self-destruction.

Until August 1992, anti-Semitism in *Magyar Fórum* and elsewhere within the HDF failed to elicit even the mildest rebuke from the bal-conies of power. But, sensing the hour at hand to make a bid for the party leadership, Csurka in an eight-page manifesto in *Magyar Fórum* went further than ever before, unleashing a storm of criticism from across the Hungarian political spectrum and abroad. In the tract, entitled "Setting the Record Straight," Csurka describes the "global financial conspiracy" that was preventing Hungary from emancipating itself of the vestiges of communism. His general thesis is that a communist-Jewish-liberal continuum has managed to preserve political and eco-nomic power in Hungary from 1945 to the present. After 1945, he writes:

> the returning Hungarian Jewry, which was terribly devastated after the German occupation, saw the Communist Party as the only guarantee for a renewed life and the only guarantee that a situation like 1944 would never be repeated. This was not only because every member of the Moscow-led Hungarian Communist quartet was Jewish, but even more because the domestic left-wing communist residue also enjoyed financial support from the former liberal bourgeois Jewry.
>
> After all, Hungarian Jewry's sense of homeland became greater than ever during the Kádár regime. In this sick and obsolescent period, Budapest

and Vienna were the two metropolitan cities where the Jews exercised an open or hidden influence and where they could be a determining factor.

Csurka continues, trying to show how a small, cosmopolitan elite has maintained "the hegemony of the Hungarian Jewry" throughout the change of governments. As proof, he says that reserves at the Hungarian National Bank dropped by fifty percent when the HDF won the election. Although the HDF is in power, he says, it is powerless at the hands of the aligned old nomenklatura, the liberal opposition and international financial institutions. "What we are actually talking about here," writes Csurka, "is a struggle between two sides: a national center . . . and a leftist bloc, which, though unmatched in its anti-communist radicalism, has been trying to preserve power continuously since 1945."

The anti-Hungarian world conspiracy theory is just one point, and by no means the most outrageous, of the article. Csurka goes on to say that the heads of television and radio, as well as the nomenklatura, must be removed—by force if necessary. "If the president of the republic continues to resist [sacking the presidents of Hungarian Radio and Television at Antall's request] then all measures are justified, any force is permissible; for none of these measures matches the illegality of refusing to approve the dismissals." Also, Csurka claims that the 1945 Yalta agreement will expire in 1995, when "the life of every post-Trianon state created around us will be different." The basic question, he argues, "is whether a new Hungarian generation will come to the fore, a generation able to avoid these new dangers or make use of these new dangers that will create a new Hungarian Lebensraum." Finally, after remarks on the "genetic reasons behind [Hungary's] degeneration" and the "failure of the laws of natural selection," he comes to Antall. It is time, says Csurka, for the ailing Prime Minister (he has cancer of the lymph nodes) to choose and train a successor. Although Csurka refrains from nominating himself, his ambitions were a secret to no one.

If Csurka had hoped that his August manifesto would snap Hungarian politics from its summer doldrums, then he succeeded with flying colors. Excerpts of the article appeared in newspapers around the world, no doubt reinforcing Csurka's belief in an international plot. HDF liberals, such as parliamentary deputy József Debreczeni, had words as scathing as those of the opposition for Csurka's latest fiasco. Debreczeni asserted that the essay was "full of anti-democratic, anti-communist, and anti-Semitic elements, which could without a doubt be equated with Nazi ideology." Antall, under heavy pressure to finally come down on Csurka, distanced himself from the tract, but stopped short of reprimanding Csurka or expelling him from the party, as many observers felt that he ought to have done. The attack on Antall, however, opened a rift between the two men that would eventually result in a full break in early 1993.

The extent to which Csurka's anti-Semitism finds resonance in the population is difficult to gauge. Surveys show anti-Semitism in Hungary less virulent than in Czechoslovakia and Poland. While Hungarians of Jewish origin do hold a disproportionately high number of positions in both the public and private sectors, especially the media, the vast majority of Hungary's approximately 80,000 (less than one percent of the population) are thoroughly assimilated, in fact, one of the most assimilated Jewish communities in Eastern Europe. Nevertheless, anti-Semitism has a long and ugly history in Hungary, which still finds expression in a popular, often unconscious, distrust of Jews or supposedly Jewish traits. During the election campaign, one often heard such offhand remarks as "Yeah, the Free Democrats have the best policies, but, you know, they *are* a pack of Jews." The anti-Semitism that first emerged against the Jewish elite in the late nineteenth century culminated in WWII, when Hungarian collaborators sent nearly 600,000 Jews to their deaths in Nazi concentration camps. The early 1944 deportations to Auschwitz, which claimed the lives of two-thirds of those who were incarcerated, occurred not under the rule of the fascist Arrow Cross, but at the bequest of Horthy's elected military dictatorship. The Red Army marched into Budapest to find only 200,000 surviving Jews in the country.

The legacies of the hardline communist regimes of Béla Kun (1919) and Mátyás Rákosi (1947–1956), both of Jewish origin, only fueled charges that communism, no less than capitalism, constituted a Jewish conspiracy against the Hungarian people. Yet, four decades of communist rule did precious little to address the prejudices that had flourished in Hungary prior to its takeover. Like its counterparts through the region, the Stalinist Rákosi regime, with an overwhelmingly Jewish party leadership, not only turned a blind eye to the atrocities of the Hungarian Holocaust, but showed itself perfectly willing to play to anti-Semitic sympathies in the population. In order to broaden its diminutive base among the masses (the party boasted only 2000 members as of 1945), the communist party employed a plebeian-proletarian brand of Hungarian nationalism and opened its membership to the "small Nazis" as well as tens of thousands of former Arrow Cross fascists. During its consolidation of power in the early fifties, the regime moved ruthlessly to purge Jews from their professional as well as political positions. Interestingly, the regime's class-based rhetoric didn't single out the victims as Jews (nor were they solely Jews), but rather, like Csurka, as "alien" or "unreliable" elements in society.[12] During Stalin's frenzied purge of Jewish party leaders throughout the East bloc in 1952, Rákosi's zeal managed to save him from the fate of his Jewish colleagues, at least for a few years. Although the revolution and the change of regimes in 1956 put an end to the crude anti-Semitism of the Rákosi clique, Kádár also declined to confront the legacy of Hungarian anti-Semitism as a deeply rooted phenomenon in Hungarian society.

In post-communist Hungary, the whitewash of the country's WWII legacy has taken on altogether different proportions. One good measure of its scope has been Antall's approach to the personage of Horthy and the Hungarian role in WWII. On the one hand, Antall has stopped short of endorsing a posthumous rehabilitation of Horthy or using state funding to return the Admiral's remains to Hungary from Argentina. But, at the same time, in a controversial January 1992 speech, Antall commemorated Axis-allied Hungary's bloody 1943 defeat (40,00 Hungarians lost their lives) to the Soviet Army at the Don River as a great act of patriotism. Characteristically, Antall portrayed Hungary as the sole victim of the battles, despite the fact that they were fighting next to German troops. The noble thing about the Hungarian soldiers' heroic stand was their commitment to the nation, not why they were fighting:

We must pay respect to and honor all of those who took part in the Don battles—to the generals and the privates, as well as the "working soldiers" [*munkaszólgálat*—involuntary draftees, including many Jews, socialists and communists, forced to serve, unarmed, on the front lines]. There are those who ask us to atone for all of the sins and mistakes over a half a century. . . . Our soldiers fought courageously and with determination, sacrificing their lives for their country and we are proud. A people can't live without heroes. . . . We must restore the 1000-year-old honor of the Hungarian military. Neither in a political or military sense do we have anything to be ashamed of.[13]

Drawing parallels between the Don battles and the present, Antall depicted a continuity in Hungarian resistance to Soviet domination, which culminated in the HDF's electoral victory. The truth of this, he asserted, was something that the West has thanklessly ignored.

According to Free Democrat deputy György Gadó, the anti-Semitism of the Horthy era is simultaneously denied and manipulated in political debate today. "The commonly heard claim today is that the Germans forced the Hungarians to implement its Final Solution policies, that anti-Semitism is a German thing," says Gadó. "This is a complete and total lie. The Hungarian Holocaust was carried out with Hungarian hands, and that is something that no one today will acknowledge." Gadó, a practicing Jew, has come under intense fire from conservative circles for his outspoken criticism of the anti-Semitism in political discourse. The conservatives have waged an all-out campaign to discredit Gadó, sparing no venom in labeling him a "liberal inquisitor," a "Hungarian hater," and a "closet Bolshevik." The nationalists charge that the unwarranted fuss over anti-Semitism only tarnishes Hungary's international image, casting doubt upon its democratic credentials and thus jeopardizing its acceptance into the European mainstream. "In Hungary, it's not anti-Semitism that is seen as posing an impediment to democracy," says Gadó, "but the mere mention that it exists." The result is that the subject of anti-Semitism is off-limits for public debate, while the national populists manipulate it with impunity.

THE KNIGHTS OF THE HOLY CROWN

Not far behind the national populist factions in parliament lurks an even nastier ultra-right in Hungary. On their own, the panoply of splinter parties that make up the extra-parliamentary ultra-right pose no direct threat to Hungarian democracy. Yet, time and again, links between the ultra-right and the right-wing of the ruling coalition show that the ideas of blatantly neo-fascist elements have an ear in the Hungarian parliament and government. The scandal surrounding the ultra-right journal *Hunnia*, whose title refers to the Magyars' legendary ancestors, the Huns, provides just one example. The monthly, dedicated to "the self-protection of the Hungarian spirit," is the "intellectual" organ of the extra-parliamentary right. Since its first issue in Autumn 1989, its sixty or so pages have tackled "the Jewish question" head on, sparing the flowery prose of the nép-nemzetis. Most of *Hunnia* is essays, poems and historical tracts from the 1920s, '30s and '40s, revealing a scarcity of contributors as well as readers. Many of the contemporary pieces come from Australian, Canadian, and U.S. exiles, who also fund the journal and distribute it in their exile communities.

Under *Hunnia*'s editor, Ferenc Kun-Szabó, a relative nonentity during the Kádár years, the journal stops at nothing to exaggerate and lament the excruciating tragedy of Trianon, of Bolshevism, and of 1956 for the Magyar people. In polemic after polemic against international Zionism, Israel is branded a "fascist," "racist," and "Marxist" regime, whose final goal "is to create a world government under control of Zionist-oriented Jewish bankers." It's representatives, naturally, are the Hungarian Jews who "blame us with pleasure for the death camps, when they forget about the deaths camps that they erected after 1919 and 1945."

Little was heard about the obscure journal with a circulation of not more than a few thousand until April 1991, when *Hunnia* ran a translated excerpt from a certain Viktor Padányi's book *The Great Tragedy* (published by Minerva Books in Australia in 1977.) The piece, which perpetrated the familiar "Holocaust lie" thesis, brought even the Interior Ministry to its feet. In the disputed article, entitled "A Few Words about the Tragedy of the Jews," the author first claims that only "tens of thousands of Jews" actually lost their lives during WWII, although in the course of the article he expands the number to 1.5 million.[14] Citing numerous sources, Padányi argues that the allies deliberately falsified statistics about the Holocaust in order to pave the way for the "Jewish revenge," namely communism. As for the 1.5 million "missing" Jews, Padányi provides an explanation which he claims is valid "even if the Jews hadn't provoked the inevitable hatred that they received, allied as they were with the enemy." First, he argues, many Jews perished simply because they found themselves living in the middle of a war zone. Second, since 1945, many of the missing Jews have been found. And last, the majority of Jews that were actually killed died in the clutches of the Bolsheviks, before, during, and after the war.

Even so, he continues, the measures against the Jews in fascist Europe cannot be posed as a moral issue since the racial laws fell within "the right of nations" to protect themselves:

> The point is that the given nations wanted to do it and, as nations, had a right to do it. . . . Part of democracy also means the right of nations to make mistakes. . . . Germany knew that the Jewry couldn't be trusted in a state based upon racial supremacy, and the Jewry was aware of this too. In my opinion, the mass emigration of the Jews would have been the correct solution, but the League of Nations didn't dare attempt it. When the war started, the Axis powers stood there with a certain part of the population working and thinking for the enemy.

Although the Interior Ministry initiated an investigation at the request of Free Democrat deputies, no action was ever taken against the periodical.

Hunnia, which continued publishing as usual after the affair, found itself the focus of dispute again in January 1992. In front of a full session of parliament, one HDF deputy openly protested *Hunnia*'s absence on the table where the deputies normally pick up the newspapers, charging that the liberal opposition had deliberately withheld the publication. The parliamentarian's claim that the move violated freedom of speech provoked an outcry from the opposition, as well as denials that they had purposely withheld it. In the end, *Hunnia* remained in parliament, with the HDF's full backing. "The media blames the populist wing of HDF," decried Csurka in the February 13 *Magyar Fórum*, "but the question is what are they so flustered about? The media considers (*Hunnia*) extreme right-wing. That's just what the communists said a few years ago about *Tiszatáj* (a mainstream literary periodical.)"[15]

The Hungarian ultra-right spans a gruesome field of interrelated parties, amongst them the Hungarian National Alliance, the Christian National Union, the Hungarian National Party, and the National Smallholders Party (the right-wing sister-party of the Independent Smallholders), as well as others with equally opaque, ultra-nationalist convictions. Although the ultra-right parties boast neither the numbers nor the potential appeal to make a bid for political power, their sympathizers represent a sizable, active constituency, one that the right-wing parliamentary parties would gladly see in their own dwindling camps. The extreme-right's actual numbers range from estimates of several thousand to over five thousand—small in total terms but not an insignificant figure considering the Free Democrats' 1993 membership of less than 20,000 and the HDF's of 27,000. The bulk of the ultra-right's mostly senior adherents are hard-core, embittered anti-communists, the right-wing "counter-revolutionaries" that the communist regime hounded, imprisoned, and tortured in the name of communism. Many come from the ranks of the lumpen and reactionary elements of the 1956 revolution, who now make their homes in the numerically strong National Federation of Political Prisoners or the 1956 Alliance. The former victims demand revenge against the powers that put them behind bars, that sent their relatives to perish in Soviet work camps. The sources of the ultra-right's funding, its leadership takes no pains to conceal, are Hungarian exiles abroad who were expelled from or fled the country after WWII, 1947, or 1956. At the same time, a younger constituency, in the form of a growing neo-fascist Skinhead movement, has found common ground with the extremists of their grandparents' generation.

At the entrance of Budapest subway stops, the stony-faced old radicals solemnly displayed the movement's twelve-page agitprop organ, *Szent Korona* (Holy Crown), which sold for twenty forints (twenty-five cents). The Holy Crown refers to Hungary's legendary first King, and later Saint, Stephen, whose 1001 A.D. coronation marked the birth of the Hungarian empire as well as the nation's Christianization. Until it folded in late 1992, the chief demand of the viciously racist, anti-

Semitic weekly had been the dismissal and persecution of all former communists active in the bureaucracy and private sector, as well as the return of all property confiscated from Hungarians after 1947. Under its editor-in-chief, Dr. László Romhányi,[16] a key figure in the former anti-communist underground, *Szent Korona* had built up a circulation estimated at close to five thousand, roughly a quarter of that of the Free Democrats' highly acclaimed weekly *Beszélő*. *Szent Korona* made its first splash in Hungarian public life in early 1991, when the Interior Ministry began legal proceedings against Romhányi for "incitement" against Hungary's minority groups. The proceedings sparked an uproar since the government based its charges on a communist-era statute designed to silence opposition voices. "Instead of trials and accusations," protested *Szent Korona*, "we request one statistic. . . . From where, and how much wealth have the Hungarian Jews stashed away? How many live among us? How many appear in parliament? How many are bank directors? How many work in the press, radio, television and the universities?"[17] Romhányi's lawyers managed to hold up the trial for months, demanding that the court conduct genealogical tests on prospective judges to determine if they were of Jewish or Romanian origin. Finally, the Constitutional Court ruled that the statute in question violated freedom of speech and threw the case out.

In late 1991, the *Szent Korona* troops could be found at their headquarters on Budapest's outskirts, in the Jurta Theater at the edge of the sprawling Peoples' Park. Until 1988, the theater, under Romhányi's direction, had functioned as the nerve center of the entire anti-communist opposition. But the parliamentary parties, says Romhányi, struck a pact with the devil, taking away the communists' political power with one hand, and giving them economic power with the other. Outside the Jurta's entrance stands a black marble bust of Cardinal József Mindszenty, the radical priest behind right-wing forces in the 1956 revolution. A real life theater-of-the-grotesque, the musty building bustles with a cast of characters straight out of a modern-day Edgar Allen Poe tale. Two Skinheads, open black jackets over hooded maroon sweatshirts, stroll into the building with casual familiarity. Muttering to herself, a tiny hunchbacked woman sorts stacks of the latest *Szent Korona* in the foyer. Furled flags and banners lie tossed in a corner heap amongst discarded props and other cobwebbed paraphernalia. A few Independent Smallholder politicians from the southern city of Szeged are also on the scene, mingling with the paper sellers who have dropped by for the new issue.

In their cramped attic offices sit Romhányi and Imre Bosnyák, a *Szent Korona* editor and leading figure in the Christian National Union. In his late seventies, Bosnyák's shrivelled physique and craggy, scarred face bear witness to his nearly two-decades-long incarceration. As a fascist, Bosnyák sat in one of Horthy's jails for several years, followed by a ten year stint in a Soviet camp after the war and then another three years in a Hungarian cell again for his role in 1956. "The Jews call us fascists, they call our younger members 'Nazi-Skinheads' and other such nonsense," says Bosnyák, his gravelly voice cracking as his anger rises. "I admit that I'm a revisionist, Trianon never was and never will be acceptable, but there are no fascists or anti-Semites here. That's an invention of the Jewish press. Our youth are good national patriots, not Nazis!"

Just back from a working trip in Paris, Romhányi nods. The forty-seven-year-old theater director is almost dapper, his longish dark hair slicked back behind oversized ears to the collar of a tight blue-and-green checked polyester jacket. But as he speaks, rapidly, darting off on long, disconnected tangents, he cuts a figure no less unnerving than the rest of the Jurta's dramatis personae. Romhányi admits that the Hungarian National Alliance, the umbrella organization of ultra-right, sees pretty much eye-to-eye with the right wings of the Democratic Forum and the Independent Smallholders, whose supporters, he claims, make up a third of the Alliance's membership. "Everything in *Magyar Fórum* is true," he says, his quick, jerky movements contributing to his aura of a door-to-door salesman. "The problem is that Csurka and all just talk and talk. They're too hesitant to put their words into action, even though power is in their hands."

In the complex topography of the historical Hungarian right, Romhányi singles out the 1938 Hungarian constitution as the modern masterpiece of the Magyar political genius. He dismisses the fact that 1938 also marked the introduction of racial legislation in Hungary as only incidental to the constitution that he claims best captures the spirit of the 1222 Golden Bull, a bill of rights proclaimed during the reign of Hungarian King Andrew II. On the office wall hangs a map of Central Europe with contemporary Hungary darkly outlined within the borders of the Habsburg Empire. Above the map, the battle cry of the interwar revisionists: "*Nem. Nem. Soha!*" (No. No. Never!) Romhányi envisions the resurrection of Greater Hungary through the creation of a democratic federation, in which all of the former countries of the Hungarian Crown would democratically elect to rejoin a Hungarian-led empire.

The extremist stands of the Jurta radicals lie far from the mainstream of public opinion. Amidst the country's economic stagnation, growing social polarization, and unemployment, however, a certain segment of the youth has shown itself dangerously susceptible to the lure of far right demagoguery. A militant Skinhead youth culture existed in Hungary at the time when Kis, Csurka, and Romhányi still shared the stage at the Jurta. Now, however, the concerted effort of the *Szent Korona* circle (which still exists despite Romhányi's incarceration) to incorporate the growing youth movement into their ranks tacitly recognizes the youth militants as a political constituency. As a bridge between the parliamentary right and the violent neo-fascist right, the *Szent Korona* groupings aim at forging a broad ultra right consensus. Top Skinhead leaders acknowledge their loose, often strained relations with the *Szent Korona* circle, although their structures and programs remain fully independent. At meetings of the Hungarian National Alliance, a dozen Skinheads line up in front of the podium as a precautionary security force.

Among other places, the continuum that stretches from the HDF to the Skinheads comes to light in the HDF-backed demonstrations against the media. At demonstrations, which Csurka promotes over the air, well over 100 Skinheads regularly join several thousand anti-press antagonists in front of the Magyar Television building in central Budapest. Side-by-side, old ultra-rightists holding placards such as "God can forgive but '56ers can't" and teenage Skinheads cloaked in Hungarian flags hurl aggressive threats at the police barricades and journalists alike. "Who do you guys write for, *The Jerusalem Post?*," two denim-clad thugs intimidatingly asked me and my colleague Bob Cohen from *Budapest Week.* "Well then go back to Israel where you came from!" Afterwards, HDF spokesmen refused to condemn the hostile anti-Semitic tone of the demonstration or the harassment of suspected "Jewish provocateurs."

Charges of cooperation between Skinhead groups and the authorities climaxed in October 1992, when 300 Skins, some clad in Nazi-uniforms and waving Arrow Cross flags, succeeded in forcing President Árpád Göncz, a writer and respected democrat, from the podium at a ceremony commemorating the 1956 revolution. The young fascists booed and whistled until Göncz, himself imprisoned for his activities in 1956, left the stage. Observers, including opposition parliamentarians, say that the youths were aided by plain-clothed Border Guards, transported to the demonstration by the Interior Ministry in army trucks. The guards apparently first distributed leaflets and small Hungarian flags and then shouted alongside the Skinheads. Skinhead leaders admitted that they had been in contact with the police the entire day and that the police had authorized their demonstration at the ceremony. The Interior Ministry denied the accusations and protested an official inquiry into the scandal. It admitted however that the Border Guards were there in an "orgnaizational role" but that they took no part in the harassment of President Göncz.

As disturbing as the proliferation of neo-fascist ideas in Hungary may be, the new surge hardly represents a mass social trend. While the Skinhead and neo-fascist movements have indeed prospered as a result of the country's economic and political paralysis, their potential appeal to broader constituencies remains limited. Meanwhile, the HDF national populists have suffered the backlash of their association with the governing power, as well as the never-ending saga of Mr. Csurka. In fact, since 1990, opinion polls have charted a precipitous decline in its popularity and membership. By early 1993, HDF's support had sunk to eight percent. Csurka consistently winds up at the lower end of popularity surveys. If only temporarily, the nationalist passions that surfaced so vehemently in early 1990 over the ethnic violence between Hungarians and Romanians in Transylvania ebbed as worsening economic conditions presented the average citizen with worries closer to home.

One intriguing 1991 Times-Mirror study testified to the ultimate hollowness of the right's nationalist exhortations. Despite relentless television programming that highlights the hardship and persecution of ethnic Hungarian minorities in surrounding countries, in addition to the government's anti-Romanian tone, the poll showed more Hungarians (forty percent) with a negative opinion toward ethnic Hungarians from Transylvania than toward Romanians (thirty percent)! It seems that the Hungarians' ethnic solidarity with their long-lost brothers in Romania rubbed off once they were faced with thousands of Hungarian Transylvanians on the streets, hawking their folk crafts and seeking employment for substandard wages. The ruling party's anti-Semitic overtones seem also to have had a boomerang effect. Though hardly a laudable figure in and of itself, the eleven percent of Hungarians with negative attitudes toward Jews fell considerably below the corresponding number in Poland (thirty-four percent), Czechoslovakia (twenty percent) and even France (fourteen percent).

However erratic nationalism's pull, various forms of populist demagoguery, national and otherwise, will undoubtedly remain a factor in Hungary. While disenchantment with the HDF resulted in gains for the liberal opposition parties, particularly Fidesz and the HSP, the majority of Hungarians express a crisis of confidence in the entire party spectrum. The reality of the free-market transition has quickly displaced the thin faith that Hungarians had in an instant *Wirtschaftswunder* on the Danube. Voter turnout dropped from sixty-five percent in the first round of the general election to just over forty percent nationwide in the late 1990 municipal elections. In many towns and villages, less than a quarter of eligible voters showed up on election day. The Hungarians' unhappiness with the adventures of the free market, however, has yet to produce a credible left or social democratic alternative to the mainstream consensus. The growing gap between the electorate and the unresponsive political parties, coupled with increasing economic hardship, leaves the door open for populist options to capitalize upon discontent.

The realignment in the air for the entire political landscape in Hungary will also see a reconfiguration of the right. Csurka and his nép-nemzeti allies set the process in motion in 1993 when they formed the *Magyar Út* (Hungarian Way) Foundation. Magyar Út, say its founders, is a "mass movement" whose goal is to "protect Hungary for Hungarians" and "to bring about changes in the Democratic Forum." The organization, which excludes Freemasons, self-confessed atheists, and homosexuals, seeks to strengthen Hungarian ownership in banks and industry and purge the media. "We are at home and we will be the owners here," Csurka told the 2000 supporters at the movement's first congress. Hungarians, he said, should not be afraid to use "civil disobedience" to resist the selling of banks to foreigners. In June 1993, upon Csurka's official expulsion from the HDF, he and five other parliamentary deputies founded the Hungarian Justice Party (HJP), which is expected to function as the political arm of the Magyar Út movement. The HJP and Magyar Út are just two of the new alliances that will certainly play a role in the 1994 elections. Whatever other constellations emerge, their components are already part of Hungary's new political culture.

Chapter 4

HUNGARY
BLACK IN THE LAND
OF THE MAGYARS

By communism's final years, most people regarded the official propaganda with attitudes that ranged from indifferent skepticism to outright derision. One may have "lived the lie," as Václav Havel described life under communism, but one knew all along that there was not an ounce of truth behind it. Yet, in Hungary, as throughout the former East bloc, there was at least one bit of disinformation that most people somehow seemed to buy. Even after the communist leaders had packed their bags in disgrace, Hungarians sincerely insisted that racism did not exist in their country. As if repeating it from a textbook, students, teachers, and professionals would mouth the same words as the party apologist: that there isn't and never has been racism in the good land of the Magyars. If pushed on it, some would admit, as if surprised to think of it that way, that anti-Semitism was a form of racism that some Hungarians had once subscribed to a long time ago. Resentment against Roma, however, people tended to put in a category all its own, not quite deserving of such an ugly title. The same applied to the "Arab money changers" who, popular wisdom had it, made millions illegally exchanging Hungarian forints for hard currency in Budapest's train stations. In fact, many Hungarians' response to racism is to point out the "anti-Magyar racism" practiced against the ethnic Hungarian minorities in neighboring countries. How can racism in Hungary even be an issue when ethnic Hungarians in Romania, Slovakia, and Serbia are the victims of such persecution?

With the exception of a handful of dissident sociologists, most people honestly believed that racism had been eradicated in Hungary. To the Magyars' credit, many third world guests admitted that the severity of racism in Hungary was significantly milder than in other Eastern European countries. Duke, a thirty-five-year-old South African political exile and member of the African National Congress, had spent nearly a year in Bulgaria before he requested a transfer to Hungary. "It was just unbearable in Bulgaria," he explains. "We weren't even allowed in bars and discos. People would hang out of windows and make monkey sounds as we went by. It seemed like some kind of fashion or craze to be racist." After the hell of Bulgaria, the softer prejudices of the Hungarians seemed like tolerance itself. Duke, who worked as an agronomist in the rich farm lands of eastern Hungary, felt that he was the first person of color many of the locals had ever seen. "After a bit they'd come up to me and in all innocence ask if my skin coloring didn't come off when I washed or if I had ever seen bread before I came to Hungary." At such naivete he just laughed. But in major cities like Budapest, Szeged, and Debrecen, the violent racism of Skinhead gangs was no joke for people of color. By and large, however, the state did its best to contain the sporadic aggression against foreign students, guest workers, and native Roma.

About a year after the 1990 elections, foreign students in Budapest say that they noticed a distinctly new tension in the air of the capital city. On the streets, Skinhead gangs had found a new self-confidence, traveling in larger and larger packs, attacking foreign students in broad daylight. Almost overnight, the presence of police patrol squads in their hip-length, steel-gray jackets doubled and tripled in the popular tourist districts. The students quickly discovered, however, that the police force had not been bolstered for their protection. Whether innocuously sitting on a bench or eating a Big Mac at McDonalds along the swanky Váci Street, any person of color was fair game for spot identity checks. Those who couldn't produce valid legal papers upon demand were rounded up and detained. Some were deported immediately, while others disappeared into mysterious, inaccessible detention camps.

Third world people like Duke found it difficult to believe that this was the same Hungary that they had come to a few years earlier. Over a matter of months, the explosion of racism became an integral part of the changes that have so radically transformed the face of Hungarian society. Armed with their own racist notions of ethnic purity and national exclusiveness, the ruling Hungarian Democratic Forum (HDF) was complicitous in fueling aggression against people of color. When it seemed to work on their behalf, they gladly turned a blind eye to right-wing violence.

The new police policy coincided with two simultaneous influxes of non-Hungarians into the country. One came from the South and the East: political and economic refugees fleeing eastern Europe, the Middle East, and even Asia through the now porous borders of southeastern Europe. The second consisted of a boom in tourism from Western countries, whose hard currency the state depended upon, not least to service its massive national debt. Hungarian officialdom seemed not only to put these two groups in very separate categories, but also to feel that the former posed a distinct threat to the latter. Under fire for police policies, Budapest police chief János Bodrácska defended the crackdowns: "We don't want these color spots in Budapest. We don't want them on our necks. What are they doing here? They are a disgrace to everyone. These are not special raids on foreigners, but on all the undesirable persons who spoil the streets of Budapest."

On one account at least, Bodrácska was completely right. The offensive was not against foreigners as such. Hungary bends over backwards to lure the thirty million plus tourists (three times the size of the population) a year to its country. And with the exception of a pickpocket or the occasional dishonest taxi driver, white tourists usually pass their vacations in Hungary with little more to complain about than indigestion. The police raids targeted foreigners with darker skin, regardless of whether they were illegal aliens, political refugees, legal residents, tourists, businessmen, diplomats, or students.

Like its Central European neighbors, Hungary has been put under direct pressure from the European Community countries, and Germany in particular, to tighten up its immigration requirements and border controls. With the Iron Curtain gone, the West Europeans stipulated that a new buffer zone was needed to keep refugees and immigrants off their doorstep. The Central Europeans have fallen obediently into line. In Hungary, the parliament set processes in motion to restrict immigration requirements, formerly among the most liberal in Eastern Europe. Between October 1991 and October 1992, Hungary refused entry to 900,000 foreigners, most of whom came from Romania and the former Soviet Union. Hungary, however, had no comprehensive law on foreigners that stated the conditions for entry, residence, detention, and expulsion. And until the parliament could hammer one out, the matter was left in the hands of the police. "The bottom line here is that it is the exclusive competence of the police to determine an individual's right to stay in Hungary," Interior Ministry's Chief of Security Károly Nagy told reporters in 1991.

The word seemed to have come from high up that third world peoples were persona non grata in democratic Hungary. The Ministry of Labor, for example, issued a nearly all-inclusive list of professions— from technical positions to unskilled jobs—for which foreigners would be ineligible. The ministry explained that there was an abundance of Hungarians looking for work who had to be accommodated first. Under pressure from international business groups in Hungary, it later modified the decree, noting that restrictions would *not* be "strictly applied." The subtext of the ministry's explanation was clear: Certain, but not all, foreigners working in Hungary were responsible for the rising unemployment among Hungarians. Even old apparatchiks like Security Chief Nagy, it seemed, were learning a few lessons from the West. "Xenophobia," he told the weekly *Heti Világgazdaság*, "could be avoided if we don't copy the mistakes made by the Western European countries. There was a time when they opened their doors to immigrants, and as you can see today, they've become the prisoners of their own policies."

From the sound of it, one would think that Hungary was being overrun with foreign nationals. But, in fact, the number of foreigners residing in Hungary is a tiny percent of the population in contrast to that in West European countries. In 1992, only 131,000 registered foreign nationals lived in Hungary, roughly half of whom were ethnic Hungarians from neighboring states.

The official measures against foreigners came at the same time that racial violence also took on a new character. The first rash of street violence climaxed in a fatal January 1992 mishap in Budapest's Kőbánya-Kispest subway station. The incident ignited when a group of several Hungarian youths started insulting and then shoving two Nigerians, one of whom they knew from the Váci Street shopping fare where he worked as a sandwich-board advertising man (one profession not off-limits to foreigners) for one of the new sex shops. The Nigerians pushed back, attracting the attention of a few nearby Skinheads who came to their comrades' aid. Backed into a corner, one of the Nigerians pulled out a pocket knife and stabbed out blindly. By the time the melee was over, a sixteen-year-old Hungarian boy lay fatally wounded on the ground.

The killing sparked a furor in Budapest. Hungarian television repeated an interview with the boy's weeping mother, saying what a decent and tolerant Hungarian her son had been and that he wasn't a Skinhead and didn't even know any Skinheads and that he had always done well in school too. The broadcasts never mentioned that the Nigerian had been defending himself and had only killed the boy by accident. The media portrayed the incident as cold-blooded murder, and from ordinary Hungarians the tragedy produced an outpouring of sympathy for the dead boy. From Skinheads, it set off a new flourish of attacks against people of color.

For weeks afterward, the Kőbánya-Kispest station was transformed into a vigil for the dead boy, manned by local Skinheads and visited by thousands of Hungarians. Against the background of Hungarian flags, people laid flowers and lit candles around the boy's photographs. Graffiti such as "Niggers go home!", "Jews go home!", and "An animal killed one of our brothers!" adorned the walls. The thugs, under the eyes of on-duty policemen, beat up any dark-skinned foreigner unfortunate enough to stray into the vicinity.

Over the ten days that followed the brawl, twenty-five racist attacks were reported in Budapest alone. Three Sudanese students, for example, ran head on into a mob of thirty Skinheads looking for the "black murderer." A young Nigerian man fell prey to a similar band. When the police arrived, they arrested the Nigerian. At one o'clock in the afternoon, before 100 witnesses, Skinheads beat up an Ethiopian student at a central market place. "Even if they are outnumbered six to one, it is always the foreigners who are considered guilty," explains Márton Ill, president of the Martin Luther King Association (MLKA), a group founded in 1991 to bridge the divide between Hungarians and foreign nationals living in Hungary. In their makeshift office at the Budapest Technical University, Ill and a handful of other students man the new telephone hotline, which foreign students can call should they run into trouble or need an escort home after dark. "The police are so hostile toward people of color that we recommend that they always have someone from the organization with them at the police station," says the twenty-six-year-old engineering student, his face pasty and eyes bloodshot from successive nights on hot-line duty. "In ninety-nine percent of the cases," he says, "no one at all is arrested. And when an arrest is made, the offenders are prosecuted under the penal law for assault, rather than for racial discrimination. There are students who are so scared that some have just picked up and gone home." The Yemenese and Sudanese governments openly considered calling their students home, but instead issued a formal protest.

RACISM UNBOUND

Racial intolerance, of course, was not born in 1989, as the persecution of Roma and Jews during different periods of Hungarian history testifies. One of Hungary's foremost sociologists and a leading democratic voice during communist rule, Ottília Solt, claims that the sudden flare up of racism against foreigners is inextricably linked to the question of Hungarians' racial prejudices toward the approximately 500,000 Roma minority, about five to six percent of the population. Racism surfaced so quickly and with such vehemence, she asserts, because the structures of racist thinking were already firmly in place. "The racist logic behind discrimination against Roma and foreigners is exactly the same," says Solt. "People simply transferred their prejudices from the Roma to foreigners, from one people with darker skin color to all of the others. One hears that in the language that people use against both groups; it's practically identical. Now they're all thrown in the pot and treated the same way, whether they're Hungarian Roma, Chinese businessmen, or African students."

There is plenty of evidence to bear out Solt's thesis, which is all the more remarkable considering the vast differences between native Roma, living in Hungary for centuries, and foreigners, the majority of whom have arrived in Hungary only in the past few years. On the streets or in the boulevard press, one hears the standard cliches of the "lazy", "work-shy" or "criminal" Gypsy regularly applied to the diverse communities of third world peoples in Hungary. One opinion poll showed that Roma were by far the most disliked group in Hungary, with seventy-nine percent of those asked expressing negative feelings toward the Roma. Before it was only the Roma who police herded up in Budapest's tourist districts and hauled off without explanation. But now, foreigners with dark skin pigment receive the same treatment.

One of the most widely repeated stereotypes about Roma in Hungary is that they deplete the social system, disproportionately draining the state of housing, education, and welfare funds. Under the communist regime, many people privately leveled the same charges against the infinitesimal number of foreigner students or guest workers in Hungary. Since 1989, however, all foreign students have paid hefty tuition rates in hard currency. Yet, the sentiments expressed in the following letter in a Budapest weekly echo the popular cliches that still abound: "The presence of African students now and the racial friction resulting from their presence can be attributed to the former regime inviting them in the first place. The average Hungarian has a hard time feeding his family as it is. He views the presence of third world students as an expense he cannot afford. . . . The Magyar people must be allowed to cleanse themselves from within and rid themselves of the various parasites that have infested their country."[1] The author's charges are just about the same as those traditionally directed against Roma, although no one would claim that it was the communists who invited the Roma to Hungary.

Actually, the first nomadic Roma settled in eastern Hungary in the early fifteenth century, suffering discrimination over the years that ranged from forced assimilation to lynchings and mass deportation. During WWII, Hungary proceeded less ruthlessly than its German or Croatian allies in carrying out anti-Roma legislation. Nevertheless, some 30,000 to 40,000 Hungarian Roma perished in Nazi concentration camps. Although the postwar regime tried to combat the widespread hostility toward the *cigány*, it also succumbed to age-old patterns of prejudice. The state, for example, denied the Roma minority the same status and privileges that it granted the much smaller German, Serb, Romanian, Slovak, and Croat minorities. School textbooks contained racist passages that propagated the notion of the "genetically inferior Gypsy." And Roma school children with particularly severe learning problems were often deemed "mentally retarded" and institutionalized.

For the police state, the cliche of the "Gypsy criminal" was useful. By spreading fear and distrust of the Roma, the regime could justify a strong professional apparatus to "protect" the law-abiding Hungarian citizenry. From 1954 to the early sixties, the state required all Roma to carry special black identity cards. "The state financed a special propaganda campaign to stigmatize the Roma as criminals, to create a climate of fear and resentment," claims Ágnes Daróczi, a Roma ethnographer at the Hungarian Institute of Culture in Budapest. She and other specialists note that although crime among Roma is indeed high, the crime rate is not higher than among non-Roma with similar levels of education and standards of living. "As the system began to weaken, certain circles saw this as a cheap ploy to preserve their own power and influence," says Daróczi, one of Hungary's foremost Roma intellectuals. Just one example was the police-sponsored television cop show "Blue Light." The show portrayed all ethnic Roma as law breakers, from prostitutes to murderers. The police, of course, were the heroes, valiantly raiding nests of Roma crime and apprehending the culprits. "Roma were clearly being blamed for increasing social tensions and rising criminality," says Daróczi. "The answer was a tough police force." Against the protests of Roma intellectuals, the state published 200,000 copies of the book upon which the Blue Light series was based.

"Even the works of Marx and Lenin didn't get state support like that," says Daróczi.

The complexity of the question of the Roma in Eastern Europe can hardly be underestimated. Despite increasing urbanization, the majority of Roma still live in the country, in squalid, overcrowded housing, most without electricity or running water. Even by the late 1970s, only 1.5 percent of Hungary's Roma had skilled work. Most held the unskilled or menial jobs that no one else in the village wanted. Studies in the mid-sixties showed less than a third of Roma to be literate. While ambitious campaigns during the communist era to educate the young generations of Roma made a significant dent in Roma illiteracy, the dropout rate of Roma from secondary school is still nearly sixty percent.

In true Stalinist fashion, the communist regime addressed the Roma question in terms of their "assimilation" into Hungarian society (actually, the same philosophy behind Roma policy since Maria Theresia's reign). Regardless of their unique attributes, the Roma were to be turned into good Hungarian workers, who lived, worked, and spoke like the average Hungarian. Anticipating a rise in their standard of living, the Roma initially welcomed their boost into the twentieth century. In many ways, however, the hasty, underfunded attempt to stamp out the "cultural backwardness" of the Roma population only backfired. The communist regime's housing policy, for example, opened new opportunities for Roma to move out of their rural squalor, into low-cost, but comparatively modern housing projects in or on the outskirts of major cities. The infamous "Gypsy rows," however, ghettoized the minority amongst a majority unprepared for their new neighbors. Tension increased as the new conditions, slum-like though they were, resulted in a huge Roma population boom. By refusing to address the underlying cultural uniqueness of the Roma community, the government simply transferred whole communities into new ghettos, transporting their problems along with them.

The spark that finally ignited the volatile relations between Hungarians and Roma was unemployment. By the end of 1992, joblessness had soared to eleven percent nationwide, with no end in sight. In industrial regions, the figures often exceeded a third of the population. "Hungary is a country in which there was little to no unemployment just a few years ago," explains sociologist János Ladányi. "Even though the figures today aren't exceptional compared with those in the West, this is a new phenomenon for people here. They don't know how to cope. There is almost a natural need for them to blame somebody. And today communism is associated with some wonderful social welfare system that in fact never existed. A typically conservative argument, it's said that there were too many benefits for the poor, and the Roma of course are the poorest of the poor. So now it's said that the Roma were oversubsidized and that's the source of our problems now. There's no truth to this, but that's what people think and say."

Resentment toward the Roma ghettos came to a head first in September 1990 in the eastern cities of Eger and Miskolc, two of the cities hardest hit by industrial shutdowns and unemployment. Trouble had long been brewing between locals and Roma in Eger when some eighty to 100 Skinheads, clad in the standard outfits of their Europe-wide counterparts, raided houses in the Roma quarter, beating their inhabitants, including pregnant women, children, and elderly people. The police stood by as they ransacked the flats, smashing furniture and windows.

The Eger assault was the first of many that Roma would endure in the course of the next few years. In September 1992, a molotov cocktail attack burned to the ground the houses of two Roma families in the southeastern village of Kétegyháza. The house owners, both with criminal records, were then assaulted by villagers. The police, denying that the action was directed against the Roma community, said that the arson was an "illegal retaliation" for "acts committed against the Kétegyháza citizens." Just weeks later, local field guard in the village of Tura shot down a Roma man and his wife at point blank range for stealing pears. Although the police launched homicide proceedings against the guard, the Roma community protested that the government was complicit in the Autumn wave of violence.

In a passionate address to parliament, Roma deputy Aladár Horvát claimed that the conservative government had not "taken a single step for the improvement of Roma society." He continued:

> The government, our democratic government, completely disregards the
> interests of the Roma minority. In fact, its policies have only deepened

the Roma people's misery. Right-wing government forces, using racial prejudices and bitterness as tools, have incited the people against one another, people whose fates are equally hopeless. In the name of the majority, they encourage one portion of society to use this tool against another, the minority. . . . I say this not only in light of the attacks in Eger, Miskolc, Rákospalota, Győre, Aranyosapáti, Kétegyháza, and Tura, but in light of the Hungarian government's policies over the last two years. For the third year now, the government has rejected our knowledge, our will to help, and our proposals.

We demand the recognition and protection of our minority rights. We demand the right and opportunity for schooling for our children, to a healthy life, and to equal chances in society. We demand severe punishment of racial discrimination and the protection of universal human rights.

The Roma community continues to trust in the sense of justice and the solidarity of Hungarians. We trust that we shall be able to go out on the street tomorrow without fear of being lynched, without fear for our children. We trust that the police will not give Skinheads a free hand in their reign of terror. And we have to trust that the Hungarian Republic does not further increase the deprivation, misery, defenselessness, and humiliation of our people. We have no other choice but to help each other. Thank you.[2]

The government issued no response to Horvát's appeal.

HEIRS OF THE ARROW CROSS

The latent racism that erupted in 1990 encompassed the breadth of society—from the person on the street to the government. Yet, a growing, organized Skinhead movement stands behind the lion's share of the violent attacks against people of color. A subterranean Skinhead scene first emerged in Hungary in the early 1980s, just about the time of their East German comrades. As in the GDR, the youths' earliest expression of right-wing sympathies came in the form of a virulent anti-communism. Initially, though, the Skins had little specific politics behind them, and mixed in with other embryonic forms of opposition subculture.

In and out of prison, the young, largely working-class male Skinheads and their followers maintained the movement mostly through the underground music scene, which enjoyed significantly more leeway than in other East bloc countries. By the mid-1980s, a number of Skinhead *oi* bands had come together, drawing upon their members' earlier experiences in punk, heavy metal, and Ska groups. The texts of bands such as *Oi-Kor* (Oi-Age), *CPG* (Coitus Punk Group) and *Mos-oi* (Oi-Smile) dealt with classic Skinhead themes such as foreigners, communists, Roma, brawling, drinking, and national pride, as well as the Hungarian minority in Transylvania. One of the original Budapest oi bands, the 1982-formed Mos-oi, flouted some of the strongest lyrics. In their "Immigrants' Share," for example, they sang:

> We'll get rid of everyone we don't need,
> Including the garbage immigrants.
> The immigrants' fate can only be death,
> We'll have to drive out all of the Blacks,
> For the Arabs—to be sure—machine guns are waiting,
> Over Palestine atomic clouds are gathering.

In another song, the Roma are their target:

> The flamethrower is the only weapon I need to win,
> All Gypsy adults and children we'll exterminate,
> We can kill all of them at once in unison,
> When it's done we can advertise: Gypsy-free zone.[3]

The band's language is clearly fascist, advocating the use of machine guns, flamethrowers, and atomic bombs to exterminate their racially inferior foes. Interestingly, already in 1982 the right-wing underground had equated Roma and foreigners, and both groups with the communist system. At this early stage of development, the group's anti-communist bias was so strong that it directed its hatred against the Palestinians rather than Jews or Israelis.

In the late 1980s, the number of Skins in Budapest and other cities swelled to perhaps as many as 800 countrywide. In 1987, the first wave of violence against Roma and foreigners brought as many as sixty Skinheads together at a time for joint attacks. The movement simultaneously developed an ideology that legitimized its actions. Radical neo-Nazi

Skins found a paragon in Hungary's WWII fascist dictator Ferenc Szá-
lasi, the leader of the German-aligned Arrow Cross party, installed to
power in late 1944 at Hitler's directive. The state kept a tight reign
on the movement, locking up its adherents for a year or two when they
could. At the same time, the state took no more pains than did the East
German, Czechoslovak, or Polish regimes to address the neo-fascist
youth movement as a domestic social symptom rather than a West-
inspired aberration.

With the capitulation of the single-party state, the Skinhead movement suddenly found itself not only with new space within which to
operate, but also with an ever larger mass of disillusioned, socially
alienated youth to draw upon. Throughout 1990 and 1991, the presence
of Skins on the streets of Budapest and at soccer matches, particularly
those of their favorite team, Ferencváros, skyrocketed. At the Ferencváros games, fans shouted insults such as "dirty Jews!" and "stinking
Gypsies!" at their rivals. Spraypainted swastikas appeared—and remained for months at a time—on building walls and monuments. The
outbursts of violence against Roma and foreigners of color in late 1990
and 1991 brought the Skinhead phenomenon into the public spotlight
for the first time. In early 1992, Budapest police sources estimated the
total number of Skinheads in Hungary at between 1500 and 2500, with
about one-fifth of that constituting a hard neo-fascist core. As in the
former GDR and elsewhere, the youth are mostly industrial working-
class boys in their late teens and early twenties, concentrated heavily
in the communist-constructed social housing projects.

While the Skinhead scene is locally organized, and fractured within
itself as well, an extensive network of national and international contacts
keeps ideas, propaganda, and even weaponry flowing between groups
and across borders. The early Hungarian Skins had been in touch with
counterparts from East and West Germany, Austria, Spain, and the U.S.
since the mid-1980s. The full relaxation of travel restrictions has only
expanded those liaisons. In 1991, for example, Vienna Skinheads devoted an entire issue of their publication *Skinhead Erwache!* (Skinhead
Awake!) to the Hungarian Skin scene and Austro-Hungarian Skinhead
joint ventures. Heavily intoxicated, the Viennese Skins made the three-
hour train trip to Budapest to join their Magyar pals at soccer matches

and at the Viking Club, gladly lending a hand in beating up the foreign students or Roma that happened to cross their paths. The publication noted how much easier it was for Skins to organize gigs in Budapest than it was for them in Vienna. One writer described the Budapest scene as such:

> There's no more trouble with the punks, because in Hungary the Skins put an end to that problem four or five years ago. But it's different with the niggers and the Gypsies. The Gypsies have gotten really uppity and in a few years will be difficult to control at all. There are many more Gypsies there than there are here [in Austria.] So it's certainly going to get hot in Budapest/Hungary and the Skins aren't going to have it so easy any more. Yes, yes, capitalism brings its children—niggers, Turks, Gypsies, etc., that come to leech off other countries.

The Austrian Skinheads here simply substitute the Hungarian Skins' critique of communism for theirs of capitalism, claiming that capitalism is even responsible for the presence of Roma in Hungary!

Next to the Skinheads, and at times linked with them, a much smaller but more sophisticated Hungarian neo-Nazi movement has surfaced, whose international contacts constitute the backbone of its existence. Little is known about the isolated neo-Nazi cells that worked conspiratorially in Hungary prior to 1989. Yet it is clear that as of 1990 international neo-Nazi organizations took a keen interest in Hungary, actively encouraging the growth of a neo-Nazi movement that could serve as a bridgehead to all of Central and Eastern Europe. Behind the concentrated *Drang nach Osten* stands the highly conspiratorial international development arm of the National Socialist German Workers Party (NSDAP-AO), whose headquarters sit in Lincoln, Nebraska, under the leadership of the well-known neo-Nazi Gary Rex Lauck. The U.S.-based Nazi group's goal is the "establishment of a National Socialist state in a free, sovereign and newly united Greater German Reich." It's first priority, which it pursues legally and openly from the U.S., is the annulment of the Nazi party's ban in Austria and Germany. The Lincoln headquarters also oversees the distribution of copious propaganda material, such as stickers reading "Lift the NS Ban!" and "Boycott Jewish businesses!", all marked with red swastikas. While the

NSDAP's close working relationship with the German extreme-right is extensively documented, evidence that the organization first set its sights on Hungary came into public light in 1991, when the NSDAP AO's German-language organ, *NS-Kampfruf*, announced the first issue of a Hungarian publication, *Új Rend* (New Order). Along with *NS-Kampfruf*, *Új Rend* joins the English NSDAP newspaper *New Order* and the Swedish *Sveriges Nationaella Förbund* as the vehicles of the Nazi's propaganda drive. In the broken Hungarian of an exile, the pilot issue of *Új Rend* calls its comrades to arms: "Since the world Jewry is internationally active, we National Socialists must also wage a worldwide battle against it!"

Although Austrian intelligence sources claim that high-level Austrian-Hungarian neo-Nazi cooperation dates back at least to early 1990, Hungarian authorities first took action against the neo-Nazi underground in January 1992, a belated response typical of the Hungarian officials' treatment of ultra-right activity. A dawn raid in the northeastern city of Györ broke up a seven-member paramilitary commando unit and confiscated uniforms, light weaponry, and neo-Nazi propaganda. The leader of the National Socialist Action Group, István Györkös, an unemployed fifty-two-year-old electrical engineer, admitted that he had been in contact with the NSDAP-AO, as well as Austria's leading neo-Nazi figure, Gottfried Küssel, for over a year.

The same judges that had sentenced liberal opposition critics with a swift crack of the gavel just a few years ago, first released the ringleaders on the grounds of "insufficient evidence." In a press statement after his release, Györkös stated that in his opinion the wartime Arrow Cross legitimately "championed the idea of pure Hungarianism." Later he was sentenced to a one-year suspended jail sentence. When the group originally put up "foreigners out" posters around Györ with an address to write for more information, it received only a mild response. But the television publicity surrounding the raid, which broadcast the group's mailing address for up to thirty seconds at a time, resulted in an immediate subscription boom for *Új Rend*, said the Györ organizers. The group asserted that it will continue to pursue a neo-Nazi agenda, but now through legal, democratic means.

However openly brutal the racism of Skinheads and neo-Nazis, similar but more muted sentiments permeate deep into Hungary's halls of power. At its best, the ruling nationalist HDF has ignored the plight of minorities, stalling minority legislation or trying to cut funds for minority programs. As for the violence, whether attacks against students, pogroms against Roma, or police brutality, the country's national conservatives have refused to protest clear human rights abuses. In fact, it was a Christian Democratic parliamentarian who acted as the legal counsel for the Skinheads behind the 1990 Eger violence. In front of parliament, one HDF deputy openly asked whether African pygmies were really human beings. At a press conference on the eve of the March 1990 election, I asked then-candidate József Antall, soon to be the new prime minister, how his party justified Hungary's growing relations with the white government in South Africa in light of his own party's emotional defense of the human rights of the Hungarian minorities. He became visibly ruffled and shot back at me heatedly: "Let me ask you, why has the world protested so loudly against the situation in South Africa for years, and yet never said a word about the ethnic Hungarians in Transylvania? Who has ever cared about the Hungarians who have suffered so much?" In other words, the suffering of the historically wronged, ill-treated Hungarian nation justifies its insensitivity toward other suffering peoples. The legacy of its own oppression gives it the right to oppress others.

The conservative right's racism derives from its understanding of the Magyar nation as an ethnically pure, organic society. All "others," that is, non-Hungarians, are implicitly second-class citizens or peoples. In the middle of the fray as usual, HDF Vice President István Csurka, clearly alluding to the Roma community, if not all people of non-Magyar ethnicity, wrote in *Magyar Fórum*: "We must end the unhealthy practice of blaming the Skinheads for all that is bad among the youth, while leniently tolerating other sicknesses, crimes, and cultural crimes. We can no longer recoil from the fact that there are also genetic reasons behind degeneration. We must acknowledge that disadvantaged strata and groups of our society have been with us for too long, groups where the severity of natural selection has not worked. . . . Our society should now support the strong and viable families, organized for work and performance. . . ."[4] Csurka openly endorses a racial hierarchy in which certain "strong and viable" groups should receive priority over those genetically "disadvantaged strata" that natural selection has somehow failed to weed out. The role of the state, then, is to lend natural selection a helping hand in ridding society of inferior races in order to halt its "degeneration." Should any parliamentarian in Germany or France, including those on the far right, be so foolish as to utter such words in public, they would surely lose their seats at once. But in Hungary, the use of such fascist terminology has gradually become a routine part of political discourse.

ESCAPE FROM KEREPESTARCSA

The heavy-handedness of the Hungarian bureaucracy's treatment of its unwanted guests illustrates just how close to the surface lies the mentality of the recently disposed regime. In former East Germany, most of the communist apparatchiks were immediately expelled from their positions, if their positions continued to exist at all in the united Federal Republic. West German counterparts came in to fill the gaps or instruct the lower echelons of the old system how to function in a manner befitting Western democracy. Although the Germans' on-the-job training clearly has not eradicated racism, nor will it, it constitutes a first step toward replacing the ethos of the past with a new set of liberal values. The rest of the former East bloc had no such ready reservoir of uncompromised, skilled personnel at its disposal. With certain exceptions, most desks at the Hungarian Interior Ministry are still filled with the same people appointed, trained, and promoted under communism. The same bureaucrats, who sanctioned the arrests of bespectacled dissidents at illegal demonstrations just a few years ago, continue to justify their behavior today with the same kind of convoluted logic.

Perhaps the grisliest example of that continuity in Hungary has been the revelations about Kerepestarcsa, a "detention camp" for illegal aliens. An hour outside of Budapest, the quiet little hamlet of Kerepestarcsa would be as inconspicuous as any other sedate Hungarian village were it not for its high-walled prison. During the Second World

War, the Axis-allied state deported Jews and other "enemies of the nation" to Kerepestarcsa. After the communists took power in 1947, the workers' state filled the cells again. Empty temporarily during the 1956 revolution, the wave of reprisals in the aftermath of the revolution's suppression put Kerepestarcsa back in business. During the seventies and eighties, the Interior Ministry used the decaying facilities as a police academy. By 1990, the camp had yet another function. Kerepestarcsa's new capacity, unknown to the public until January 1992, was to hold "illegal aliens" until they could be deported to their native countries. Only when human rights activists got wind of something foul did Kerepestarcsa's new purpose come to light.

The story of Ali, a nineteen-year-old Iraqi Kurd, was just one of many of the tales to come out of the camp. In the aftermath of the post–Gulf War Kurdish uprising in northern Iraq, Ali escaped from his village in northern Iraq into Turkey. By foot, bus, and hitchhiking, he made his way to Bulgaria and then to Romania. From Romania, he and six other Kurds slipped across the border into Hungary, moving across the country by night. Their final goal was the Austrian border, the West. As they attempted to enter Austria through the forest, they lost their way. Forced to backtrack, they ran straight into a Hungarian border patrol. After four days in the local Sopron prison in western Hungary, Ali was sent to Kerepestarcsa. For the next four months, with the exception of two short-lived escapes, the detention center was Ali's home.

Inside Kerepestarcsa, twenty to thirty prisoners (or "detainees" as the officials called them) were crammed into tiny, dark rooms. The officials made no distinction between those inmates who were politically persecuted in their native countries and those who were economic refugees. Even students and unknowing tourists found themselves cast into Kerepestarcsa's cells. The camp authorities separated the several hundred prisoners according to their own specious notions of ethnicity or race—black Africans in one building, Arabic persons in another, Asians in a third, and East Europeans, mostly Romanians and Albanians, in a fourth.

"This was a place for animals, not for humans," explains Ali in his Pidgin English. "It was very, very dirty. I had never seen people live like this." Two weeks before I spoke with him, he and a young Romanian woman had escaped for a third time by digging a hole beneath a barbed-wire fence. Hidden for the time being in the flat of a Budapest human rights activist, the skinny, baby-faced Kurdish boy spends day and night in the high-rise for fear of being spot-checked on the street. He sleeps, showers, and watches Hungarian television. He has given up hope of receiving political asylum, as he and his companions had planned. Now, he admits, all he wants is to be back in Iraq.

Independent observers confirm the camp's squalid conditions. Toilets are always stopped up and flooded, rooms lack electricity or lighting and a putrid, all-pervading stench fills the air. Meals there consist of soup, bread, and tea. Ali and other Muslims, who refused to eat the thin, pork-based soup, lived only on bread and tea. For exorbitant prices, often ten times the normal price, detainees could buy extra rations from the guards. Observers say that the majority of inmates clearly look undernourished, many anemic or weak from other illnesses. The prisoners spend the days cooped up in the bunk houses, allowed outside only if they paid the guards $10 or $20 to make a phone call. Otherwise, contact with the outside world is off-limits. One group of eight Chinese tourists spent more than three weeks in Kerepestarcsa because authorities refused to call the South African embassy where their valid passports were being processed for visas.

Brutality in the camp was routine. "They sprayed gas in our faces as if it was a joke," says Ali. "The really bad guards would wake you up in the morning with gas or their big sticks." In early December the inmates staged a riot which finally alerted the outside world to the camp's existence. "We tried to do everything that we could to resist or let people know what's going on here. We shouted and broke the windows and burned the beds. We wanted to speak to Mr. Alex [a guard reputed to be in charge] but they only brought about 100 police who beat and teargassed us." At one press conference, camp officials admitted that the protest was not the first of its kind: Between July and December 1991 specially trained police had been ordered into Kerepestarcsa on several occasions to quell unrest.

After an official two week news black out, reporters, opposition parliamentary deputies and human rights observers finally gained entry to the camp. The first visitors were appalled to find such diverse categories of people as refugees, immigrants, illegal residents, temporary residents, and even students and tourists all thrown together—and with no legal recourse. According to Hungarian law, authorities can legally hold aliens for a maximum of six days. "We all found the new function of this camp very disturbing," said Éva Blénesi, a Budapest-based human rights specialist. A Romanian-born ethnic Hungarian, she described the conditions as equivalent to the darkest asylums and orphanages that she had visited in Romania. "The only thing that has really changed at Kerepestarcsa over the years has been the color of its inmates," she says. "The people there have always been those who are in some way 'unpleasant' for the regime in power."

An Amnesty International report also harshly criticized the violation of basic human rights in Kerepestarcsa. Yet, in typical style, neither the camp authorities nor their bosses at the Interior Ministry found legitimate cause for the uproar. Interior Minister Péter Boross characterized Amnesty International as the kind of "oversensitive liberal philanthropists that you find in every country." Referring to the 1956 Hungarian revolution, he added that "Amnesty International should have been here when hundreds of people were hanged by the communists, but you didn't hear them then." As one reporter pointed out, Amnesty International was not established until 1961. Prime Minister Antall also played down the revelations stressing that xenophobia was "no worse" in Hungary than in other European countries. The international community, both Boross and Antall insinuated, was once again unfairly picking on Hungary, the real victim of injustice.

Those who deny the existence of racial prejudices in Hungary today are fewer and farther between. Unlike the Prime Minister and his conservative colleagues, a wide array of forces has coalesced to take action against xenophobia in Hungary. In September 1992, more than 50,000 Hungarians took to the streets to protest against racist violence and right-wing extremism. Hungary's President, Árpád Göncz, a respected author and democrat, personally met with groups of foreign students and third world guests, apologizing on behalf of all Hungarians for their treatment. Among the political parties, the three liberal opposition parties, the Alliance of Free Democrats (AFD), the Federation of Young Democrats, and the Hungarian Socialist Party, all endorsed anti-racist stands, roundly criticizing both the insensitivity and racism of the ruling coalition. In the 1990 elections, the AFD placed several leading members of the Roma community on its ticket, landing two of the Roma candidates in parliament. With the exception of the 1990–92 Czechoslovak parliament, Hungary's is the only legislature in the former East bloc to have Roma deputies. The Roma community itself has also made great strides in organizing its members. From the dozens of small and diverse groups that mushroomed in 1990, thirty-nine organizations have banded together to found the Roma Parliament, a democratic forum for Roma issues.

The forces of tolerance have immense handicaps to overcome in their struggle against racism. The latent racism in Hungarian society came to the surface with plenty of ready weaponry at its disposal. In the face of nationalism, widespread ignorance, and economic catastrophe, democrats emerged from single-party rule sadly empty-handed. During the communist era, even research on racial prejudices was banned. "Combatting racism through democratic channels means starting from scratch, from the very beginning," said one social worker. "Our project must be to create a whole new culture more accepting of diversity. I don't have any illusions. We have a long way to go."

Chapter 5

ROMANIA
CEAUŞESCU'S REVENGE

Dawn has just broken along the jagged rim of the Carpathian basin, shrouding the valleys of western Romania's tremendous mountain chain in a light, translucent mist. On the bridge leading into the Transylvanian city of Tîrgu-Mureş, an army roadblock halts all traffic coming from the single-lane overpass. A squat tank planted squarely at its center overlooks the sullen outskirts of the historic city and its Romanian and ethnic Hungarian inhabitants. Kalishnikovs slung casually over their shoulders, soldiers in long khaki-brown wool coats and dish-shaped steel helmets inspect every vehicle. Only three months after the December 1989 revolution, in which over 800 persons lost their lives, violence has flared again in Romania. Unlike the overthrow of President Nicolae Ceauşescu's dictatorship, this time the March 1990 killings in the northwestern region of Transylvania pit the Romanian majority against the ethnic Hungarian minority. Although nationalist conflict has long marred relations between Romanians and Hungarians in the historically disputed region, the fierce explosion of ethnic tensions so soon after the revolution catches all but its architects off-guard.

On the bridge, one lanky, unshaven guard checks the Romanian licence plates of our mud-splattered Dacia. Two hours west of Tîrgu-Mureş, in the provincial capital of Cluj-Napoca, another ethnically mixed city, Welsh photographer Maggie Morgan, German journalist Erich Rathfelder, and I had swapped our Budapest-rented Mercedes for the battered Romanian make. Although Tîrgu-Mureş looks calm twenty-four hours after the clashes that claimed thirty lives, the city remains under martial law, and the army has orders not to allow any Hungarian transport through the checkpoints. As the sentry peers through our grimy windshield, his simple peasant face evokes the television images of the revolution, of the soldiers, the "heroes of the revolution," who had supposedly battled hold-out units of the Securitate, Ceauşescu's feared paramilitary police. In the euphoria of victory, TV screens flashed pictures of demonstrators swarming over the army's tanks and soldiers embracing beautiful Romanian girls with long, raven-black hair. As he flips quickly through our passports I wonder what role this young recruit had actually played in the opaque reality of Romania's prime-time revolution. Had he fired on demonstrators before orders came to abandon Ceauşescu and "join the people?" His round, expressionless dark eyes reveal nothing. He tosses his cigarette over the bridge's stone wall and looks up uneasily at the growing queue behind us. He steps back and waves us on into Tîrgu-Mureş.

Even as the morning lengthens, the city's rough cobblestone streets remain eerily empty. Schools are closed for the day and the shops tightly shut. Debris from the three day melee still litters the gutters and sidewalks. Overturned, burned-out cars and broken glass make a trail to the central Square of the Roses, the scene of the past days' encounters. Romanian troops ring one end of the oblong square, where half-a-dozen tanks stand poised near the giant black marble statue of the 1848 revolutionary Avram Iancu. At the foot of the monument, the candle and pine-branch memorials to the revolution's dead lie trampled and scattered about. Up a tiny side street, an elderly Hungarian man patiently boards up the ransacked office of the Hungarian Democratic Union of Romania (HDUR), the newly founded political organization of the country's 1.7 million–strong minority. In Tîrgu-Mureş—called Marosvásárhely by the ethnic Hungarians, Neumarkt by the German Saxons—about half of the population is Hungarian. His daughter, the man says, gesturing with the hammer in his hand, won't let her children outside the house. Like most of the Hungarian community, she has bolted her doors out of fear. The army presence, he warns, is only a temporary solution. "During the revolution, when we were on the streets together, Hungarians and Romanians were brothers. We thought that our victory might be a fresh start for the nationalities in Transylvania." He shakes his head. "But now it's worse then ever before."

A short walk from the HDUR office, the man points out the headquarters of *Vatra Românească* (Romanian Cradle, or Romanian Hearth), the ultra-nationalist Romanian organization founded in January 1990 that spearheaded the vicious attacks on Hungarian demonstrators. Until the violence, little had been heard about the regional ultra-nationalist movement that would come to have a central part in postcommunist Romanian politics. The two soldiers guarding the wrecked office show us inside, explaining how the ethnic Hungarians returned the Romanians' assault with reciprocal venom. They claim that the Hungarians had unfairly provoked the Romanians. Or that was what they had heard, at least. One upended file cabinet still contains a handful of the organization's literature. Back on the street, safely around the corner, our guide looks over the tattered carbon copies of the "Romanian cultural organization's" early proclamations. They extoll the glory of the Romanian people and the sanctity of the "unitary Romanian state," warning Romanians of the need to protect themselves against the designs of Hungarian separatists. The old man winces and shrugs, "There's nothing here that Ceauşescu didn't say."

ROMANIA'S FAVORITE SON

But as the Hungarian gentleman well knew, post-communist Romanian nationalism had already shown a face far more menacing than that which underpinned Ceauşescu's particular brand of "national communism." As Romania's many ethnic minorities would learn, the Tîrgu-Mureş violence signaled only the first stage of a nationalist groundswell which would make Ceauşescu's chauvinism look bland. The essence of the hatred and distrust, of the resentment and fear, that had ignited the ethnic clashes in Transylvania, had been an integral component of the communist dictatorship's *Staatsraison*. Although Ceauşescu's twenty-five-year tyranny irrevocably blackened the name of communism, his flamboyant adulation of Fatherland, patriotism, and the "unitary Romanian national state" survived the revolution un-scathed—as did the bulk of the police state's massive apparatus that was so inextricably intertwined with that ideology. In Tîrgu-Mureş, as throughout Romania, it became clear that although the revolution had severed the dictatorship's head, its body and its soul were still very much alive. That reality cast a black cloud over the flickering hope that finally, this time, Romania might wrest itself from its centuries-long history of despotism and ethnic strife.

The kind of nationalism that surfaced with such vehemence in Tranyslvania replicated the essence of Ceauşescu's bombastic "national communism," the most exaggerated form of its kind in the East bloc. Shortly after the communist take-over in Romania, the "native faction" within the ruling Romanian Communist Party (RCP) gradually turned toward an official nationalist policy and cautiously tried to shed the unwanted straight-jacket of Stalinist internationalism. Not until the forty-seven-year-old Ceauşescu took the helm in 1965, however, did Romania markedly distinguish itself among its neighbors. Politically, Romania's break with the Soviet Union climaxed in 1968 with Ceau-şescu's open defiance of Warsaw Pact forces' invasion of Czechoslovakia, a stance that brought the country within a hair's breadth of military confrontation with Big Brother. In a country whose historical antipathy for Russia was as deep as its sympathy for socialism was thin, the course of national independence won Ceauşescu the Romanian population's sincere admiration. Abroad, Romania's independent foreign policy at the height of the Cold War (actually more bluster than deed) earned it access to hard currency loans, privileged trade status, and lavish praise from the West.

The regime's efforts to free the country from Moscow's fetters constituted only one aspect of its nationalist campaign. The Ceauşescu regime also accelerated the "re-Romanization" of Romania, a step-by-step unthawing of the national values, symbols, and culture that had been briefly put on ice. In every sphere of society, Ceauşescu sought to restore to the Nation the prominence and place that it had enjoyed during the interwar years. Although now under the banner of communism, Ceauşescu's national vision fired the imaginations of both the intelligentsia and the rank-and-file. As despised as Ceauşescu had become in poverty-stricken Romania by the Winter of 1989, the self-anointed *Conducător*, or leader, became a popular national hero almost overnight in the late sixties. With certain self-imposed restrictions, the discourse that Ceauşescu garnished in communist jargon tapped the same themes that had dominated Romania's pre-1945 discourse—the country's historic glory, the origins of Romanian ethnicity, the nature of the "national essence," and, perhaps most vociferously, the preservation of national unity. The state slowly rehabilitated national figures, from poets to medieval peasant crusaders, as the forerunners of Romanian Marxism-Leninism. A bizarre personality cult around Ceauşescu posed a continuum from the medieval princes Michael the Brave and Ştefan the Great to Romania's favorite son, Ceauşescu himself. In the 1980s, when Ceauşescu's disastrous economic policies bore their meager fruit, a cold, hungry population abandoned their leader. Yet, in contrast to other East bloc countries, no organized democratic opposition, even among intellectuals, arose from the popular misery. The conditions of the police state, of course, went a long way toward thwarting oppositional initiatives. But, perhaps more importantly, it was the nationalist convictions that Ceauşescu, the intelligentsia, and the people embraced that preempted the emergence of a democratic opposition such as Solidarity in Poland, Charter 77 in Czechoslovakia, or Hungary's Democratic Opposition, all movements committed to values such as political pluralism, human rights, and civil society. So successfully had Ceauşescu reestablished the hegemony of the interwar national discourse, opposition to the despot never managed to extricate itself from that framework.

The state's recourse to nationalism, needless to say, dazzled the many ethnic and national minorities within Romania's borders less than it did the Romanians. After a short period of domestic liberalization in the 1960s, Ceauşescu initiated a ruthless anti-minority campaign under the heading of "homogenization," a euphemism for assimilation. The Ceauşescu plan for a brave, new Romanian world sought to eviscerate the cultural identities of the Hungarian, Serbian, German, Roma, and other minorities in Romania. Not coincidentally, the policies fomented tension between the Romanian majority and their co-inhabitants—a strategy that helped divide potential opposition to the regime, as well as to divert frustration from the country's economic dire plight. The regime concentrated its efforts in Transylvania, where resentment, particularly between Romanians and Hungarians, had a long and tragic history.

Those historical animosities furnished the raw material for Ceauşescu's nationalist propaganda, just as they do today for the contemporary Romanian ultra-right. The rival historical claims of Transylvania's nationalities and the memories of past injustices are critical to their identities and never lie far from the surface. In just about any Hungarian or Romanian household in Transylvania, the same standard, self-glorifying, and self-pitying accounts of either nationality's history in the region can be heard almost verbatim. The Romanians tirelessly assert that Transylvania is an "ancient Romanian land," first settled by the modern Romanians' Daco-Roman ancestors in the first and second centuries. The Daco-Romans, they claim, survived wave after wave of foreign invasion, valiantly preserving their Latin-based tongue and cultural traditions. At long last, born in 1859 of the unification of the two original Romanian principalities, Moldavia and Wallachia, Romanians heralded the Kingdom of Romania as the penultimate culmination of their two millennium-long struggle for unity and independence. Not until the signing of the WWI peace treaties, however, did nationalists see their dream of "Greater Romania" fulfilled. Remarkably, after Romania's last minute reentry into the war, the victorious Entente powers awarded Romania a disproportionately handsome array of territories, thus more than doubling its size. The addition of Bukovina from Austria, Bessarabia from Soviet Russia, southern Dobrudja from Bulgaria, and Transylvania from Hungary presented the Romanian state with a conglomeration of ethnic minorities that now made up more than a quarter of the population. The new regions and peoples, many of whom resented Romania's unfamiliar rule, brought about the state's determination to consolidate national unity, to create a national consciousness capable of maintaining its fragile new structure.

Over a glass of homemade *palinka*, peach brandy, the ethnic Hungarians in Romania will tell you that they arrived in the western Carpathians in the ninth century, to find only sheep and a smattering of Slavonic tribes. Romanians, the Hungarians assert, had fled south of the Danube and, although they later returned and came to form a majority of the population, the Hungarian Kingdom ruled over the territory until the Turks conquered it in 1526. Thereafter, Transylvania enjoyed various forms of autonomy under Ottoman and then Hungarian-administrated Habsburg rule from the seventeenth century until 1918. A short stroll around almost any Transylvanian city or town tells the story of its Habsburg legacy. The faded pastel colors of the Jugendstil architecture can be seen throughout the monarchy's former domain, from Croatia to Slovakia, sub-Carpathian Ukraine to northern Italy. The uniquely Romanian feature of most Transylvanian cities is Ceauşescu's barren rust-stained concrete highrises, many today only half-built eyesores, falling apart on muddy construction sites. During the late eighteenth and nineteenth centuries Transylvania boasted a rich cultural tradition, relative prosperity at the crossroads of trade routes, and a reputation for peaceful coexistence among its many peoples. Neither interwar Hungary nor ethnic Hungarians in Romania ever accepted the post-WWI loss of the region and, with Hitler's blessing, Hungary reoccupied northern Transylvania from 1940 to 1944. Finally, after Axis-allied Romania's quick switchover to the Allies' ranks in August 1944, Romania retook the Hungarian-occupied region with the Red Army at its side.

Ceauşescu and his hagiographers made certain that Romania's temporary WWII loss of Transylvania to Hungary left an indelible imprint on the collective Romanian consciousness. Propaganda continually reinforced the national obsession with unity and sovereignty that had plagued Romania since its inception. Whether during the interwar years, the communist era, or today, nationalists insist that Romania is a "unitary state"—a centralized Romanian state and not a federation of different regions and peoples. Their fears reflect the fact that Romania *is* a young, ethnically mixed, regionally disparate state, all factors which, in the twentieth century at least, make up a certain recipe for political instability. In his book, *Transylvania: An Ancient Romanian Land,* Lieu-

tenant-General Ilie Ceauşescu, "PhD," the President's brother and favorite pseudo-historian, mouths the official rhetoric that both Romanians and the Transylvanian minorities became accustomed to over the
years. Ceauşescu deems the region the "hearth of Romanian habita-
tion", whose "forced incorporation" into the Habsburg Empire was an
"historical accident . . . contrary to a long, natural evolution toward
Romanian political unity in the Carpatho-Danubian area." In the regime's standard "Romania-speak," found in any school book or newspaper, he writes:

> In today's Romania, dynamic and prosperous, held high in regard all over
> the world, a united people inhabiting a unitary territory stands before the
> contemporary world proud of its glorious historical traditions, ready at any
> moment to defend its fundamental assets: independence, sovereignty, ter-
> ritorial integrity, its belief in a more dignified and better way of life, in
> the communist ideal. The seventieth anniversary of the foundation of the
> unitary Romanian state [1988], celebrated by the Romanian people in an
> atmosphere of powerful enthusiasm, emphasizes the Romanian people's
> indestructible unity around the Communist Party, the vital center of the
> nation. Today, too, as throughout Romanian history, the idea of national
> unity is a catalyst for the whole people's will to be themselves, free, in-
> dependent, and sovereign in its ancestors' land.

The passage speaks volumes about the character of Romanian regime. Typically wooden, the aggrandizing rhetoric binds the nation to
the Communist Party in a single entity, making unity around the nation
inseparable from allegiance to the party. Ceauşescu portrays communism as nothing less than the highest and purest form of nationalism,
with the RCP the "vital center of the nation." At the very middle of
the concentric circles stands the President and Party General Secretary,
his brother Nicolae. Everything in Romania radiates outward from the
"Giant of the Carpathians": the party, the nation, and the people, in
that order of priority. The language also gives one a taste of the regime's
anti-Hungarian and anti-Russian sentiment as well. From what are Romanians "defending" the "independence, sovereignty and territorial
integrity" of their "ancestors' land," if not from Magyar irredentism
or Soviet domination? And, despite the religious imagery, the scien-

tifically socialist state calls upon "natural evolution" in the last instance
to underpin its claim to Transylvania.

In practice, Ceauşescu's homogenization measures in Transylvania
represented his final, paranoid drive to realize national unity through
the creation of an ethnically pure state. The Romanian communists
believed that the only certain way to be "masters in their own house,"
a phrase repeated *ad nauseam*, was to insure that no one else lived there
but Romanians. The campaign's first phase saw the restriction of cultural privileges, such as the elimination of bilingual signs in traditionally
Hungarian regions, cutbacks in minority language school instruction,
and the shortening and then final removal of Hungarian, Serbian, and
German language broadcasts. In an effort to dilute the Magyar concentration in Transylvania, the regime resettled Romanians en masse
from the eastern regions of Moldavia and Wallachia to Transylvania.
In the early 1980s, as Ceauşescu's popularity waned, his march against
the minorities took on ever more draconian features. As part of a new
"systemization" campaign, bulldozers razed traditional villages and
whole sections of historic cities. Concentrated in Transylvania and Bucharest, the goal of the drive was to destroy 13,000 villages a year until
the year 2000, moving their former inhabitants to new "agro-indus-
trial" living complexes. The state's tone toward the Hungarian minority, as well as Hungary, became ever more abusive. The regime
accused the minority of revanchist ambitions to return Transylvania to
Hungary, a conspiracy in which the other minorities were actively
collaborating. The press obediently fanned the flames of suspicion.
When the first demonstrations in December 1989 broke out in the
western city of Timişoara, the regime decried the unrest as the reactionary, separatist, imperialistic work of Hungary and its ethnic agents
in Romania. At that time, however, the demagoguery found not a tidbit
of sympathy.

BLOOD SPILLS IN TRANSYLVANIA

In the chaos of the revolution's aftermath, the provisional National
Salvation Front (NSF), at first a diverse transition body of reform com-

munists, democratic dissidents, and prominent intellectuals, including
many ethnic Hungarians, moved quickly to consolidate power across
the country. One of the Front's first moves was to propose constitutional
guarantees to protect individual as well as collective rights for ethnic
minorities, an impressive step by any account in southeastern Europe.
The minorities formed independent organizations and revived previously banned publications and broadcasts. The emboldened Hungarian
minority made far-reaching demands, such as the reestablishment of
the historic Hungarian Bolyai University in Cluj and the introduction
of mandatory bilingualism.

As much as the revolution had temporarily united the nationalities,
the minorities' move to assert their rights found little sympathy from
a majority suckled on Ceauşescu's propaganda. As the focal point of
the ethnic question in Ceauşescu's Romania, Transylvania was home
to an entire apparatus whose primary task had revolved around the
"management" of the ethnic minorities. The most numerous and feared
sections of the Securitate, for example, had been based in Transylvania.
Its officials and informers permeated the bureaucracy at every level. The
post-revolutionary realignment of political forces left the old apparatus
in a precarious spot, with its functionaries' privileges and futures hanging in balance. Immediately after the revolution, it was unclear what
direction the Front would eventually take and what would happen with
the remnants of the old system, from the village party leaders and local
police to the upper echelons of the army and Securitate units. A January
1990 decree that forbade the former nomenklatura from joining political parties exacerbated their sense of impotence and anxiety. It was
this scenario that gave birth to the extreme nationalist movement *Vatra
Românească*.

Upon taking power, the National Salvation Front integrated much
of the Securitate into the army, postponing a more final decision on its
ultimate fate for three months. In some cities, such as Cluj, plainclothes
Securitate officers occupied the same buildings as they had before, but
with a lower profile for the time being. In others, Ceauşescu's trusted
henchmen seemed, for the moment at least, to have mysteriously vanished. "The establishment of Vatra Românească as a nationalist cultural
association was a very clever, mafia-style solution for those people who

were banned from public political life, but who wanted to organize themselves," explains Smaranda Enache, a former dissident from Tîrgu-Mureş and today one of Romania's most respected democratic oppositionists. "The initial leadership, a handful of doctors, lawyers, and academics, represented only the tip of the iceberg. Behind these less compromised figureheads stood high-ranking army and Securitate officers, police, judges, diplomats, and so on, all of those involved in implementing Ceauşescu's homogenization policies in Tranyslvania. Their strategy was to convince public opinion that their institutions were indispensable to the country, to create a new legitimacy for themselves in order to regain their pre-revolution roles and privileges." The raw material of their plan was the fear and anxiety that they had already cultivated during the dictatorship. The instruments to manipulate those emotions, the communist regime's expansive, professional network of disinformation, was still firmly in their hands.

As early as January 1990, hostile reactions to the initiatives of the Hungarian minority began to surface in the press. The ethnic Hungarians, unhappy with the pace of reform, staged several demonstrations in February, which attracted as many as 40,000 persons in Tîrgu-Mureş. Romanians staged counterdemonstrations. In early February, Vatra Românească held its first known public meeting in Tîrgu-Mureş, voicing clear opposition to Hungarian demands for separate schools. In a mid-March interview with the Bucharest daily *România Liberă*, the Vatra's recently named President, Radu Ceontea, elaborated the new organization's rationale in familiar words:

> After almost a thousand years of foreign domination in Transylvania, it is difficult for the Hungarians to forget their behavior as rulers. These absurd claims [for minority rights] ... are designed to give them not only the rights that they had in the past, that they have now, and that they will have in the future—maintained in line with Romania's new democratic status—but also "special" rights that are not specific to minorities. ... Romania is not a multinational state but a national unitary state in which different percentages of minorities live. And no minority is permitted favors just because its ancestors were oppressors for centuries!"[1]

Ceontea, even more explicitly and aggressively than Ilie Ceauşescu, emphasizes the ethnic nature of the Romanian state, in which other nationalities live as "guests." The minorities, he says, will receive no more rights than those generous privileges that Ceauşescu had granted them. Ceontea magnanimously concedes to "maintain" those "rights" that existed under the dictatorship in "democratic" Romania. Any additional rights he considers "favors," which Romanians will withhold from the Hungarians as punishment for the legacy of Hungarian rule in Transylvania.

The simmering tempers of February came to a boil in early March, when ethnic Hungarian students and teachers in Tîrgu-Mureş launched peaceful strikes to protest the Bucharest government's postponement of measures to reopen a number of Hungarian schools. Vatra Româ-nească, making its presence felt for the first time, called for more counterdemonstrations. On March 19, several hundred Vatra supporters gathered in the Square of the Roses, chanting "Hungarians want to take back Transylvania!" and "Death to László Tökes!" (the ethnic Hungarian pastor from Timişoara whose arrest in mid-December 1989 sparked the first demonstrations of the revolution). The demonstrators then began randomly attacking Hungarian pedestrians and barging into the offices of the local administration. Before the hours-long rampage had climaxed, busloads of local Romanian peasants arrived on the scene, intoxicated and armed with axes and clubs. The peasants' later testimony revealed that they had been paid and armed by Vatra leaders, who had been working in tandem with the local mayors. As the police stood idly by, the mob stormed the HDUR office, trapping prominent Hungarian leaders in the attic.

Shocked by the events, the Hungarian community, and many Romanians as well, organized a nonviolent counterdemonstration of 20,000 in the main square the next day, demanding an investigation into the violence. At the march's fore was a yellow, red, and blue Romanian flag, a symbol of the minority's allegiance to the Romanian state. But by early afternoon, Romanian nationalist forces had amassed across the square. Police moved in to separate the crowd and ten light Soviet tanks pulled up in front of each group, effectively drawing the battlelines. As stones and bottles began to fly, about a hundred Roma, in their wide-brimmed black hats and colorful scarfs, marched in, singing in Hungarian, "Don't worry Magyars, the Gypsies are behind you!" Molotov cocktails, prepared from a nearby gas pump, ignited the tanks and abandoned automobiles before they were extinguished with hoses that both sides had been using as weapons. The fighting levelled off for a bit until fifteen buses carrying over 1000 peasants showed up again. "The peasants didn't wait for a minute but went straight at the Hungarians," said one observer. "They knew what to do. It was complete chaos by then, a full-scale battle." About an hour later, Hungarian reinforcements showed up in the form of 500 or so Székelys, a local ethnic Hungarian people with medieval roots as militant tribal warriors. The majority of the city people fled as the Székelys and the Roma, armed with knives and farm tools, clashed with the Romanian peasants into the early morning hours. By the time army units and police reinforcements intervened, the grotesque feudal melee had left several hundred people injured and over two dozen dead.

The army's belated intervention and the government's ambivalent response the following day betrayed the complex behind-the-scenes compromise that had been shaping up between the reform communist leadership, the Securitate, and nationalists. Prime Minister Petre Roman issued several mild statements about the "regrettable events," without even mentioning the lives lost or distinguishing between the Romanian agitators and the Hungarian victims. Rather, Roman calculatingly played the national card by giving credence to the ultra-nationalists' charges, legitimizing the Vatra and its backers as a potent political constituency. In the following weeks, local councils were restructured and Vatra representatives installed into top positions. On March 25, the Bucharest government adopted a decree creating a "new" secret information service. It explained that "the dismantling of the Securitate had seriously compromised Romania's security, and timely intelligence would have permitted the authorities to react more quickly to the violence in Tîrgu-Mureş." The Securitate was back, its plot a grand success.

LIFE WITH VATRA

Before the dust had even settled in Transylvania, the Romanian press from Timişoara to Bucharest was echoing the nationalists' charges that the Hungarians had attacked the Romanians first and that only Romanians had been killed. Wild rumors circulated about Hungarian troops and busloads of agent provocateurs from Hungary crossing the borders into Romania. The Transylvania violence, they maintained, was the work of Hungarian separatists, organized and financed from abroad. Even the most moderate of Romanians seemed to buy the line of people such as Vatra Vice President Ion Coja, a university professor, who insisted, that "the feeling of uncertainty among Transylvania's Romanians is particularly strong, because the Hungarian minority has put the lives of Romanians there in danger. This was a result of a lack of authority on the part of the government, the police, and the army. The HDUR is responsible for countless attacks on Romanians as well as for questioning Romania's possession of Transylvania."

In Hungary, the violence provoked cries of protest from across the political spectrum. At torchlit demonstrations in Budapest's spacious Hero's Square, the air crackled with the stuff of war. Hungarian politicians publicly raised the issue of redrawing the borders for the first time since WWII. Despite protests from other parties that the move would only exacerbate tensions, the nationalist Hungarian Democratic Forum (HDF) insisted upon sending a delegation to the trouble spot. The action-reaction spiral of nationalist tension sent the Vatra's membership skyrocketing to over four million in Transylvania, making it the largest political force in the region. In Hungary, the saber-rattling just days before the first round of the elections may well have tipped the final scales in favor of the HDF nationalists.

The call for a strong-arm police or military response to "Hungarian separatism" played effectively upon many Romanians' historical fears, as well as a psychological need for security and order. Above all, the nationalist demagoguery found resonance among two groups of Transylvanian Romanians. The first group consisted of those people in northwestern Transylvania who had experienced, or whose families had suffered, Hungarian occupation during the 1940s. The second, and larger group, included those Romanians who had resettled in Transylvania from eastern Romania during the Ceaușescu years. Paradoxically, those Romanians who had experienced Hungarian injustice most directly, as well as those who had no experience with the Hungarians at all, took the nationalist line most to heart.

Driving back from Tîrgu-Mureș along the winding, potholed road to Cluj, we picked up two Romanian hitchhikers, at odds between themselves over the recent violence. Dan, a twenty-six-year-old engineer from Cluj, wasn't sure what to make of the conflicting reports that he had heard about the battles. His grandmother was half Serbian, his wife an ethnic German, a Transylvania Saxon. He had always lived among Hungarians, had many Hungarian friends and, like most Transylvanians, understands a bit of each of the languages. "I've never had problems with the Magyars," he explains. "We were all in the same boat during the dictatorship. Things were bad for all of us. If I ever ran out of sugar or something, I could always just go next door and ask my Hungarians neighbors. It was no problem." But now, he knows, things are different. Neighbors, best friends, and co-workers aren't speaking to one another.

As the little automobile clatters noisily along the road, his mate, Liviu, explains that he sees things differently. He rejects the claim that that Romanians and Hungarians suffered equally, or, as the Hungarians would have it, that the minorities were persecuted more than the Romanians. Since Ceaușescu was a communist first and foremost, and not a Romanian, he had suppressed Romanian national culture as well. "The Hungarians always had relatives in Hungary to bring them coffee, medicine, and the like," says the handsome, young mechanic. Liviu's family moved to Transylvania from near Iași in Moldavia in the late 1970s, and although he knows many Hungarians, he's not particularly close to them. Under Habsburg rule, he says, the Hungarians owned everything and the Romanians did the dirty work. "Now businesses and factories will be privatized. Who in Romania has money to buy them?", he asks rhetorically. "Nobody. But the Hungarians can get the capital from Hungary. They can buy Transylvania right out from under our feet." In no time at all, he insists, Romanians could become "second-class citizens" again.

LITTLE NATION COMPLEX

As much as contemporary ultra-nationalism resembles Ceauşescu's national communism, nationalists reach much further into Romania's past for their historical bearings. In Romania today, nationalists have dredged up anti-Semitic, often neo-fascist, Romanian traditions that even Ceauşescu dared not call upon by name. During the communist era, the state and its cultural elite cautiously at first and then ever more brazenly exhumed conservative nationalist thinkers such as Romania's poet laureate Mihai Eminescu, philosopher-poet Lucian Blaga, and historian Nicolae Iorga. Banned completely after WWII, the cultural establishment saw to it that selected volumes of their works were gradually reprinted and their writings included in school curricula. The contemporary ultra-nationalists, however, as well as a good part of the so-called democratic opposition, have rehabilitated the pantheon of Romania's most conservative national prophets, from Eminescu to philosopher Nae Ionescu, the spiritual father of Romanian fascism. Any one of many newspapers or journals publish numerous poems or excepts from the array of Romania's pre-1945 national thinkers. The ethnic nationalism of their historical forefathers serves a number of important functions for Romania's post-communist nationalists. For one, by binding "Romanian blood" to Romanian land, the historical Weltanschauung rationalizes Romanian dominance in every sphere of cultural, political, and economic life. For the former nomenklatura, whose privileges had been based on their relationship to the state, the claim of ethnic superiority provides a new justification for the maintenance of their privileges.

Integral to Eastern European nationalism past and present is the inferiority complex of the small, young, long-suffering nation. Whatever its impassioned spokesmen may profess, the history of modern national identity throughout most of Eastern Europe dates back only to the late nineteenth century, a reality that they tend to compensate for with myths that locate national traditions as far back as the imagination stretches. As those same spokesmen rightly argue, if selectively, the history of their people is usually a tragic one, marred by invasions, occupations, world wars, betrayals, and economic and natural catastrophes. Although the national cultures often boast a rich heritage of poetry, literature, and music, their achievements have gone relatively unrecognized on the world stage, particularly in comparison to those of the Western European nations. In Romania, the interwar "rebirth" of the national identity expressed the small, misunderstood nation complex through an exaltation of all that was specifically Romanian in culture and tradition. One current of the movement possessed strongly isolationist, anti-Western, anti-cosmopolitan overtones, and viewed modernization and industrialization as foreign, Jewish-led processes that undermined Romanian tradition.

Ceauşescu may well have draped his stand against Moscow in a pro-Western cloak, and proceeded with industrialization at breakneck speed, but in his nationalist ideology he also harbored the same suspicions. He extolled all that was Romanian as superlative simply because it was Romanian. What was Romanian was beyond reproach, and the Romanian President above all. Ceauşescu set his court poets to work, for example, to show how one tradition or another in Romanian literature, philosophy, and other disciplines actually preceded and informed major Western cultural achievements. In one telling statement about literature, Ceauşescu said:

A not very becoming practice has developed, comrades, to look only at what is being done abroad, to resort for everything to imports. This betrays also a certain concept of considering everything that is foreign to be better, a certain prostration before what is foreign, and especially before [the West]. Time has come for [resorting first] to [our] own forces and only afterwards to appeal to import. There are books printed in tens of thousands of copies and which make an apology of the bourgeois way of life, while good Romanian books cannot be printed because of lack of paper.[2]

The very tone—humble, patient, self-pitying and misunderstood—is typical of almost all East European nationalisms. The poor Romanians, the tone suggests, are simply asking for what they deserve, what history and fate have wrongly denied them. The Romanians must therefore stand up for themselves, for their own culture, their own values and traditions, rather than allow some foreign power to dictate their destiny.

That which is foreign, which is other, the logic implicitly continues, is out to destroy Romanian identity and culture.

In the context of a bloc-divided Europe, Ceauşescu's anti-Western polemics hardly stood out as extraordinary. The same anti-Western, isolationist sentiment, however, reiterated by Ceauşescu's same court poets in post–Cold War Europe has entirely different implications. Behind the ultra-nationalists' critique of "Western cultural imperialism" lurks a rejection of the democratic values and principles that are meant to underpin a Europe united from the Atlantic to the Urals. In terms somewhat mild for his ilk, the Vatra's Coja explained in a 1990 interview:

> When you ask me why Romanians must be nationalistic, I would answer that it is necessary in the face of the idea of a united Europe, the notion of an internationalized world. Before long it will come to a dilution of the individual national cultures and identities. There is already an Anglo-Saxon cultural model . . . that has taken hold among our youth and threatens to destroy the national identities of individual peoples. It is from this point of view that Vatra Românească tries to expose the elements that threaten to destroy the Romanian identity.

The gist of Coja's criticism of "internationalism" is just about identical to that heard in nationalist circles from Paris to Moscow. A standard, homogeneous "Euro-culture," they maintain, threatens to water down all that is unique and specific about their own national cultures. And like the arguments of the National Front in France or the Pamyat parties in Russia, Coja's defense of national values against the encroachment of Western ideas and life-styles is simultaneously a rejection of a united Europe. By retreating into "Romanianism," the nationalists reject the democratic assumptions of liberal political culture. The Romanian ultra-nationalists pander to the same sentiment to rally opposition against market reforms, European integration, foreign investment, the United Nations, and democratic opposition parties. Their misgivings about "Europe" and the West have less to do with degenerate American pop culture, as Coja implies, than they do, for example, with provisions for the guarantee of individual and minority rights. The nationalists opt for the priority of an undefined "national culture," accountable only to their own interpretation of Romanian tradition. In effect, nationalists can fill their ambiguous notion of "national tradition" with whatever suits them best. It provides them, for example, with a ready alibi against "foreign pressure" to respect democratic principles. "We'll do it our way," they respond. It means that in the name of Romanian or French or German tradition, nationalists can justify whatever they like, so long as they link it to their national history.

ROMANIA'S GENERAL ION ANTONESCU

The nationalism that first appeared in Transylvania spread like fire through the rest of the country, showing once again that ultra-nationalist elements need not occupy the official seats of power in order to impact official policy and public opinion. The Front's promises of minority rights faded quickly and its leadership, which mass defections had pared down to its reform communist core, showed itself ready and willing to parrot the Vatra's jingoism. Prime Minister Petre Roman, the grandson of a rabbi and son of a Spanish mother, seemed particularly eager to court the nationalists. In the future, the Front would team up with the Vatra's political arm, the Party of Romanian National Unity (PRNU), as a regular coalition partner. The Front, however, wasn't alone. The opposition "historical parties"—the National Liberal Party and the National Peasants Party—also lacked the courage to abstain from the nationalist chorus. With the floodgates of nationalism open, the basic tenets of the Vatra Românească ideology soon came to dominate the thinking across virtually the entire Romanian political spectrum.

No example better illustrates the worrying breadth of the nationalist consensus in Romania than the reappraisal of Romania's 1940–44 Axis-allied military dictator, Marshal Ion Antonescu. During the Ceauşescu years, particularly in the 1980s, the state noticeably softened its line on the wartime leader, perhaps, some observers speculated, with an eye toward his eventual rehabilitation. But today in postrevolution Romania, hardly a voice of dissent is to be heard above the roar of good words for "Romania's Marshal."

Politicians and the press alike herald Antonescu as a "great Romanian patriot" for his three year campaign against the Red Army on the Eastern Front. Under Antonescu's command, German-allied Romanian troops recaptured Bessarabia in 1941 and continued on across the Ukraine all the way to the Bug. The fiftieth anniversary of the Romanian army's attack on the Soviet Union on June 22, 1991, saw the Romanian press flooded with unrestrained praise for the Marshal and his noble campaign. The government-friendly daily *Adevărul* paid typical tribute: "A disgraceful lie ... has soiled this date for the last forty-five years, as well as the 1156 days leading up to August 23, 1944 [the day Antonescu fell from power and Romania switched over to the side of the Allies]. Communist totalitarianism shrouded this period in diverse labels and tendentious value judgments, with the intention of incriminating the entire Romanian people." *Adevărul* was just one of many publications to publish or quote the text of the General's speech that opened the eastern front:

> From the very beginning of my governance, from the very beginning of our national struggle, I have promised to lead you toward that victory which will erase the stain of shame from the annals of our people, banish the shadow of humiliation from your brow, and remove its burden from your shoulders. Now is the hour that the holiest of struggles begins—the fight for our ancestral rights, for our Church, the fight for the eternal hearths and altars of Romania. Soldiers, I order you to cross the Prut! Destroy the enemy to the East and to the North! Free your brothers languishing under the crimson yoke of Bolshevism! Unite the ancestral soil of Bessarabia with the body of the homeland, join the princely forests of Bukovina to your fields and meadows. Soldiers! Today follow the triumphal path of Ştefan the Great to demand back what your forefathers had struggled for! Forward! Be proud that the centuries have placed you here to guard justice and defend Christendom. Be worthy of your Romanian past!

On June 1, 1991, the forty-fifth anniversary of Antonescu's execution, only the representatives of the party of the Hungarian minority remained in their seats during the minute of silence parliament observed for Romania's "greatest anti-communist," the man who re-liberated eastern Bessarabia. "Despite the numerous efforts to erase this great patriot from our memory," wrote the liberal opposition daily *România*

Liberă (Free Romania) one year before on that date, "his name, so closely bound with the unification of Greater Romania in 1918 and then the desperate struggle for national unity and integrity between 1941 and 1945, was never forgotten. . . . After forty-four years, history has at last allowed the Romanians to shed a tear and light a candle for Ion Antonescu."[3]

The gush of praise for Antonescu neglects the people who really shed tears during the pogroms, massacres, and deportations of the Marshal's rule. Although Antonescu was primarily a military man and not an ideologically committed fascist, his short partnership in power with the fanatically fascist Legion of Archangel Michael, also known as the Iron Guard, hardly betrayed his innermost convictions. The Marshal's four year rule sent over 300,000 of Romania's nearly 800,000 Jews and tens of thousands of Romas to their deaths, mostly in forced labor camps. In *Eichmann in Jerusalem* Hannah Arendt describes how, "In Romania even the SS were taken aback, and occasionally frightened by the horrors of old-fashioned, spontaneous pogroms on a gigantic scale; they often intervened to save Jews from sheer butchery, so that the killing could be done in what, according to them, was a civilized way." Even before Romania joined forces with Hitler, Antonescu stripped all but a handful of Romania's Jews of their citizenship and introduced, according to Arendt, "anti-Jewish legislation that was the severest in Europe, Germany not excluded. . . . Hitler himself was aware that Germany was being outdone by Romania, and he complained to Goebbels in August, 1941, a few weeks after he had given orders for the Final Solution, that 'a man like Antonescu proceeds in these matters in a far more radical fashion than we have done up to the present.' "[4]

In Romania today, the extent of the Holocaust's denial is virtually unparalleled among the former Axis allies. Even self-acclaimed democrats play down Romanian collaboration with Hitler's Germany as the ultimately necessary compromise of a small nation wedged between the European superpowers, the closest being the Soviet Union. "I know what Hannah Arendt wrote," said the President of the National Liberal Party Radu Câmpeanu in one interview, "And it's a shameful lie!" Democrats, reform communists, and nationalists alike contend that Antonescu's policies actually saved the lives of Jews. Although some of the General's later policies did spare Jewish lives, the prevailing historical cover-up circumvents any Romanian responsibility at all for the horrors perpetrated in the name of the Romanian nation, as well as the possibility that similar propensities still survive in Romania. The early consent of the National Peasant Party and the National Liberal Party, leading members of the "democratic opposition" at the time, to the rehabilitation says plenty about the shallowness of Romanian democracy.

Perhaps even more distressing has been the muted reaction of Romania's democratic intellectuals. At the Bucharest offices of the Group for Social Dialogue (GSD), a forum of the country's top critical thinkers, GSD Vice President and leading figure in the Civic Alliance movement, Gabriel Andreescu, looks down at his feet at the mention of the Antonescu debate. No, he, at least, doesn't put Antonescu on the pedestal of a national hero. "But his rule had both positive and negative sides," says Andreescu, steering away from a potentially controversial critique, "which we couldn't look at objectively during the Ceauşescu era. Some kind of reevaluation is necessary." Some of Andreescu's colleagues at the GSD periodical *22* are even less inclined to swim against the tide. "I was taken aback to learn that Romania is being held responsible for the liquidation of more than 400,000 Jews during the war," wrote one well-known opposition journalist. In the same issue the editor of *22* wrote, "The presentation of Romania as a land in which the extreme right flourishes unchecked, and other such charges, is deeply unpatriotic."[5]

The staunchest opposition against the moves toward an official rehabilitation of Antonescu have come from the leaderships of the Hungarian and Jewish minorities. Bucharest's chief rabbi Moses Rosen maintains that the Antonescu reappraisal is an insult to Romania's Jews as well as to the Romanian people themselves. "It's almost impossible for us to believe that the 300,000 Jewish victims of the Holocaust are not even being acknowledged," said Rosen in a 1991 interview.[6] He argued that there were many instances of Romanian people sheltering and saving the lives of Jews during the wartime terror. "Now," explained Rosen, "extremists appear, in my opinion neo-fascists, and identify the whole Romanian population with Antonescu. What a moral catastrophe! Hitler had other allies such as Horthy in Hungary or Petain in France, but nobody has come up with the idea to identify France with Petain." According to Rosen, the simultaneous reappraisal of Antonescu and his emergence as the symbol of the extreme right could have long-term consequences for Romania. "What is worrying is that no one today will present themselves as an anti-fascist. This enables the far right to agitate unhindered. Those who fight against communism," said Rosen, "can not forget the other evil—fascism."

ROMÂNIA MARE'S NOSTALGIA

Though somewhat slower off the block than Vatra Românească, ultra-nationalist forces outside of Transylvania coalesced soon after with an agenda of their own. The Bucharest-based *România Mare* (Greater Romania) Party, centers around a sixteen-page weekly by that name, which espouses chauvinism and xenophobia with few equals in all of post-communist Eastern Europe. Whereas Vatra Românească emerged as a regional force in an ethnically mixed and historically disputed area, *România Mare* set about agitating similar phobias across all of Romania. In contrast to Transylvania, the relatively homogeneous regions of eastern Moldavia and southern Wallachia neither know the conflicts of living with a large ethnic minority, nor have they any positive experience of interethnic coexistence. With the channels of propaganda already in place, the extremists' immediate success in whipping up ethnic suspicions where they had no rational basis was startling. Four months after *România Mare* first hit the newsstands in June 1990, its circulation jumped to 600,000, the largest of all of the Romanian weeklies. In May 1991, the publication spawned its own party, complete with women and youth sections.

Were one to take *România Mare's* paranoid scenario of Romania's situation seriously, a police state would be the logical solution. The weekly portrays a Romania on the brink of collapse, threatened by enemies from all sides. Its crude, though often imaginative, conspiracy theories call the people to arms against every possible kind of anti-Romanian plot, be it Hungarian revanchism, Roma anarchism, CIA sabotage, or international-Jewish financial domination, to name just a few of their favorites. No minority, regardless of its size, is spared derision. The first line of attack is usually directed against the "fascist, irredentist, Asiatic-Mongolian" Hungarian minority and its Israel-aligned Horthyist commanders in Budapest, the Hungarian government. "Do you know what we will do when we come to power?" *România Mare* asks its readers. "We will peel the skin off the Hungarian fascists and kick their asses over the border until they arrive in their stall, called Hungary."[7] Among the paper's routine subjects of ridicule is the Hungarian Pastor László Tökes, "the Romanian peoples' enemy No. 1." The weekly regularly castigates Tökes as a member of the Hungarian secret service, not to mention a machine-gun-toting terrorist, a fierce Romanian hater, a notorious rapist, and a homosexual. The very same taunts are interchangeably turned against rabbi Rosen, as well as a number of democratic intellectuals also on the radicals' "top-ten list of national traitors." A standard part of *România Mare* is its crass jokes: "Who is an anti-Semite?," runs one typical jibe. "Someone who hates Jews more than necessary."[8] The Soviet Union's dismemberment has made the Russian and Ukrainian minorities in the former Soviet Republic of Moldavia, roughly the territory of Romanian Bessarabia before its 1940 annexation, lively new targets. The question of Moldavia's reunification with Romania has brought with it ethnic violence in the eastern region of Transnistria heavily populated by Russians. "The bells toll for our brothers across the Prut," warns *România Mare*, referring to the ethnic Romanian majority in Moldavia. "The historical banditry of the Russian cossacks is raising its ugly head once again. The danger looms, innocent blood is flowing, Romanians come to the aid of your brothers! Nations across the world, dam the bloody tide of Slavs into civilized Europe!"[9]

The party's ringleaders resemble those behind Vatra Românească, and, periodically, ally themselves with their Transylvanian counterparts. The *România Mare* clique, however, comes from even higher and more compromised positions within the Ceauşescu hierarchy, not least from the very top echelons of the Securitate and the army. According to democrat Smaranda Enache, the power base of Vatra Românească encompasses a much broader strata of the old system than does that of the *România Mare* leadership. "Vatra Românească includes many members of the administrative and technocratic elite who not only want to maintain their former privileges, but also to extend them into the future. They have gradually shown themselves open, for example, to political compromise, to free market initiatives, and even cooperation with Hungarians, so long as they benefit from it. The *România Mare* group, on the other hand, comes from a somewhat different strata—they were the most conservative representatives of Ceauşescu's instruments of repression. If Vatra represents the corpus of the old system in Transylvania, then *România Mare* represents its head in Bucharest. Repression was their raison d'être and it remains the only profession that they know."

A cursory look at the curriculum vitae of *România Mare's* leadership attests to a heinous array of forces at work. The two names brandished in bold letters across *România Mare's* masthead—Eugen Barbu, Director, and Corneliu Vadim Tudor, Editor-in-Chief—figured among Ceauşescu's most radical nationalist hagiographers. Beneath them in the party hierarchy stand Mircea Muşat and Radu Teodoru, two infamous communist hacks who have made come backs as the party's vice presidents. Under the dictatorship, Muşat's claim to fame was as the main censor in the field of history and a vocal proponent of the nationalist line. The retired Air Force colonel Teodoru is widely suspected of having been a high-ranking Securitate officer. The army is also highly placed in the party, personified by the executive secretary, retired lieutenant general Teodor Paraschiv. Paraschiv served in the Romanian Army's General Staff and as a high-ranking officer on the staff of the army contingent in Transylvania.[10] The revamped Old Guard reveals the continuity of its allegiances nowhere more clearly than in its outcry over the handful of trials against the top-ranking Securitate and military brass accused of having ordered their units to fire on the people during the December revolution. The Romanian revolution, claim the ultra-nationalists, was a foreign, primarily Hungarian-inspired plot against the Romanian nation, in which foreign agents spilled innocent Romanian blood.

The figures of Barbu and Tudor are hardly new to the fray of Romanian politics. In the communist cultural weekly *Săptămîna* (The

Week), Ceauşescu's acolytes mixed their unbounded "love for the communist party" with a virile ultra-nationalism unique in postwar Romania. The propagandists pushed the outermost limits of national extremism in a communist state, sometimes venturing onto territory that even forced Ceauşescu to step in and draw the line. A 1980 scandal over an anti-Semitic *Săptămîna* editorial thrust its editor-in-chief Barbu into the spotlight a second time within two years.[11] In early 1979, Barbu had been exposed for literary plagiarism, undermining his reelection to the Central Committee. In the unsigned *Săptămîna* piece, it was Tudor's pen that vilified those Romanian intellectuals who had abandoned the Romanian state and the communist party. Such traitors, he wrote, are but "teachers of the democratic tarantella clad in stinking mantles, Herod's strangers to the interests of this nation . . . who occasionally succeed in making one dizzy with their display of trafficker patriotism. We have no need for lazy prophets, for Judas who lack the Romanian dimension of self-sacrifice in their easily purchasable blood." The blatant anti-Semitism is particularly striking in the context of Ceauşescu's Romania, where little simply "slipped" through the censors' hands. The international outcry over the editorial forced Ceauşescu to publicly condemn anti-Semitism for the first time ever, and *Săptămîna* to print a vague apology. But neither the state nor the Writers Union took action against Barbu or Tudor. *Săptămîna* and like-minded periodicals continued publishing material along the same lines.

Still today, Barbu, Tudor, and their Old Guard allies remain wedded to the ideals of dictatorship. The chaos of the moment, they plead, can only be halted through the reimposition of military rule. Although Antonescu is now the recipient of their thickest laurels, the *România Mare* ideology combines its fascistic nationalism with an unabashed nostalgia for the good old days of Ceauşescu communism. The *România Mare* Party defines itself as "center-left" and panders to a growing public sympathy for the security and order of the communist regime. The appeal to the Ceauşescu era is strongest in its economic program, which holds "liberal" market policies to blame for the economy's post-revolution tailspin. There the extremists have plenty with which to agitate. From 1989 to mid-1993, unemployment jumped to over eleven percent. While shop windows displayed food products only fantasized about during the infamous "Ceauşescu winters", price liberalization caused food prices to rise 1,360 percent between 1990 and 1993. Gross domestic product and industrial output plummeted, the latter falling by over a fifth in 1991 and 1992, and with no end in sight. In response, the *România Mare* Party program promises a return to full employment and social security. One typical *România Mare* article asks, "My God, brother, why did you kill Ceauşescu?" The same issue contains the following homage to the executed leader in classic national communist rhetoric:

> Why do we tremble before the Hungarians? Why don't we simply expel all of the Hungarian extremists and Gypsy thieves? Or are we so scared of the West? Even if we were, we wouldn't be so naive as not to see what the West wants to do with our country. It wants to destroy it, to ruin it, to reduce us to slaves and in no way bless us with its civilization. Ceauşescu knew well what the West had up its sleeve: Hungary was to be awarded western Romania and Bulgaria the South. Our existence as a state was to be terminated. There were always those who disapproved of socialism because it recorded ever greater successes and we didn't have to beg for foreign aid, even though we had to tighten our belts—we did it with our heads held high. I can only say that no lord, no king, nor any government ever did more for the Romanian people than the socialist government. Millions of apartments were built. In the cities, housing complexes blossomed, as well as wonderfully furnished schools, and factories in which there was always enough work. Romanian society is now splitting into two antagonistic classes—poor and rich, slaves and slave-owners. May the *România Mare* Party mobilize all Romanians to free this land from the Western-financed Hungarian traitors, the heathen bootlickers, who we should not tolerate on our ancestral soil.[12]

The passage illustrates just how reactionary opposition to the post-communist governments' market transitions can look. And the hostile anti-Western sentiment strikes a sensitive nerve among many in a climate of economic crisis and insecurity. In Romania, a party so blatantly neo-fascistic as *România Mare* is generally considered extreme left. With their pseudo-leftist jargon, the posturing of groups like *România Mare* as the defenders of social justice tends to fill the gap that a progressive left alternative to the market consensus might occupy, were such organized forces to exist in Romania. *România Mare*, for example, has been just about the only political force to protest the IMF-advocated economic policies, an issue which would occupy a place on the agenda of most Western leftists. The twisted and tangled definitions of right and left can only be understood in terms of the nature of Ceauşescu's national communism, and the relationship of today's political forces to that ideology. Perhaps one of the best examples is the close ally that *România Mare* found in the successor to the Romanian Communist Party, the Socialist Labor Party (SLP). The two parties, one neo-fascist, the other neo-Stalinist, would occupy the polar ends of most political spectrums in the West—that is, if their militant breeds had counterparts in Western Europe. The two parties, however, represent different strains from within the hard-line wings of the old apparatus, whether from the RCP, the army, or the Securitate. The common heritage and interests enable *România Mare's* staff writers to contribute to *Socialistul*, and vice versa.

The SLP is just one of *România Mare's* on-again, off-again allies in the wild landscape of the Romanian ultra-right. A jungle of ultra-nationalist periodicals clogs every newsstand in Romania. Weeklies such as *Europa, Politica, Phoenix, Naţiunea, Expres,* and *Renaşterea Bănăţeană*, just to name a few, espouse the *România Mare* line in varying degrees of refinement, depending upon the political interests of its backers. Despite frequent bitter exchanges, each accusing the other of fascist sympathies, the rival factions have tended to have a single effect in influencing Romanian opinion and discourse. They succeeded in thrusting their ultra-nationalist opinions into the public forum, forcing more moderate parties and politicians to respond. Precisely this impact upon public debate appeared to be the first priority of the ultra-nationalists during 1990 and 1991.

That aim also seemed to be shared by their monied backers from the Romanian exile. Right-wing Romanian, sometimes former Iron Guard, exiles in the U.S., Canada, Germany or elsewhere, contribute regularly to the ultra-nationalist press, often with views even more fascistic than those of the Romanian editorial boards. By far the most influential of all of the emigre provocateurs is the former Iron Guardist and Ceauşescu-patron Iosif Constantin Drăgan. Having amassed a fortune in Italian exile, the elderly entrepreneur returned to Romania in 1990 to encourage ultra-nationalist currents, a mission he pursued with equal vigor during the Ceauşescu dictatorship. The radical multimillionaire finances the gamut of ultra-right publications through his publishing trust Europa Nova. In 1990 he was elected the Honorary President of Vatra Românească. Bookstore windows throughout Bucharest display his historical opus, *Antonescu, the Marshal of Romania and the War of Unification.*

Until the September 1992 elections, *România Mare* and its cohorts agitated primarily through their periodicals. Many observers heralded the elections as a victory for the opposition democrats in the Democratic Convention, a coalition of democratic parties opposed to both the fractured NSF and the ultra-nationalist parties. Although President Ion Iliescu won another term at the country's top post and his party topped the polls, the Democratic Convention emerged as their chief rivals.

The first serious national electoral debut of the ultra-nationalists, however, overshadowed the democrats' gains. With a combined fifteen percent of the vote, the election catapulted the nationalist extremists from their editorial offices into parliament, establishing them as one of the major electoral power blocs in Romanian politics. The PRNU, the România Mare Party and the SLP all cleared the three percent hurdle necessary for parliamentary representation, with eight, four, and three percent of the vote respectively. The PRNU's presidential candidate, Gheorghe Funar, ran third behind Iliescu and the Democratic Convention candidate with eleven percent of the popular vote. Although on their own the radical parties' single digit showings may look meager, the PRNU has quadrupled its support since 1990 and won a number of seats outside Transylvania. And, in a fragmented parliament, the trio wields significant power. In fact, in the wake of the elections, a governing coalition between Iliescu's Front and the nationalist-communist bloc seemed like one of the president's few viable alternatives. Some observers speculated that only the fear of Western reprisals prevented Iliescu's party from overtly joining forces with the ultra-right, which agreed to support the minority government. Whatever the case, the rightist radicals now not only have a voice on the national political stage, but are also key players in Romanian politics. One of the *România*

Mare Party's first proposals to parliament was to officially ban the party of the Hungarian minority.

THE BOYS OF THE ARCHANGEL

The ultra-nationalists formerly loyal to the Ceauşescu regime constitute by far the country's largest and most dangerous ultra-right force. Yet, other, in some ways even darker stripes of radicalism have also surfaced in Romania. Like the *Szent Korona* radicals in Hungary or the Confederation for an Independent Poland, its proponents tend to be the hardcore, ideologically committed anti-communists, amongst them those who suffered the communist regime's persecution. In Romania, this far right tendency first appeared in the ranks of the Romanian Student League, the organization at the forefront of the postrevolution democracy movement. In Spring 1990, before the democratic opposition to the ruling Front had organized, the Student League and its charismatic, bearded twenty-eight-year-old leader Marian Munteanu rallied opposition around demands for democratic reform and a new ethic of moral integrity in political life. But even in its earliest days, the first phase of its radical right-wing development was plain to see in some of the League's top leadership.

In April 1990, a month before the first elections, the League was at the height of its popularity. The thousands of young anti-communist demonstrators in Bucharest's central University Square looked to Munteanu and the League for leadership and inspiration. The NSF, maintained the young revolutionaries, was nothing but a cosmetically revamped holdover of the dictatorship, whose autocratic leanings had become increasingly transparent.

The spirit in the dirty, congested "communist-free zone" of University Square was one of hope, civility, and determination. Ragged, sunburned students played guitars and wrote songs, still basking in their newly won liberty and a lingering illusion of power. In afternoon marches through the city streets, the protestors' witty jingles echoed playfully off Ceauşescu's monstrous high rises. A month after the Tîrgu-Mureş events, the demonstrators had also added "Transylvania and Bessarabia are Romanian lands!" to their repertoire of chants. In the shade of his makeshift tent, Heinz, a twenty-one-year-old Transylvania Saxon, explained that a distinctly nationalist tone had grown louder in the square over the past few weeks. But the nationalism among the protesters, he said, had fortunately not reached the pitch of that within the Student League itself. He handed me a copy of the League's newspaper *Glasul* (The Mirror) opened to a cartoon that featured a Hungarian horseman leading a charge toward Bessarabia. The accompanying articles heaped insults upon the Hungarian minority in terms as primitive as those of the Vatra. "One hears this kind of thing particularly from the League's leadership, and Munteanu is no exception," explained Heinz. "That's why most students with minority backgrounds have quit the League."

The *Glasul* issue took me to the publication's third-story editorial office across from the technical university, and there to its editor-in-chief, Sorin Drăgan. Atop one desk, an old fan strains to circulate air in the stuffy room. A single typewriter clatters periodically from behind the thin wall. Drăgan, a twenty-two-year-old technical student, roused himself from a cot in the corner. Working day and night, he apologizes, he tends just to catnap when time permits. In a white T-shirt and dark jeans, his short, jet black hair ruffled from sleep, Drăgan resembles any of the thousands of Romanian students in the capital. Yes, he explains in suspiciously meticulous English, the recent Transylvania pieces were his doing. "Today, all other issues fade in comparison to the national issue," he says, the first prerequisite of which is ousting the NSF from power. "Communism was an absurd, nihilating force, which erased the idea of the nation from the consciousness of the Romanian people," says the serious young man. "Any real opposition today has to be nationalist, that is, thoroughly anti-communist and armed if necessary. The people have suffered too much. We can't have any scruples."

At first, Drăgan's nationalist line barely sets it apart from most of the reigning chorus. Most of the opposition parties would concur with Drăgan's general thoughts about the Front, about reunification with Bessarabia or about the dangers of Hungarian nationalism. But Drăgan's terminology and the values he accents raise the eyebrows of anyone familiar with philosophy of the interwar Romanian fascist movement.

Drăgan, for example, lays particular stress on the centrality of religion, namely Romanian Orthodoxy, to Romanian nationalism. A tinge of messianism colors his talk of Romania's tragic "search for destiny." A new, well-equipped, well-trained army, he says, "should be a normal part of our lives." His critique of Ceauşescu's industrialization policies emphasizes their devastating effect on "spirituality of the Romanian *Volk*," the centuries-long bearer of which has been the traditional peasantry and the villages. A romantic notion of the good fight permeates his vision, which he pledges to "carry on underground, if necessary."

The young journalist's articulate presentation of the principles of the Legion of the Archangel Michael betray his well-informed grasp of the violent fascist movement, particularly its early stage, which also sprouted from the soil of student politics. He admits that he has read the works of the fascist philosopher Ionescu, who he refers to as a "fine proponent of Romanian national values." "All Romanian nationalist movements have been based upon the general ideals of the Iron Guard," he explains. In its later stage, he concedes, one, less intellectual element of the Legionary movement took that vision to an extreme. Yet, given the circumstances at the time, Drăgan feels that he can neither condemn nor condone those acts. "It's said that Gypsies and Jews were killed. I'm not so sure. The movement was positive in principle, even if its ideals culminated in certain excesses," he says. Since nationalist movements have been the most vigorously anti-communist of the century, the communists branded all right-wing or even conservative opposition as "legionnaire," explains Drăgan. "Personally, I would be flattered to be called a legionnaire. It denotes the highest enemy of communism. If I had to chose between communism and Hitlerism, well, I would avoid communism. Hitler, at least, had the decency to speak directly, and not with cheeky lies."

The tradition that Drăgan recalls from the darkest pages of Romanian history is one that even the *România Mare* extremists keep at arm's length. Although the apparatus ultra-nationalists regularly employ Guardist language and subscribe to many of the movement's fascist principles, theirs is first and foremost a politics of power, ideology the means of its preservation. The result is more akin to the principles of the military-man Antonescu or even those of their late mentor Ceauşescu than it is to the mystical, reactionary romanticism of the Legion's interwar leader Corneliu Zelea Codreanu. In the 1920s and '30s, Codreanu's legionnaires wove a mystical religious fanaticism into their version of Romanian nationalism, setting themselves on a messianic mission in the name of their patron saint, the warrior angel Michael. The youthful movement's idealist ethic of purity and self-sacrifice, its cultist vision of the true and the divine, wouldn't even have occurred to Ceauşescu's former cronies. During the postwar years, the state wiped out the remnants of the Iron Guard as such. (In doing so it conveniently killed two birds with one stone. The smallest of all of the communist parties in Eastern Europe, the RCP freely opened its doors to thousands of legionnaires, boosting its membership while simultaneously taking care of the problem of the Guard.) Others rotted away in jails until their deaths. Abroad, Guardist cliques reestablished themselves in exile, publishing newspapers in Great Britain, Canada, and the U.S. Not until the 1989 revolution did the movement reemerge in Romania—and when it did it came from the halls of the universities—just as it had in the 1920s.

The Student League's hour of glory ended as abruptly as it had begun. On June 18, 1990, just weeks after the NSF's landslide election triumph, the government ordered in truckloads of miners from the nearby Jiu Valley to clear University Square. With pick handles as clubs, the coal-blackened miners mercilessly beat the demonstrators and ransacked the opposition groups' offices. Drăgan, severely injured, fled to Budapest and then on to Vienna, where he applied for political asylum. The miners nearly beat Munteanu to death, landing him in an intensive care unit for several months. Upon his recovery, Munteanu briefly joined forces with the newly founded democracy movement Civic Alliance. But before long it became clear that his nationalist convictions were stronger than the new opposition could tolerate. After his graduation from the university, Munteanu went on to found the Movement for Romania, an ultra-nationalist, Christian fundamentalist organization with a close affinity to the interwar legionary movement.

Although publicly Munteanu rejects the title of legionnaire, observers from the democratic opposition were not the only voices to immediately note parallels between the two movements. In Timişoara, the Iron Guardist monthly *Gazeta de Vest* (Western Gazette) is one of the several groups who openly claim the legionary mantle for itself, and it hails none other than Munteanu as the movement's new leader. The March 1992 *Gazeta de Vest* sports a Munteanu quote on its masthead: "What will happen if the disaster in progress continues for the next ten years? We will stand before a depopulated country of broken and drained people. This will be the consequence of the present anti-Romanian and anti-national policies." The fascist tabloid calls for Codreanu's rehabilitation, as well as that of Timişoara native Horia Sima, the Iron Guard's leader after Codreanu's 1938 murder. *Gazeta de Vest* also serialized the infamous twenty-four-part "Protocols of the Elders of Zion," a turn-of-the-century forgery that purports to expose the contents of a secret meeting of world Jewry in which the "Elders of Zion" plot to foment war, disease, and economic collapse as the first stage in a bid to rule the world. The March issue greets Munteanu's Movement for Romania as a legal party dedicated to "the belief in Jesus and the defense of the Romanian nation. This movement carries forth the historical ethic of martyrdom, of serving God and the nation, omnipotence and brotherly love."

Munteanu's movement belongs to a shadowy underworld of neofascist subculture in Romania similar to that of the neo-Nazi groups in Germany. The student leader says that the major difference between the Movement for Romania and the pre-1938 Legion is that his organization is "democratic" and spurns violence. (Other explicitly Guardist parties, composed mostly of elderly former Legion members, say that the Munteanu group does not deserve the title of the Legion for exactly this reason.) But like the interwar movement, Munteanu's group is rigidly hierarchical, fundamentalist, mystical, and ritualistic. Its members, who wear black shirts with the movement's insignia on their sleeves, are sworn to secrecy and loyalty. Should they disobey an order or betray the movement in any way, they are automatically expelled. All members are required to have a thorough knowledge of Codreanu's works and the legionary interpretation of Romanian history. The group's meetings begin with prayers said beneath a portrait of the original Iron Guard leader. Observers estimate the movement to have a following of several hundred members, mostly (male) students and frustrated youth, with clusters of support in the university cities of Bucharest, Cluj, Iaşi, and Timişoara. Whether so radical and quirky a movement could gain broader support is unclear. Munteanu remains a popular, compelling figure, who could well attract a certain following among young people looking for a sense of belonging and a radical outlet for protest.

ROMA IN THE CROSSFIRE

Romania's roughly 2.5 million Roma have been caught in the crossfire between the nationalities, on the one hand, and social tension emanating from the country's economic disintegration, on the other. The country's largest minority, more than ten percent of the population, has had to pay for post-totalitarian freedom as no other people in Romania. Although the ultra-right has led the charge against those they deem their genetic inferiors, hatred and wrath against the Roma comes from all segments of society and from across the political spectrum. In the two years that followed the revolution, more than seventeen instances of mob violence left at least five Roma dead and unknown hundreds injured. For the most part, police stand by as citizens burn down Roma villages or attack Roma families. The hostility combined with mass unemployment, grinding poverty, and one of the lowest standards of living in Eastern Europe, has prompted thousands of Romanian Roma to flee their homes, even to Germany where Skinheads await them with molotov cocktails. In a putrid little Roma ghetto outside of Cluj-Napoca, one women, pregnant and with three dirty, sickly children around her skirt, summed up the feelings of many Roma: "It was much better for us under Ceauşescu. Then we were all equal. Now we're third-class citizens. The Romanians are first, the Hungarians second, and we are at the very bottom."

After the change of powers, it didn't take long for the Roma to understand that they had become the all-purpose scapegoats for Romania's every problem. However diverse the circumstances, there seemed to be a foreknowledge that popular opinion would accept the Roma as guilty. With so few Jews left in Romania, the Roma, one sociologist surmised, serve as the country's new Jews. [That, however, has in no way eliminated anti-Semitism. See Chapter 8.] In December 1989, as relief aid came flooding into Romania from abroad, wild rumors circulated that Roma had poisoned blood supplies and pillaged local stocks of food and medicine. Another popular myth making the rounds at the same time was that Ceauşescu hadn't been Romanian at all, but rather Roma or part Tartar and part Roma (How could a pure-blooded Romanian ever have committed such crimes against his own people?). In fact, Romanians had long tended to associate the Romas' "privileges" with communism, with Ceauşescu, and with the minority's alleged eager collaboration with the Securitate. (One Roma organization responded to these charges in the newspaper *22*: "How many of us were RCP members? How many of us participated in the songs of praise for Ceauşescu, hung his portraits on the walls, parroted his slogans, and wished him a long, happy life? We'll tell you: None!")

The first pogrom struck in early January 1990 in the village of Turu Lung, when 1000 villagers marched to the hamlet's Roma quarter and set fire to houses. The villagers, incensed over political differences that the Roma expressed at a town meeting, burned thirty-six of the forty-one Roma dwellings to the ground and attacked the Gypsies with makeshift weapons.[13] Transylvania's Roma learned directly after the March 1990 Tîrgu-Mureş violence that they would play a useful role to the government as a political scapegoat. Of the thirty-one people investigated in connection with the event, twenty-four were Roma, five were ethnic Hungarian, and two were Romanian. In the end, the court convicted seven Roma alone of offenses such as disturbing the peace and possession of illegal weapons. Again, in June 1990, after the onslaught of the miners on Bucharest's University Square, it was finally a handful of Roma whom police paraded across the television screen as the guilty parties.

Visitors to Romania can't help but shudder at the deep, emotional racism of average, otherwise quite reasonable and open-minded Romanians toward the Roma. The post-Ceauşescu crash of an already decrepit economy has only worsened tensions, as Roma unemployment and crime has soared. In a paradoxical, two-sided manner, the Roma's fate in Romania is closely bound with the introduction of a market economy. One reason for the new wave of violence against the Roma is Romanians' sheer frustration with their own economic deprivation, and their fear of crime and social disorder. The Roma, however, traditional traders and wheeler-dealers, also represent the spirit of the free market unregulated, speculative, profit-oriented business dealings. Roma businessmen, for example, were the first to take advantage of the new space for entrepreneurship, making quick and sizeable profits on small-scale buying and reselling. Although these Roma constitute a tiny minority of the Roma population, just as Jewish businessmen and bankers were only a minute fraction of German Jews in the Weimar Republic, Romanians have directed their outrage at them.

Romania's free press has chimed in unscrupulously against the Roma, publishing letters, editorials, and articles that rival the panegyrics of *România Mare*. Roma are routinely referred to as "thieves," "black-marketeers," "beggars," "criminals," and "whores" with racist adjectives such as "brown," "sun-burned," "chocolate-colored," or "coffee-colored." Just one month after the revolution, a reader of the Timişoara newspaper *Renaşterea Bănăţeană* wrote: "I would take the same measures against the Gypsies as did Antonescu." Since then, the advocacy of genocidal policies has become common in the ultra-right press. "A bullet only costs a couple of lei," *România Mare* reminds its readers. Even the tone in the papers of the democratic opposition and the government is frightening. A report on the selling of bottled beer in the August 10, 1990 *Adevărul* accused the Roma of being the real profiteers of the revolution, as well as police informers: "The flourishing trade with bottled beer is dominated exclusively and authoritarianly by the Gypsies. All day long they lie in ambush for the beer truck. They are shameless. Well-organized, they storm the trucks. . . . Because they are entrepreneurial and prepared to commit any type of vandalism, they raid the shops and warehouses, threaten or beat up the owners. . . . And because of their years-long collaboration as informers for the police, it is impossible to catch them. . . . They move from tree to tree like sparrows. And I say sparrows so as not to insult the crows." The national minorities, too, have willingly contributed to the Roma people's defamation. One piece in the Timişoara German-language weekly, *Die Neue Banater Zeitung*, described the Roma presence in the Timişoara marketplace as: "Noise, riffraff, blood-curdling laughs, goods lying on the bare earth. . . . Have we made a revolution for tramps and garbage?"

How can one explain the frightening intensity of this primitive, coarse hatred circulating in Romania today? The fear and the anxiety of change, the frustration of economic deprivation, and the manipulation of chauvinism from the press and politicians have all contributed to the prevailing mood. But perhaps, as Romanian-German author Richard Wagner suggests, a further explanation lies in the uniquely distorted nature of Romanian society that evolved under the Ceauşescu dictatorship. Romanian democrats point to the complete neglect of morality and moral values in communist Romania. The average person, simply to survive, was forced to fight bitterly, without consideration, even against friends and neighbors. Since aggression had no outlet, it built up, not only against others, but against one's self, too, for one's own consciously hypocritical actions. Wagner, who left Romania for Germany in 1987, explains: "The people fought for their daily bread, not for freedom of speech. It was a daily struggle for survival, and it was everyone against everyone. One had to push to the front of every queue, one had to protect oneself against informers. It required tricks and compromises, just to get by—nasty compromises, denunciations, petty undetectable crimes. Being on the brink of bare existence, always afraid of being pushed into the abyss of nothingness, makes one immoral. The people were thrown into a cycle of suffering, and sank in the vicious circle of dictatorship. Thus they became their own tormentors."[14]

After the regime's ouster, the survivors saw themselves as the victims of the dictatorship, Wagner argues, and, with the figureheads of the regime overthrown and executed, their pent-up wrath no longer had an immediate object. Although the object of their anger should have been themselves, they directed it instead against those who reminded them of their guilt: against the national minorities who supposedly profited from communist internationalism; against the Roma who supposedly collaborated with the secret police; against Jews who supposedly stood behind socialism and against the democratic dissidents and the emigres, who stood so high and mighty after communism's collapse.

In Transylvania, time has done nothing to heal the wounds of the Tîrgu-Mureș violence. The rise of the ultra-nationalists to positions of political prominence has only inflamed nationalist tensions and continued to polarize relations between ethnic Hungarians and Romanians. In local elections, the electorate has split along ethnic lines. "There's no politics in Transylvania," one democratic activist told me. "It's just one nationality against the other." In Cluj-Napoca, where a quarter of the 400,000-strong population is Hungarian, the PRNU's militant new president Gheorghe Funar was elected mayor. A former small-time communist leader, Funar's first moves in city hall were to outlaw bilingual signs, even those on traditionally Hungarian institutions, ban several international conferences, limit the jurisdiction of Hungarian schools, and thwart a number of Hungarian joint-venture projects. Ethnic Hungarians may no longer display the Hungarian flag or sing their national hymn. The minority's hopes of resuscitating the historical Bolyai University—closed under Communist rule—are now as remote as they were during the Ceaușescu years.

Shortly after Funar's February 1992 victory, I stopped by to speak with the new mayor. Unfortunately, Funar was in France but his vice mayor, Liviu Medra, grudgingly agreed to speak with me after a litany of excuses, half-threats, and stipulations that I had become used to hearing from nationalist politicians. ("The Western press just doesn't understand the Romanians," he told me. "You journalists live in Budapest and soak in all of the Hungarian propaganda. We're busy men here. Why should we waste our time?")

A short, heavyset man with a dark five-o'clock shadow, he explained that the new measures were aimed at nipping Hungarian separatism in the bud, and went on to give me half-a-dozen examples of the Hungarians' "disloyalty" such as the celebration of certain Hungarian holidays and the singing of provocative national songs. "Cluj is a Romanian city; it always has been and it will stay that way. What would you think if you came to Cluj as a Western tourist and saw Hungarian signs everywhere?," he asked half rhetorically. I responded that I would interpret it as an expression of Romanian tolerance and magnanimity. He shook his head. "No, people would think that this is really a Hungarian city, and we can't have that." Did he really think that these new restrictions were the way to gain the Hungarians' loyalty, I asked him, or weren't they certain to push the minority in other direction? He shook his head again. "It is not our job to win the Hungarians loyalty. First they must prove it to us if they want these kinds of special favors." As I left the office after about an hour of similar dialogue he lifted his big arm up around my shoulder, looked me in the eye and said: "I want to tell you just one thing. The Romanians have never in their entire history shown intolerance toward other peoples. Never."

The moderate leadership of the Hungarian minority, whose sympathies lie with the Democratic Convention, has urged patience from their constituencies. "These are clearly the policies of the past," said Peter Buchwald, the party's Cluj president. "They are an extension of Ceauşescu's drive to wipe out Hungarian culture from Transylvania, and we are going to fight them as we had for the past twenty-five years. There's nothing more that we can do." But other, more nationalist voices within the minority consider the time ripe for more decisive action. Maverick HDUR party leaders from the near-ethnically homogeneous region of Széklerland in central Transylvania have become increasingly outspoken about regional autonomy, a privilege that the Székleys, who consider themselves ethnically Hungarian, enjoyed until 1956. In the Romania-speak of the Vatra-PRNU nationalists, terms such as "autonomy" or "self-government" are code words for Hungarian separatism, which, in fact, pretty much describes the wishes of the radical Székleys leadership. In cities such as Cluj, where the Hungarians are a minority, the Székleys' nationalism reverberates negatively, undermining even minimal cultural rights for the Magyar population there.

The Romanian nationalists' fears of regional fragmentation and instability could well become a self-fulfilling prophesy, just as their strong-arm backers desire. In addition to Transylvania, the other variable of Romania's delicate national equation is eastern Bessarabia, known as the Soviet Republic of Moldavia from its 1940 annexation until 1990, when the independent republic's Romanian majority restored its Romanian name, Moldova. The territory of Bessarabia has passed between Romanian and Russian hands seven times since 1812, and could return to Romania once again. Squeezed between Romania and the Ukraine, the population is two-thirds ethnic Romanian and the remainder primarily Russian and Ukranian. Although the ethnic Romanian Moldovans boast a regional identity of their own, nationalist elements in the Moldovan Popular Front have pushed to put the diminutive territory of 4.3 million people on a path toward unification with Mother Romania. The trajectory scares no one more than the national minorities, who have taken up arms against the Romanian leadership in the predominantly Russian-speaking swath of Moldova east of the Dniestr River. Only to complicate matters further, the northern and southern sections of the original territory of Bessarabia now belong to the Ukraine, while the Transnistria region, formerly Ukraine, sits within Moldovan borders.

In short, this scenario raises the specter of other nationality conflicts in the future, and thus gives plenty of ammunition to Romanian ultra-nationalists on the home front. Since even the Romanian Moldovans balk at the thought of unconditional unification under Bucharest's wing, one possible compromise could be some kind of political autonomy for the region within the state of their Romanian brothers. Should the Moldovans strike an agreement with Bucharest over a form of self-government, the regime could well find itself faced with a full-scale mutiny in the Szeklerland. The nationalist dynamic that Romanian radicals have set in motion on Romania's eastern and western frontiers could facilitate the country's internal combustion, perhaps bringing some kind of military dictatorship to power in order to hold the country together by force. On a smaller scale, this is just what the nationalists accomplished in Tîrgu-Mureş in 1990. With wars in the Balkans to the south and in the former Soviet Union to the east, the years of 1990–93 may go down as some of the most democratic of Romanian history.

Chapter 6

THE CZECH REPUBLIC
SKINHEADS WHO CRY

Prague—that city where reality fuses with dreams, and dreams
turn into visions of horror.

Siegfried Kracauer

On the night of March 25, 1991, Pavel Opořenský strolled
through one of Prague's narrow, cobbled streets toward the
home of some old acquaintances. Opořenský, a thirty-eight-
year-old sculptor, had only recently returned to his native city of Prague
after eleven years of self-imposed exile in New York City.[1] Like other
artists, writers, and intellectuals, he had fled the repression of Czechoslovakia's dictatorship, returning after the 1989 Velvet Revolution to
make his contribution to the country's cultural rebirth. As he approached the quiet little Vyšehrad Park, the bearlike, 200 pound–plus
Opořenský spotted a pack of Czech Skinheads with some Austrian
buddies. On their way to hear the Skinhead band Orlík they sang
German songs and shouted "Sieg Heil!" Opořenský claims that he tried
to avoid the marauding youths. But here the stories of the sculptor and
of the Skins—which a packed courtroom would later hear in full—take
very different turns.

According to Opořenský, he had already passed the dozen or so
youths when he heard a scream and looked back to see a small man
running franticly toward him, with the Skins in hot pursuit. As four
of the Skinheads fell upon the man, a second man wielding a pocket-

knife appeared on the scene. The newcomer attempted to intervene against the Skins, or so goes the Opořenský version, when the youths pulled out *tongas*—flexible, lightweight steel billy clubs—and one a full-size hunting knife. Another Skinhead then whipped out a tear-gas canister and gassed the second man in the face. The blast dropped him like a stone, sending his shrieking wife to his aid. According to Opořenský, a Skinhead, screaming at the top of his lungs, rushed the couple with a heavy municipal garbage bin raised over his head.

At this point Opořenský entered the fray. He intercepted the charging Skin, knocking him and the dumpster to the ground. "I wanted to smash his face in. I was so upset, so repulsed, so exhausted from watching the scene," he told a reporter from the biweekly *Prognosis*. In self-defense, he claims, he pulled out his own weapon, a razor-sharp eight-centimeter German pocketknife. He tried to scare the boys off, warning them: "OK, come on, let's go. I'm used to such bastards in New York." But they kept coming at him. When seventeen-year-old Aleš Martinů swung his tonga at the sculptor, he countered with a stab to the boy's neck, which neatly severed a main artery near the collarbone. With twelve more Skinheads coming after him, Opořenský fled to a nearby police station. When the police showed up at the scene of the skirmish, the street was tranquil and deserted.

The Skinheads and several other witnesses tell different, though no less confused stories of the night's events and the circumstances of Martinů's death. Some of the Skinheads claimed that Martinů defended himself as an enraged Opořenský repeatedly charged him with his knife. Another version has Opořenský wrestling down the troop's leader, stabbing Martinů only by accident. Witnesses from the street and various windows offered still other, conflicting stories: After the knifefight, for example, Opořenský ran across the street, where bystanders heard him say "I got it all the way in him, the bastard. All the way to the hilt." The statement was a piece of evidence that would later be used against him when he stood trial for manslaughter. None of the four Skinheads directly involved in the melee appeared before the court that tried Opořenský. Martinů was dead, one was never identified, an Austrian Skin fled home, and the gang leader, wanted by the police for other crimes, went into hiding in Switzerland.

The trial and its bizarre circumstances captured the public's attention in Prague. Some of the Czech boulevard press and sensational, mass-circulation magazines portrayed the Skinheads as the victims, as a bunch of simple, frustrated Czech boys looking for a cause. The glossy monthly *Reflex* ran a touching story entitled "When Skinheads Cry." The cover photo showed a dozen weeping teenage Skinheads huddled around Martinů's casket, clutching each other in grief. Martinů's corpse was clad in his Skinhead uniform—high black boots, green flight jacket, jeans rolled up at the ankles. Among scattered flowers, across the dead boy's chest lay some army dog tags, a cross, and a shotgun shell. Orlík played at the funeral, the same group the gang was off to see on the fated March night.

Martinů's father, a law-abiding carpenter, waged his own campaign to clear his son's name. The portrait that emerges of his boy indeed reveals a very "normal" Czech kid, born and socialized in the later decades of the Czechoslovak Socialist Federal Republic, the period of "normalization," as the regime referred to the years following the 1968 clampdown on the Prague Spring reform movement. "Aleš wasn't a criminal," he told reporters at the trial, where he was surrounded by his son's Skinhead friends. According to Mr. Martinů, Aleš "just wanted to help people." Although his father had hoped that he would play professional hockey, Aleš wanted to be a policeman or a security guard, maybe even an elite "Black sheriff" with an all-black uniform and German shepherd. For years Aleš had danced in a local dance troupe, one of whose members was a black African. The troupe members say Aleš and the African boy got on well together. They were friends and the black boy cried when he heard about Aleš' death. Aleš quit the group, however, for the exhilarating world of Skinhead violence, machismo, and comradeship. When Mr. Martinů learned that Aleš was carrying a tonga, he reprimanded his son. "I told Aleš that he didn't even know how to use the thing." Aleš responded that he had only to show it to Roma in order to send them running.

During recesses, the bespectacled Mr. Martinů showed court reporters photos of Aleš, a sweet-faced, happy kid with long, gangly limbs. One recent photo showed the boy laughing in his new bomber jacket with his head freshly shaven. One arm was feebly extended in the Hitler salute, another wrapped jokingly around his brother's neck, as if mocking his new role. "Everybody wanted to do their part in the revolution," explained Mr. Martinů. But while students led the demonstrations, working-class youth were left out. "So they became Skinheads and focused on the problem of crime committed by Gypsies, Vietnamese, and Arabs," which says his father, was "higher than acceptable." In the months preceding the brawl, the Martinů family had been robbed twice. Aleš's Skinhead friends describe the seventeen-year-old as a follower, proud just to be a member of the gang. "He didn't like blacks, that's true," attested one Skin pal. "But when there was a fight he would stand in the crowd and shout 'beat him, beat him!' He never kicked or beat anyone himself."

In the end, after a much publicized and drawn out trial, the court cleared Opořenský. While the verdict meant nothing to the dead Aleš Martinů, the spectacle gave Czech society some unanticipated grounds for introspection. Some asked what it was that took such an average, healthy boy like Aleš Martinů down such a road. Fascist Skinheads in Berlin or Vienna was one thing, but in Prague? Just who were these Skinheads, and how far into mainstream society did their hatreds reach? Others asked why the police persecuted good Czech kids for doing the job that the police didn't seem up to themselves. Perhaps these young people could be trained, some suggested, and form patrols to protect neighborhoods.

These were all questions with answers that lay uncomfortably close to home. The fated confrontation on the dark streets of Prague was a clash between two very different cultures in postcommunist Czechoslovakia. The much publicized legal showdown was hardly a simple matter of good versus evil, of democracy versus fascism. There was plenty of evidence to cast just doubt upon Opořenský's credibility and actions. The trial reflected a deep schism in Czech society, one that pitted the dissident against the average guy, the emigre against the local, the artist against the worker, the Prague Spring generation against those who had never hoped for anything more than a telephone, a flat, and a car. Though the average Czech detested the communist system, it was only a tiny minority of dissident intellectuals who actively touted the moral, democratic ideals of Czechoslovakia's 1989 Velvet Revolution. In the hands of playwright-philosopher Václav Havel, that vision took him from the prison cell to the presidency overnight, and on the streets of Prague and Bratislava in November 1989, the Czechs and their Slovak brothers seemed in unanimous consent with the dissidents' starry vision. The events of the following years, however, would present a much more diverse picture of Czech and Slovak societies.

BLUE VELVET

Even before the 1993 division of Czechoslovakia into separate Czech and Slovak states, the Czech lands—Bohemia and Moravia-Silesia— seemed the best prepared of all of the East bloc countries to make the leap to something close to Western democracy and market capitalism. Nationalism among the 10.3 million Czechs has historically tended to take a "civic-democratic" form, closer to that of postwar western Europe than that of other former communist states. A unique privilege in the region, the postcommunist 1990–92 Czecho-Slovak Federal Republic (CSFR) could look back upon a democratic interwar tradition. When Havel assumed the presidency in 1989, he intentionally linked postcommunist Czechoslovakia to the 1918–38 Czechoslovak Republic, or the so-called first republic. The interwar republic, the first form of modern statehood for either nationality, is synonymous with its founder, the liberal humanist Thomáš Masaryk. In word as well as deed, Havel went to great lengths before the country's 1993 split to link his own office to the personal legacy of Czechoslovakia's founding father.

Though not without its own shortcomings, the first republic survived as a working parliamentary democracy until German troops snuffed it out in 1938. The republic had pursued a relatively enlightened policy toward its many ethnic and national minorities, granting its German, Hungarian, Ruthene, and Polish citizens far-reaching rights. Yet at no point did the many nationalities of the interwar Czechoslovakia ever subscribe to the common "Czechoslovak" national identity that its founders had envisioned. The Czechs, including most Moravians, who speak Czech, thought of themselves as Czechs. The Slovaks, who speak their own closely related Slavic tongue, proudly considered themselves Slovaks. From the inception of the secular interwar republic, the Slovaks sensed a distinct Czech arrogance coming from Prague, which took a condescending, paternalistic view of less-developed, rural, Catholic Slovakia. The Slovaks' resentment over their de facto junior status in the republic fueled a virile nationalism that eventually welcomed Nazi Germany as a national liberator. The strained relationship between Czechs and Slovaks, however, never degenerated into armed hostilities, a nearly unique achievement in the region.

Under the WWII Nazi German protectorate, the Czechs behaved with renowned docility, neither collaborating with the occupying forces in great numbers nor resisting them with remarkable heroism. Anti-Semitism and anti-Roma feelings ran high in parts of the population, which the Germans exploited to wipe out nearly all of the Czech Roma population. Perhaps the most disreputable act in the history of Czech nationalism came immediately after the war's end. After tense relations with the three million Sudeten Germans during the first republic, the ethnic Germans' whole-hearted collaboration with Nazi Germany was the last straw for the Czechs. With the end of German occupation, the postwar government confiscated the ethnic Germans' land and property in Bohemia and sent them packing to Germany. Anti-German propaganda continued to flow well into the late fifties, until Prague finally heeded protests from East Berlin.

During their tenure, the communist powers kept nationalism more or less under wraps in the Czech lands and Slovakia. Although Prague was once again the locus of power and decision-making, underdeveloped Slovakia benefited enormously from the common state (a fact that few Slovaks today will acknowledge). When Slovak nationalism did raise its head in communism's final decades, it came mostly from populist currents within the Communist Party. Though not without its own nationalist undertones, the reform communist liberalization movement of the legendary Prague Spring followed spiritually in the footsteps of the first republic. The movement for social democratic reform, for a "Third Way" between communism and capitalism, captured the essence of the Masaryk's vision, even if it never breached the confines of the Leninist party state. The tragic crushing of the Prague Spring signalled a resumption of the neo-Stalinist status quo, which most Czechs and Slovaks served humbly until 1989.

THE MARCH OF THE RIGHT

The peaceful 1989 November revolution and its personal symbol, Havel, embodied all that was noble and moral, democratic and liberal in the Czech character. It was not long afterward that a darker side of that personality showed its face. In April and May 1990, a year before Aleš Martinů's death, a wave of ethnic violence against Roma and Vietnamese workers made headlines in northern Bohemia. In the northern cities of Nový Bor, Děčín, Teplice, Bílina, Chomutov, Česká Lípa, and Liberec, racist Skinheads and a confused hybrid of Nazi-punks lit into unarmed groups of Roma with clubs, chains, and iron pipes. According to the Prague daily *Lidové noviny*, local police forces took little or no action against the agitators. Although at first confined to the youth scene, mostly at discos and concerts, the aggression soon boiled over into the community at large. Roma tell of large crowds gathering around as young thugs kicked and beat Roma unconscious. "This isn't the first open hostility against Gypsies," one Czech student from Děčín told me at the time, "but now it happens everyday."

Simultaneously, Skinhead troops vigorously intensified their campaign against Czechoslovakia's 46,000 foreign workers, the majority of whom were Vietnamese. On May 1, 200 Skinheads raised havoc in central Prague, turning on a Canadian tourist group after they had beaten up or dispersed all the Roma and Vietnamese from the main square. Vietnamese students at the Electrical Engineering College in Plzeň appealed to President Havel to take immediate action to address the deteriorating relations between the peoples. "We have been informed about people who have been injured or even killed," wrote the students. The freshly founded Civic Roma Initiative, Charter 77, and the Czechoslovak Helsinki Committee, among other human rights groups, also issued formal protests against the terror.

Havel's response, though quick and well-intentioned, failed to penetrate to the source of the deep-seated prejudices and social tensions in

Czech society. "Since the explosion of freedom, we have witnessed in this country the inherent irresponsibility and some of the dark and evil sides of the human character," reflected the philosopher-king at a May press conference. Havel echoed widespread rumors at the time that disillusioned elements of the old apparatus, particularly the security forces, stood behind the violence. Such elements still occupied most of the bureaucracy and some of them may even have thought that they could still destabilize the new democracy with their old tricks. Many newspapers, for example, that were the channels of communist disinformation only months ago, pinned the blame for the recent clashes on the Roma. As Havel implied, the feeble police response could well have been ordered from above as a ploy to influence the restructuring of the Interior Ministry. In such a scenario, the threat of chaos or anarchy would have provided grounds for old apparatchiks to try to maintain the security apparatus. Nor is there any reason to rule out collaboration between neo-fascist Skinheads and the communist regime's former henchmen. Yet, racial tensions and ethnic animosity existed in the Czech lands long before the dictatorship's frontmen lost their jobs. The friction had been brewing for years and finally found expression once the police state's brakes had disappeared. Havel must have known all too well that racism, as a social phenomenon, was a problem that the new democratic state would have to confront as such, and not as some irremediable flaw in human nature.

Actually, it was while Havel pondered the human condition from behind bars in the mid-1980s that an underground world of neo-Nazi *oi* bands and Skinhead hate culture found an audience in Prague. By 1987 or 1988, any tourist could see classic Skins, their exposed ears sticking out from their round, razored heads, at central cafés in the Prague Old Town. At beer halls, they openly fraternized with German and Austrian Skinheads. Demonic, heavy metal bands like Orlík and Bráník stirred hatred against the standard Skinhead enemies—punks, Roma, foreign workers, and third world students—as well as Slovaks and tourists, the last for swamping their beloved Prague. The hardcore Nazi-skins located their ideological forefather in the small anti-German Czech fascist movement of the 1920s and 1930s.

In the 1989 revolution's immediate aftermath, legal Orlík concerts drew as many as 600 Skinheads at a time. Their stage sets brandished full-size color posters of Miroslav Sládek, the leader of the newly formed ultra-right wing Republican Party, an organization from which Czechs would hear plenty more in the future. Orlík's seething lyrics whipped teenagers like Aleš Martinů and his mates into a frenzy. The song "Blackbird," for example, links third world nationals with the country's new democratic forces: "What kind of blackbirds are around?/They are the unions and the independent parties/But I have better ideas without the blackbirds/I call that, my country, Fatherland/ And that could only be—Skinhead state!" In a matter of months, the numbers of Skinheads and their fellow-travellers seemed to double and triple. By 1992, experts estimated about 1000 active Skins in Prague, 500 in Plzeň, and roughly 2000 in northern Bohemia. Their supporters ran into the tens of thousands.

The Republican Party's early appeal to Skinheads didn't prevent a plethora of even more ostentatious ultra-right groupings from taking shape. A pseudo-intellectual Skinhead group, New Czech Unity, waged a war against alcohol and drugs, as well as "Gypsy parasites." It promoted an ethic of physical work and camaraderie, which it based on Bohemian myths from the Middle Ages. Along with other neo-fascist white supremacist groups, from the Ku Klux Klan to the White League (Bílá Liga), Czech Skins and neo-Nazis organized their most impressive show of strength since the revolution on November 24, 1991. To cries of "Gypsies out!", "Bohemia for the Bohemians," and "Gypsies to the gas chambers!", as many as 1000 assorted right-wing hooligans marched through the central Wenceslas Square, American Confederate flags dangling from sticks. Police intervened only to stop scuffles between the right-wingers and a 500-strong counterdemonstration of Roma and young Czech anarchists. The leftists with brightly colored punk coiffures and black leather jackets yelled "Fascists out!" and "The Roma must stay!" The Skinhead march broke away from the counterdemonstration and wove its way in and out of several Roma neighborhoods until police finally disbanded it four hours later. "If this crowd had been any larger," said the Prague deputy chief of police, "we would have needed water cannons and tear gas." But since December 1989, he noted, such means were no longer at his disposal.

THE CZECHS' MATES

The fact that Czechoslovakia's third world guests were among the first targets of Skinhead terror came as little surprise to the victims themselves. In their letter to Havel, the Vietnamese engineering students underlined the yawning cultural and communication gaps that had grown between the two peoples. In the late 1970s, the Vietnamese government offered the services of its workers to the shorthanded Czechoslovak economy to help pay off debts that it had accrued during the war years. From the moment that they landed at the Prague airport, the Vietnamese workers had no illusions as to their purpose in Czechoslovakia: They were the flesh-and-blood form of value in a primitive process of barter. Quartered in workers' hostels, the foreign nationals received the barest language training and only a brief introduction to Czech society. Their families and children were forbidden to join them. The state put them to work at the most menial of jobs and promptly forgot about them.

According to Uyen Phem Huu, a computer engineer who has lived in Prague since 1980, the trouble began shortly after the first workers came to Czechoslovakia. As a young student Huu experienced the formidable barriers between the two cultures. "There wasn't even a common language with which Vietnamese and Czechs could speak to one another," he says. Upon arrival at the factory, for example, every Vietnamese worker was given a Czech name. "It was really impossible to find a friend at their workplace because we naturally knew them only by their Vietnamese names. The Czechs couldn't understand why the Vietnamese workers didn't learn Czech right away when they couldn't even be bothered to remember a couple of foreign names."

He points out, however, that the pre-1989 period was also relatively quiet and in many ways quite pleasant. The Vietnamese in Czechoslovakia considered themselves fortunate to escape the turmoil and grinding poverty of their homeland, if only for a couple years. During the communist years, says the slight, neatly dressed man, discrimination took more subtle forms than it does today. Vietnamese workers say that the chief source of friction was their purchase of "Czech" commodities. The Czechs looked at them as if they were thieves when they bought goods with their unconvertible *koruna* to send back to their families. "At that time people couldn't afford to hit someone in the streets," says Huu. "Often you just wouldn't be served in a restaurant or picked up by a taxi. But that was one thing. Now there's democracy and that means they can hit whoever they want and get away with it."

In democratic Czechoslovakia, the postcommunist government took care of the "guest worker problem" with a simple administrative stroke of the pen. In late April 1990, at the peak of the first outbreak of violence, the government announced that all foreign workers must leave the country before 1995. The expulsion of the 46,000 workers, the government claimed, would help insure jobs for Czechoslovak citizens in the new market economy. The terror spree on the streets seemed to propel the process along. By late spring 1990, every seat on the Prague to Phenom Phen flight was booked months in advance.

One problem that cannot simply be put on an airplane and flown away is that of the Roma. As throughout Eastern Europe, the 500,000 to 600,000 Roma in the Czech lands and Slovakia are the poorest, least educated, and most discriminated against of peoples. In one opinion poll, a staggering ninety-one percent of those Czechs and Slovaks asked expressed antipathy toward Roma. Since Nazi measures claimed the lives of almost all of the Bohemian and Moravian Gypsies, most of those in the Czech lands today are Slovak Roma, repatriated there after the Sudeten Germans' expulsion. Communist policies, though making dents in chronic problems such as substandard housing and illiteracy, perpetuated and institutionalized many of the racial prejudices that flourished prior to WWII. The regime treated the minority as a genetically inferior, second class of people, with a worthless culture better plowed beneath the Czech and Slovak cultures. Through heavy-handed policies of integration and assimilation, the state tried to extinguish the unique Roma identity. It suppressed the Romany language and traditions, liquidated rural settlements, and outlawed nomadic wandering. The campaign ended up robbing the Roma of much of what was constructive in their traditions, turning many of the younger generations into lumpen Czechs.

The most Orwellian of the communist policies toward Roma included the coerced and sometimes involuntary sterilization of Roma women. Although the official decrees never explicitly referred to Roma by name, the testimonies of former administrators, doctors, and Roma women expose a clear-cut policy designed to regulate the "large, unhealthy population" of Roma by sterilizing women. The government's first course of action was to offer lucrative monetary incentives (as much as a full year's wage in Slovakia) for Roma women to undergo sterilization. Other women report that after abortions or Caesarean sections doctors had sterilized them without their consent. The first protests came in 1979 from the Charter 77, the Czechoslovak human rights and democracy movement. The Chartists accused the state of violating the penal code on genocide, which included "whoever seeks to destroy fully or partially any national, ethnic, racial, or religious group . . . [such as] measures in order to prevent reproduction among this group." The government paid the dissidents no heed and continued with the sterilization policies until 1989.

Immediately after the 1990 elections, both the federal and state governments undertook a number of moves to guarantee the Roma minority full human rights. The second largest minority in both the Czech Republic and in Slovakia, the Roma now finally have status as national minorities. Roma culture has flowered and a panoply of independent groups and periodicals have sprung up, although tribalism and infighting have kept them from acting as an effective political force. But, as the excellent 1992 Helsinki Watch study on Czechoslovakia's Roma underlines, the prejudices of the past continue to permeate Czech society today. According to the report's authors: "The attitudes of doctors and government officials who promoted the sterilization of Roma women are still present in some hospitals where women are placed in segregated and overcrowded maternity wards. Teachers and government psychologists still transfer capable Roma children to special schools for the mentally handicapped. In some schools, Roma children still sit in separate rows in the back of the room; other schools contain only Roma children." The racist, undemocratic consensus against Roma in the Czech Republic stretches from the bureaucratic elite to the beer hall regulars. It is a chauvinism that the right has found most useful in exploiting against its democratic opponents.

Human rights experts like Dr. Tomáš Haisman, head of the federal

Department of Human Rights and Humanitarian Issues from 1990–
92, insists that Czech society is already "divided into two races—blacks
and whites." Modern democracy, he says, offers the Roma no means
to overcome the social and economic barriers of this division, but instead
ossifies their position on the outermost periphery of society. Three key
concepts, argues Haisman, symbolized the 1989 revolution: freedom,
democracy, and the market economy. "You extend these concepts to
the situation of the Roma people and you have a real horror story," he
says. Freedom for the Roma, he explains, means the freedom of the
minority to express themselves as they wish, which is not necessarily
conducive to good relations with their Czech neighbors. For the
Czechs, on the other hand, freedom is the freedom to take action against
the Roma. Democracy, Haisman sees as the codification of the present
political status quo, the assertion of the will of the Czech majority over
the Roma minority. And the free market, he argues, will only entrench
the Roma at the bottom of the economic hierarchy. "The race question
here will be a central source of conflict here for a long time," says
Haisman. "In the U.S. during the 1950s and 1960s there emerged
some very aggressive fighters for the rights of blacks. This is the kind
of thing that will have to happen here for things to really change."

BEER HALL NATIONALISM

For a few fleeting months in 1989 and into 1990, the petty, nasty side
of Czech nationalism—intolerance, spitefulness, cowardice, and sub-
servience to authority—vanished along with the dictatorship that epit-
omized its ethos. The Skinhead violence of spring 1990, however, signalled the resurgence of that ethos and its metamorphosis under
democracy. The actions of teenagers like Aleš Martinů openly, angrily
vented the emotions that their parents' generation had dutifully held
in check. By 1991, a new, popular form of Czech chauvinism had
clearly asserted itself throughout Bohemia and Moravia. Unlike its eastern relations, the Czechs' "beer hall nationalism" was not centered
around territorial expansion, religious identification, national indepen-

dence, or minorities abroad. More in step with Western Europe's New Right culture, it played primarily upon the racial prejudices and economic anxieties of the lower and middle classes. With a potent economic populism, Czech nationalists (as well as the reformed communist party) surged to fill a gap in Czech political culture that progressive left-wing or social democratic parties would also try to fill in Western Europe. Despite the Czechs' strong social democratic traditions, such forces hadn't sufficient time to establish themselves, much less to redeem the tarnished name of the left.

The Czech lands' beer hall nationalism raised its head first and most fiercely in northern Bohemia. Formerly the heart of the ethnic German Sudetenland, the northwestern region had flourished before WWII as the republic's prosperous industrial belt. Driving today through northern Bohemia, the hub of the communist state's heavy industry, travellers encounter one grimy town after another where the power plants of Bohemia's "black belt" expel layer upon layer of sulfur dioxide–rich soot over streets, buildings, and playgrounds. Although pollution throughout the Czech lands and Slovakia ranks among the worst in Eastern Europe, the official "ecological disaster zone" in northern Bohemia is exceptionally nightmarish. The average lifespan of its residents is three or four years less than that of other Czech and Slovak citizens, which in turn is three to five years less than that in neighboring countries. In some areas, infant mortality is twelve percent higher than in other regions of Czechoslovakia. In winter, when cold fronts trap the pollution over cities and towns, the air quality is sometimes so bad that schools are closed down and children, pregnant women, and the sick are bused out to mountain resorts.

The advent of economic "shock therapy" brought inflation and unemployment to northern Bohemia; although among the lowest levels in Eastern Europe, they were nevertheless a trauma for the Bohemians. The first to lose their jobs, of course, were the Roma. In some places unemployment hit as much as half of the Roma population (the rate for all Czechs was three percent in 1992.) Crime also jumped to previously inconceivable levels. Although Roma make up only two percent of the Czech population, they accounted for eleven percent of all crimes and fifty percent of crimes such as pickpocketing and burglary. At the same time, the Czechs experienced another "threat" in the unprecedented wave of immigration crossing their country from Eastern Europe en route to Western Europe.

Since 1991, journalists from northern Bohemian cities have talked in terms of "running race wars" between Roma and Czechs. Splattered across walls is graffiti such as "Death to all Gypsies!", "Genocide for the Gypsies!", "Chop the Gypsies to bits!", and "Gypsies back to Slovakia!". Violence is a daily phenomenon, which between December 1989 and mid-1991 claimed the lives of nine Roma. Some Roma mothers refuse to send their children to school because of the Skinhead bands that stalk the grounds. The press has chimed in, using racist adjectives when they speak of the Roma and demanding new, tougher police measures to address the problem. One local newspaper in Chomutov published a statement by a group called Death Squad, that threatened to begin "liquidating all unadaptable Roma." By 1993, several cities had passed ordinances that gave local authorities the right to evict troublesome Roma from their apartments (on grounds such as overcrowding, lack of hygiene, etc.) and expel them from the cities without court orders.

The sentiments of the Skinheads clearly had a resonance that extended beyond marginal youth gangs. The average burgher, too, shared many of the prejudices that the Skinheads acted upon with violence. According to Charles University sociologist Václav Trojan, "the first violence was a barometer of deeper social tensions within society." The former dissident argues that these "antagonistic feelings had been building up for years here, and then were finally given the signal to explode." Ordinary citizens, for example, formed "self-defense" squads, sometimes with hired mercenary Skinheads, to protect their communities from "Gypsy criminality." Police forces have come under heavy pressure to crack down on Roma, or at least to cut the Skinheads slack to do the dirty work for them. "Local communities have shown clear popular support for the violence, for the Skins, and for the police," says Trojan. "One can't say that this racism is restricted to a lunatic fringe." Even in Prague today many restaurants have "whites only" signs. According to a report issued by the Institute for Criminology in Prague: "The populace sympathizes with anyone who at least verbally, but better 'in reality' stands up for their protection. . . . Thus, for example, Skinheads are forgiven and ultimately supported by a considerable part of the population, which mistakes their racist, fascist intolerance with the protection of the society from criminality."[2]

The organized political manifestation of this hatred is the ultraright Republican Party, which soared onto the Czechoslovak political stage in less than two years. The spectacular gains of the obscure Association for the Republic-Republican Party of Czechoslovakia in the summer 1992 elections was one of the most painful of the many kicks that Czech democrats would take that year. Although the radical free marketeers of Finance Minister Václav Klaus' Civic Democratic Party (CDP), an offshoot of the original Civic Forum movement, captured the Czech elections, the party of Foreign Minister Jiří Dienstbier and the former Charter 77 dissidents garnered only 4.3 percent of the Czech vote, just short of the five percent necessary to win seats in parliament. The Republicans, on the other hand, scored the underdog upset of the elections, marching into the legislature with over six percent of the Czech total, more than 600,000 votes. Their showing, up dramatically from less than one percent in 1990, landed the populists eleven seats in the 200-seat Czech National Council.[3]

Until the 1992 elections, the crude Czech nationalism of the Republican Party had found expression only on the streets and on building walls. When the Republicans' president Miroslav Sládek first showed his face in Prague's squares in late 1989, it was exactly that sentiment that he set out to capture. From early on, he aimed his message at the disillusioned and displaced in Czech society, at the little man who had about as much in common with Václav Havel as a Thuringian peasant had with Goethe. In the those first blissful days of new freedom and sugarplum dreams of free market prosperity, Sládek's angry appeal found resonance almost exclusively among the Skinheads and their sympathizers. The young, clean-cut former bureaucrat openly courted the young militants, casting the Republicans as the party for social security and law and order. For some reason, his pre-December 1989 post as a small-time censor in the official Central Bureau for Press and Information didn't bother the young thugs. More important was the Republicans' early demand to expel all Vietnamese and Cuban guest workers from Czechoslovakia. In rabble-rousing, virulently anti-communist soapbox speeches, Sládek wove a simple net to catch the inevitable fallout from the crisis conditions of the economic transition. Sládek saw his constituency in the same social strata that the ultra-right Republican Party in Germany targeted with such impressive results. In fact, the German Republican chief, Franz Schönhuber, noted the two parties' affinities from the start and managed to overlook his Czech counterpart's strident anti-German rhetoric to send congratulatory greetings to its first party congress. The Czech party adopted the Germans' logo as their own.

As social crisis set in and the revolution began to lose its glitter, Sládek pounded the pavement all the more tenaciously. He relentlessly traversed the country, painting an opaque picture of society in which communist conspiracies and impenetrable networks stacked the deck against the average citizen. While Civic Forum's leadership made policy from on high in the Hradčany Castle, he peddled his message directly to the people. At aggressive, highly charged demonstrations, he rallied against the "communist agents" in Civic Forum, against the secret police–staged revolution and against "Gypsy criminality." From top to bottom, Sládek insisted, former communists permeated the economy and the political bureaucracy. Among the Republicans' foremost demands were a full purge and ban of all former members of the Communist Party, regardless of their function during the dictatorship. All former communist leaders, the Republicans demanded, should be tried and sentenced. So deep ran Sládek's phobia that he even charged Havel with having been a Communist Party member. Like most of Sládek's wild accusations, he hadn't a speck of evidence to back up the charge. The president's office wryly parried the joust: "Václav Havel was never, at any time, a member of the Communist Party, or for that matter of any other party."

As Sládek's star rose in late 1990, he tried to distance himself from his jack-booted shock troops. But the issues with which he had first won the Skins' hearts remained central to the Republicans' agenda. "Security," for example, gets top billing in the party's program, which calls for new laws that would enable the police to "intervene quickly and responsibly"—although against what or whom it doesn't specify.

The manifesto also demands a beefing up of the security apparatus that Sládek claims to have detested so in its communist form. In Sládek's vision of a new Czechoslovak police state, the death penalty would also be reinstated and prison space increased.

Only after numerous efforts and a hand from the U.S. Czech exile community did I get the chance to speak with Mr. Sládek in person. In the Republican Party's three-room office on the outskirts of Prague, Sládek greeted me with a big smile and a firm handshake. His animosity toward the press was common knowledge and had more than once initiated scenes of name-slinging and even fistfights. "Let me first say that I don't like you, journalists that is," he says as we seat ourselves in a small back room overlooking a snow-covered yard. "It's awful what they write about me," he adds in his servicable English, smiling. A bigish, handsome man, with broad shoulders, intelligent blue eyes, and short brown hair, Sládek comes off as relaxed and personable. Dressed casually in jeans and a black-and-white sweater, he speaks with his legs stretched out before him and laughs often and easily. He looks to be in his late thirties or early forties, but his exact age, he says with a smile, is "top secret."

What sets the Republicans apart from all of the other parties, he explains, is that it remains a "Czechoslovak" party, even after the country's division. "We were the only party that fought against the break-up of Czechoslovakia until the very end," he says. Now, the party demands the reunification of Czechoslovakia. "The division of the country was completely undemocratic," he says. "It was the work of two men, [Czech Prime Minister] Klaus and [Slovak Prime Minister Vladimír] Mečiar, and not the will of the Czechs and Slovaks. A popular referendum would show that there was clear support for a united Czechoslovakia." The Republicans also insist that Subcarpathian Ruthenia (now in the Ukraine) be reincorporated into a "Greater Czechoslovakia." Historically, the region had indeed fallen within the borders of Czechoslovakia during the 1918–38 republic, but became part of the Soviet Union in 1945. Sládek makes regular visits to the eastern region, where he raises the Czechoslovak flag and promises supporters there that one day they will return to Czechoslovakia. According to Sládek, he is "the most popular politician" in all of Subcarpathian

Ruthenia, and given the chance, ninety percent of its inhabitants would cast their votes to "rejoin" Czechoslovakia.

Sládek's "Czechoslovakism" stands out as a peculiar anomaly amongst the ethnic-oriented nationalists of the East European right. He says that he is a "Czechoslovak nationalist" and continually refers to "Czechoslovakia," to the legacy of Masaryk, and to the first republic. "But wasn't Masaryk a liberal social democrat?", I ask him. "Isn't Masaryk also the political mentor of your archenemy President Havel?" Sládek laughs. Havel, he says, doesn't deserve the mantle of Masaryk. "Havel is a puppet in a puppet show prepared by the communists years ago," he says, the smile disappearing from his face. "Havel too was behind the country's break-up and he will go down in history as the worst president since that of the WWII German protectorate. Just look at what he has done. He amnestied all of the criminals, emptying the jails onto the streets. He even apologized to the Sudeten Germans who destroyed Czechoslovakia for the first time in 1938." The picture of Havel as a figure of moral integrity, maintains Sládek, is a product of pure propaganda, spread by the Western press. "The picture that Czechs have of Havel is of an alcoholic, a man who always has a mug of beer in one hand and a cigarette in the other. Can you imagine John Major or Bill Clinton appearing before the public like this?"

For all of the party's undemocratic trappings, it is the Republicans' explicitly racist anti-Roma proposals that land Sládek and friends squarely in the category of a neo-fascist party. In its program, again under "security," the party vaguely mentions its intention "to solve the problem of the Gypsies by resettling them." In standard Eastern European phraseology, "resettling" tends to be a polite term for expulsion, in this case sending recently repatriated Roma populations (mostly Slovak Roma) in Bohemia and Moravia back to their former places of residence. Once in parliament, the Republicans sponsored a draft law, drawn up by the prosecutor-general, to give local police broad special powers to control "undisciplined groups of migrants." The draft law, clearly aimed at Roma, stipulated that people who did not live permanently in a municipality could remain there only with the prior consent of the local authorities and then for no longer than five days within a given six-month period. Police could monitor apartments without search warrants and fine or imprison "illegal" occupants.

According to Sládek, the proposals, which sparked an outcry from human rights and Roma groups, are a "normal thing," and have the full support of local administrations and populations. For years, he explains, Roma from Slovakia, Hungary, Poland, Germany, and even France had come to the Czech lands to take advantage of the communist regime's generous social benefits. Now, they continue to drain the state of funds, and have caused crime to quadruple. "If the police had the powers, it would be easy enough to take care of this problem," he explains. "These Gypsies don't have a lot of furniture or anything like that. They could easily be put on trains and sent back to where they came from." Publicly, Sládek offered a new Alfa Romeo sports car to the first police force that rids its town of Roma. As for human rights, Sládek smiles and laughs again. "You know," he looks at me, "last year I was in Los Angeles at the University of California and some professor asked me about this law and human rights. I said to him: 'If you want some Gypsies of your own, just let me know, we have an abundance.' I don't interfere into your problems with blacks, let us take care of Czechoslovakia. I think we know what's best for us."

Klára Samková of the Roma Civic Initiative (RCI) claims that the Republicans' proposals "violate just about every international statute on human rights that exist." But, says the human rights lawyer, "Sládek is in parliament today because of his hateful rhetoric against the Roma. He used this issue again and again, and that was enough for many people. You don't have to have a program in the Czech Republic, you simply have to say that you will send away the Roma and they'll vote for you."

Where the Republicans scored their biggest electoral victories was, not surprisingly, in northern Bohemia—also the site of even stronger showings from an alliance dominated by the reform communist party. Economists note that when it comes to economic policy, the Republicans and the Communist Party of Moravia and Bohemia (CPMB—the only "reformed" communist party in Eastern Europe brash enough not to change its name) share quite a bit of common ground. The ultra-right and the CPMB-led Left Bloc took big constituencies from the democratic parties by arguing against full-speed-ahead privatization and the dismantlement of social services. Though experts contend that Sládek doesn't know the first thing about economics, his populism found an ear amongst the lower and middle classes, particularly among men in their twenties. In addition to the Roma issue and social demagoguery, the Republicans' anti-German posturing may have helped amass the fifteen to twenty percent tallies that the party chalked up in some Bohemian towns. In the former Sudetenland, Sládek's stoked anxieties about the expelled ethnic Germans returning to claim their prewar land and factories, as well as fears of German capital buying up Czech industry.

REPUBLICANS OF A FEATHER?

The Republicans' pathological anti-communism and hard anti-German stand has helped make it some interesting friends abroad. Like every right-wing extremist party in the former East bloc, the Republican Party has well-heeled allies in the Western exile communities that fund its mission. Although the Republicans' Western contacts appear to be nothing on the scale of nationalist parties in Croatia, Hungary, Romania, or even Slovakia, the case of the Sládek confidant, U.S. businessman Miloš Vobořil, serves as an all too typical example. Vobořil was born into a wealthy, land-owning Czech family in central Bohemia before WWI. In 1939, the Germans confiscated his family's estates and factories, sending the Vobořils, at the time the sole Czech importers for General Motors, into hiding. After the war, the family returned and set up shop once again until the postwar nationalization measures left the Vobořils empty-handed again. After his father committed suicide, Miloš fled communist rule, going first to Belgium and then to the U.S. As an entrepreneur, he remade his family's lost millions, and even delved some into U.S. politics. As a self-described "unofficial foreign policy advisor" on Eastern Europe, Vobořil claims that he pulled some weight in the Reagan White House, as well as with conservative U.S. Republican Party senators such as Al D'Amato and Robert Dole.

When the walls in Eastern Europe tumbled, Vobořil received a call from one of his father's former associates from GM in Detroit. As a consultant to GM, Vobořil returned to Czechoslovakia in early 1990 to negotiate a joint venture deal with the Czech automobile giant Škoda. But the Germans got the better of the Vobořils once again, and Volkswagen took Škoda for the bargain basement price of $750 million. While in Prague in the spring of 1990 Vobořil went shopping for some political pull and met Sládek. According to Vobořil, the Czech Republicans were "the only party with a real Reagan doctrine—free enterprise, low taxes, export-oriented" and, above all, vehemently anti-communist. Although the political philosophy of Klaus' Civic Democratic Party was much more in the spirit of Reaganism than the Sládek party, the Republicans gave Vobořil the "in" he coveted into Czech politics. Vobořil in turn helped fund the party and forge connections between it and his conservative chums in the U.S. In April 1992, Vobořil took Sládek and his party secretary, Jan Vík, on an insider tour of the Washington establishment, arranging meetings with people in the White House, the Congress, and in the influential Czech community in Chicago. Illinois Governor Jim Edgar commended Sládek for bringing "true freedom and democracy to one of America's newest allies, Czechoslovakia." Illinois Congressman William Lipinski addressed a letter to then-Secretary of State James Baker protesting slander charges that Sládek "may face" for his errant accusations against Havel. The slander charges, in fact, were never brought against Sládek, although not as a result of Lipinski's letter.

The mere presence of the Republicans in the Czech legislature adds to the very different face of Czech politics in the aftermath of the 1992 elections and Czechoslovakia's split. Along with most of the former Charter 77 dissidents, all talk of civil society, expanded forms of democracy, and the like have vanished from political discourse. Although Havel was reelected president (only of the Czech Republic the second time), the Republicans immediately gave him a taste of what they had in store for him. Preceding the vote, in the debate broadcast live over Czech television and radio, Sládek and his deputies staged a scandalous two-hour filibuster before parliament, during which they harangued and insulted Havel, calling him a cow, a communist agent, a cigarette smoker, a beer drinker, and a lackey of the Germans. Most deputies there walked out of the hall in disgust. ("That was our first time on television," Sládck told me. "I was pleased. We came off well.")

Human rights organizers see no good coming from the country's division or from the conservative tint of the new political establishment in the independent Czech state. "Our two years of grace are over," says Roma spokesperson Samková, who had slipped into parliament in 1990 under the Civic Forum umbrella. Oddly enough, her group, the RCI, stands as firmly behind full-speed-ahead privatization as Klaus' CDP, despite its disproportionate implications for Roma. Samková's efforts, however, to put the RCI under the Klaus party's wing during the 1992 election campaign fell on deaf ears. "They said that they were sorry, but that they simply didn't want to risk the white vote," explains Samková, whose party ended up with only 50,000 votes, far short of that necessary for seats in parliament. "We agree that the economic problems here must be solved first, but that mustn't necessarily exclude all other problems. The CDP doesn't see how human rights and minority issues are useful to it. If something doesn't bring them immediate economic profit, it's expendable." Now, Samková admits, her only resource is to knock at the doors of power, politely asking for favors.[4]

SLOVAKIA'S WAY

However murky the uncharted waters of sovereignty for the Czechs, the nationalist leadership in Slovakia has wasted no time in steering its very own little Slovakia the way of the Balkans. A combustible mixture of nationalism, economic crisis and minority problems has beset the independent new state with instability from its first days. In contrast to the Czech Republic, whose economic prospects appear among the most promising in the region, Slovakia is struggling to wrest itself from a desperate postcommunist tailspin. In 1992, Slovakia registered a twelve percent unemployment rate and a twenty percent drop in industrial output. Slovakia received only eight percent of Czechoslovakia's total foreign investment in 1992. Though Slovakia is now finally free of the Czechs' "economic tutelage" and "exploitation," as Slovak nationalists have it, few independent economists see statehood bettering the country's general lot. In fact, now cut off from the Czech Republic's access to the West and squeezed between Hungary, Ukraine, Romania, Austria, and the Czech Republic, the 5.3 million Slovaks face a potential for instability that has never loomed so large. The first phase of Slovak independence has done little to assuage critics who fear that Slovakia could easily turn into a nasty conundrum of autocracy and nationalist conflict.

One of the main sources of apprehension is Slovak nationalism, which, unlike that of the Czechs, bears the unmistakable imprint of ethnic nationalism. For the Slovaks, who endured nearly 1000 years of Hungarian rule, the single historical precedent of an independent Slovakia is the 1939–45 Nazi-puppet Slovak State. Under its Führer, Father Jozef Tiso, the clerical-fascist regime instituted rigorous racial legislation against Slovak Jews and Roma. Before the war's end, the dictatorship had sent some 70,000 Jews, almost the entire Slovak Jewish population, to the German extermination camps in Poland. Although the Slovak fascists never boasted the backing of a popular majority, the Slovak State embodied the reactionary ultra-nationalism that had taken similar paths elsewhere in Eastern Europe.

The vast majority of Slovaks in postcommunist Slovakia also rejected an openly extreme variant of Slovak nationalism. Slovak moderates point to the Slovak National Uprising of August 1944 against the fascist state as more indicative of the Slovak character than the wartime quisling regime. The nationalists, on the other hand, deny or minimize the atrocities of the Slovak State. Whatever its faults, they say, at least it was Slovak.

At no time between the communist regime's 1989 overthrow and Slovakia's 1993 rebirth as an independent state did most Slovaks support a full break with the Czechs. Nevertheless, amidst rising national sentiment and discontent with the breakneck pace of the Czech-led economic reform, the Slovaks handed a solid victory to the national populist Movement for a Democratic Slovakia (MDS) in the 1992 elections. Under its controversial leader Vladimír Mečiar, the MDS campaigned on a platform of greater autonomy for the Slovak Republic, which would include a deceleration of the Czechs' free-market transition program. In the familiar mold of national populism, Mečiar, a burly former heavyweight boxer, exhibited a worryingly authoritarian style, and an aggressive intolerance toward criticism when under fire.

As a party, the MDS fused Slovak fears about the crumbling economy with reckless nationalist slogans. In other words, Slovakia's plight was the fault of Czech economic policy. Yet, never during the campaign did the MDS advocate the overnight sovereignty for Slovakia that it soon found plunked in its lap. The strongman Mečiar's election to Slovakia's top post set in motion a dynamic that even its initiators couldn't brake. From the Czech side, Klaus, all too pleased with the thought of ridding the Czechs of underdeveloped Slovakia, rejected Slovak proposals for a Czech-Slovak Union or some looser type of confederation. It was to be "all or nothing," and by January 1, 1993, the dreams of radical Slovak nationalists had finally come true—a fully independent Slovakia lived again.

It didn't take long after assuming office for the MDS nationalists to confirm the democrats' worst suspicions. The government, heavily laden with former communists, showed itself bent upon bringing the media, as well as other public institutions such as universities, under its single authority. As prime minister, some of Mečiar's first moves in office were to renationalize the publishing house that prints all of the newspapers in the Slovak capital of Bratislava and to obstruct an international joint venture that would have guaranteed the financial security of Slovakia's leading independent daily, *Smena*. Television came back under direct government control. Mečiar used every instrument at his disposal to bring the media in line with the government's wishes. In Mečiar's words, all that he wants is for the media to present "a truthful picture of Slovakia." Those journalists who fail to print "the truth," Mečiar's truth, could become subject to new proposed laws against libel and slander.

The trajectory of other ruling national populist parties, such as the Hungarian Democratic Forum or the Croatian Democratic Community, shows that political and economic exigencies will more likely than not push the MDS leadership further and further in the direction of extreme nationalism and autocratic options. That possibility worries no one more than Slovakia's largest minority, the 600,000 ethnic Hungarians in southern Slovakia. In Czechoslovakia, a multinational state, the ethnic Hungarians comprised three percent of the total population. In independent Slovakia, however, an ethnically defined nation-state, the minority accounts for over ten percent of the people, a whole new scenario for majority-minority relations.

The Slovaks' road to independence has done nothing to quell Magyar anxieties about being trapped in hostile territory. The ethnic Hungarians vigorously lobbied for the continuation of the Czechoslovak federation. In the event of independence, the ethnic Hungarian parties argued, they would seek constitutional guarantees for collective minority rights and expanded autonomy within Slovakia in order to protect their culture and rights from nationalist intrusions. Mečiar swiftly squelched the Hungarians' demands, stubbornly insisting that the minority already enjoys "a higher level" of rights than is normally the case in Europe. In abusive flurries, he blasted the ethnic Hungarians as "subversives" and "separatists" whose aim is to cast doubt upon Slovakia's territorial integrity. The Slovak nationalists insist that the ethnic Hungarians' aim is to "turn the Slovaks into a minority in their own country." Tension between Mečiar and ethnic Hungarian parliamentary deputies flared to new heights during Slovakia's debate over its new constitution in autumn 1992. When the MDS and its allies voted to change the wording of the preamble from "We, the citizens of the Slovak Republic" to "We, the Slovak nation," the Hungarians marched out of the parliament in protest. The change, they charged, officially enshrined the Slovaks as the dominant nationality in Slovakia, relegating minorities to a second-class status. Since independence, regional Slovak authorities have set about removing signs with Hungarian place-names and in some places banned their mention on state television. Relations between Slovakia and Hungary have hit an all-time low, with Mečiar and Hungarian nationalists exchanging crass insults of the kind one heard in Yugoslavia in 1990.

With the exception of the Hungarian minority parties, nationalists of one shade or another define the breadth of the Slovak political spectrum. The MDS's closest partner in parliament is the radical Slovak Nationalist Party (SNP). The SNP, the first of the major parties to advocate full sovereignty for Slovakia, captured fourteen percent of the 1990 popular vote with the slogan: "From the nation, with the nation, working for the nation." Although the SNP's share of the 1992 vote dropped to nine percent, a fall explained mostly by the new presence of the nationalist MDS, its anti-Magyar rhetoric played particularly well among Slovaks in central Slovakia, the home of most of the ethnic Hungarian minority, as well as in Bratislava.

Alongside the SNP lives a host of extremist splinter parties and organizations. The "cultural movement" *Matica Slovenská* portends to defend Slovak culture from Magyarization. The movement's vitriolic propaganda against Hungary and the Hungarian minority in 1990 and 1991 caused an early flush of ill will between southern Slovakia's cohabitants. The neo-fascist Slovak People's Party (SPP), a right-wing offshoot of the SNP, is probably the largest of the peripheral ultra-nationalist parties, such as the Party of Freedom, the Party of National Unification, and the Movement for a Free Slovakia, all of which failed to win seats in parliament. The anti-Semitic SPP heralds itself as the successor of the interwar fascist Hlinka's Slovak People's Party and openly defends the record of the Nazi-controlled state. Skinhead groups are just as active as in the Czech Republic, if not more so, and have launched their own wave of terror against Roma and foreign students.

The radical nationalists staged their most impressive show of strength in March 1991 at a ceremony of as many as 10,000 people in Bratislava to lay a cross on Tiso's grave. The following day, March 14, the fifty-second anniversary of the Slovak State, the crowd gathered again to hear a broadcast tape of Tiso reading his 1939 Declaration of an Independent Slovak State. The main square rang with shouts of "Independent Slovakia!" and "Czechs, Jews, and Hungarians out!" For some inexplicable reason, President Havel, in Bratislava for the day, appeared on the scene to have a few words with the militants. Before he could open his mouth, however, the mob rushed his entourage, kicking and spitting on the president. "Death to Havel!", "Judas!", and "Czechs are greedy!," the incensed crowd screamed as bodyguards pushed Havel into his limousine and sped away. Since 1991, the commemoration has become an annual affair, although since the SNP withdrew its support for the ceremony the crowds have thinned to less than half the size of that on the first demonstration.

The partition of Czechoslovakia, as smoothly as it transpired, has added several new destabilizing dimensions to a region with no shortage of potential disasters. The most worrisome at the present appears Slovakia's tense relations with the Hungarian minority and Hungary. The Slovak's insensitive policies have hardly endeared the minority to the new state. Mečiar is certain to find himself against the ropes as the economic situation continues to worsen in the short term, a fact that all but the government economists concede. When he comes out punching, the Hungarians could well be his target, if not the Czechs, the Jews, the opposition, or the press.

One of the saddest aspects of Czechoslovakia's break up is the loss of the federation as a positive, democratic example of a multinational state in Eastern Europe. The legacy of Masaryk's Czechoslovakia was of a political, civic state, defined primarily by its citizens, and not by a single nationality. And, as a multinational state, it worked. Until January 1, 1993. The separation of the Czechs and the Slovaks marked the termination of the region's most sucessful multinational state into two ethnic polities. The logic of division is the same as that behind the disintegration of former Yugoslavia into separate, homogeneous nation-states. The difference, in addition to a far more congenial history between the Czechs and the Slovaks, is that few nations in the Balkans have such clearly marked historical and ethnic borders as the Czechs and the Slovaks. Lingering questions of former federal property, debt, and legislation will certainly irritate Czech-Slovak relations, but neither the borders nor Czech or Slovak minorities in the other state (30,000 Czechs in Slovakia; 300,000 Slovaks in the Czech lands) will arouse the passions that lead to conflict.

Now, however, both the Czechs and the Slovaks are guided by a rationale different from the Staatsraison of Czechoslovakia. They are now nation-states, with borders and constitutions defined according to ethnicity. The upshot of that rationale is most obvious in Slovakia, where a large and potentially separatist minority lives along its southern border. In the Czech Republic too, the increased tension between Czechs and Roma reveals the logic of pure ethnicity in play. When Moravian nationalists demand a separate state from the Bohemians, they are simply taking this thinking one step further. The loss of Czechoslovakia is the loss of a constructive model for different nationalities to live together peacefully in a single state.

Chapter 7

POLAND
CHRIST OF NATIONS

I f one concept captured the essence of the Solidarity movement
during the Polish August of 1980, it was that of "civil society."
For the opposition movement, centered around the newly formed
independent trade union, the notion of a participatory, open, public
realm was initially both its means and its end. The idea of civil society
was an attempt to create an independent sphere of discourse, a "second
society" alongside the state in which people lived and behaved as if
free. The early Solidarity movement constituted a conscious protest
against power, against authority, against ideology, and against politics
as such. The strategy of former sixties student-movement radicals such
as Jacek Kuroń and Adam Michnik, the left wing of Solidarity, was
expressly "anti-political." Their aim was to reinvent the independent
society that the communist state had negated. Although the Polish
opposition rejected the standard labels of "right" and "left," "socialist"
and "capitalist," their demands extolled an anti-authoritarian, participatory ethic that had long been the hallmark of the European left.[1]
Perhaps there was even a tinge of anarchism to the opposition's idea
of a "permanently open democracy" in which autonomous citizens
would realize themselves as acting subjects as they created a pluralistic

civil society. The notion of community stood at the heart of the Polish opposition's project. It was not, however, an exclusive community of the working class, of the nation, or of a certain religion, but a broad community of citizens, an amalgam of diverse individuals who coexisted and interacted in society as a whole.

Although the democratic oppositions in East Germany, Slovenia, Czechoslovakia, and Hungary also latched onto the concept of civil society, only during those brief, exhilarating months in Poland did an entire society in a communist-ruled country put the idea into practice. Society came alive, ordinary people took the initiative, and a spirit of mutual respect and camaraderie prevailed. But the radical vision of a society based upon self-organization, social justice, and participatory democracy did not extend through the whole of the Solidarity leadership. The Polish opposition was broad and heterogeneous, with social democratic, liberal, and Christian strains within it. Other far less influential, right-wing and nationalist groups also existed outside of Solidarity. For the more conservative opposition, "participation" didn't imply self-government, but, for example, the individual's freedom to practice his religion or, among nationalists, the "independence" of the Polish nation. Whatever Solidarity's internal differences, however, the leadership and membership united under the new union's banner in opposition to the communist party's corrupt ethic of power, its dogmatism, its repression, and its intolerance.

Since 1989, Poland has seen independent society establish itself in a way unimaginable during the communist era. The system based upon free elections and a chaotic but more or less functioning parliament has enjoyed a popular legitimacy, even if trust in the institutions of democracy has plummeted dramatically since their inception. Yet today the emerging political culture is a far cry from the spirit of the Polish August. The former Solidarity consensus has given way to a much sharper political division between a Christian nationalist right and a liberal center. In Solidarity's wake, conservative, populist, and Catholic national tendencies barged to the fore in a crowded political landscape. Whether in the form of parties, such as the militant Christian National Union (CNU), or in individual politicians, such as President Lech Wałęsa, these conservative elements have sought to construct a

new Poland upon the twin pillars of Catholicism and Polish nationalism.

Behind the scenes, the real prime mover of postcommunist Polish
conservatism has been the Polish Roman Catholic Church. At first
cautiously, and then with striking audacity, the arch-conservative
Church hierarchy has battled to impose its vision of a fundamentalist
Catholic state upon Poland. Over ninety-five percent of Poles are Catholic, and Catholicism is deeply entwined in the Polish national identity.
The Church emerged from the miasma of communism with tremendous popular authority and clout as the granite fortress of anti-communist opposition and Polish tradition. For a Catholic nation under
communist rule, the nomination of Cardinal Karol Wojtyła to the Holy
See in 1978 and his stirring visit to Poland the following year united
the Poles as never before.

As longingly as the Church awaited communism's end, the advent
of democracy in Poland proved a mixed blessing. On the one hand, the
demise of single-party rule freed the Church and practicing Catholics
from the strictures of the secular state. The Church now enjoys freedom
that was unthinkable just a few years ago, and has placed itself squarely
at the center of public life. Yet, pluralism and multi-party democracy
have also deprived the Catholic Church of its former privileged position
as the one autonomous, noncommunist institution in Poland. Even for
devout Catholics, the Church is now one of many voices competing
for popular influence. Democracy has opened society to new trends, to
diverse opinions, and to challenges to centralized power. Perceiving
new, perhaps even further-reaching threats to its former hegemony,
the Church has gone to controversial lengths to preserve and expand
its leverage in Polish society. It has flexed its considerable muscle to
make its Christian agenda the order of the day in Poland, dangerously
blurring the separation of Church and state. The ecclesiastical hierarchy
has fostered intimate links with those political parties who endorse
traditional Catholic values. Among Catholics and non-Catholics alike,
the encroachment of the Church leadership upon the affairs of state
has provoked great uneasiness about the course of transition. Polish
democrats, opposed to the Church's intrusions into the political process,
see their country at a historical crossroads: one path leading to a "nor-

mal" western democracy, the other to an authoritarian Poland of de facto theocracy.

THE CHURCH OF THE NATION

What distinguishes Polish nationalism and conservatism from its counterparts throughout the region is the central role of the Polish Catholic Church. Catholicism and nationalism converge in Poland as closely as religious and national identity dovetail anywhere in Eastern Europe. The Roman Catholic Church established itself in Poland in the Middle Ages, and, during Poland's many partitions and annexations, the Poles preserved a common national identity through Catholicism and the Church. During the nineteenth century, when Poland was completely wiped off the map of Europe, the great Romantic poet Adam Mickiewicz coined the epithet "Poland, Christ of Nations." In times of occupation, churches served as a refuge for Polish language and culture, protecting Polish traditions from (Orthodox) Russification or (Protestant) Germanization. In spirit as well as deed, the Church helped mount resistance against Poland's foreign conquerors. Nazi Germany's campaign against the Poles and the Catholic clergy during the Second World War further strengthened the bond between the Church and the nation, between Catholicism and national independence. True to its past, the Catholic Church established itself as the guardian of the nation again during the communist era. The Church and its prelates, such as Cardinal Stefan Wyszyński (Primate of Poland 1948–81), readily accepted the mantle of the "church of the nation."

Heroic though the Church looked when it emerged from communism, the Catholic hierarchy's relationship to the ruling authorities had in fact always been one of tactical compromise. From 1955 onwards the state tolerated Catholicism and the Church. Rather than risk the consequences of open victimization, the communist authorities hoped that by acknowledging the Church they could gradually undermine its influence and at the same time win popular support. In the 1960s the communist regime could even boast of the Church's statistical growth—more priests, monks, and places of worship than at any time in Polish history. For its part, the Church hierarchy assumed that the communist state would survive indefinitely. While rank-and-file clergy were often openly critical of the regime, the episcopate showed itself more than willing to meet the state halfway when compromise proved expedient.

The ecclesiastical leadership's complex relation to Solidarity in the early 1980's underlines its ambivalent role. While the Church lent Solidarity its moral support, and activist priests held masses in the Gdańsk Lenin Shipyards, the hierarchy kept its distance from the union, and especially from Solidarity's radical democrats. "In those stormy months," recalls Michnik, "the Church functioned as a catalyst for compromise and as an emergency brake. With the praises of the official propaganda and great authority over the population, the episcopate stood by its line that compromises must be found. Until the signing of the August agreements [which legalized Solidarity], the Church hierarchy held fast to its belief that the founding of independent unions was impossible."[2] The upper echelons of the Church, argues Michnik, were distrustful of a mass social movement that might spiral out of control and undermine its influence over its flock. With the state, the Church knew what it was dealing with. The Solidarity radicals, with leftist aims and broad popular support, seemed to pose a greater, unknown challenge to the Catholic leadership.

For many Poles, however, the Church's record appeared spotless. A short walk through any Polish town reveals the intensity of the Poles' faith. Hardly a skyline exists without a cross-topped steeple; young people in jeans jackets proudly brandish crucifixes around their necks; and public places such as post offices, banks, or grocery stores adorn their walls with images of the Virgin Mary. Every year hundreds of thousands of people make their pilgrimage to the Jasna Góra monastery in Częstochowa, the country's holiest shrine, to worship at the sacred icon of the "Black Madonna." When in June 1992 a group of conservative deputies publicly questioned the political credentials of Peasant Party leader Waldemar Pawlak, President Wałęsa immediately sprang to Pawlak's defense: "No worries gentlemen, he's been to Jasna Góra more times than I have!"

In the countryside, it is the local parish priest to whom people look for guidance. "We're building a church!" is a common sign in the rundown villages in eastern Poland, worst hit by the economic squeeze. For a foreigner, the celebration of Corpus Christi in the southern city of Cracow is a spectacle that evokes images of the Middle Ages. An army of monks and nuns sing hymns and kneel in solemn devotion on the flagstones of the city's thirteenth century market square. In the Baroque St. Anne's church in the university quarter, local believers attend a candlelight wake for the unborn child.

At the same time, much of the younger generation see Catholic dogma conflicting with their modern lifestyles. For many Poles Catholicism is more habit than conviction. While Polish doctors imposed an "unofficial" (and illegal) ban on abortion in 1989—on pain of being struck off the medical register—some estimates put the abortion figure as high as 800,000 a year, one of the highest rates in Europe. And despite calls for the re-introduction of Catholic values, hard pornography and contraceptives are readily available at street kiosks. Religious convictions have not stopped young Poles from experimenting with drugs and premarital sex just as freely as their counterparts in the U.S. or Western Europe.

Along with their faith, the Poles also cherish their Polishness. In light of Polish history, national independence is understandably at the heart of Polish nationalism and usually takes anti-German or anti-Russian shades. Poles today, however, tend to see neither Russia nor the united Germany as the most pressing threat to national sovereignty. In fact, it is the intentions of the independent Ukraine which Poles currently distrust most. Anti-Semitism, too, has long been part of Polish nationalism and Catholicism. The tragic fate of Polish Jews in the twentieth century has failed to eliminate anti-Semitic feelings, which persist today despite the presence of fewer than 5000 Jews in the country. For the most part, however, Polish nationalism tends to look mild in contrast to the chauvinistic nationalisms of many of their neighbors. One factor that has kept extreme nationalism under wraps is the fact that Poland, unlike so many of its former East bloc partners, has only a minute percentage of national minorities within its borders. In fact, Poland has never in its history been so Polish. Most of the ethnic Germans in now-western Poland were expelled after WWII, and most of the Jews that survived the Holocaust emigrated during the communist era. And though ethnic Polish minorities live in the eastern territories lost to the Soviet Union after WWII (in Lithuania, western Ukraine, and Belarus), most Poles want no more than to see these minorities enjoy basic human and cultural rights within their present borders.

THE CHURCH COMES OUT

After the imposition of martial law in 1981, the Church gradually moved ever closer to the opposition, which, though outlawed, maintained its immense popularity among the population. In negotiations between state and opposition the Church acted as the negotiator, the ostensibly neutral middleman. Only during the Spring 1989 election campaign did the Church hierarchy unequivocally throw its weight behind again-legal Solidarity, and once it did, it did so with full force. The Church provided the unprepared Solidarity civic committees with logistical assistance such as office space and meeting halls, xerox machines and organizational advice. From the pulpits, priests informed their parishes about electoral meetings and procedures. Clergymen allowed religious celebrations to be turned into political rallies, which even included the blessing of Solidarity banners and candidates![3] Although the Church's backing for the Solidarity candidates was pretty much evenhanded, there were a few exceptions that presaged developments to come. In five cases, the Church rejected Solidarity candidates on ideological grounds. One candidate was a physician who practiced abortions. The Church also made certain that its men, such as Solidarity leader Wałęsa, kept their hands firmly on the Solidarity rudder.

The dizzying pace of history in late 1989 and 1990 soon confronted the Church with an entirely new political landscape. The collapse of the Soviet bloc and the dissolution of the Polish United Workers Party in 1990 left a gaping power vacuum in Poland. Internal divisions within Solidarity split the former opposition into liberal-reform and conservative-national camps. The Church not only saw power slipping from its hands, but a new adversary arose from the ashes of communism—Western liberalism.

One of the best examples of the Church's deep distrust of liberalism was the rise and fall of Prime Minister Tadeusz Mazowiecki. Mazowiecki, a liberal member of the Catholic intelligentsia and former close advisor of Wałęsa, had been appointed Prime Minister with the Church's consent. The Mazowiecki government took it upon itself to bring religious instruction back into the schools. The same government offered the Church special tax breaks and returned its confiscated property before the claims of other former owners had even been processed. Measures to introduce a ban on abortion also came to the fore. And Mazowiecki, a good Catholic, dutifully supported the Church on the abortion issue too. Yet, the Prime Minister represented a brand of Catholicism and political liberalism that lay on a collision course with the beliefs of the conservative Church. Mazowiecki belonged to a circle of critical Catholic intellectuals committed to an "open Catholicism," one with a more modern Christian message for contemporary society. Equally, if not more suspect was the political agenda of Mazowiecki and his liberal cabinet. In 1990, their program was nothing out of the ordinary in Eastern Europe—a market economy, a "return to Europe," constitutional democracy, and the independence of a popularly elected government. In fact, it was what most East Europeans then referred to as "normal." At the time, perhaps even Mazowiecki wasn't aware of the Church's intransigence toward the changes transforming the former Soviet bloc before its eyes—a factor that would contribute to his downfall in the elections a year later.

To its longtime secular critics, the Church's coming out revealed nothing new. Even compared to other Catholic churches in Europe, the Polish Roman Catholic Church stands out as a particular anachronism, a church suspended in a bygone, premodern thinking. Unlike churches in the West, the Polish Church's first priority in the postwar decades was to defend itself (indeed its very existence during the Stalinist fifties) from the incursions of the state. Under siege, the Church defensively retreated behind its high walls, experiencing none of the liberalizing influences of the postwar ecumenical councils and synods, most notably the 1965 Vatican II reforms. The internal structure of the Church remained rigidly hierarchical and its dogma orthodox and inflexible.

For progressive Catholics, who had hoped to persuade the Church hierarchy to shed its bunker mentality under different conditions, the onset of democracy was a bitter disappointment. "The Polish Church remains the last totalitarian institution in Europe," remarked one critical priest wryly. The conservative Polish prelates entertained no thoughts of "catching up" with their Western counterparts. On the contrary, with a like-minded Polish Pope as their legitimazation, the Polish Church sees itself as the last bulwark of pure, uncorrupted Catholicism in Europe. Its mission is not to be reformed, but to counterreform European Christendom, to bring deliverance to the morally ill West. The Church's starting point is naturally Poland, which, it claims, has also suffered acute moral devastation from four decades of communism and the gnawing influence of Western culture. How else to explain such a high abortion rate among Polish women? Or that good, church-going Catholic men read porn magazines? It is this perception of spiritual corruption, of believers and society gone astray, upon which the Church justifies its interventionist steps into society and politics.

The Polish Church's spiritual mission has the stamp of approval from the very highest office of the Vatican. As early as his 1979 visit to his native Poland, Pope John Paul II espoused the idea of a "Christian Europe" united by transcendental, moral values. Since the fall of communism, the pontiff has vigorously promoted his vision to throngs of worshipers on return trips to Poland, as well as on historic first tours of Hungary and Czechoslovakia. Communism is no longer the major deterrent to the restoration of Christian civilization, as Pope Wojtyła had emphasized in the past. Today the Western culture of materialist consumption and moral laxity present the Catholic Church with its greatest obstacle.

In a 1991 sermon in northern Poland, the Pope spelled out the impending dangers confronting Catholics in postcommunist society: "Don't let yourself get caught up by this civilization of desire and consumption, which, taking advantage of various means of propagation and temptation, has infiltrated our society. Is this civilization or anti-civilization? Is this culture or anti-culture?"[4] In Czechoslovakia, the

Pope similarly warned of replacing communism with the "secularism, indifference, hedonistic consumerism, practical materialism, and moral atheism" of the West. Central Europe, the Slavic Pope said, could act as a bridge uniting "a Europe from the Atlantic to the Urals" in "a new unity." That unity, however, is not the common respect for human rights and democracy that underpins the Conference on Security and Cooperation in Europe's notion of a Europe from the Atlantic to the Urals, but a Europe united by Christianity. The pontiff implies that Poland should be the model Christian state, a beacon for the rest of Europe. Soon after communism's capitulation, the Pope quickly turned his homeland into the frontline of the Vatican's new reconciliatory *Ostpolitik*. On his 1991 pilgrimage to Poland, the Holy Father made highly publicized visits to the eastern border cities of Przemyśl, Łomża, and Białystok, where thousands of Uniate Ukrainians, Lithuanian Catholics, Orthodox Russians, and Belarusians poured over the border to hear his message of reconciliation and unity.

The intrusion of the Catholic Church into matters of state has a long history in European Christendom, and even today the logic for an interventionist Church policy in the earthly realm calls back to the medieval debates of the early Church fathers over free will and salvation. According to Christian doctrine, there are two roads to salvation: a life of good and moral deeds, and divine grace. In a society so corrupt as that of modern Europe, or in the case of young East Europeans cursed with the original sin of communism, the individual is severely restricted in his ability to choose the good. Human beings, in other words, are not capable of exercising their free will in a moral way under such immoral conditions. One avenue, presumably a longer-term strategy, is for the Church to rejuvenate the faith and morality of its followers through its teachings during Church services on Sunday mornings, for example. Catholics then should intuitively choose the good.

The Catholic Church in Poland, however, insists that it reach further with its message than the last row of pews. Religious education in schools and a media that respects "Christian values" should also be inundating followers, and, in the case of the media, non-believers too, with the word of God. Another alternative, a kind of damage-control strategy, is to limit the possible evils and temptations from which the individual can choose. This solution implies a social straightjacket that binds the individual by limiting his choice. If abortion is outlawed or pornography banned, the individual cannot sin by choosing them. The damage-control opinion brings the Church even more overtly out of its spiritual confines into the social and political spheres. Its recourse must be to civil law, and civil punishment for those who break it.

According to Wojciech Lamentowicz, professor of law at Warsaw's Polish Academy of Sciences, the Church's interventionist philosophy reverses the roles of Church and state that existed under communism: "Now we have to protect democratic values not so much from a powerful, authoritarian state, but from a powerful, authoritarian Church. The Church, which before had been the defender of the people, has become the new obstacle to self-expression." Lamentowicz argues that Poland's Catholic hard-liners see a "strong nation and a strong government united in the body politic, mediated through some sort of strange discourse by the Church. The Church unites the nation and government in one holy alliance of forces in favor of decency and a moral life." The logical consequence, he says, is that all public space would come under the supervision of this strong, moral government, with the Church standing behind it as the final judge.

Although the Church's conservatism may not have surprised Poland's democrats, the boldness with which it moved to realize its vision of a Catholic state shocked even its sharpest critics. In Poland's young democracy, with nearly thirty little-known parties competing in the parliament, the Catholic Church is by far the most powerful political actor in the country. "The Church is the only national organization, which is highly centralized, well-organized, well-disciplined, endowed with considerable material resources, and has at its disposal many channels of information, as well as the direct backing of a Polish Pope," explains sociologist Andrzej Flis. According to Flis, few politicians have been willing to risk their careers by opposing the Church's wishes. "The Church exerts its pressure through many channels, and since 1991 it has done so openly, without any discretion, which is a good yardstick of its strength."

Neither the episcopate nor individual bishops, for example, have hesitated to pass judgment upon the wording of the new constitution, upon economic policy, or upon foreign policy, much less upon social issues. Poland's first three noncommunist prime ministers all had the Church's tacit approval. In the 1990 presidential race, it seemed to be Wałęsa—the traditional Catholic, father of seven children, with a holy medallion permanently stuck to his breast pocket—who had the Church's support over Mazowiecki. One month before the vote, Church bishops circulated a pastoral letter about the elections that was read aloud in all Catholic churches. The letter said that it was the duty of all Poles to elect to public office "trustworthy people who accept the Christian code of ethics and are guided by Poland's raison d'état." Although officially neutral on the contest, the Church's preference for Wałęsa, particularly in the final runoff with the emigre businessman Stanisław Tymiński, was plain.

Nearly all the political parties have felt themselves forced to weigh the possible reaction of the Church to their programs. The hierarchy wields incredible influence over politicians, and during the first years of postcommunist democracy, few mustered the nerve to openly defy it's bidding. One of the most blatant examples of Church intrusion has been its heavy-handed campaign to have abortion criminalized. From Primate Jóset Glemp, Poland's highest-ranking bishop, to priests in village parishes, the Church's representatives fiercely lobbied politicians and believers to support the bill. Parliamentary deputies received letters from the episcopate urging them to vote the bill through, and bishops summoned top politicians to personal tête-à-têtes. At masses, local clergyman launched pulpit tirades against "mother murderers" who slaughtered their own babies. The abortion bill that the Church favored would have introduced the most extreme legislation in Europe, alongside Ireland. Not only would terminating a pregnancy be illegal, but both women and their doctors would be subject to two years imprisonment. Exceptions would be made only if a woman's life—and not simply her "health"—was endangered. Even in cases of rape or incest the law would offer no protection. The bill would also have put an end to prenatal screening and "morning-after" contraception methods.

The Church's four-year campaign finally paid off in January 1993, when the ruling five-party coalition struck a compromise deal to avoid its own collapse and probably fresh elections. Brushing aside demands for a referendum on the issue—over a million signatures had been collected in less than three weeks—the government managed to force through a watered-down version of the original bill. Much to the dismay of Catholic conservatives, the new bill avoided the punishment of women and permitted abortions in cases of rape and incest. "Why," argued one pro-church parliamentarian "should a child be punished for its father's mistakes?" In truth, the political compromise satisfied neither the right nor its critics. For the opposition, centered around the referendum committees, the new law practically meant an end to womens' choice on abortion. For the right, it sanctioned murder. Primate Glemp appeared in parliament shortly after the vote to join deputies in a celebratory mass for this "great step forward," but Catholic radicals vowed in defiance that the struggle for their original project would continue.

The ubiquitous presence of the Catholic Church in society has led Michnik and other critics to warn of a looming "Iranization" of postcommunist Poland. Some observers, such as sociologist Flis, argue that the situation is potentially even more menacing than in Iran. "Iran is clearly a theocracy, where the clergy exerts power directly, as heads of state and in the legislature," he says. "As politicians, the religious men inherently bear responsibility for their decisions and policies." In Poland, however, the Church leadership extends its influence into political life from behind the scenes, without directly assuming public posts. It is not the Church that passes unpopular bills, such as the ban on abortion or special tax breaks for itself, but politicians, who, in the end, must answer to their electorate. "The gravest threat to Polish democracy is the separation of power from responsibility," explains Flis. "The Church is a classic case of power without responsibility. They press and influence politicians, but formally the politicians make the decisions that follow Church policy. This puts the Church in a very comfortable position. It is involved in politics and not involved in politics. And if you look at the Church's legacy during communism, this is really nothing new."

THE CHURCH'S CRUSADERS

As the first fully free elections to the Sejm, the Polish parliament, approached in Fall 1991, the Church's misgivings about democracy spinning out of control grew large. In place of the communist party and a united Solidarity, new parties mushroomed with programs that spanned the political spectrum. At first, the Catholic hierarchy, though officially neutral again, ambiguously stressed the importance of electing parties that "guaranteed the preservation of national identity and Christian values." But as the campaign intensified, and the center-liberal Democratic Union jumped in the polls, the Church seemed to panic. "Unofficial" posters appeared and lists circulated that named the parties approved by the Church. Top on the lists, and clearly the Church leadership's favorite, was Catholic Election Action, an alliance led by the fundamentalist Christian National Union (CNU). The lists, which varied in composition, also recommended the conservative-right Center Alliance, several Christian democratic parties and, in some cases, the neo-fascist National Party. Conspicuously absent from the fliers and posters was the Democratic Union, the party that united the former Solidarity left with the progressive Catholic intelligentsia.

A resolution passed at the bishops' conference stated that only parties which "respected the rights of the unborn child, the law of the family, and Polish Christian tradition" could enjoy the mandate of real Catholics. The episcopate had officially banned agitation from the pulpit, but when an unsigned letter was sent from the conference to all dioceses explicitly stating which parties and candidates to vote for, it was clear that the "official" ban would not be heeded. On the eve of the elections, Bishop Józef Michalik addressed a "mass for the fatherland" with the following words: "It would be an evil if a Catholic nation once again found itself in a situation in which it was governed by a non-Christian parliament. A Catholic's responsibility is to vote for a Catholic, a Christian for a Christian, a Moslim for a Moslim, a Jew for a Jew, a Freemason for a Freemason, and a Communist for a Communist. Let everyone vote according to his conscience."[5]

Whether or not the Church's meddling tipped the scales in favor of the conservative Christian parties remains unclear. Fifty-eight percent of the electorate opted not to vote at all. The two biggest vote winners were the Democratic Union with 12.6 percent (significantly less than early polls had predicted), and the reform communist party with an unexpectedly impressive 11.6 percent of the vote. Nevertheless, in the end it was the right, led by the Catholic Electoral Action/CNU (nine percent) and the Center Alliance (8.5 percent), that put together a multi-party ruling coalition. Poland's new prime minister, the first chosen from a freely elected parliament, was Jan Olszewski, a conservative Catholic attorney associated with Center Alliance.

In office for an almost uninterrupted spell since the 1991 elections, the CNU has proved itself the Church hierarchy's loyal foot soldier. Most observers agree that the CNU program accurately mirrors the views of the Church leadership, and that the CNU as a party acts as God's anointed servants in the nitty-gritty of day-to-day politics. Just like the Church, the CNU envisions a Poland thoroughly steeped in "Christian values" (as they repeat ad nauseam), a national Catholic state prepared to combat both the residual legacy of communism and the Western evils of consumerism and moral permissiveness. Founded by right-wing intellectuals and professionals in 1989, the party's antipathy toward the West includes a biting critique of the market economy. In the 1991 campaign, the CNU scored big points branding the ruling liberals the "architects of recession." The party's vague, pseudo-leftist economic program promised a rejection of Finance Minister Leszek Balcerowicz's tough monetarist line, a stop to the influx of foreign capital and Western goods, and an emphasis on welfare.

Independent economists agree that beyond sloganeering the CNU lacks even the basic outlines of a viable economic plan. And indeed, the evangelicals concede, their priorities lie elsewhere. Their mission is the "rebirth" of the Polish nation, at the cornerstone of which lies the traditional, close-knit family: a hard-working, dedicated father, a devoted housewife and mother, and respectful God-fearing children. The guiding light of the CNU's social policy is the Vatican's Child and Family Rights Charter, which condemns abortion, divorce, pre-marital sex, and the use of contraception. In a CNU Poland, Poles would be protected from the West's culture of smut and sleaze, from pornography and American television.

Polish Matters, the CNU's monthly journal, outlines the party's vision of the "rebirth" of Poland. It identifies "Christianity, Church, Fatherland, and Honor" as the principles that disillusioned Poles must observe to soothe the pain of material hardship. For the CNU, the Polish renaissance depends on a revolution of the soul grounded in the political and moral re-education of youth. "The young generation must be morally pure and physically strong," they say, "for a strong and healthy organism is the tool of a beautiful soul." The young Pole must assume the role of a "moral crusader" if he is to overcome the norms of the young "petty criminal, alcoholic and anarcho-pacifist," for, "a true Catholic is not a meek little lamb who easily reaches compromise." Responsibility for social and economic failure is laid squarely at the feet of the ubiquitous "enemies" of the Polish nation: the "pseudo-tolerant" left (including the liberal center), the "intelligentsia who appropriate the title of intellectuals," the elites—"barbarians in love with Western prayer beads and tinsel," and even scholarship students who have come into contact with the "demoralized West."

The problem is not merely the enemy within. Other, far more threatening dangers lie at the core of the CNU's apocalyptic vision of post–Cold War Europe. Poland is portrayed as a country worn out by communism, abused by its neighbors and isolated from the world. "Infanticidal Western Europe, the quintessential traitor," is largely to blame for this. In language reminiscent of their communist predecessors, the authors of *Polish Matters* reserve their greatest wrath for Germany—"the fourth Reich." "Europe of 1992 is the Europe of the German nation," they declare, a pan-German enterprise directed against Poland. The tiny German minority in Poland is seen as "the conveyor belt of German raison d'état," their claims for political and cultural recognition dismissed as treason or "fifth columnism." For party radicals, Polish raison d'état also means defending the Polish cultural diaspora and promoting the rebirth of Catholicism in the eastern territories lost to the former Soviet Union. Their holy duty is to establish a protectorate for the Polish minorities in Lithuania, Belarus, and the Ukraine. "Be prepared for belligerence," beseech the authors of *Polish Matters*, "a mighty Poland in a de-Christianized Europe has a strong mission to fulfill," a mission justified by "the richness of the Polish culture of the soul and religious belief."

Although it describes itself as a Christian democratic party, the CNU's ideology is at odds with the basic assumptions of even the most conservative Christian democratic parties in Western Europe. Its advocates may insist that "nationalism defends democracy," but what the ideology lacks is precisely a democratic component. The party sees itself as the executive of Church law in the political sphere. It does not therefore tout a political program so much as an evangelical mission, which, by definition, is answerable only to God, not to an electorate. Even if it chose to, the CNU would have difficulty drawing upon the meager Christian democratic tradition that existed in Poland before WWII. The closest historical precedent for the CNU is the interwar National Democratic party, led for more than thirty years by Roman Dmowski. Though near to the Catholic Church, Dmowski's chauvinistic, anti-Semitic party was first and foremost a national party, fueled primarily by hostility toward Poland's aggressive neighbors, Germany and the Soviet Union, as well as its domestic minorities, most notably Jews and Ukrainians. In contrast to contemporary Poland, however, the Church played a secondary role in the interwar Dmowski party. In the CNU today, it is the Christian element that receives the greatest emphasis, and nationalism second.

Nation and spirit are inextricably bound in the political program of the CNU and the Church. As much as CNU's diatribes often sound like abstract moralizing, its agenda is part of a much larger political program. Inherent in that program for the creation of a mighty Catholic Poland are Orwellian policies of eugenics and social engineering. According to CNU philosophy, the Polish nation is both an ethnic community—of Poles, and a spiritual community—of Polish Catholics. Containing both elements, the nation thus functions as the critical link between the two communities, the earthly and spiritual. The creation of a vital spiritual community, per CNU, depends upon a strong Polish nation, that is, upon a community of ethnic Poles devoted to Christianity. The most elementary unit of that ethnic community is the (Catholic) family. The construction of a Catholic nation-state must therefore start at the root of the nation's weakness, the family and its contemporary moral crisis. On the family, or ethnic, side of the equation, the CNU project is essentially eugenic, aimed at the improvement of the species through controlled reproduction. Nearly homogeneous Poland, where the gene pool is virtually closed, is the perfect laboratory for a policy of eugenics. Basically, Poles only have to reproduce more pure-blooded Poles to build the great white Catholic Poland that the CNU and the Church dream of. Although unsaid, such logic implicitly rules out "interbreeding" with people of other nationalities or religions. The ethnic component of the CNU vision thus also sheds new light on policies such as the banning of abortion, which, presumably supported on purely religious grounds, also have ethnic implications. The other side of the equation, that those Poles be true Catholic Poles, implies a policy of social engineering aimed at the youth. The indoctrination of the new generation with Christian ideology must, of course, be supervised by the Church and political forces under hermetic conditions, a Poland closed to external influences.

POLES APART

As mighty as the Catholic Church may be, its activism and the zealotry of the CNU have provoked a popular backlash. Many Catholics deeply resent the Church's influence in politics, and object to the hierarchy's ultra-conservative stances on social issues. "Even the Pope is open to criticism today, which certainly wasn't the case a few years ago", remarked one journalist from the liberal Catholic weekly, *Tygodnik Powszechny.* Surveys show that public trust in the Church as an institution has fallen off drastically since communism's demise. From 1990 to early 1992 confidence in the Church dropped from a high of eighty-five percent to a low of fifty percent. In early 1993, the Church's disapproval rating (forty-six percent) was higher than its approval rating (forty-one percent) for the first time. Among the institutions included in the 1993 poll, approval was highest for the army (seventy-two percent) and the police (sixty-seven percent.) Ever more outspoken opposition has made itself heard from democratic Catholic circles, as well as from within the Church itself. Liberal currents in the clergy have focused their energy on internal reforms in order to loosen the hierarchy's grip on decision making and Church policy. And although they have scored some important victories, they remain unable to affect the Church's most controversial positions.

Just off Cracow's bustling main square, behind the stark, thirteenth century Gothic Church of St. Mary, the women in the regional Democratic Union headquarters insist that the overwhelming majority of Poles are fed up with Church policy. At a long table overlooking the street, Democratic Union activists, Natalia, twenty-two, and Brygida, twenty-seven, stuff envelopes with fliers that promote a popular referendum on the abortion question. They know that neither the Church nor most politicians, including many in their own party, want the emotional issue to come to a plebiscite. For one, surveys consistently show that over seventy percent of Poles oppose the outlawing of abortion. Second, the Church and the political establishment fear that a popular vote could bitterly divide the country. But Natalia insists that "society is already split over this question." She feels that a referendum "is the only truly democratic way" to settle the controversial issue. For Natalia, a psychology student at Cracow's Jagiellonian University, the abortion question is no simple matter. As a practicing Catholic, she doubts that she could ever have a pregnancy of her own terminated. At the same time, women, she feels, should have the right to make their own choice. The number of abortions performed each year in Poland, she insists, could be lowered through education. "There are many Poles who don't even know how to use contraceptives," she says, citing statistics that only eleven percent of Polish couples use contraception. "And if the Church prevails, it will stay that way. The rate of unwanted pregnancies will remain high and women will simply travel to doctors abroad."

Brygida, the referendum campaign's regional director, agrees with her co-worker. She points out that neither she nor Natalia consider themselves "feminists." In fact, by the look on her face, she seems to consider it a pretty nasty slur. Also a Catholic, Brygida associates "feminism" with the old communist Women's League, and today with the Parliamentary Women's Circle, laden with women from the reform communist party. The Democratic Union, she stresses, is "nonideological," and therefore doesn't try to "exploit" women's issues for political gain. Poland's foremost liberal party wouldn't even take a stand on the abortion bill. But that doesn't upset Brygida. No position at all is better than that of the CNU. "They want to throw women back to the dark ages," she protests. "They see women as subordinate, second-class beings, as nursemaids who live to please their husbands with babies and meals." Even if women accepted this servile role, she notes, most Polish men couldn't possibly support a family of even three people with their single salaries. And as unemployment forces women out of the workplace, many couples are already thinking twice about more-than-one-child families, she says.

Across the square, the Cracow CNU chairman, Paweł Pytko, manages his party's regional affairs. The hushed office has the aura of a hi-tech funeral parlor. Behind his desk, outfitted with jet-black, state-of-the-art office technology, a big wooden crucifix stands next to a framed red, white, and blue certificate from the 1992 Republican National Convention in Houston, Texas. With his neatly trimmed mustache and black polyester suit, Pytko would blend unnoticed into the fundamentalist sections at the convention. Pytko, in his mid-forties, rejects charges that the CNU is overly prudish on matters of the flesh. He, for example, has nothing against people informing themselves about contraception. In contrast to the West, however, where even teenagers may require this kind of information, Polish adolescents, he explains, don't encounter these problems at such tender ages. Under such circumstances, sexual education would be tantamount to promotion.

"What we don't want is to turn Poland into Sweden," says Pytko, a country which he points out has the highest suicide rate in Europe. I look at him frankly puzzled. What relation does the availability of contraception have to the Swedish suicide rate? "That's simple," he responds, taking a moment to sort out his thoughts. "In a country like Sweden, where sexual relations are casual, where pornography is commonplace, and where values are relative, people feel alienated from one another. These societies have lost their closeness. The individual is alone, and the world is meaningless for him." His argument is the same as that of the ultra-right in Germany or Belgium, Hungary or Croatia: Modernity leaves the individual stranded, staring into an existential abyss of morally empty choices, each as meaningless as the other. The family, the nation, and religion restore a purpose to human existence, securing the individual in a tight community of blood and faith.

The unpleasant reality of the twentieth century, however, means facing it, and turning it back at all costs. The Church and the CNU, for example, have publicly condemned both homosexuality and the contraction of the AIDS virus as "sins." Although not going quite as far as some Russian ultra-rightists, who propose the extermination of homosexuals, or even the Romanian government, which refuses to revoke the communist law criminalizing homosexuality, Poland's Catholic conservatives have come down hard on those who "deviate" from the heterosexual "norm." In an interview with the Warsaw daily *Trybuna*, CNU vice-chairman, Stefan Niesiołowski, outlined CNU's thoughts on the matter, essentially the Vatican line on homosexuality and AIDS:

Niesiołowski: TV programs that deride priests and the Church are clearly an attack on the right of people to respect their religion and their vision of God. The assault on the Christian ethic is particularly visible in the area of sexual ethics and ideas about marriage. There are TV shows today that try to impose upon people the idea that the teachings of the Church are somehow at odds with reality. We want to introduce a Christian system of values because if we don't, there is the danger that it will be replaced with a different ideology: one that embraces the easy way of life, the avoidance of sacrifice, hedonism, contempt for other individuals, for the fatherland and for tradition.

Trybuna: Are there other legitimate systems of values in Poland?

Niesiołowski: The conflict here is essentially whether all ideologies should have equal status. Can you have on the one hand a Christian ideology and on the other a system of values in which homosexuality is treated as normal or which accepts drug addiction and sodomy? On the one hand, the family, and, on the other, two perverts, each with their own television program? Homosexuals in the West have managed to win great privileges for themselves. I will

257

never accept this, nor will I ever accept a law that treats perversion as normal. This would quickly lead to other problems. Even now people with AIDS are becoming incredibly aggressive, demanding privileges at the cost of others.

Trybuna: How would you deal with the problem of AIDS?

Niesiołowski: People with AIDS are mainly perverts and drug users. They usually only have themselves to blame. Very few get the disease by way of blood transfusions. If somebody gets syphilis he doesn't suddenly gain widespread understanding and sympathy. However, for some strange reason AIDS creates a halo of secrecy around itself and provokes sympathy. And yet AIDS is just a particularly acute and terminal form of venereal disease.[6]

The Niesiołowski interview sparked sharp protests from Lambda, one of several new gay organizations in Poland. It pointed out, for example, that most of Poland's several thousand registered HIV-cases became infected through needle-sharing, not through sexual intercourse. According to Lambda spokesman Jerzy Krzyszpień, statements like Niesiotowski's are a conscious form of manipulation, an attempt to stigmatize homosexuality as a sickness and perversion. Most Poles, even practicing Catholics, he feels, are relatively tolerant of sexual diversity. "The problem is that most people know very little about homosexuality, and with this kind of demagoguery they could easily be persuaded otherwise."

Homosexuality has been legal in Poland since the 1920s, and even the CNU have not yet made an issue of reintroducing a legal ban. During the communist era, the state observed, harassed, and intimidated homosexuals. For the public, homosexuality was either a non-issue, or, as the propaganda had it, a variation of bourgeois Western decadence. Only foreigners received AIDS tests. "Very slowly homosexuality is coming into the open here," says Krzyszpień, "and people are a little surprised that it is more prevalent than they thought. That's why this absurd talk of 'privileges' and perversion is so dangerous. We're worried that there will be a negative reaction as we try to secure even the most basic rights that gays and lesbians have in the West."

Every small step forward for gay activists meets stiff resistance from the bureaucracy. Health department officials tried to remove mention of anal sex from the first-ever safe sex pamphlet for gay men, for fear of "promoting" homosexuality. Under Church pressure, a safe sex poster campaign begun in the late 1980s was halted. "Even if they're not anti-gay, officials don't want to risk their positions," says Krzyszpień. "They say that the Western Europeans may have their ideas about it, but that we'll do it our way, and that means doing nothing to offend the Church." The result is public ignorance, growing hostility toward homosexuals and drug users, and fertile soil for the rapid spread of HIV and AIDS.

In Summer 1992, thirty HIV-positive children became the victims of the misinformation surrounding HIV and AIDS when villagers chased the children and health officials from two houses that had been purchased for them outside of Warsaw. The children were then moved to another village in the vicinity, where the local citizens staged nightly protests. The demonstrators claimed that they could be infected with the virus through mosquitoes, air, and the sewage system. In the end, the villagers attacked the childrens' residences, as well as foreign medical teams that had come to inspect the sites. One night the clinics mysteriously caught fire and burned to the ground. The police attributed the fire to lightning and made no arrests after a perfunctory investigation. The villagers' actions provoked an outburst of criticism from health officials and much of the media. The Church, however, saw it differently. Primate Glemp called the media coverage "a misuse of the concept of tolerance" and "a humiliation of the victimized citizens." People shouldn't close their eyes to the fact that AIDS is a result of "social disorder," said Glemp, and that "curbing the epidemic is primarily the responsibility of the individual."

The CNU saw great hopes of implementing its "re-Christianization" program when it entered the right-wing Olszewski government. The watchword of the fragile seven-party coalition that assumed power in late Winter 1991 was "de-communization," which meant a general cleansing of state and society from undesirable communist elements. For Olszewski, the root cause of Poland's crisis was the continuing rule of the nomenklatura, whose destruction the government made its top priority. In practice the much-promised breakthrough amounted to little more than firing existing civil service personnel and appointing "trusted" replacements, usually from the CNU. In economic policy too, the government was begrudgingly forced to continue shock therapy.

As Olszewski's rhetoric became more abrasive, so support for the coalition dwindled. The government's final act came in early June 1992 when the Minister of Internal Affairs circulated a list of parliamentary deputies suspected of being agents of the communist security services. Though bound to secrecy, deputies eventually leaked the list to the press. On it were scores of top politicians including irreproachable former Solidarity leaders, formerly jailed nationalist leaders, and even the chairman of the CNU. Soon afterwards the State Security Office put the army on alert, ordering troops to guard the television and radio buildings. Rumors abounded of a putsch. On June 4th, while parliament was debating the political vetting, regular programing was suddenly cut, and Olszewski appeared live on both television channels. His dramatic appeal to the nation that a communist takeover was in the making proved to be the final nail in the coalition's coffin. A vote of no confidence was passed, and the Minister of Internal Affairs was unceremoniously escorted from the ministry building.

POPULISM'S MANY FACES

Typical of populist fortunes, the CNU's attempt to exploit dissatisfaction with the country's economic woes ran aground once it found itself sharing power. As part of the ruling coalition, it too was responsible for 1992's forty-five percent inflation rate and the fate of Poland's 2,000,000 unemployed. Populism is most potent when invoked from outside of power, where empty promises and amorphous programs are relevant only in so far as they effectively capture frustration or fear. The most easily peddled populisms are usually those with the least specific ideological content. Rather, populist parties tend to have broad, ambiguous, politically vague programs that appeal to the lowest common denominator of the most people. Thus, nationalism and economic populism often go together hand in hand. The requirements couldn't be more minimal—one only has to be a member of the nation and want more money.

Though populism can take progressive forms, in Eastern Europe populist parties tend to veer to the right politically, while taking anti-market positions on economic issues. Opposition to the full-speed-ahead market reforms, for example, is a part of every populist movements' platform. The blame for economic failure is dished out generously: to communists, liberals, the IMF, Jews, and other nations. On strictly economic issues, the thin, wishful programs of right-wing populists are often identical to those of the reform communist parties. To its discredit, postcommunist Poland has proven a fruitful breeding ground for populisms, which have blazed spectacularly before fizzling out and dissipating into the thin air from which they came. Both as parties and grassroots movements, the Poles have been the quickest of their former East bloc brethren to organize themselves. Perhaps a legacy of their Solidarity past, workers, farmers, the socially dispossessed, and even sinister former communist elements have shown themselves capable of turning disillusionment into political muscle.

The most disturbing of Poland's populist ventures was the mercurial campaign of Stanisław Tymiński in the 1991 presidential election, a farce so successful that most Poles woke up the next morning wondering if it had all just been a bad dream. Although Wałęsa eventually defeated the emigre businessman, Tymiński's quixotic run for the country's highest office was all too real. In the first-round vote, the dark horse Tymiński beat Mazowiecki and four minor candidates to meet Wałęsa in the final runoff. As much as the post-Solidarity parties would have liked to write off the "Tymiński Phenomenon" as a fluke, it revealed that a considerable part of the population was dissatisfied with the policies of the Mazowiecki government, politically disoriented and receptive to the hollowest of demagoguery.

After twenty years abroad, Tymiński, a "self-made millionaire" with Polish, Canadian, and Peruvian citizenships, arrived unannounced on the Polish political scene in Autumn 1990. A complete unknown, with a dubious curriculum vitae that stretched from the wilds of the Amazon jungle to libertarian politics in Canada, Tymiński portrayed himself as the prodigal son who had left Poland with nothing and returned a wealthy industrial kingpin. Although his boasts were often wildly exaggerated at best, his message was simple and clear: He knew the ropes of capitalism and he would make Poland rich, just as he had made his fortune in the West. Suspiciously soft on communism, he inveighed against the agents of conspiracy, from the IMF to Wałęsa, for obstructing Poland's prosperity. He appealed to the little man, the losers of the economic transition. Yet unlike most populists, Tymiński didn't vow to "slow things down." While Mazowiecki proposed to continue with shock therapy and Wałęsa countered with vague calls for "acceleration," the Canadian businessman said that he would do it all "faster." How, he didn't say, simply "faster," as if he and he alone possessed the magic formula for Poland's overnight metamorphosis from rags to riches. For a political program, the candidate submitted his self-published book *Holy Hounds*, a "textbook for the free market," that combined self-help maxims and an anti-Western economic critique with the author's own bizarre mystical beliefs. During the first-round campaign, as the former Solidarity leaders battled it out between themselves, neither the media nor his opponents paid much attention to Tymiński.

Even once the press finally zeroed in on the candidate, exposing Tymiński for the crackpot that he was, his popularity remained strikingly high after his first-round finish behind Wałęsa. On closer scrutiny, it came to light that Tyminski had been in contact with the communist security service for years while abroad. At press conferences he often contradicted himself about his past, feigned ignorance of even knowing the name of the former security police and, more than once, simply refused to answer the questions, standing completely silent for minutes on end. At times he seemed to condone the 1981 imposition of martial law, which had opened Poland to unnamed "internal threats." In fact, many disgruntled former communist apparatchiks found a new home in Tymiński's Party X, the vehicle through which he tried to maintain his momentum after his defeat to Wałęsa. Although Party X failed to come up with concrete programs any more coherent than that of their leader, it filled its empty carriages with traditional populist baggage—anti-Semitism, authoritarianism, and national chauvinism.

In an appeal to its targeted constituency, Party X labelled itself "the party of pain." "The Polish nation has been cheated," said Tymiński at an April 1991 rally. "No one wanted communism and no one wants it now, but people also do not want to be told what to do by foreigners. The Poles have become a tool of international manipulation," he warned, "and Poland is ruled worse than under communism."[7] The more defined its ideology and leadership became, the more dramatically Party X sank in the polls. In the parliamentary elections, Party X gained only three seats in a 460-seat Sejm. While Party X faded away soon afterward, the sentiment upon which it had fed remained a volatile and unknown factor in Polish politics—one which would raise its head again under different guises.

The very election that turned Party X into an ex-party saw another renegade populist organization by the name of the Confederation for an Independent Poland (CIP) stage an upset victory of its own. Unlike Tymiński and Party X, the CIP and its unquestioned leader Leszek Moczulski were no newcomers to Polish politics. As it likes to boast, the CIP predates even the Solidarity movement. In 1979 it was the first dissident group to establish itself as a political party. Under journalist and military-history buff Moczulski, the CIP represented a nationalistic, patriotic alternative to the communist party as well as Solidarity. Then, as now, the CIP held fast to uncompromising demands for Poland's "full independence" from foreign powers and ideologies. During the seventies and eighties that power was the Soviet Union and the ideology was communism. The CIP radicals charged Solidarity's "crypto-communists" with "insufficient patriotism" for their willingness to compromise with the communist party. In contrast to the Solidarity leadership, which advocated a "gradualist" approach to political reforms, the CIP never swayed from its insistence that Poland could realize its freedom only with the termination of Soviet domination—"here and now." The price that Moczulski and the CIP leadership paid for the purity of their dissidence was high. During the seventies and eighties, Moczulski spent a total of nearly ten years in prison, an understandably traumatic experience that many today feel has left its mark upon the eccentric leader.

The repression of the communist regime reduced the CIP to a tiny conspiratorial core of several hundred members by the late 1980s. It resurfaced as a legal party in 1989, however, with its will unbroken. The CIP refused to join the negotiations between Solidarity and the government on the grounds that the communist party constituted an illegitimate partner. From the sidelines, Moczulski and his company vilified Solidarity and the Mazowiecki government for their continued collaboration with the communist party. In the presidential race, Moczulski finished dead last with 2.5 percent of the vote.

The CIP's fortunes were soon to change. The Tymiński challenge had dramatically exposed popular discontent with the *Solidatura* and its new offspring. Suddenly, for the first time since its inception, the CIP found itself in the position to capitalize upon its decade-long status as the outsider, as the diehard opponent of power and the status quo. "We never compromised with the communist party, we are not responsible for the present mess," the CIP alone could say. In the 1991 parliamentary campaign, the CIP stuck adamantly by its principles of old. "National independence," however, no longer meant the overthrow of communism, but an "internal independence" aimed at settling accounts with the "paid traitors and stooges of Russia" still in the bureaucracy or economy. They shrilly attacked the liberals' economic plan as an unpatriotic, communist-aligned sell-out of the nation. Their own economic program came straight from the pages of textbook populism. The CIP's extravagant promises included doubling wages, raising spending, cutting taxes, and protecting domestic industry and agriculture. "We have to give people money—then the economy will work well," said Moczulski. In the end, the CIP took 7.5 percent of the vote, enough to make it the third largest party in parliament.

Even after their electoral success, in true CIP spirit the party declined to enter into any of the diverse and unwieldy coalition governments of later months. Today, their plan of action remains a populist one, taking their program of national values, patriotism, protectionism, independence, justice, and moral integrity directly to the people, to villages and towns in the country. On economic grounds, the CIP plank finds resonance particularly among the lower middle class, those Poles hit hardest by the economic reforms. Their proposal for worker buyouts of factories appeals to those people without capital to invest themselves. Ideologically, although the CIP itself steers clear of excessive nationalism and anti-Semitism, hardcore nationalists form a second pillar of CIP support. Despite its own self-definition as a nationalist party, the CIP doesn't fit the category of most typically chauvinistic East European nationalist parties. While it occasionally makes noise about the Polish minorities in Poland's lost eastern territories, the recovery of the eastern lands is not part of its program. And although Catholic, the CIP maintains its distance from the Church, stressing, again, its independence.

Above all, the CIP is a populist and statist party, whose enigmatic personality is tied to the man whose portrait decorates their office walls, Poland's interwar military ruler Marshal Józef Piłsudski. Historians are still locked in debate over the Marshal's diverse legacy. Some see Piłsudski as a relatively benevolent figure, a champion of Polish independence, whose "gentle" dictatorship ensured a degree of prewar stability that was the envy of Poland's neighbors. Others point to Piłsudski's penchant for strong-arm methods, his belief that the "evil in men's souls could be scrubbed clean by military spit and polish," and to the political and ethnic repression of his regime. Poland's interwar period pitted Piłsudski, the socialist-turned-dictator against Roman Dmowski's right-wing National Democrats. While the National Democrats stressed ethnic homogenization and national regeneration, Piłsudski represented the ideals of the military man that he was—honor, chivalry, and a strong, authoritarian state for a strong, independent Poland.

It is this vision, Piłsduski's fierce defense of Polish independence, as well as his clear commitment and unwillingness to compromise, for which the CIP so esteem their hero. The CIP have made the words on Piłsudski's gravestone their own: "To win and then rest on your laurels is a defeat. To be beaten but never to give up is a victory." The party sees Poland today confronted with a situation similar to that of the interwar years: political and economic chaos looming on one side, the Church and its allies on the other. A powerful state is necessary to maintain internal stability against the looming danger of revolution and anarchy. As they continue to forsake a role in power while maintaining and expanding links with their constituency, the CIP seems to be one of the few parties that can guarantee itself a place in the future of Polish politics.

The CIP emerged in the elections from dozens of other radical parties, who, though not in parliament, continue to maintain a low profile on the fringes of political discourse. Among the many ultra-right and neo-fascist groups that have tried to forge a working alliance are Polish National Rebirth, The Polish National Party, The Polish Independence Party, The Conservative Monarchs Club, and National Awakening. The largest and most prominent ultra-right party is the National Party (NP), which in 1992 merged with the European Commonwealth of Poles headed by Maciej Giertych, longtime advisor to Cardinal Glemp. The NP envisages a Poland "run for Poles and by Poles—and not by minorities," such as Jews, cosmopolitans, and freemasons. The denim-clad battalions of NP malcontents regularly propagate their own brand of diplomacy in Polish towns and cities. In June 1992 some several hundred NP Skinheads gathered at the Grunwald monument in Cracow, commemorating the victory of the combined Polish-Lithuanian armies against the Teutonic knights in 1410. A few days earlier, three of the NP's members had been arrested in connection with the brutal murder of an East German lorry driver in the industrial suburb of Nowa Huta. With banners bearing fascist insignia the group marched angrily into the city center, their burly leader Bolesław Tejkowski at the fore. Once in the main square, launching a cacophony of shouts and jeers as they passed the editorial offices of ("Jewish") *Gazeta Wyborcza*, the marchers ceremoniously burnt the European Community and Israeli flags to cries of "Poland for the Poles!" and "Out with Judeo-Solidarity!"

The NP has not shied away from contacts with its "Aryan Slavic brethren." Since 1991 it has been a member of the Slavonic Congress, an international fascist organization established in St. Petersburg. As Zdzisiek, a young Skin, explained during a March 1992 demonstration in the border town of Zgorzelec: "The Church tells us to love everybody. I don't love the fucking Church. I have my own Slavonic God. Światowid is not merciful, he's just." In addition to the NP, Poland's several thousand Skinheads also boast a number of their own local organizations, with contacts in the U.S., Germany, France, Czechoslovakia, and Germany.[8] Violence against punks, foreign students, Ukrainians, and Roma is common course in larger cities. In Silesia in western Poland, Skinheads regularly break up meetings of the ethnic Germany minority, which cultivates its own connections to the same ultra-rightist German groups that encourage the Polish Skinheads.

The sense of belonging, meaning, and identity that Skinhead groups provide young people is also a need that many religious sects prey upon. Throughout Eastern Europe, groups such as the Moonies and Hare Krishna lost no time in establishing a foothold once communism had passed away. In Poland, the ritualistic Catholic group *Opus Dei* (God's Work) has set up shop, with, it appears, the full blessing of John Paul II. Although the size of the highly secretive organization's membership is unknown, both young people and clergymen acknowledge that Opus Dei has penetrated their ranks. The writings of Opus Dei's founder, the late Spanish priest Jose Maria Escriva de Balaguer, have been translated into Polish and are easily obtainable. Like other religious sects, the Opus Dei functions as an ersatz family for its mostly younger members, demanding the individual's unquestioned devotion, as well as money. Complete with medieval ceremonies, secret oaths, and the like, Opus Dei demands lifelong servitude and obedience to its creed. Every aspect of life is regulated, from work and education to contacts with family and friends. Escriva's book *Camino* (The Path) is a list of formulaic aphorisms such as "Humble yourself. Don't you know that you are a garbage bin?"

The Polish Pope revealed his sympathy for Opus Dei and its leaders almost immediately upon his rise to the papal seat. His tenure has seen Opus Dei loyalists soar to the highest positions in the Vatican. Pope Wojtyła circumvented the normally fifty-to-one-hundred-year-long process of canonization to have Escriva beatified only seventeen years after his 1975 death. The beatification, which rested upon a few minor and dubious miracles, raised eyebrows throughout the Catholic establishment. Indeed, Opus Dei seems to have a special role in the Pope's Christian Europe as the right-wing counterweight to progressive forms of European Catholicism, which Pope John Paul II has no more sympathy for than he did with Liberation Theology in Central America. The Pope has apparently urged the leader of Opus Dei in Rome, Cardinal Alvaro del Portillo, to take up his activities in Poland.[9] Since 1986, the organization has set up school exchanges with Polish children and owns several houses in Poland where its devotees live.

Since 1989, the heady days of communism's demise have given way to widespread pessimism over the country's future. While the benefits of the old regime have dissipated, the gains promised by the new system have not yet appeared for a sizeable part of the Polish population. At times, frustration has taken the form of spontaneous protest. In 1992, for example, radical farmers encouraged by the militant Farmers Self-Defense Union organized road blockades, sit-ins, and a defiant march on Warsaw. At the time there was even talk of setting up "Peasant Battalions"—armed militia to protect debt-ridden peasants from prying bailiffs and cheap EC imports. Other forms of resistance have been organized along more traditional lines. Solidarity and the ex-communist trade unions have, independently, lent their support to workers' protest against the government's policy of bleeding state enterprises dry of public funds. A wave of strikes in the industrial heartlands of Silesia and Southern Poland in the summer of 1992 threatened to bring down the government. Workers' demands included pay rises, an end to the payroll tax, and, in some cases, a degree of autonomy and self-management. The liberals, however, guided by the principle that "the best industrial policy is no industrial policy," stuck fast to their guns. And though the government could, with some satisfaction, point to 1992 as the first year of economic growth, the price has been massive cuts in public spending, falling standards of living, fifteen percent unemployment, and a continuing crisis in public finances.

The harsh experience of the transition has been something of a rude awakening for a society that once believed it was enough to banish communism for Poland to become a new Japan. Calls for a return to the authoritarian solutions of the past are sustained even by the ruling liberals, who demand "special powers" for the government. Since 1989 the legitimacy of Poland's nascent democratic institutions has been gradually eroded, while public trust in the organs of law and order has steadily grown. Paradoxically, only the first, quasi-democratic elections in June 1989 brought electoral satisfaction, with Solidarity winning all but one of the contested seats. By contrast, the 1990 presidential race destroyed the myth of Solidarity in an acrimonious war of words, while the forty percent turnout in the 1991 parliamentary vote produced a fragmented parliament condemned to a future of weak coalition governments. Simultaneously, the polarization of political forces has signalled a rightward shift in political culture. Parties such as the CIP, which three years ago was considered "extremist," or Center Alliance, which then constituted the "right wing" of Solidarity, now find themselves firmly in the center of the political spectrum. New left-wing alliances hope that they may be able to stem the tide of fundamentalism. But their task will be a difficult one. The Church, though it has suffered defeats, is unlikely to abandon its political mission. Nor, it seems, will anyone be able to make it do so.

Chapter 8

ANTI-SEMITISM
WITHOUT JEWS

It was all too hopeful to think that Europe's New Order might be one free of anti-Semitism. In many ways, the conditions have never appeared so favorable. For one, there are few Jews left in most of Europe. In Germany, Austria, Poland, Romania, Slovakia, the Czech lands, as well as the Balkans and the Baltics, Hitler's Final Solution policies decimated the thriving Jewish communities that had composed nearly half of the world's Jewry. In the East bloc, most of those who escaped the Holocaust later fled the hostile "anti-Zionist" campaigns of the communist states. Of the five million Jews who lived in non-Soviet Central and Eastern Europe on the eve of WWII, only 700,000 survived to see the war's end. Today just over 125,000 Jews remain in their ancestors' homes. Only Russia (with nearly two million) and Hungary (about 80,000) still have significant Jewish populations.

Furthermore, one might have thought that the incomprehensible horror of the Holocaust, of six million exterminated Jews, would have left people with more sympathy toward the remaining Jews, or at least have deprived anti-Semitism of any popular currency. In Western Europe, though anti-Semitism does live on, its open declaration is a social taboo that few dare to breach in public. Also, with the fall of the Soviet empire, Israel ceased to be the official foe of the Eastern European states, a status that had generated thinly disguised anti-Semitic propaganda for decades. One of all of the new democracies' first foreign policy moves was to re-establish the diplomatic relations with Israel that had been severed during the June 1967 Arab-Israeli War.

Nevertheless, anti-Semitism is alive and flourishing throughout Eastern Europe, even in the virtual absence of Jews. As before WWII, anti-Semitism is a staple of the far right movements, central to their way of thinking, if not explicitly to their programs. There are hysterical anti-Jewish movements like the Russian ultra-nationalist Pamyat groups, one of whose twenty-two program points includes nineteen against Jews. Many other less flamboyant nationalist parties, including ones that have come to power, have also recycled prewar (and postwar communist) cliches about international Jewish conspiracies and plots of world domination.

Opinion polls taken in 1990 and 1991 show that between about one-fifth and sometimes as many as nearly one-half of people in Eastern European countries harbor anti-Semitic feelings. The strength of anti-Semitism varies from country to country. One comparative poll conducted by the American Jewish Committee shows anti-Semitic attitudes in seventeen percent of Hungarians, twenty-three percent of Czechs and Slovaks, and forty percent of Poles. Alongside the passive anti-Semitic burgher, extreme anti-Semites make their presence felt, and the lives of Jews uncomfortable. Since 1989, synagogues and Jewish buildings in nearly every Eastern European state have been defaced with anti-Semitic graffiti. With so few living Jews, anti-Semites in Germany, Poland, Romania, Czechoslovkia, and elsewhere have directed their hatred against Jews long dead, vandalizing cemeteries and knocking over gravestones. Most Jews in Eastern Europe have assimilated into the dominant national cultures, and hold their national identity, as Hungarian, Pole, or Russian, as dearly as they do their Jewish identity. On the streets, however, Jews report sporatic harassment, such as anti-Semitic slurs or being spat at in the face. In schools, Jewish children complain that they sometimes encounter anti-Semitism from classmates, in the form of swastikas scrawled on their desks or taunts of "Christ killer!" or "Jewish swine!" Public figures of Jewish descent have received vicious hate mail, including death threats and neo-Nazi propaganda.

Today's anti-Semitism, however, as disturbingly familiar as it sounds, is not a simple throwback to that of the 1920s and '30s. In contrast to the interwar era, anti-Semitism today doesn't threaten the Jewish communities in Eastern Europe to the extent that it did then. There have been no attempts to reintroduce anti-Semitic legislation or trends of systematic persecution. Even in Russia, where anti-Semitism is most virulent, that animosity has not manifested itself in pogroms or other forms of concerted violence against Jewish persons. In terms of physical security, other national minorities, such as the Roma, live in much greater danger. Opinion polls in almost every country consistently show Jews either in the middle or at the bottom of surveys that rank negative feelings toward different minorities, usually well below the likes of Roma, Arabs, blacks, and Russians. Today other minorities top the new fascists' hit lists.

Though the essence of the new anti-Semitism has much in common with what came before, it invokes the evil of Jewry under new historical conditions, with a content specific to those circumstances. The new anti-Semitism defies the traditional categories of medieval Jew-hatred or Christianity's time-honored prejudices against the Jewish people. Nor is it the same as Nazi racism or the communist regimes' "anti-Zionism." Admittedly, the anti-Semitism of the East European right contains more of the characteristics of traditional religious and ethnic anti-Semitism than does that of Jean-Marie Le Pen, Franz Schönhuber, or Patrick Buchanan. In Hungary, the national populists' charges of Jewish blood contaminating the "essence" of "pure Hungarianness" is clearly racial. In Poland, Romania, and Russia, Jews are still castigated for deicide. Yet, while age-old biases remain in circulation, and often lie at the root of popular anti-Semitic attitudes, they are noticibly less conspicuous than they were before WWII.

Whatever its proponents may say, the new anti-Semitism has less to do with actual Jews than it does with an abstract image of the "the Jew." Above all, it is the common stereotypes attributed to Jews that the anti-Semite fights, the *collective picture* of Jews that survived both the Holocaust and the Cold War. Beneath its traditional guises, one of the chief focuses of today's anti-Semitism is the West, with its secular ideologies and modern values. Anti-Semitism is implicit in ethnic nationalism, and nationalists use the "Jews" or "Jewishness" as euphemisms for the "imported," "foreign" values that they oppose, from socialism to Western pop music and international law. The receptivity of average people to anti-Semitism constitutes a valid litmus test for a society's propensity to undemocratic right-wing ideologies. The contemporary anti-Semite is also the racist, the homophobe, the conservative Catholic, and the provincial nationalist. "Whenever the shadow of anti-Semitism arose in public life," notes Adam Michnik, comparing France and Poland, "it was an unmistakable signal that people with anti-democratic, intolerant views were on the political offensive. Today ... when anti-Semitic opinions are expressed in Poland, Jews are not the issue. The question is whether or not there will be a Polish democracy."

THE JEW AS SYMBOL

As much as contemporary anti-Semitism reveals a mind that persecutes all who are "other" from oneself, the extreme right's singling out of Jews is by no means completely random. Some observers argue that because there are no longer even ostensibly objective grounds for Jew-hatred (i.e., no Jews), the anti-Semite could just as well settle upon Turks, blacks, or even "bicyclists" as the object of his frustration. This is the classic scapegoat theory, which contends that through no actions or qualities of their own, Jews have always been picked out as guilty for every imaginable problem. The scapegoat theorists are basically the same as those who endorse theories of "eternal anti-Semitism,"[1] arguing that anti-Semitism will always exist no matter what the circumstances. The Jew is suspect by nature for having nailed Jesus to the cross, and he can do nothing to absolve himself from that original sin. Both schools of thought point to the conflicting nature of the accusations made against Jews: the lowly, dirty Jew; the wealthy, powerful Jew; the Jew as capitalist, entrepreneur, usurer; the Jew as communist and revolutionary; the Jews who stick to themselves; the Jews who infiltrate gentile society; the Jewish individualist; the Jewish collectivist; the Jew as religious fanatic; and the Jew as atheist. Whatever the circumstances, the anti-Semite will find a reason to pin his misery on the Jew. And in the context of postcommunist Eastern Europe, where the need to locate the "guilty" in someone other than one's self is particularly acute, the dark, elusive stereotypes of "the Jews" make them ready candidates.

Postcommunist anti-Semitism, however, tells us more than that Jew-hatred continues to function as a kind of all-purpose xenophobia, although it does that too. The new anti-Semitism has a distinct content, an ideological pattern that is part of every far right movement in the region. The right draws upon anti-Semitism to express its opposition to, as Michnik points out, European democracy in its broadest sense. As it is used from Rostock to Tirana, Moscow to Paris, those particularly "Jewish" qualities that the right singles out are inevitably tied to European modernity, as a conscious protest against liberalism and the idea of a united Europe, against human rights and democratic values. Just as in Soviet polemics against "Zionism" and "Free Masonry," the Jews are vilified as the agents of Western ideas, life-styles and economic forms. As contradictory as anti-Semites' diverse charges against Jews seem to be, the stereotypes all have a common denominator. Today's anti-Semites use the stereotype of the "urban," "cosmopolitan" Jew to paint all that is modern as alien and treacherous. When the anti-Semite charges the Jews with Bolshevism and liberalism in the same breath, the claims are not wholly indiscriminate. The anti-Semite rejects the common Enlightenment values that underpin both ideologies: their internationalism; their shared notions of equality, technological advancement, and reason; their emphasis on urban culture; and so forth. The continuity enables the anti-Semite today to call the dictates of the International Monetary Fund (IMF), an institution with the values of free-market capitalism etched in its soul, part of a grand "Judeo-Bolshevik plot."

Most of the stigmas that the contemporary right employs have been part of modern anti-Semitism since the late nineteenth century. For many people, the Jews, with prominent positions in banking, commerce, and high culture, became symbols for liberalism in Eastern Europe. In politics, business, and science, people of Jewish origin were at the forefront of modern, progressive trends that made their way from West to East. Always a minority among the dominant nationality, with a worldwide religion and bonds that transcended the borders of states and empires, the Jewish communities represented the international (or the non-national) over the national. Nationalists often lumped the Jews and the Germans together, branding both as the proponents of foreign ideologies that were alien to the native, peasant-oriented nationalisms of the day. The abstract, international component of Judaism gave rise to theories of an "all-powerful Jewry" and a "worldwide Jewish conspiracy." The infamous "Protocols of the Elders of Zion," for example, supposedly documented a Jewish plot to take over the world. Although the texts, which appeared in Russia at the turn of the century, had been forged by the Czar's secret police, they had a mass circulation during the interwar period throughout Eastern Europe. Since 1989, the Protocols have resurfaced in every postcommunist country. Those who take the bogus papers as real continue to claim that a small clique of evil people manipulate world events from behind the scenes.

The communist regimes repackaged the old conspiracy theories, which fit in neatly with their own megalomania of plots, spies, sabotage, and betrayals to explain the deficits of their systems. Official anti-Semitism under communism was a potent instrument in the hands of rulers lacking popular support. Paradoxically, it was the heavy presence of Jewish socialists in Eastern Europe's prewar and postwar communist parties that made anti-Semitism so attractive to Stalin and non-Jewish communists. Even before the 1917 October Revolution, "the Jew as revolutionary" had become another standard stereotype. Although only a negligible percentage of Jews actually identified with Marxism-Leninist ideology, the upper echelons of the tiny prewar communist parties in Eastern Europe were indeed disproportionately filled with Jews. Of the forty-nine Commissars of the short-lived 1919 Hungarian Soviet Republic, thirty-one had Jewish heritage. The activities of the Comintern, headed by East European Jews, quickly won the label of a "Judeo-Bolshevik world plot," a cliche that would long outlive the Comintern itself. In the immediate postwar period, communists with Jewish backgrounds often took over prominent, unpopular positions in the police or the security apparatus, or the highest-ranking position in the ministries of trade and commerce. The first postwar leaderships of the orthodox Stalinist regimes were punctuated with Jewish names. In the top Politburo positions one found Anna Pauker in Romania, Rudolf Slánský in Czecholsovakia, and Mátyás Rákosi in Hungary. Those very regimes, however, showed little sympathy for Jews who were not communists. In an inversion of prewar stereotypes, the "Jewish capitalist" became the "subversive enemy of the people," while the "Jewish revolutionary" became the representative of the ruling power. As Paul Lendvai argues, the essence of the stereotypes remained unchanged.[2] The Jew was "alien," "rootless," and "anti-national." In countries that had actively collaborated with Nazi measures, "the Jews' " new position as the Kremlin's servants hardly endeared the surviving Jewish communities to the population. According to Lendvai: "The corporate Jew was not only detested as a corporate Communist, but also as a colonial ruler in the service of Soviet power. To make matters worse, the hated Jews appeared to grow more powerful and conspicuous in inverse proportion to their vastly diminished number. It was the political prominence of the Jews more than anything else that bred the enormous power of anti-Semitic resentment among the humiliated and suppressed East European nations." The fact that most Jewish citizens in these countries suffered as much, if not more, from their hard-line policies, such as nationalization of property, did nothing to dampen popular animosity.

The first wave of Moscow-engineered purges in the early 1950s calculatingly tapped the passion of that antagonism. Looking to stabilize the shaky East European regimes, Stalin decided that the Jews were to be made responsible for Stalinism. In the extensive housecleanings of the Jewish Old Guard, "Zionist" appeared for the first time alongside traditional anti-Jewish adjectives, such as "rootless" and "cosmopolitan." "Zionism" became a heresy on a par with "bourgeois nationalism," "Titoism," and "Trotskyism"—all interconnected and essentially one. In 1951, Slánský was arrested, tried in one of the most excessive of the Stalinist show trials, and hanged in 1952. That year Pauker also fell in Romania, and Jewish communists throughout the communist apparatuses were exposed as "enemies of the people," as co-conspirators in a worldwide Zionist plot. The anti-Zionist drive "spelled the destruction not only of the Jewish tormentors of non-Jews and Jews but also for the collective existence of the Jewish communities in general. The old and new roots of anti-Semitism, the social resentment of the expropriated urban elements, and the nationally motivated Jew-hatred of the "new class" of party officials and government bureaucrats had turned into an explosive political force."[3] That force, masked as anti-Zionism, was one that the communist regimes would turn to again and again over the decades. Swaddled in communist jargon, the authorities' denunciation of Zionism resurrected the same cliches that abounded before the war: the Zionist, or, better said, the Jew, was the faceless enemy, now an agent of "capitalist imperialism."

THE IMF'S AGENTS FROM TEL AVIV

It wasn't long after the fall of communism that a postcommunist anti-Semitism began to take shape. During those initial months before nationalism burst onto the scene with such ferocity, there was little vocal opposition to all that entailed "Europe" and "the West." This time, the East Europeans believed, the West would not let them down as it had so many times in the past. But as nationalism swelled and economies only worsened, anti-Semitism shot to the surface. It emerged so quickly because it was already there. In organized form, political parties exploiting anti-Semitism came from two sources. One was the nationalist factions that existed within every communist party throughout Eastern Europe. Whether in Poland or Slovakia, Romania or Hungary, these currents had long relied on anti-Semitism to denounce both the illegal democratic oppositions, as well as internationalist and liberal elements in their own communist parties. In Romania, those forces had coalesced around the Securitate-cultural weekly *Săptămîna*, in Poland in the official Patriotic Grunwald Association, in Hungary in the National Patriotic Front (NPF). Another source of anti-Semitism came from the corner of the opposition, namely nationalists (including emigre groups) who opposed both communism and the liberal democratic oppositions. As the Hungarian Democratic Forum's collaboration with populists in the official NPF showed, these currents often had more in common with each other than they did with either their fellow oppositionists or fellow communists.

Next to Russia, anti-Semitism in Romania is among the most rabid and open in Eastern Europe. A clear case of anti-Semitism without Jews, Romania has a Jewish community of about 17,000 in a country of 23 million (.08 percent of the population.) Of the more than 750,000 Romanian Jews who lived in prewar Romania, about 350,000 survived the Holocaust. Under Ceauşescu, who "sold" Jews to Israel just as he dealt ethnic Germans to Germany—allowing them to emigrate at per head rates—all but 18–20,000 Romanian Jews had left the country by 1989. ("Romania has three things to sell the West," said Ceauşescu, "Germans, Jews and oil.") Unlike Czechoslovakia and Poland, however, the regime never openly exploited anti-Semitism. This was primarily a result of its independent pro-Israel foreign policy, which enabled Romania to maintain lucrative relations with the state even after 1967. Nevertheless, inside the Romanian Communist Party and state apparatus, ultra-nationalists such as *Săptămîna* editors Eugen Barbu and Corneliu Vadim Tudor [see Romania chapter] took Ceauşescu's chauvinistic national communism to its logical conclusion, penning anti-Semitic texts that smacked of interwar fascism.

The case of anti-Semitism in Romania tells us much about the character of the new anti-Semitism. In spring 1991, ultra-nationalists succeeded in stirring anti-Semitism to fever pitch in the Romanian press. The two prime instigators of the hatred were the weeklies *Europa* and *România Mare*, the latter the mouthpiece for Barbu, Tudor, and the renamed Securitate. The hysteria reached a crescendo with the publication of a series of fiercely anti-Semitic articles in *Europa*, another pro-Securitate publication whose obsession with Jews and Jewish conspiracies rivals that of the worst Russian ultra-nationalists. The editor of the tabloid, Ilie Neacşu, a former small-time communist apparatchik, claimed that 5000 Jews had taken over most of the key positions in Romania. He and other authors charged "Judeo-Hungarian finance" and "Jewish ministers" with undermining the Romanian national economy, and trying to turn Romania into a "Mediterranean colony." The paper urged that only "genuine Romanians" be allowed to hold positions in trade, industry, and in the universities, and that "anti-Romanianism" be a legal offense just as anti-Semitism can be prosecuted.[4]

By mid-1991, this kind of paranoia had become routine for *Europa*. But both *Europa* and *România Mare* went even farther in the spring and summer of 1992, explicitly calling for their readers and the government to take action against Romanian Jews. *Europa* demanded that the Interior Ministry and the Ministry of National Defense "prove their patriotism" in these "difficult hours, when jackels and hyenas are biting into the body of the country with rare cruelty."[5] "We have the right to round them up and judge them severely for their odious crimes," wrote *România Mare*. "And if the wrath of the people cannot be appeased, then the flight from Egypt is going to look like a picnic in retrospect."[6] The newspapers' appeals to violence found no resonance in the population, and the new tone of their polemics finally mobilized the government, the Jewish community, and opposition democratic forces to initiate legal action against the newspapers. The government, itself not below fanning the same emotions, condemned the "legionary, Iron-Guardist" attitudes in the Romanian press and announced that it would draw the attention of the *Europa* articles to the Prosecutor General as a "case of incitement to pogrom."

The charges drew no retractions or apologies from the ultra-nationalists. The Romanian Information Service, the renamed security service, stated that it found nothing anti-Semitic about the pieces. In a May 1991 issue of *Europa* Neacşu responded to critics:

> I cannot accept the fact that those who constitute this ethnic group should occupy the majority of decision-making functions in the state apparatus, in teaching positions, at the radio and television, and in the written press. All that is missing is for them to penetrate military institutions, to turn our churches into synagogues, and then we can also move our capital to Tel Aviv. We should not forget that forty-five years ago, the carriage of communism had been helped on its road by more decendents from Israel than by genuine Romanians. All that, without even mentioning all those [Jews] who had important party and state functions throughout these years. . . . If we defend the interests of Romanians and we point our finger at the opportunists, does this make us fascists?[7]

Different shades of the same prejudices can be found in most of the Romanian media, even in the publications of the democratic opposition. At the same time, neither pogroms nor physical attacks have actually materialized against the handful of mostly elderly Jews in Romania, as they have regularly against the Roma. In fact, emigration for Jews, now easily done, leveled off in 1991 and 1992.

The subtext of the ultra-right's anti-Semitism is perhaps more important than its intentions toward Romania's Jews. For one, the ultranationalists invoke anti-Semitism against all of their political opponents. "Down with the Jew Iliescu!" proclaimed one piece of graffiti that I saw against the Romanian president, whose Romanian ethnicity is above suspicion. Posthumous charges of Jewishness also swirled around the name of Elena Ceauşescu. The ethnic Hungarian Pastor László Tökes is regularly labeled part of the ubiquitous Jewish conspiracy. *România Mare* defames former dissidents such as the poet Mircea Dinescu and the liberal ex-Minister of Culture Andrei Pleşu as "foreign-blooded traitors" and "dark-skinned individuals."[8] In other words, the Jews include everyone who is foreign, unpopular, or guilty of the ills that beset the nation. For nationalists, evil always comes from others and never one's own people.

Anti-Semitism in Romania often strikes out at that which is international, Western, and liberal, including capitalism. Although the percentage of Jewish ownership or Israeli investment in Romania is a fraction of one percent, *România Mare* accuses "Judeo-Hungarian finance" of undermining the country and holds responsible Romania's "Jewish ministers for the destruction of the economy."[9] The picture of capitalism as a dark, international plot designed to "turn Romanians into the slaves of the West" fits traditional Jewish stereotypes, and makes it prime fodder for the far right. The Jew is the hidden, destructive force, the "invisible hand" of market forces. Who will profit from the free market if not ordinary Romanians? If not "us" than it must be "someone" else—the Jews and the foreigners. Anti-market nationalist forces staunchly oppose foreign investment as the "sellout of Romania to Jewish international capital." The conspiracy theories play upon popular anxieties of an invasion of investors from abroad who would shut down factories or extract profit (formerly known as surplus value) from the Romanian economy. The parallel between these arguments and those made against "Western imperialism" only a few years ago is hardly accidental. For the former apparatchik nationalists, the privatization and denationalization of the centralized economy loosens their own hold on state-owned property.

For ordinary people, with little experience in the world of politics and economics, recourse to a "Jewish plot" is an easy, universally applicable way to grasp complex processes. Just like communist propaganda, it portends to explain everything and claims always to be right. What, for example, could be more unfathomable to an Eastern European peasant than the workings of the IMF? The IMF is an international, capitalist institution that has set strict austerity guidelines for their country which have accelerated its economic tailspin. The IMF virtually dictates a country's economic policies, even if the country, such as Romania, is not officially a member of the fund. In addition, the IMF is a institution that the average person cannot see, appeal to, or hope to combat. Even the East European governments throw up their hands, explaining, "This is what the IMF demands. There's nothing that we can do about it." It dwells somewhere beyond the reach of ordinary people, making decisions in distant Western offices that adversely affect their lives.

The nationalist gutter presses from Moscow to Bratislava routinely link the IMF to the "Jewish world conspiracy." As in *Europa*, the IMF is portrayed as an instrument of a Jewish plot directed from Israel, whose one goal is to "transform the Romanian people into cesspit cleaners, dog catchers, refuse collectors, and porters serving individuals who are foreigners to the nation and to the country."[10] The Hungarian national populist István Csurka, the incarnation of Satan as far as Romanian nationalists are concerned, plays the same tune. He explains the "hegemony of the Hungarian Jewry" in terms of the continuity of Jewish financial and political power from the Jewish-led communist take-over to the present: "The communist henchmen, murderers, and torturers were supported by the occupying Red Army at that time. Today, the financial elite is supported by the IMF." According to Csurka, the Jews' "hidden [political] influence" is possible only through their worldwide financial network. "Although the economic restructuring demands of the IMF do not include political requirements in so many words, they nevertheless contain such hidden requirements. . . . For the Hungarian financial sphere, the change of regime has meant the preservation of all of its influences, as well as the preservation and development of good relations with Western capital, the facilitation of the comrades' survival, and the continued hiding of things that need to be hidden."[11]

The rantings of ultra-nationalists may understandably find an echo in some peoples' prejudices. Compare the IMF's role in Eastern Europe with Hannah Arendt's description of traditional European stereotypes of Jews: "We find the Jews always represented as an international trade organization, a worldwide family concern with identical interests everywhere, a secret force behind the throne which degrades all visible governments into mere facade, or into marionettes whose strings are manipulated from behind the scenes. Because of their close relationship to state sources of power, the Jews were invariably identified with power, and because of their aloofness from society and concentration upon the closed circle of the family, they were invariably suspected of working for the destruction of all social structures."[12] The IMF possesses all of the insidious characteristics of the "Jewish world conspiracy" with one critical exception—it's not Jewish.

For the ultra-nationalists, the Jew represents everything that is "anti-national," and in Eastern Europe that also implies Western democracy. The Jews are not only the agents of economic imperialism, but of cultural imperialism too. "The cosmopolitan Jews"—whether in fact artists, former dissidents, intellectuals, or democratic oppositionists—are held responsible for the "import" of foreign ideas. In this sense, anti-Semitism is an ideological construct that goes hand in hand with the isolationist philosophy of ethnic nationalism. In Romania, for example, the event that symbolizes that country's break with its past, that supposedly ushered in a new era of European democracy to Romania, was the December 1989 revolution. In theory at least, Ceauşescu's overthrow severed Romania from its legacy of dictatorship, tyranny, and secret police forces. As different as reality has proved, the December revolution remains associated with the ideal of Romania's "return to Europe," with the triumph of justice, and the rule of law. It is no wonder then that Romania's ultra-nationalists view the revolution as national treason. They maintain that the uprising was a "Israeli-Hungarian plot," engineered by the Mossad, the Israeli secret service, and the CIA. The voices of *România Mare*, *Europa*, and company outspokenly oppose the meager handful of trials begun against Securitate officers who have been charged with giving orders to fire upon demonstrators. "Why are the Jews keeping Nicu Ceauşescu behind bars?",[13] asks one *Europa* headline about the president's son, the former head of a regional Securitate division. *Europa* doesn't really believe that the courts are packed with Jews, or that they will convince their readers that they are. "The Jews" here are synonymous with the rule of law, with international requirements for the respect of human rights. In effect, it's the West, Western opinion and pressure, that is responsible for keeping *Europa's* Securitate comrades behind bars.

HISTORICAL AMNESIA

Romania is just one of the countries in which sweeping revisionist interpretations of its wartime history have raised eyebrows abroad. The Romanian, Croatian, Slovakian, and Hungarian states were all closely allied with Nazi Germany during WWII, and in each country native collaborators sent Jews and other victims to their deaths in concentration camps. Even in the German-occupied Czech lands and Poland, as well as the Baltics, there was collaboration with, or in many cases at least sympathy for, the Final Solution measures. "At least the Nazis are taking care of our Jewish problem," said many Poles. Under communism, the ruling powers diplomatically turned their heads and refused to acknowledge the extent of domestic complicity in the Holocaust. The communists tended to attribute the crimes of the war period—the discrimination, the pogroms, the deportations—to Germany and "fascist cliques" at home. The people, the propaganda implied, had never really participated in the policies of the German-allied leaderships.

The close of a discredited era gives countries the unique opportunity to reevaluate the former official versions of history. In postcommunist Eastern Europe, however, that occasion has failed to prompt a critical reevaluation of the communist regimes' obfuscation of their countries' roles during WWII. To the contrary, nationalist and right-wing forces have used the opportunity to exonerate even the leaders and movements responsible for the Axis-allied states' genocidal policies. Those leaders' "patriotism" is couched in terms of "anti-communism," and they are glorified as the loyal defenders of the nation against Soviet Bolshevism. (None of the collaborationist leaders have yet been rehabilitated, and only in Romania, in the case of Antonescu, does this appear at all likely.) While even most radical nationalists don't dispute the reality of the Holocaust altogether (the explicitly pro-Nazi parties do), they refute or minimize their country's participation in wartime atrocities.

Croatia is a case in point, where nationalist President Franjo Tudjman, even before he came to office, had been at the front of the campaign to clear Croatia of a reputation among the most sinister in Eastern Europe for its WWII war crimes. During its 1941–45 reign, the brutality of the Nazi-allied regime under Ante Pavelić, leader of the fascist *Ustasha* movement, even prompted protests from the German Waffen SS officers assigned to Croatia. The sheer numbers alone, as shocking as they are, say nothing of the Ustasha's primitive methods of massacring Serbs, Jews, and Roma. Although reliable figures are hard to come by (that's exactly the source of debate), independent scholars estimate that about 500,000 Serbs and 200,000 Croats perished during the war years. By 1945, Croatia had rid its territory of over eighty percent of its Jews and Roma. The symbol of the Croatian Holocaust is the Ustasha's notorious concentration camp Jasenovac, where at least 150,000 to 200,000 victims, mostly Serbs, lost their lives. Even during the Tito decades, Serbs and Croats jousted over the Jasenovac numbers. Serb nationalists claimed that at least 700,000 people died at the camp. Revisionist Croatian historians put the figure at "only" 60,000, a vast discrepency that speaks volumes about the chasm dividing Serbs and Croats today.

A historian by trade, Tudjman's position on Jasenovac and the quisling Independent State of Croatia was radical even by the standards of Croatian nationalists. In his book published in 1988, appropriately titled *Wastelands: Historical Truth,* he asserts that only 40,000 inmates perished at Jasenovac, and of those many were actually killed by Jews in control of the camp apparatus. Tudjman's book amounts to an apologia not only for wartime Croatia and its atrocities, but also for Hitler's Germany and the Final Solution. His contorted argumentation and obscure examples are those of ultra-right historians everywhere who try to prove "Holocaust lie" theses.[14] Tudjman doesn't completely deny the "Holocaust" [his quotation marks], only the numbers—six million murdered Jews is an "exaggeration"; its horror—communal suicide is a Jewish tradition; and its premediated logic—the Nazi leadership had tried to win an independent state for Europe's Jews in Madagascar, but were finally forced to fall back on other solutions to the "Jewish problem." In the end, he writes, excusing the German people as well, "the exclusion of Jews from German and European life by way of gradual extermination . . . was only revealed to a narrow circle of Nazi faithfuls, and remained hidden to the majority of Germans."

The primary ambition of Tudjman's book is to lift the "unjust" stigma of the "Jasenovac myth" from Croatian nationalism. Certainly, the Jasenovac numbers had been at times overblown, and the communists did nothing to clarify the real circumstances of the enormous brutality that occurred during the war period, much of which transpired between warring nationalist factions and not between the partisans and "fascists" as the communists would have had it. But, for Tudjman, "historical truth" means exonerating the Croats. Jasenovac, he claims, was not really a "liquidation camp" but a "labor camp" in which Jews lived privileged existences in private flats with their families. He approvingly quotes "eyewitness" sources who claim that Jews "managed to grab all the important jobs in the prisoner hierarchy" or "took the initiative when it came to preparing and provoking not only individuals, but also the mass murders of non-Jews, communists, partisans, and Serbs." According to Tudjman, Jews "to a large extent ran the 'selection process,' i.e., they chose which prisoners would be 'liquidated,' and, partially, they even handled the executions." The Ustasha commanders were "responsible only for designating the 'prisoner' in charge of prisoner management." The Jews, who the Ustasha benevolently trusted, took care of the rest.

The Jews' extermination of the Serbs and Roma was in keeping with a people who, according to Tudjman, authorize mass murder to save its race. Though admitting that it "seems exaggerated," Tudjman quotes one former Bosnian inmate: "The Jew remains a Jew, even in the Jasenovac camp. . . . Selfishness, craftiness, unreliablity, stinginess, deceit, and secrecy are their main characteristics." The Jews' penchant for genocide runs deep, implies Tudjman, making it only a "small historical step" from "Nazi-Fascism" to "Judeo-Nazism," the latter embodied in the Israeli repression of the Palestinians. "All of this is happening in the mid-eighties," writes historian Tudjman:

> when world Jewry continues to have the need to remind us of its victims during the "Holocaust," by even trying to prevent former UN Secretary Kurt Waldheim from being elected as president of Austria! There was no general reason for this, seeing as, during WWII, (in the rank of a minor officer of the German army), he was neither an inflictor of "war crimes" nor was he in the position to make decisions as to their execution. But just as one can be deaf and blind as to what is happening under one's very nose on the orders of Israeli generals and its government, so this also testifies to the fact that historical narrow-mindedness and stupidity fully prevail, and Jewry is obviously no exception to this.

Tudjman neglects to mention that Waldheim served during the war years in occupied Yugoslavia, in an advisory capacity to the Croatian government.

With free elections and the explosion of nationalism across Yugoslavia, the quarrels that nationalist historians had once waged from libraries (or prison cells) became the charged rhetoric of the nationalist leaderships and, indeed, the raw material of war. When Tudjman, a former partisan general (he fought against the Ustasha fascists!), became president in 1990 he renamed Zagreb's central Square of the Victims of Fascism to the Square of the Croatian Great Kings. The new Croatian guide books eliminated mention of the wartime state's fascist Staatsraison, and schools dropped their regular trips to Jasenovac. Tudjman, though he expressly distanced himself from the Ustasha state and Pavelić, made much of their symbolism and language his own.

Historical whitewashings such as that in Croatia are not only anti-Semitic, but they exacerbate anti-Semitism. Symbols such as Jasenovac and Auschwitz are testaments to the fact that the Jews suffered more than the Croats or the Poles during the war. For peoples who feel that they have suffered immensely over the centuries, this truth is a denigration of their own traumas. And, to look the suffering of the Jews in the eye, of course, means owning up to their own complicity. In Eastern Europe, the frank, self-critical admission of wrongdoing seems far beyond the means of nations whose self-esteem was further maligned by four decades of communism. It implies sacrificing their inflated myths of past glory and goodness, their nation's noble struggle against injustice, foreign invasion, and occupation.

In Eastern Europe today, these myths are the very cornerstones of the nationalist regimes' legitimacy. They are also one of the last ostensibly noble things that many people have left to feel good about. The existence of these historical black spots force the culpable to try all the harder to reverse the victim-persecutor relationship. They feel accused and react against it by labeling the Jews as the agents of communism, or in the case of Croatia, of fascism. It was the Jews, they say, who forced communism upon the innocent nation. The nationalists equate the crimes of "Jewish Stalinism" with those of their nation during the war (if they admit that they occurred at all). The "Jews' crimes against the Romanians" thus cancel out the Romanians' "alleged" crimes against the Jews. The historical slight-of-hand exonerates the nation both of its wartime past, as well as its responsibility for communism. And, conveniently, it sets up the Jews as the most likely candidate for the nation's next misfortune.

This "reversal of guilt" back onto the Jews in Eastern Europe parallels the kind of anti-Semitism that is most prevalent in Germany and Austria. More so than in Eastern Europe, traditional racial and religious anti-Semitism has fallen off considerably in postwar Western Europe. In contrast to pre-1945 anti-Semitism, the "new anti-Semitism" in Western Europe no longer has the potential to politically mobilize significant parts of the population. As Professor Herbert Strauss, former director of the Institute of Anti-Semitism Research in Berlin, argues, "No politician [in former West Germany] can build a mass popular party which relies upon a racially grounded anti-Semitism to attract voters. That was the case with the Nazis, who projected responsibility for crises, social tensions, class struggle, and fears about communism onto the Jews, effectively turning them into scapegoats. That can't happen anymore because Jews in the West are integrated and accepted in way that they never were in the Weimar Republic."[15] And, Strauss adds, there are simply too few Jews in Germany for such charges to have credibility.

Nevertheless, anti-Semitism persists in Western Europe too, and not all so independently of political discourse as Strauss and others may suggest. Surveys done during the 1980s in Germany and Austria (and France as well) consistently show general anti-Semitic biases in about a third of the populations. In one German study, for example, more than forty percent of the respondents thought of Jews as "cunning" and "clever," while only eleven percent described Jews as "honest." Negative stereotypes such as that of the "greedy and manipulative" Jew are still widespread. About a third of those asked felt that "Jewish influence" in the world is too great.[16] About half of the group with generally negative feelings toward Jews (and more in Austria) have strong anti-Semitic orientations, and then about half again (five to seven percent) fall into the category of "extreme" anti-Semites. Most of those who profess anti-Semitic prejudices have no contact whatsoever with people of Jewish origin, and their antipathy, in fact, is consistently greater towards other groups, such as blacks, Arabs, and Roma. Not surprisingly, the anti-Semites are more likely to vote for conservative or extreme right political parties. The surveys also show that positive impressions of Jews have risen and that a majority of Germans, particularly among young people, reject any kind of anti-Jew prejudices at all.

In place of traditional anti-Semitism, researchers in Germany and Austria have located a more prevalent "secondary anti-Semitism," which has more to do with the peoples' relationship to their past than to actual Jews. Numerous surveys show a clear impatience among Germans to finally and definitively "draw a line" between the Nazi past and the present. "Secondary anti-Semitism" is the resentment that many Germans feel toward Jews—or Israel—for not allowing Germans to simply "forget" the past. In a 1986 study conducted by the Allenbach Institute for Demographics, for example, seventy-two percent of Germans agreed with statement, "I was born after the war and have nothing to do with the war or the persecution of the Jews. I don't feel guilty." Two-thirds of those asked felt that less should be said about National Socialism forty years after the end of WWII. They agreed that contemporary Germany should finally make a full break with the past. The same proportion said that they would rather avoid a discussion with their friends over National Socialism and the Holocaust. A majority also expressed unhappiness with a feeling of unique obligation to Israel so long after the Holocaust. As the study's authors concluded: "The desire to forget is strong. The present danger is not one of a flaming new anti-Semitism, but rather the eagerness to turn away from history. The numbers clearly speak of breaking with the past, of not wanting to hear more about it, and not wanting to discuss it any longer. . . . We are threatened here with the loss of history. The majority views the past only as a burden, and not as unrenounceable, valuable knowledge, that must be preserved at all costs."

The Germans' (and Austrians') resentment over their moral debt to the Jews has transformed traditional stereotypes, once based on living Jews, into a new kind of anti-Semitism without Jews. Older Germans are fed up with being reminded of their complicity in or relationship to the crimes of the Third Reich. Younger Germans resent having to bear responsibility for the legacy of their grandparents' generation. As Strauss explains: "The psychological needs of the Jews contradict those of the Germans. For the Jews, the history of the Holocaust is a trauma that they still feel and live with. On the German side it is also a trauma, but one that they desperately want to forget so that it doesn't continue to pain them. The Germans' aversion to their shame turns into resentment against those who caused the shame." In other words, the Jews are responsible for giving "us Germans" a bad name. Like the Eastern Europeans, the Germans project their guilt onto their former victims. Unlike the Easterners, however, the West Europeans don't have forty years of communism to use against the Jews.

While blatantly racial anti-Semitism has lost its political legitimacy in the West, the success of the New Right parties shows that politicians can also exploit secondary anti-Semitism. In Germany, the right-wing Republican Party (REP), for example, goes to great lengths to play down the uniqueness and Germanness of WWII and the Holocaust. By sanitizing the Nazi past, the Republicans relieve ordinary Germans of the moral responsibility that they obviously feel is unwarranted so many years after the fact. "Will you please finally leave us in peace," REP chief Franz Schönhuber admonishes the leaders of Germany's Jewish community to standing ovations at REP party congresses. In typical form, he accuses the German Jewish organization of "agitation" against "good German patriots." "We can't stand to hear more of your drivel," he says. "We won't let ourselves be humbled any longer!" It is not anti-Semites but outspoken Jewish voices, Schönhuber claims, who are responsible for anti-Semitism. In Austria, the yuppie ultra-rightist Jörg Haider, Western Europe's most successful New Right candidate, beats the same drum. The Austrians have nothing to be ashamed of, he says, soothing their consciences. They were only "doing their duty." Haider steers clear of overt anti-Semitism, while shifting blame for the war off the shoulders of the Austrians and onto those who refuse to let the issue just fade away.

FROM BELOW, FROM ABOVE

The first studies of popular anti-Semitism in "transitional" Eastern Europe consistently show the persistence of negative attitudes toward Jews among large parts of the populations.[17] In Slovakia, thirty percent of those surveyed shunned the idea of having Jews for neighbors (the figure was half as high in the Czech lands). Over eighty-five percent of Slovaks, however, declined to have Roma as neighbors. Another poll showed only twelve percent of Hungarians had unfavorable opinions of Jews. Interestingly, the studies show a lower rate of popular anti-Semitism in Hungary than in most other countries, although Hungary has twice as many Jews as the five other former East bloc countries combined. The Poles, on the other hand, with only several thousand Jews, tend to have deeper anti-Semitic prejudices. A third of Poles seem to feel that its 5000 or so Jews have "too much power in Poland." A survey of high school pupils showed more of the respondents expressing sympathy toward Jews (twenty-three percent) than negative feelings (seventeen percent). Nevertheless, a quarter of those asked opposed the thought of having a Jewish friend home for the holidays. Forty-seven percent felt that Jews had no right to be elected to the parliament. Researchers from the Center for Public Opinion Research noted that "In a country almost devoid of Jews, where no lobby or Jewish organization with the smallest political ambition exists, large numbers of people fear they are being ruled by the Jews. This evidence is strongly rooted in negative stereotypes, which even the most obvious facts are unable to change."

In Romania, where anti-Semitism flourishes in the press, only eleven percent of the respondents in one poll approved of anti-Semitic journalism. Seventy-eight percent opposed such articles. In the former Soviet Union, anti-Semitic attitudes appear to vary greatly from country to country. In Uzbekistan, thirty percent of those polled in one 1992 study agreed that "Jews must answer for killing Christ." Only six percent responded similarly in Estonia. Likewise, just two percent of Estonians believed that "Jews are mainly responsible for the disasters of the Revolution and the mass repressions of the Soviet era," while twenty-five percent in Belarus responded affirmatively. The same study revealed that there had been an increase in anti-Jewish sentiment over the year and a half since the first such poll had been conducted. The numbers, though rough, show that anti-Semitism "from below" exists throughout Eastern Europe, and not necessarily in correlation to the size of Jewish communities or the level of anti-Semitism in political discourse. The statistics, however, beg the important questions about the relationship between popular anti-Semitism and political behavior. Is anti-Semitism today simply tolerated, or is it practiced, too? Can these prejudices be converted into overt hostility against Jews, in the form of physical violence or legal discrimination? To what degree can politicians manipulate anti-Semitic beliefs to their advantage?

So far, politicians armed with anti-Semitism have been unable to sway significant constituencies with that weapon alone. In fact, voters clearly reject the most extreme of the anti-Semitic parties, and have relegated their sort to the margins of political life. But other, less flagrantly anti-Semitic parties openly vie for political power. In contrast to Western Europe, thinly veiled anti-Semitism has become part of mainstream political discourse, manipulated by major parties and leading politicians. Candidate Tudjman, for example, campaigning in early 1990 for the upcoming election, publicly stated: "I'm glad that my wife is neither a Serb nor a Jew." In the 1990 election in Hungary, which put the national conservative Hungarian Democratic Forum (HDF) into government [see chapter 3], the HDF's populist right-wing appealed to anti-Semitism in their attacks against the liberal Alliance of Free Democrats. They implied that Free Democratic candidates of Jewish origin were less than fully Hungarian, and therefore untrustworthy of political power. Swastikas and Stars of David appeared on Free Democrat campaign materials. In the end, even Free Democrat leaders felt that anti-Semitism was an insignificant factor in their loss to the HDF. Perhaps more to the point, the HDF, as a party that embodied nationalistic, racist, provincial, and anti-Semitic attitudes, won the votes of those people who had similar sentiments.

Anti-Semitism also flared during Poland's 1990 presidential election campaign. With the onset of democratic changes in 1989, anti-Jewish graffiti such as "Gas the Jews!", "Juden Raus!", etc., appeared ever more frequently on synagogues, cemeteries, and Jewish buildings. In April 1990, in Kielce, the site of an infamous 1946 anti-Jewish pogrom, anti-Semites hurled smoke bombs into a concert of a Ukrainian Jewish ensemble and, on another occasion, into the meeting of a Jewish Solidarity activist. Solidarity candidates regularly found their campaign posters smeared with Stars of David and graffiti such as Żydy ("kikes"). To those familiar with the methods of the communist security service, the source of much of the agitation during the transitional period of 1989 and 1990 was beyond doubt. Since 1980, the regime had feebly tried to blacken Solidarity's name by portraying it as a Jewish-led organization. In part, the apparatchiks still in office at the time owed their positions to the "anti-Zionism" that they had repeatedly called upon to discredit their many enemies since the late sixties. Simultaneously, outside of the state structures, new openly anti-Semitic parties, like the National Party, joined forces with a brutish right-wing underground of Skinheads and soccer fans.

For the most part, the Solidarity movement had cautiously steered clear of anti-Semitism throughout the 1980s. No sooner, however, had Solidarity fragmented into nationalist-Catholic and liberal camps in 1990, than anti-Semitic motifs came immediately to the fore. The split at the top of the trade union put Wałęsa on the opposite side of his old allies Tadeusz Mazowiecki, Michnik, and other liberals, who had recently organized a separate party. After several ambiguous remarks about the new party from Wałęsa, one journalist at a press conference asked whether he considered the new group a "Jewish party." Wałęsa's response, his first to such as question, set a critical precedent: "Well, no . . . but look at who they've got there: Michnik, Geremek, Turowicz [all leading Solidarity intellectuals, Michnik and Geremek are Jewish]. Why do they conceal their origins? I am proud to be a Pole, but if I were a Jew, I would be proud to be a Jew." For the first time, Wałęsa emphasized his ethnicity, as well as that of his political adversaries, and charged the liberals with "concealing" their Jewishness. His comment, whether consciously anti-Semitic or not, opened the door to an issue that would haunt the presidential campaign until its end.

Most observers, Michnik included, insist to this day that Wałęsa is not an anti-Semite. But in a climate in which anti-Semitism was available, noted one journalist from the liberal daily *Gazeta Wyborcza*, Wałęsa "used anti-Semitism as a convenient tool in the political struggle against his opponents, mobilizing against them, and in his own favor, an electorate that at least tolerated anti-Semitism."[18] Wałęsa's refusal to immediately distance himself from anti-Semitic innuendos sanctioned their use in political discourse. Tellingly, the prime target of the anti-Semites' fire was not even Jewish. Widespread rumors had it that Wałęsa's leading opponent in the presidential race, Mazowiecki, a lifelong Catholic and former Wałęsa advisor, was in fact a Jew. Although never coming directly from Wałęsa, he and his team pandered to the ignorance and prejudices that gave such rumors credence. On the campaign trail, Wałęsa consistently asserted that he was a "one-hundred percent Pole" and "a real Pole, born in Poland." Who then wasn't a real Pole? The insinuation was that other candidates indeed had something to conceal about their ethnic origins. His remarks about his Polishness (which he offered to prove with his birth certificate) divided candidates according to ethnic, racial criteria—one group with allegiance to Poland, and another with loyalties that lay "elsewhere." As racial as Wałęsa's distinction was, he aimed it not so much against actual Jews (there wasn't even one running) as against "political Jewishness." The liberal Mazowiecki and his Western-oriented, intellectual colleagues fit perfectly the bill of the "cosmopolitan Jews."

Throughout the campaign, Wałęsa repeatedly denied accusations of anti-Semitism, insisting that he wanted a Poland "free of anti-Semitism and chauvinism." At the same time, he refused to condemn the charges swirling around Mazowiecki or to publicize his previous good relations with Polish Jews. He shrewdly sensed that it might lose him votes. In response to the pro-Wałęsa, anti-Semitic shouts that rang out at his rallies ("Send Mazowiecki and the Jews back to Israel!", "Gas the Jews!", "When are you going to throw the Jews out of office?"), Wałęsa responded mildly or not at all. Sometimes he would condemn anti-Semitism, but always stopping short of reprimanding anti-Semites in his own ranks. The anti-Semites, it seemed, had found a home in the Wałęsa camp, and the candidate did not intend to alienate them. The Catholic Church, which seemed to be leaning toward Wałęsa, remained silent on the controversy until after the election, when it finally issued a pastoral letter condemning anti-Semitism.

It is impossible to calculate whether anti-Semitism contributed to Wałęsa's landslide victory over Mazowiecki in the first round of the election. For several reasons, Mazowiecki would probably not have fared any better had the issue never have come up at all. After the first round, the anti-Semitic posturing disappeared almost entirely. Wałęsa discarded the tool when he no longer needed it. "Wałęsa invented nothing by himself here—he simply reacted to anti-Semitic stereotypes present in the minds of his voters and in his own," wrote journalist Konstanty Gerbert who covered the affair closely. "For the overwhelming majority of Poles these stereotypes present in the minds of his voters are presumably not central ones, but they are tolerated in one's own thinking and in that of others. Using anti-Semitic language, Wałęsa proved to his voters that he was one of them." Wałęsa oversaw the introduction of anti-Semitism into Polish political life, and the majority of people and institutions accepted it without protest. Although it seemed to blow over almost at once, Wałęsa christened anti-Semitism in the politics of democratic Poland. It remains there, to be used again when other politicians find it expedient, just as Wałęsa did.

THE ANTI-SEMITIC MIND

As much as anything, anti-Semitism in Europe today reflects a way of thinking about the world. The anti-Semitic mind is the right-wing mind, and the anti-Semite the person who is available to nationalist ideologies and populist demagoguery. In the Frankfurt School's seminal study on authoritarian propensities in the U.S., *The Authoritarian Personality*, the German social critics observed during the 1940s that anti-Semitism has less to do with actual Jews than with the anti-Semitic subject and his total situation. The "place to look for the determinants of anti-Semitic opinions and attitudes is within the persons who express them," they observed. The anti-Semite, they concluded, shows a strong *propensity* to fascism and other authoritarian ideologies. More than fifty years later, the Frankfurt critics' observations are still useful. The anti-Semite in postcommunist Eastern Europe is also the potential adherent of the extreme right, whether that person is actually a member of a fascist or ultra-right-wing party or not. His is a mind that hates something that doesn't even exist, a form of thinking that uses the simplest, most available categories to make sense of society.

The anti-Semitic mind is particularly susceptible to the language of "treason," "betrayal," and conspiracy theories, whether directed toward unseen "enemies" of the working class or those of the nation. The content is easily interchangeable, since he is suspicious of all that is new or different or modern. Studies show that the anti-Semite tends to be provincial and uncultured, more often from the country than the city. His reactions are triggered by fear and anxiety, envy and spite, resentment and ignorance. He would rather be led by a strong, forceful, charismatic leader than accept the responsibility of democratic participation in society. An authoritarian leader, he believes, can march into power and chop out the rot and corruption that prevents "things from getting done." It is a personality that respects power, follows orders, and shows allegiance, when those qualities are demanded.

An American Jewish Committee study conducted in cooperation with several Czechoslovak research institutes during 1991 and 1992 presents a fascinating portrait of the typical anti-Semite in Slovakia. According to the surveys, the Slovaks most likely to demonstrate anti-Semitism are older people, those with little education, those working in semi- and low-skilled jobs, and those who live in small rural settlements. The survey found anti-Semitism associated with social and economic inertia and cultural backwardness. Roman Catholics are more likely to harbor anti-Jewish prejudices than members of other religious denominations, and Slovaks more so than the ethnic Hungarian minority in Slovakia. Those people less likely to accept anti-Semitism—and the same applied in the Czech Republic—had higher educations, are professional, young, and live in cities.

The survey compiled a list of opinions and values common to Slovaks with anti-Semitic attitudes. What emerges is a descriptive anatomy of the right-wing personality in Eastern Europe, of the potential fascist. The general Weltanschauung of the Slovak anti-Semite is also that of the lower- and middle-class supporters of right-wing and nationalist movements throughout Eastern Europe. The Slovaks with anti-Semitic biases:

- tend to be the most frustrated with the changes since 1989. They are pessimistic about their future and display greater sympathy toward the former communist regime than non-anti-Semites.
- Even more so than other Slovaks, they feel economically insecure, convinced that market reform and privatization will only hurt them. They have little faith in their own individual resources to change their circumstances. They believe that privatization will increase social inequality, enabling a few individuals to prosper at the expense of the majority. They opt for state ownership and a centralized economy over a free-market economy in which "national wealth would be sold out to foreign capital."
- They are apprehensive about opening their country to foreign influences. They fear the loss of their national identity in a united Europe and distrust the EC and NATO.
- They are skeptical that the new political establishment represents the interests of ordinary citizens and tends to be distrustful of democratic

institutions, preferring a "strongman" government that would preserve social order and prevent chaos.

- They are more nationalistic than other Slovaks and more hostile to national and ethnic minorities.
- They believe that the Czechs have consistently exploited the Slovaks. They blame the Czechs for communism and they supported the break-up of the Czechoslovak state.
- They are more favorably disposed toward the WWII Slovak state than other Slovaks, and more likely to play down the crimes of the then-fascist government.

With minor adjustments, the Slovak anti-Semite could be the right-wing nationalist anywhere in Eastern Europe. Roughly the same set of values and general opinions describes the supporters of any one of a number of ultra-right parties. Importantly, the portrait of the Slovak anti-Semite acknowledges the role of change and uncertainty in the lives of people who subscribe to anti-Semitic and ultra-right ideologies. As the Frankfurt School study underscored, a fascist potential may exist in many people, but it is the objective situation that turns that propensity into action. The person inclined toward anti-Semitism and right-wing ideology is less flexible and responsive to social change than others. Drastic changes in his personal life (the loss of a job, for example) or political or economic instability are all factors that could transform latent tendencies into action. Considering the cataclysmic changes that have affected almost everyone's life in postcommunist Eastern Europe, it is fertile ground for such ideologies.

Despite new violence and threats against Jews, there is no second Holocaust on the horizon in Eastern Europe. Above all, the persistence and tolerance of anti-Semitism speaks to the immense difficulties of building democratic foundations in the former communist countries. Whether his animus is directed against Jews or national minorities or Roma or homosexuals, the person who thinks in anti-Semitic categories spurns the consensus of a democratic civil society. The countries that refuse to acknowledge the existence of Jew-hatred and obscure their own nation's relationship to the past condone those prejudices and the societies infected by them. That nationalist leaders find it difficult to condemn anti-Semitism should hardly come as a surprise since their political philosophies are based upon ethnicity and blood lineage. In the West, though anti-Semitism exists, the postwar decades have delegitimized its use as a political weapon. In the East, anti-Semitism was naturally a taboo, but one that the communist regimes themselves regularly violated. Today it has reemerged in Eastern Europe primarily as a political weapon, and its potence, as well as the contents of its message, shed an alarming light on the nature of postcommunist political culture.

CONCLUSION

For a few fleeting moments, critics in the West heralded the collapse of communism in Eastern Europe as "the end of history," insisting that capitalist and liberal ideas had prevailed over rival ideologies once and for all. The victory cries of philosopher Francis Fukuyama and like-minded Western conservatives, however, were premature. In 1989, history did not perish—it was reborn.

The "democratic revolutions" began a reshaping and redefining of the national political cultures as they emerged from communism. Although the Eastern Europeans hoped for a qualitatively new future, they found themselves lacking the historical bearings to chart a qualitatively new course. Some looked to the West for models, while others reached back into their own national pasts. The Eastern Europeans today are in the midst of grappling with their identities—as states, as societies, as democracies, and as nations. Nascent though this process is, the outlines of a broad sociopolitical spectrum have come into focus, with old and new, democratic and authoritarian elements. On one side of the spectrum, nationalist and far right forces exert influences far greater than their equivalents in the West and have firmly established themselves as one part of the new political culture. In some countries they

301

have shown that they have the power and the allure to dominate the process of redefinition. The most extreme and horrifying case has been Serbia, where the designs of nationalists to carve out a Greater Serbia from former Yugoslavia have unleashed the bloodiest war in Europe since WWII. The Serbs have demonstrated to the world the consequences of ethnic nationalism in a multinational region. The same dynamic has the potential to ignite ethnic conflicts across the region, wherever large national minorities exist and ethnic nationalism is the order of the day. The conflicts in former Yugoslavia could easily spill over into neighboring states, bringing in Albania, Bulgaria, Turkey, Greece, and Middle-Eastern Arabic states as well. In the former Soviet Union, ethnic battles are raging in Moldova, Tajikistan, Georgia, and Azerbaijan (Nagorno-Karabakh). Even closer to the heart of "civilized" Europe, the animosities simmering in Slovakia, Hungary, and Romania could also lead to war. Where all-out wars are unlikely, say in the Czech Republic, Germany, and Poland, the same rationale of ethnic nationalism underpins national populist and racist ultra-right movements which are steadily expanding their size and influence.

The battle for the souls of Europe's newest citizens, however, is far from over. As formidable as the new nationalisms may be, democratic forces in Eastern Europe—as well as in the West—have the resources to counter their appeal and dominance. Neither the fall of communism nor the rise of nationalism have definitively closed the history books in postcommunist Eastern Europe. The region stands at a critical crossroads, at a time when both the domestic democratic movements and the international community must act decisively if they are to halt its slide into extreme nationalism and new dictatorships.

One of the most immediate courses of action to hedge the advances of the ultra-right has been for governments to take legal action against militant neo-fascist groups. In Germany, where legislation prohibiting expressions of fascism is the strictest in Europe, authorities have—if belatedly—cracked down on the most radical right-wing organizations, formally banning their activities and confiscating their propaganda materials. Positively, the state's moves signaled that such movements will not be tolerated when they put their ideas into practice. The criminalization of the ultra-right not only hampers its activities, but it also delegitimizes their ideologies in the eyes of average citizens. On the other hand, such restrictions implicitly limit freedom of speech and association. The calls for increased surveillance and special anti-terrorist units also sanction the construction of a militarized security state, the kind that conservatives have been pushing for since the late sixties. As wholeheartedly as most German progressives have backed the state's measures against the far right, many leftists find themselves in the uncomfortable position of supporting the same repressive measures that they had condemned for years when used against the radical left. Also, in practice, these measures have done relatively little to quell the activities of the right. The right wingers have simply gone underground or formed new groups under different names.

The postcommunist countries have shown themselves even more reluctant to use legal measures against right-wing organizations. So soon after the criminalization of their own ranks, democrats have mixed feelings about applying the same measures to silence other "unacceptable" opinions. In the absence of new legislation, many of the present laws against "racism" and "fascism" are the very same that were used against the democratic oppositions only a few years ago. Confirming the democrats' worst fears, conservatives in Czechoslovakia and Hungary have shown just how easily such bans can be abused. They have insisted that if "hate speech" laws apply to fascist groups, then they also must apply to "communist" ones; if the swastika is illegal, then the hammer-and-sickle must be as well. Many people also see nothing in the extreme right that warrants official prohibition. In contrast to Western Europe, many more Eastern Europeans consider these right-wing movements as "normal" or "natural" phenomena, the logical antithesis of "left-wing communism."

However wrought with contradictions the recourse to repressive measures may be, in the short term democrats have no choice but to act with all the means at their immediate disposal. At the same time, they must also recognize that legal bans and police raids address only the most visible symptoms of a much larger social problem. Neither the far right parties nor the sentiment that makes them popular can be abolished through criminalization, even if such laws were strictly applied (which sympathetic authorities and police forces are often unwilling to do). In the best of circumstances, they would only affect the extreme fringe of the ultra-right, those groups that openly incite racial hatred and violence. In Eastern Europe, movements and political parties that propagate nationalist and racist rhetoric are firmly lodged within the mainstream of parliamentary politics. Also, anti-fascist laws have been in force both in Western and Eastern Europe since WWII without stopping racist and neo-fascist sentiment from fermenting. First and foremost, the nationalist and radical rights across Europe must be confronted as historically rooted sociopolitical phenomena. National chauvinism is neither the "aberration" that the communist regimes claimed nor are Skinheads the frustrated kids that the West European establishment asserts. The new fascisms in Europe are genuine, organized, and interconnected political movements grounded in prejudices and bigotry which penetrate to the heart of society. If the democratization of Eastern Europe is to succeed, it requires a confrontation with and redefinition of these political cultures and the cultivation of modern democratic values to supplant those of the past.

Certainly, the vision of Eastern Europe's former democratic dissidents was to introduce exactly those democratic values that communism had denied. Back in 1990, the greatest obstacle to democracy seemed to be the residual strength of the communist elites. No one imagined then that in just two years the real threat would come from a new nationalist right. The dissidents, in those countries in which they existed, have experienced different fates. In Poland, the dissident-led Democratic Union is the strongest party in a fragmented parliament. In the Czech Republic, however, the Civic Movement party of Jiří Dienstbier and other left dissidents failed even to win parliamentary representation in the 1992 elections. President Havel is only faded window dressing in a country governed by conservative free marketeers. In Hungary and former East Germany, support for the parties of the former democratic oppositions stands at less than ten percent.

Though all the states of Eastern Europe now have constitutional democracies, the voice of the dissidents is in danger of being lost altogether in the roar of nationalism. To some extent, democratic forces have themselves to blame for the setbacks they have suffered. For one, both the dissidents and the West miscalculated the depth of the average person's commitment to democratic values and the market economy. As happily as the Eastern Europeans witnessed communism's downfall, they entered a new era with precious little experience of democracy and what it entailed. In the heady days of 1989, many believed that all they had to do was free themselves from communism, and a prosperous Western-style economy would rise from the ashes. In allying themselves so closely to the free market, and fusing the ideals of modern democracy to capitalist principles, the democrats and democracy were the first to be blamed when the shock therapy programs began to bite.

It is not too late, however, for democratic forces to rethink their own commitment to the free market. Since many of the dissidents have solid left-wing backgrounds, they still have recourse to the values that many of them renounced in the 1980s. Left and social democratic tendencies are also still strongly represented in the democratic parties. But in 1989, when the market appeared as a miracle remedy, those tendencies lost both their clout and their nerve. Unless left democrats reassert themselves, they leave the field open for the right to occupy traditionally leftist ground, and to link modern democracy with the hardship of the current economic transitions.

For democratic intellectuals to regain their positions at the head of the revolutions, they have a number of daunting obstacles to overcome. For one, they misjudged the size of the wedge that the communist regimes had driven between themselves and society. Western-oriented intellectuals and "cosmopolitans" had been a favorite scourge of the communist regimes for decades, and the propaganda, as in so many other cases, sunk into the minds of the citizens more than many would care to admit. The dissidents' own position in society drove that wedge in even deeper. They embodied an ethic of moral opposition, purity, and integrity that alienated them from most people. The sometimes arrogant and moralizing stances of the former illegal oppositions bred a resentment that has translated at the polls. To overcome that distance, the dissidents and intellectuals must make an effort to go more directly to the people, to speak to their everyday concerns, and to offer clear, comprehensive programs.

The former dissidents are just one potential source of a vibrant, non-communist left. So far, most of the small and fragmented left-wing parties in Eastern Europe have been unable to gain a foothold in their respective parliaments. The language of the left has been so compromised that these parties find it next to impossible even to articulate their political programs. Only in the Czech Republic, one of the few Central or East Europe countries with a non-communist leftist tradition, has a social democratic party managed to establish itself as a major opposition party. In the absence of a left, the right has successfully given pseudo-leftist demands a nationalistic twist to capitalize on popular dissatisfaction. Their success with traditionally leftist social issues attests to the fact that there is room in the fluid political landscape for a genuine progressive left.

Independent social movements and progressive trade unions have also been slow to organize. After four decades, during which self-organization, self-management, and other non-state-sanctioned initiatives were tantamount to political treason, most Eastern Europeans (the Poles an exception) have little practice in promoting their interests through extra-parliamentary means. Yet, many people feel themselves unrepresented by the existing political elites, as the low voter turnouts of recent years illustrate. Again, the right and not the democrats have gone to the grassroots to challenge the powers that be. But rather than self-organized autonomous movements with concrete programs and demands, the right has appealed to frustration with hollow demagoguery and calls for an authoritarian leader with strong-arm strategies. There is plenty of potential for broad coalitions of independent social movements, ecology groups, trade unions, left-liberal tendencies, and progressive socialists to assert themselves.

As thin as the precedents for self-organization in Eastern Europe may be, the idea of civil society was at the heart of the democratic oppositions' projects during the 1980s. In Poland, Hungary, East Germany, Czechoslovakia, and some of the former Yugoslav Republics, the illegal oppositions used the idea of an autonomous sphere of public self-organization to challenge the centralized authority of the state. Under the banner of civil society, the oppositions stressed the need for a society based upon self-activity and empowerment, human solidarity, participatory democracy, and community initiatives. The project of civil society was an attempt to cultivate a new democratic culture from the bottom up. Unfortunately, the leading proponents of civil society, the democratic dissidents, abandoned their strategy once the communist powers fell. Independent society, they argued, was now free to develop as it would within the framework of liberal democracy.

Today, although independent society exists, nationalism and chauvinism have stymied the development of a new democratic political culture. For nationalists, community is ethnic, solidarity is national, and democracy a pretext for a strong, centralized national state. Nationalists offer the bonds of blood, family, and religion to compensate for the atomization and weak fabric of contemporary society. A flourishing civil society, however, is as potent an alternative to nationalism and authoritarianism now as it was to communism during the 1980s. For a genuine civil society to blossom, democrats must once again make it their top priority, recognizing that a democratic, pluralistic state can only grow out of a new political culture and society. In the 1980s, the democratic oppositionists cast civil society as an "anti-political" alternative to the politics of the state. Today, the democrats, many now politicians, must work hand in hand with extra-parliamentary forces to rebuild and nurture a democratic political culture, which, by its very nature, can help to undermine nationalism's destructive pull.

Many of the reform communist parties in Eastern Europe portray themselves as social democratic alternatives to both the nationalist right and free-market liberals. Almost without exception, reform communist parties have weathered their defeats far better than their critics could have ever predicted three years ago. In the Czech Republic, Slovakia, and Poland, they scored impressive second-place victories in the 1991 and 1992 elections. Elsewhere, as in Lithuania or Serbia, they won elections outright. In every case, the reform communist parties have made impressive mileage out of opposing the pace of the economic transformations. These parties, however, which differ greatly from country to country, are still heavily burdened with their communist legacies. Though they profess a commitment to democracy and progressive socialism, the new converts have yet to fully extricate themselves from their old habits and thinking. In many cases, they stoop to the same populist rhetoric as the right. In the former Soviet Union and the Balkans, they espouse a nationalism as ferocious as that of the extreme right, and indeed have forged close working alliances with the most radical of the far right parties. In Central Europe, too, these parties have refused to make a credible break with the past, even though genuine left, left-liberal, and social democratic elements often exist within their ranks.

If the tide of nationalism and the resurgence of the right is to be stemmed, all progressive democratic forces must acknowledge the necessity of redefining the nature of the contemporary nation-state. In Eastern Europe, the ethnically based national state is a sure recipe for intolerance, chauvinism, ethnic conflict, and war. The concept of the ethnic nation is implicitly exclusive and racist, and, in one form or another, serves as the guiding principle of Eastern and Western Europe's far right ideologies. In order for the cohabitants of Eastern Europe to coexist peacefully in the future, they must adopt civic definitions of their nations and states. In civic states, full rights and equality derive from citizenship, available to all legal citizens of that state, and not from ethnicity, which favors members of one nationality. All the states of Eastern (and Western) Europe include minority and ethnic groups that live among the dominant nationality. Their multi-ethnicity is a fact that all of their members, as well as their constitutions, must recognize. By defining themselves in terms of the dominant nationality alone, the ethnic national state establishes a hierarchy of peoples, with some more equal than others. The multicultural and multinational character of Eastern Europe, the rich diversity of its traditions, cultures, and languages, should be celebrated as its strength. The states that provide their minorities full political and cultural rights, that grant their peoples and regions more autonomy, that practice multiculturalism will in the long run be the more democratic and stable.

Along these lines, one concept the Eastern Europeans could embrace is that of a Europe of regions and interlinking communities. Long before modern nationalism descended upon Eastern Europe, most people defined their identities in terms of their region and not strictly according to their nationality. During the Habsburg era, Transylvania's Hungarians, Romanians, and German Saxons had both a strong Transylvanian identity and a national identity as well. In Silesia, Germans and Poles took their Silesian identity as seriously as their German or Polish identity. The same is true for all of the ethnic groups that lived under one or another of the pre-WWI monarchies. The twentieth century and the enthronement of the nation-state has seen the steady erosion of these regional identities and the strengthening of ethnic national identification. Now, in the "imagined community" of the nation, Romanians in Transylvania believe that they have more in common with their fellow Romanians in far-off eastern Moldova than with the ethnic Hungarians who live next door.

In contrast to the imagined community of the nation, a Europe of civic communities could stress the common interests and goals of all peoples cohabiting in various regions and localities. Although a rejuvenation of regional identity and interests can't hope to replace national allegiance and the entrenched structures of the nation-state, it could provide a foundation for greater understanding and cooperation in multi-ethnic societies, underlining what they have in common and not what separates them. In 1989 and 1990, the collapse of the centralized communist governments immediately resulted in a renewal of multi-ethnic local and even regional initiatives. Many of these initiatives were entrepreneurial in nature, as upstart businessmen took advantage of the new space that had opened up for them. Also, non-national social movements budded whose interests centered around the environment, women's issues, the dissolution of the security apparatuses, and educational reform, among other pressing matters. These grassroots initiatives were a spontaneous, almost reflex reaction of local communities to the sudden removal of the communist system's constraints. Different nationalities came together in the same spirit of common cause which had united them during the overthrow of the communist regimes.

The tremendous pull of nationalism soon overwhelmed the fragile bonds of civic community that were forged in the days after the revolutions. Though some local initiatives and movements have managed to survive nationalism's onslaught, the prevailing trend in Eastern Europe has been toward organization along national lines and around national issues. Ethnic minorities have been forced to retreat into their own political parties to secure minimal cultural and human rights. Not surprisingly, Eastern Europe's new nationalist leaderships have done little to promote regional and multi-ethnic initiatives. Indeed, nationalists have turned "regionalism," "autonomy," and "local self-govern-ment" into code words for minority separatism. They demand a strong central authority from which all power emanates, an authority which derives its legitimacy from the allegiance of the dominant nationality. Manipulating fears and suspicions, they have been able to divide peoples by convincing the dominant nationalities that such regional initiatives threaten their country's territorial integrity and national autonomy.

As potent as this kind of demagoguery may be, different forms of decentralized, non-national political organization could help redirect nationalist energies toward the common interests and goals of local citizens. One key feature of the nation-state has always been absolute administrative control over a particular territory. Mary Kaldor of the Helsinki Citizens Assembly argues, however, that it is possible to en-visage various kinds of local and regional political organization with different but overlapping responsibilities. Local, democratically elected political units could function more as municipalities, or provinces, with responsibility for a wide field of policy-making, including local eco-nomic and cultural policy. In European Community (EC) jargon, the "principle of subsidiary" means that as many decisions as possible are made by the smallest unit of administration or the lowest layer of political organization. Of course, any such territorially based political units would have to be accountable not only to their constituencies, but to international democratic and human rights standards as well.

The decentralization of power through the delegation of respon-sibility to local government could have many benefits. Many East Eu-ropeans are disenchanted with democracy for the very reason that they feel so removed from the decision-making process in their respective capitals and parliaments. Also, after forty years of dictatorship, they have little practical experience with democracy. Democracy in Eastern Europe must be seen as a learning process, one of accepting values that are sometimes foreign to peoples raised under authoritarian regimes. By involving the citizens of local communities more directly in the decisions that affect their lives, local government would provide hands-on experience with a new political culture and help restore battered faith in democracy. Citizenship itself must be redefined to mean more than simply nationality or the right to a passport. In a civic nation, citizenship acquires an active connotation, one that involves all of its members in the workings of the polity. A broader notion of citizenship would provide citizens with several political identities, only one of which is national.

A Europe of communities could also take the form of cooperation between the contiguous border areas of neighboring states. Across Eastern Europe, state borders often artificially divide regions that have long historical identities and traditions of cultural and economic ties. A process of restoring these links and reintegrating these regions could help foster the recognition of common interests among states, and a new economic interdependence between peoples would bind their fates in a way that would help overcome ethnic animosities. The concept of a "Europe of regions" has the full support of the European Community and the Council of Europe, which oversaw the creation of the first "Euroregion" between communities in the upper Alsace region of France, the German state of Baden-Württemburg, and the Basel area of Switzerland in 1963. By 1992, there existed more than thirty organized Euroregions in Western Europe. Though the Europeans have no legal status of their own in the international community and their activities are subject to the approval of the central governments, they are given great leeway in the administration of their joint activities.

In Eastern Europe, Poland has boldly taken the lead in putting the idea of interregional cooperation into practice. In 1993, Poland, Hungary, Slovakia, and the Ukraine signed an agreement establishing the Carpathian Euroregion to encourage crossborder cooperation among local communities in all four countries. The agreement's top aim was to improve links between the border areas' infrastructures, setting up telephone exchanges and economic information centers, planning new roads, and opening new border crossings. The participants also discussed joint efforts to protect the environment and the need to develop contacts between communities and groups through cultural exchanges. The organization stressed the voluntary character of regional cooperation between the local communities and emphasized that decisions would have to conform to the laws and policies of the respective national governments. The Poles have also made progress in setting up a Neisse Euroregion that links communities in southwestern Poland, the northwest area of the Czech Republic, and the eastern tip of Germany. There have also been moves to construct a Euroregion connecting communities in northwestern Poland with border regions in Germany, Sweden, and Denmark. Although the Euroregions have met with harsh words from Polish nationalists, there is strong local support in the regions themselves.

The need for new interlinking supranational alliances and organizations is now particularly acute in light of the organizational void left by the demise of the Soviet-led structures such as the Warsaw Pact, the Council for Mutual Economic Aid, and the Comecon trading bloc. Dangerously on their own, the new democracies lack the networks to provide safeguards against political or economic isolation and against the attempt by one country to dominate others. The first, perhaps naive, hope of the new democracies was to join the Western international institutions at once. The EC and NATO were top on their lists. They soon found however that the West's commitment to their futures would often be more word than deed.

Although the West opened doors previously closed to the Eastern Europeans, access to the most lucrative and sought-after institutions remained beyond their reach. One recourse has been for the Easterners to create parallel, regional alternatives of their own. The first of these regional pacts was the Pentagonal initiative between Italy, Hungary, Czechoslovakia, Austria, and Yugoslavia. The alliance, which grew out of the Alpine-Adria Working Group of the late seventies, promoted political and economic coordination between the countries with the ultimate aim of expediting their entry into the EC (Italy was the only community member). The arrangement won high praise for its pragmatic projects to improve the neglected infrastructures of its former communist members and strengthen ties in the region. By 1991, although the group had suspended Yugoslavia, it had added Poland, Slovenia, Croatia, and Bosnia-Herzegovina to its ranks and changed its name to the Central European Initiative. As a bridge between East and West, the alliance has indicated its intent to draw Belarus, Ukraine, Romania, and Bulgaria into its work.

Another attempt at regional integration has been the Visegrad Triangle (now Quadrangle) agreement between Hungary, Poland, the

Czech Republic, and Slovakia. Founded in 1991, the alliance was first seen as a halfway house for the Central Europeans on the road to full membership in the EC, NATO, and the West European Union. The original three countries felt that their chances would be better if they banded together to push their cause. Although the Quadrangle remains a loose alliance, without institutions or formal structures, it provides a framework for meetings and regional cooperation. In many ways, the Central Europeans see the Visegrad pact and other regional arrangements as "second best" alternatives to membership in Western institutions. This being the case, they have tried to make the best of the situation. In 1993, the Visegrad partners set up a free-trade zone, lowering customs duties between the members, a milestone achievement which could eventually result in a Central European trade bloc with sixty-four million members.

With good reason the Eastern Europeans want desperately to become full members of the most prominent and established of the Western European institutions. They covet access to the EC markets in order to compensate for the collapse of intra-East bloc trade. Equally as important, the EC could provide the Eastern Europeans with a part in the structures that have promoted integration and peaceful relations in Western Europe for four decades. Full membership in the EC is a prerequisite for the "return to Europe" that East and West touted with such enthusiasm in 1989. It would buttress a civic, European identity, underscoring that the new European order is one of a Europe of citizens, and not, as nationalists insist, a Europe of nations with competing claims and fates. Once the Eastern Europeans feel themselves full members of Europe, with all of the benefits, they will also share in its responsibilities, such as the guarantee of human and minority rights and basic democratic standards. Until that time, there will be two Europes, one with a high standard of living and democracy, and another with its own lower standard.

The reluctance of the EC to admit the Eastern Europeans reflects a cold-shoulder treatment from the West that has many Eastern governments crying bad faith. And rightly so. The West, too, shares responsibility for Eastern Europe's precarious position. Eastern Europe emerged from communism with debilitated economies, societies, and political cultures that faced the greatest of odds against successful recovery under the best of circumstances. Full of hope, the young democracies staked their futures on the West, on Western-style democracy, on market economies, and on full inclusion in the West's institutions. And, in 1989, the West seemed prepared to meet the expectations of Europe's new citizens. But, as it had so many times in the past, the West backed away from Eastern Europe at one of its most critical moments of need, leaving the populations frustrated, disappointed, and open to undemocratic, anti-Western political options.

For countries attempting the Herculean task of turning their centralized, state-run economies into free-enterprise market economies, the financial aid and investment from the West was only a fraction of what the new governments had expected. The West offered no Marshall Plan, as it had to postwar West Germany, and only East Germany had a rich uncle willing to bankroll its reconstruction. Rather than desperately needed capital to rebuild industry and infrastructure, the West, through the IMF and other channels, has insisted that the Eastern Europeans meet the strictest of austerity guidelines in order to qualify for the most minimal of loans and financial aid. In practice, the IMF has proved itself merciless, even toward those countries that have broken their backs trying to meet their stipulations. When countries, such as Hungary, have failed to hit the IMF's targets, the IMF has immediately frozen their access to promised loans. The West, argued economist John Kenneth Gailbraith in 1991, was trying to sell a version of radical free-market economics to Eastern Europe that even, "we in the West do not have, would not tolerate, and could not survive. Ours is a mellow, government-protected life; for Eastern Europeans pure and rigorous capitalism would be no more welcome than it would be for us."

What Eastern Europe needs most today is a comprehensive economic aid package from the West, which, despite its own economic malaise, could afford to be far more generous than it has been. The IMF could certainly soften its shock-therapy requirements, allowing the Eastern Europeans to move more gradually toward more socially oriented versions of the market economy. Its uncompromising demand that social safety nets be cut away, for example, only opens democrats to easy attacks from the right. Significant aid could also go toward rebuilding infrastructure and protecting the environment. Almost all of the Eastern European governments have massive debts hanging over their heads, which the West could forgive or offer moratoriums on until the Eastern economies stabilize.

As long as the West insists upon laissez-faire philosophies in the East, the least it could do would be to adhere to its own principles when they could benefit the Eastern Europeans. With the collapse of the Comecon trade bloc, the Eastern Europeans have scrambled to re-direct their trade westward. Only through trade surpluses with the West, they know, can they hope to offset the heavy costs of economic transition and pay off Western loans. The Central Europeans have shown themselves more successful at penetrating Western markets than many experts had predicted, particularly in the areas of steel, textiles, and agriculture. From mid-1991 to mid-1992, exports from Poland, Hungary, the Czech Republic, and Slovakia to EC countries increased by nearly thirty percent. In response, Western Europe has fortified the walls around its own domestic markets, refusing to remove existing trade barriers and even imposing new trade sanctions on the most rapidly growing Eastern European exports. The Central Europeans have reacted with incredulity to the EC's trade wars. Hungary's Prime Minister József Antall called on the EC to "retain a sense of solidarity and not treat the region as Europe's back yard." Although the EC has granted Hungary, Poland, Slovakia, and the Czech Republic associate member status, they have dragged their feet on paving the way for their full membership. The EC acknowledges that the Central Europeans should and will eventually join the community, but the question that they refuse to answer is just when that will be. The EC claims that the poverty of the Central Europeans would place far too great a strain on an organization already beset with problems of its own. EC experts estimate that it would cost the community almost eleven billion dollars to accept the four Central European countries and that it would be unlikely that the four would have incomes equivalent to the EC's poorest members within the next two decades.

The price of exclusion however could prove much higher for the West Europeans in the long term. A rich Europe and a poor Europe, a Europe of stability and a Europe of instability, has already triggered a wave of westward economic migration. The war in Bosnia alone has put over two million refugees on the road. The Western governments, spurred on by their own far rights, have passed strict new immigration laws, erecting new walls where the Iron Curtain once stood. The West Europeans, and Germany above all, have exerted tremendous pressure on the Central Europeans to tighten their own immigration requirements, which has only shifted the problem farther East and fueled xenophobia in the respective countries. The ultimate goal of Western Europe must be to fully embrace the Eastern Europeans as the full citizens of a united Europe. The Treaty of Rome, which called the EC to life, envisioned an organization that would eventually encompass all of Europe, not just its wealthiest members. Rapid integration of the Eastern Europeans into the EC would stimulate Eastern economies and work toward staunching the flow of immigration, as well as giving the West critical leverage over the new members on issues of human rights, democracy, and the environment. Instead of forcing the Eastern European governments to abide by unrealistic economic demands, the West should make aid and investment contingent upon high standards of minority rights, freedom of the press, and free elections.

The West must also move more decisively to incorporate the new democracies into its security structures. The demise of the Warsaw Pact confronted its former members with a host of new, unforeseen dilemmas. For one, it made every member responsible for its own security policy, including the costly task of modernizing and rearming their forces against former allies who had overnight become potential foes. Also, a new security threat arose first from the Soviet Union and then from its successor states. As ethnic tensions heated up, and the wars in former Yugoslavia exploded, all of Eastern Europe has come to look like a potential battlefield, in which neighbor could be pitted against neighbor. The Central European states have lobbied NATO and the Western European Union for admission as quickly as possible—but their request has fallen on deaf ears. NATO has so far refused to give any form of security guarantees to non-members, let alone expand its scope or seriously consider the admission of new members. To accommodate the former East bloc countries, it invented the North Atlantic Cooperation Council, an institution whose role has remained unclear.

NATO, still in the throes of defining its post-Cold War raison d'être, is hesitant to take unstable and poorly equipped Eastern Europe under its wing. Nevertheless, all of the Western institutions must understand that it is in their own interest to overcome their Cold War prejudices and look east with an open mind.

The West's failure to respond constructively to the new realities in Eastern Europe has nowhere been more blatant than in former Yugoslavia. The inaction of the West in the face of Serbian aggression has set a worrisome precedent. In Serbia, nationalist and ultra-right forces have backed a war in Bosnia-Herzegovina complete with genocide, mass rapings, and the forced expulsion of millions of people. As early as 1991, during the war against Croatia, the West could have intervened to stop the fighting and show the Serbs that it was serious about enforcing democratic standards in postcommunist Europe. It miscalculated, however, in believing that the conflict in the Balkans was too costly to warrant stronger measures and that it lay outside the interests of Western Europe. Rather than insist upon a multi-ethnic solution to the crisis in Bosnia-Herzegovina, Western policymakers endorsed the logic of nationalists by proposing to divide Bosnia into ethnically based provinces. The Vance-Owen plan represented a clear capitulation to the Serbian and Croatian nationalists and to the rationale of ethnic nationalism in general. The plans for partitioning the state admit that peoples of different ethnic and national backgrounds cannot live together in multinational states. The reasoning is the same that divided Eastern Europe into nation-states after WWI and lays the ground for intolerance, discrimination, and a future of endless ethnic disputes and outright wars.

The territorial gains of the Serb nationalists show that victory is again possible for the most radical political elements in Europe, and that the West will stand by to watch it happen. The Serbs' conquests send a clear message to the far right in every country—from France to Russia—that success is within their grasp. They tell nationalists in Eastern Europe that borders aren't inviolable, that contemporary Europe is indeed a "Europe of nations" in which nations will battle out their destinies over land that is bound to the blood of their people. The West errs if it thinks that it is immune to the same viruses that have infected

Eastern Europe. The problem of the right is not one of a couple of thousand Skinheads, but of the latent prejudices and sentiments that they express in their most extreme forms, and that right-wing parties have shown themselves deft at exploiting. Today, the political and economic crises affecting Western Europe also open it to far right forces. Throughout Western Europe, the New Right parties have made striking gains in the first years of the 1990s, and their demise is nowhere in sight. The West cannot afford to take forty years of stability for granted, and neither can it shut off Eastern Europe as if the walls of the Cold War were still standing. The fates of both Europes are intricately bound, and they must work together if the Europe of the past is not to be the Europe of the future.

NOTES

INTRODUCTION

1. For simplicity's sake, I use "Eastern Europe" throughout the book to designate all of the former communist countries.

2. Eric Hobsbawm, *Nations and Nationalism since 1780: Programme, Myth, Reality* (Cambridge: Cambridge University Press, 1990); Anthony D. Smith, *Ethnic Origins of Nations* (Oxford. Basil Blackwell, 1986); Ernest Gellner, *Nations and Nationalism* (Ithaca: Cornell University Press, 1983); John Armstrong, *Nations Before Nationalism* (Chapel Hill: University of North Carolina Press, 1982); Benedict Anderson, *Imagined Communities: Reflections on the Origins and Spread of Nationalism* (London: Verso, 1991).

1—GERMANY ONE PEOPLE, ONE RIGHT

1. This figure comes from the federal Office for the Protection of the Constitution (OPC). Ninety percent of those attacks occurred against foreigners, particularly asylum applicants, and their accommodations. The annual report estimates the number of right-wing extremists in the FRG at 41,400, 6,400 of whom are militant. The highest number of right-wing attacks occurred in the former West German states of Nordrhein-Westfalen and Baden-Württemberg. The highest number of

attacks per population, however, came from the smaller former East German states of Brandenburg and Mecklenburg-Vorpommern.

Interestingly, the federal Interior Ministry computes its figures differently and counted 4900 right-wing related criminal acts between January and November 1992. Unlike the OPC, the ministry includes offenses such as racist insults and incitement to riot.

2. Wolfgang Thierse, "Deutsch-deutsche Gewalt" in *Angst vor den Deutschen: Terror gegen Ausländer und der Zerfall des Rechtsstaates*, ed. Bahman Nirumand (Hamburg: Rowohlt, 1992), 69.

3. Peter Ködderitzsch and Leo Müller, *Rechtsextremismus in der DDR* (Göttingen: Lamuv, 1990), 13.

4. *"Angst vor den Fremden"* by Anetta Kahane in Nirumand, 233.

5. Norbert Madloch "Rechtsextremismus in Ostberlin und in den Ländern der einstigen DDR" in *Jugend und Rechtsextremismus in Berlin-Ost*, (East Berlin: Magistratsverwaltung Für Jugend, Familie und Sport, 1990), 4.

6. For excellent analyses of the New Right movements see *Die Rückk..'r der Führer: Modernisierter Rechtsradikalismus in Westeuropa*, eds. Martina Kirfel and Walter Oswalt (Vienna: Europaverlag, 1991).

7. The best guide to postwar Germany's radical right is Thomas Assheuer and Hans Sarkowicz's *Rechtsradikale in Deutschland: Die alte und die neue Rechte* (Munich: C.H. Beck, 1990).

2—EAST GERMANY FASCISM IN THE ANTI-FASCIST STATE

1. *Die Tageszeitung*, September 18, 1992.

2. For just about the only examination of the GDR underground scene, see M. Stock and P. Mühlberg, *Die Szene von innen: Skinheads, Grufties, Heavy Metals, Punks* (Berlin: LinksDruck, 1990).

3. The cult-like Goths, or *Grufties*, expressed the existential meaninglessness that they perceived in their lives in head-to-toe black outfits and ghostly pale made-up faces. The Goths' mystical subculture represented a retreat from the material grind of everyday life into a spiritual world of melancholy and gloom. The dark, medieval aura that the Goths created around themselves contrasted sharply with the bright, shining future that the GDR supposedly promised them in modern industrial society. The Goths found meaning not in the present, which they saw as hopeless and senseless, but in notions of afterlife and eternal recurrence. At night, the teenagers met with candles in graveyards, performing innocuous rituals to the sounds of their favorite band, the English group, The Cure. In contrast to the punks or the Skinheads, only rarely did the Goths' pessimism translate into political convictions.

4. Loni Niederländer, *"Zur Lage und zur Bekämpfung der Skinhead- und Fascho-Szene in Berlin, Hauptstadt der DDR,"* unpublished study for the GDR police.

5. Burkhard Schröder, *Rechte Kerle: Skinheads, Faschos, Hooligans* (Hamburg: Rowohlt, 1992), 233.

6. On November 21, 1992, Silvio Meier and two friends were attacked by teenage neo-Nazis in the subway station around the corner from their squat in Berlin-Friedrichshain. Silvio, twenty-five, was killed with three knife wounds to his chest. His two companions were badly wounded.

    Silvio was one of the founders of the *Kirche Von Unten* as well as several other opposition groups. As a person, he embodied the peaceful, democratic, and humanistic ideals which he fought for politically. His name was known throughout the left-alternative scene in East Berlin and protest marches after his murder drew thousands of people.

7. Grunhild Korfus, *"Rechtsextremistische Orientierungen in der DDR-Jugend: Wie sind sie entstanden?"* in *Jugend und Rechtsextremismus in Berlin-Ost* (Berlin 1990), 13.

8. Thomas Amner, "Prozesse gegen Skinheads in der DDR," in *Deutschland Archiv* 8 (1988): 805.

9. Wilhelm Heitmeyer, *"Wenn der Alltag fremd wird: Modernisierungsschock und Fremdenfeindlichkeit"* in *Blätter für deutsche und internationale Politik* 7/91 (Bonn 1991). For a shortened English translation see *European Affairs*, "Xenophobia: Modernisation's Curse" (Amsterdam 1991).

3—HUNGARY THE GHOSTS OF CONSERVATISM PAST

1. These are 1991 figures.

2. See George Schöpflin's "Conservatism and Hungary's Transition," *Problems in Communism* (Jan.-April 1991), 60–68.

3. The working relationship between the népi populists and the national populist wing in the Hungarian Socialist Workers Party (HSWP) reflected the historical populist-urbanist tension that manifested itself even within the HSWP itself. In contrast to the party internationalists—often Jewish, Soviet-schooled Marxists who identified with the 1917 October revolution, the national communists stressed the expediency of incorporating aspects of the national spirit into state ideology. In Hungary, the 1956 revolution marked the transition from the hard-line Stalinist regime of Mátyás Rákosi, to that of Kádár, who, although installed through the force of Soviet tanks and the uprising's brutal repression, was more in the mold of the "good Hungarian" that the Soviets hoped the population would accept. Between Scylla and Charybdis, Kádár played the nationalist card to the best of his ability, striking compromises with the nationalist intelligentsia, while always aware that the tanks that brought him to power also limited his room for maneuver. Within the party, nationalists made their

voices heard particularly during the historical debates of the sixties and seventies. The nationalists, through a more plebeian notion of class struggle which incorporated all forms of historical resistence to the ruling classes, drew a line of continuity stretching from early anti-Habsburgian independence movements to the ruling communist regime. The urban, European-oriented Marxists, such as Erik Molnár or the philosopher Lukács, considered such historical conceptions primitive, relying instead upon the more classical arguments of the Marxist tradition.

4. Benedict Anderson, *Imagined Communities: Reflections on the Origin and Spread of Nationalism* (London: Verso, 1991), 159 and 114.

5. Edith Oltay, "Churches Gain New Rights, Grapple with Old Problems," *Report on Eastern Europe* (Aug. 10, 1990) 23–26; and "Church-State Relations in the Postcommunist Era," *Report on Eastern Europe* (June 21, 1991) 10–13.

6. *Budapest Week* (December 3–9, 1992).

7. Parliament eventually settled on a compromise abortion law that went into effect on January 1, 1993. The law, the less restrictive of the two proposed, enables women to elect to terminate a pregnancy in a "severe crisis situation" which is defined as a "situation that causes physical or mental shock or a socially impossible situation and thus endangers the healthy development of the fetus." Although the law is one of the most liberal in Europe, critics say that it does not go far enough to guarantee that authorities cannot refuse the operation to women in crisis situations. Also, women under eighteen years of age must have their parents' consent.

8. *Magyar Fórum* (Sept. 12, 1991).

9. *Magyar Fórum* (Sept. 5, 1991).

10. *Magyar Fórum* (Sept. 26, 1991).

11. Anthony D. Smith, *Ethnic Origins of Nations* (Oxford: Basil Blackwell, 1986), 138.

12. Paul Lendvai, *Anti-Semitism in Eastern Europe* (London: MacDonald, 1971), 306–307.

13. *Magyar Fórum* (Jan. 23, 1992).

14. "Néhány szó a zsidó katasztrofáról," *Hunnia* 18 (April 25, 1991), 2–9.

15. Even when I confronted him in person about *Hunnia*, Csurka refused to distance himself from the publication. He admitted that he finds some "very interesting things" in *Hunnia*, "much of which could appear in *Magyar Fórum*." The attempts to ban the paper or bring it to court for fascist agitation, he too indignantly rejected as a "shameful violation of the freedom of the press."

16. Romhányi was arrested in August 1992 in connection with the murder of a local tramp who lived in the vicinity of the Jurta Theater. Romhányi suspected the man of stealing a handbag that belonged to his girlfriend and locked him in the Jurta cellar after interrogating and beating him. The next day Romhányi and three others took the man out to the Buda hills to dig his own grave. They beat him up again, finally killing him and dumping his body in a garbage bin.

After Romhányi's arrest, *Szent Korona* changed its name to *Riadó* (Alarm). The

Szent Korona groupings, however, continued to exist and the content of *Riadó* remains the same as that of *Szent Korona.*

17. *Szent Korona* (May 22, 1991).

4—HUNGARY BLACK IN THE LAND OF THE MAGYARS

1. *Budapest Week* (March 5–11, 1992).

2. Hungarian Radio, September 14, 1992.

3. László Kürti, "Rocking the State: Youth and Rock Music Culture in Hungary, 1976–1990," *East European Politics and Society* (Fall 1991), 498–499.

4. *Magyar Fórum* (Aug. 20, 1992).

5—ROMANIA CEAUŞESCU'S REVENGE

1. Dennis Deletant, "The Role of *Vatra Românească* in Transylvania," *Report on Eastern Europe* (Feb. 1, 1991), 33. See also Vladimir Socor, "Forces of Old Resurface in Romania: The Ethnic Clashes in Tîrgu-Mureş," *Report on Eastern Europe* (April 13, 1991), 23–25.

2. Kathrine Verdery, *National Ideology Under Socialism: Identity and Cultural Politics in Ceauşescu's Romania* (Berkeley: University of California Press, 1991), 98.

3. *România Liberă* (June 22, 1990).

4. Hannah Arendt, *Eichmann in Jerusalem: A Report on the Banality of Evil* (Middlesex: Penguin Books, 1963), 190–191.

5. *22* (July 11, 1990).

6. *Die Tageszeitung* (July 2, 1991).

7. *România Mare* (July 17, 1991).

8. *România Mare* (May 29, 1992).

9. *România Mare* (March 20, 1992).

10. Michael Shafir, "The Greater Romania Party," *Report on Eastern Europe* (Nov. 15, 1991), 25–30.

11. Michael Shafir, "The Men of the Archangel Revisited: Anti-Semitic Formations among Communist Romania's Intellectuals," *Studies in Comparative Communism* XVI, 3 (Autumn 1983), 223–243.

12. *România Mare* (July 19, 1991).

13. See *Destroying Ethnic Identity: The Persecution of Gypsies in Romania* (New York: Helsinki Watch Report, 1991), for an excellent account of violence against Roma in Romania.

14. Richard Wagner. *Sonderweg Rumänien: Bericht aus einem Entwicklungsland* (Berlin: Rotbuch Verlag, 1991).

6—THE CZECH REPUBLIC SKINHEADS WHO CRY

1. *Prognosis* (May 29–June 11, 1992), 8–9.
2. *Struggling for Ethnic Identity: Czechoslovakia's Endangered Gypsies* (New York: Helsinki Watch Report, 1992), 101.
3. Interestingly, the autonomy-minded Movement for Autonomous Democracy-Society for Moravia and Silesia was the third biggest vote getter in Moravia, capturing twelve percent of the vote there. The Moravian regionalists demand a Czech state with a constitutional framework for territorial self-government which would put the Moravians "on equal footing" with their Bohemian counterparts. The more extreme Moravian Nationalist Party, with two parliamentary seats, insists that Moravians are a separate "nationality" from the Czechs.
4. The new government quickly showed that even the smallest favors were not going to come from its side. The new citizenship law for the Czech Republic required at least two years of residency and five years with no criminal record. This effectively discriminates against the Roma, who make up over twenty percent of all convicted criminals. Moreover, many Roma were jailed under the communists for dubious reasons like unemployment, i.e., "leading a parasitic life."

    Klaus and his allies have also tried to toe a pragmatic line on the proposed anti-Roma legislation. "Prague has been quite supportive of the whole campaign," one human rights activist told me in early 1993. "What is remarkable is the extent to which leading politicians legitimize Skinhead violence. Klaus and others have tried to strike a balance between Skinhead violence and Roma crime. Publicly they try *not* to take sides."

7—POLAND CHRIST OF NATIONS

1. David Ost, *Solidarity and the Politics of Anti-politics: Opposition and Reform in Poland Since 1968* (Philadelphia: Temple University Press, 1990).
2. Adam Michnik, *Der Lange Abschied von Kommunismus* (Hamburg: Rowohlt, 1992), 27–28.
3. Krzysztof Kosela, "The Polish Catholic Church and the Elections of 1989," *Religion in Communist Lands*, 18, 2 (Summer 1990), 129.
4. Jan B. de Weydenthal, "The Pope Appeals in Poland for a Christian Europe," *Report on Eastern Europe* (June 12, 1991), 21.
5. *Gazeta Wyborcza* (Feb. 22, 1992).

6. *Trybuna*, No. 257 (Nov. 11, 1992), 1–2.

7. Louisa Vinton, "Party X and the 'Tymiński Phenomenon'," *Report on Eastern Europe* (Aug. 9, 1991), 9.

8. Some Skinheads have acknowledged contacts with the Ku Klux Klan headquarters (*Blick nach Rechts*, May 25, 1992). The ultra-right Germany-based Schiller Institute, a front for the activities of the U.S. fascist millionaire Lyndon LaRouche and his wife, approached several of the right-wing political parties, offering them money and logistical assistance. The case was immediately handed over to the Interior Ministry, which issued warning letters to several prominent politicians. There was no evidence that any funds were accepted from the organization. (*Die Tageszeitung*, Sept 8, 1992.)

9. *Die Tageszeitung* (Feb. 12, 1992).

8—ANTI-SEMITISM WITHOUT JEWS

1. See Henryk M. Broder, *Der ewige Antisemit: Über Sinn und Funktion eines beständigen Gefühls* (Frankfurt am Main: Fischer Verlag, 1988).

2. See Paul Lendvai's classic *Anti-Semitism in Eastern Europe* (London: MacDonald, 1971) for an excellent account of anti-Semitism under communism.

3. Ibid., 81.

4. Prominent voices in the Romanian Jewish community claimed that Jews might well have to flee Romania for their lives. Bucharest Rabbi Moses Rosen even proposed an airlift of Romanian Jews to Israel should the provocations continue unabated.

5. *Europa* 24 (May 1991); Michael Shafir, "Anti-Semitism without Jews in Romania," *Report on Eastern Europe* (June 28, 1991), 20–32.

6. *România Mare* (June 21, 1991).

7. *Europa* (May 1991); Shafir, 26.

8. *România Mare* (May 31, 1992).

9. *România Mare* (June 21, 1991).

10. *Europa* (May 1991); Shafir, 27.

11. *Magyar Fórum* (August 20, 1992). See also the volume *Kirekesztök: Antiszemita írások, 1881–1992* (Budapest: Aura Kiadó, 1992) for the quoted Csurka text as well as many other contemporary and historical examples of Hungarian anti-Semitism.

12. Hannah Arendt, *The Origins of Totalitarianism* (New York: Harcourt Brace Jovanovich, 1951), 723–755.

13. *Europa*, 65 (March 1992).

14. U.S. historian Robert Kaplan puts these ideas into the proper perspective: "Holocaust revisionism exists in the West, but only among the most hard-core anti-Semitic and

academically marginal elements: kooks, that is. But Tudjman is an elected president of a new country. And though his rash leadership may have led Croatia into an avoidable war, he is by no means the most hard-line of Croatian politicians. The truth is, this book is well within the mainstream of ideas that have exploded upon the Balkans with the collapse of communism." *The New Republic* (Nov. 25, 1991).

15. *Die Tageszeitung* (April 25, 1990), interview.

16. *"Ausmass und Formen des heutigen Antisemitismus, 1949–1987"* conducted by the Institute for Demographics (Allenbach) and the Center for Anti-Semitism Research (Berlin).

17. *Antisemitism: World Report 1992*, (London: Institute of Jewish Affairs, 1992), 43–71. See the IJA's annual World Reports for summaries of recent studies and country-by-country documentation of anti-Semitism across the world.

18. For an extensive account of the controversy, see Konstanty Gerbert, "Anti-Semitism in the 1990 Polish Presidential Election" in *Social Research* 58, 4 (Winter 1991).

INDEX

INDEX